UNACCOUNTABLE

UNACCOUNTABLE

How Elite Power Brokers Corrupt Our Finances, Freedom, and Security

JANINE R. WEDEL

PEGASUS BOOKS

NEW YORK LONDON

UNACCOUNTABLE

Pegasus Books LLC
80 Broad Street, 5th Floor
New York, NY 10004

Copyright © 2014 by Janine R. Wedel

First Pegasus Books cloth edition August 2014

Interior design by Maria Fernandez

Library of Congress Cataloging-in-Publication Data is available.

ISBN: 978-1-60598-582-4

10 9 8 7 6 5 4 3 2 1

Printed in the United States of America
Distributed by W. W. Norton & Company

Again, to my parents, Arnold and Dolores Wedel

*And to the memory of Antonina Dachów and Erna P. Harris,
each one a force of nature who changed my life*

Contents

Preface   ix

PART I   IN ONLY OUR OWN WE TRUST   1

CHAPTER 1   New World, New Corruption   3

CHAPTER 2   Unaccountability, Structured   30

CHAPTER 3   Inside the New Corruption   48

CHAPTER 4   High Priests and the Gospel of Anti-Corruption   74

CHAPTER 5   Privatizing Media, Performing "Truth"   101

PART II   THE NEW CORRUPTION AT WORK   145

CHAPTER 6   Spies, Company Men, and the Melded Company-State   147

CHAPTER 7   Thought Leaders and Think-Tankers   178

CHAPTER 8   Professors, Physicians, and Prestige for Hire   205

CHAPTER 9   "Grassroots" and Nonprofit Organizers   226

PART III   RESTORING THE PUBLIC TRUST   253

CHAPTER 10   What Is to Be Done?   255

Endnotes   275

Acknowledgments   375

Index   379

Preface

You might expect a book called *Unaccountable* to begin with tales of the "wretched excesses" of the one percent. Or with the in-your-face corruption of bad apples straight out of *The Wolf of Wall Street*. But gaudy excess is almost by definition easily visible, unmistakable. Unfortunately, the most damaging corruption today—violation of the public trust—is not so readily seen. Nor is it uncommon or limited to isolated incidents. It is not about bad guys or aberrant, illegal behavior.

I wrote *Unaccountable* to bring to your attention the invisible corruption that has become *business as usual* when it comes to how so much power and influence work nowadays. I come to this work as a social anthropologist—not the stereotypical one who dons a pith helmet to live among a long-lost tribe in Borneo, but one who has spent her career in exotic places like Washington and Warsaw as a participant observer in think tanks, government agencies, and academic institutions. As an anthropologist who has long studied how systems and organizations actually work (as opposed to how they purport to work), it is my job to identify and explain patterns. I wrote *Unaccountable* to show that the modes of operating that have taken hold with this new kind of corruption have become part of our ecosystem.

These practices may look benign—they are performed by eminent and respected people who have inside information and who mostly think they are doing the right thing. They believe they have unique expertise and the personal integrity to regulate themselves and act on our behalf. But they are beyond our accountability; neither law nor ethics holds them responsible for their actions. I ask: Who does more harm to our livelihoods and security, and who helped to create more inequalities: the lone wolf like Bernie Madoff who knows he's corrupt (and eventually lands in jail), or the financial operators who, buoyed by their peers, push the limits of the law with reckless trading that brings down the economy? The players you will meet in *Unaccountable,* and others like them, are insidious and difficult to detect, and they do more damage than you might think. I wrote *Unaccountable* because, unfortunately, what you don't know and can't see *can* hurt you and threaten—even upend—your finances, freedom, and security.

I wrote *Unaccountable,* too, because more and more we feel like we're outsiders, excluded from a system we used to know how to negotiate but no longer quite do. Figuring things out is not as straightforward as in the past. We're subject to new ways of influencing and organizing influence that are not as obvious as they were just twenty-five—or even five—years ago. Increasingly, we sense a division between outsiders and insiders and that the insiders are working on their own behalf, even as they purport to have us, the public, in mind. The rest of us are left on the outside, knocking to get in. We see bits and pieces of stories in the media, or experience them in our own communities, stories that give us pause or make us angry at being excluded. But we don't quite know what makes the system tick.

You may have heard the term *shadow lobbyist* floating around. Linda Keenan and I coined it several years ago in our featured column in the Huffington Post to characterize a common type of today's influencers. We offered many examples week to week. Since then, the shenanigans of shadow lobbyists have attracted increasing attention in various outlets, including the *New York Times*, drawing on the work of the Center for Responsive Politics, and more recently, *The Nation*, in a more encompassing treatment.

But while reporters and other observers are ever closer to getting the gist of the new corruption, they're still not quite there. Their stories are mostly centered on Washington—Capitol Hill and K Street lobbyists. Even the imagery that editors select to accompany the articles often showcases the U.S. Capitol. The media's primary targets are predictable, such as how K Street has evolved in recent years, or what former elected officials are doing. But what about former Executive Branch officials or staff? Academics? Think-tankers? The use and abuse of media?

In fact, today's most destructive corruption and unaccountability in influence-wielding are broad in scope. And they extend far beyond Washington and far beyond the United States. The new corruption I document almost certainly touches nearly everywhere.

Moreover, if we view the players being exposed as aberrations, we're less inclined to look into how they operate, who and what they're connected to, and the systemic changes that have produced them. We won't know how to spot them, what we're up against, or how to effect change.

As I said, as an anthropologist it is my job to lay out the patterns—to show how the pieces of the influence puzzle fit together. It's also my job as an anthropologist to point out the connections. Indeed, social-network analysis—charting how people are linked to each other and to organizations—originates largely in social anthropology. *Unaccountable* connects the dots—not just of players, their roles, affiliations, and networks. It explores relationships among systems: Cultural trends we see in media also rear their head in finance. It also ties together multiple and seemingly disconnected threads across a wide range of public and private arenas. The connections you will discern by reading *Unaccountable* at first may seem unrelated, but in fact they can help you make sense of the world around you.

Today's ways of influencing are not limited to one arena or another like "finance," "media," or "politics." The lack of clear boundaries, indistinct identities, melded missions, and focus on "performance" that we see in the media, we also see in think tanks, academia, "grassroots" organizations, and government. Corporate websites now sometimes look like news outlets; news outlets' products, like a collection of press releases; philanthropy, like influence-laundering. And high-powered players move agilely across arenas, say, retiring from the military and government and joining a private equity firm while assuming multiple university associations. Synthesizing a range of unfolding phenomena of global relevance, *Unaccountable* provides an encompassing view of modern-day influence.

I've chosen exemplary cases that show how the mode of organizing influence has changed from the recent past and how unaccountability is thereby heightened. Every day, the media offer up more stories from which to choose—indeed, until the minute this book went to press, I was continually including new ones.

As you read *Unaccountable*, your own examples will occur to you as you see them in action in your communities and countries. In them, you'll find yourself identifying the different forms of organizing influence spelled out in the book, and you'll be equipped to make the connections among players and arenas. Like an amateur anthropologist, you'll have the tools to take effective action.

Since I've been writing and speaking about the new corruption, people as far-flung as a city planner in Columbus, Ohio; a farmer in Saskatchewan who serves on a Canadian agricultural board; and a political scientist in Israel have enlisted my analysis to help them understand the players and patterns in their own circumstances.

Unaccountable draws heavily on examples from investigative journalists, as well as (of course) my own fieldwork, interviews, and experience. It is informed by perspectives from political and other social sciences and by research ranging from that of anthropologists and practitioners of finance to philosopher-sociologists of science and to media studies conducted by research institutes. And yet, *Unaccountable* is decidedly the work of an anthropologist.

The book is divided into three parts. Part I—*In Only Our Own We Trust*—lays the groundwork for understanding the new corruption. I explain the "structured unaccountability" that is today built into our corporate and government organizations, how the "High Priest" economists and their approaches to the anti-corruption "industry" helped blind us to the corruption that matters most, and why the personalization of media and "performance" of truth today pervade finance, politics, and beyond, not just media.

Part II—*The New Corruption at Work*—takes unaccountability from a different angle, with modes of organizing as the point of departure. We'll look at how a variety of types of players and entities, ranging from consulting firms to "think tanks" and universities to "nonprofits" and "grassroots" organizations, all coordinate influence to sway policy and public opinion.

Finally, in Part III—*Restoring the Public Trust*—we'll look at what can be done to counter the effects of the new corruption and how we can begin to trust public institutions again.

PART I

IN ONLY OUR OWN WE TRUST

CHAPTER 1

New World, New Corruption

W hat does "SWIMNUT" know that the world's supposed experts on corruption or the elites who gather each year for skiing and schmoozing in Davos do not?

This anonymous commenter was responding to an online article about the 2013 ranking of the world's most corrupt countries, as measured by the best-known international arbiter of corruption, the organization Transparency International. In TI's survey, the experts canvassed perceive Somalia, North Korea, and Afghanistan as the worst transgressors. But "SWIMNUT" sees it differently:

> Not quite sure how corruption is defined but I think the US needs to be included as one of the most corrupt "civilized" countries in the world. . . . In the US . . . we have created a political elite that extorts hard working people for their own political and financial gains.

"SWIMNUT" wasn't the lone voice of skepticism. Well over half of the 180-odd commenters to this article targeted the United States as an offender that was grievously under-scrutinized.[1] Amid the usual partisanship, name-calling, and crackpot conspiracy theories that one finds in comment sections, many of these readers conveyed undeniable threads of truth, ones I've been weaving together for decades.

> From "kolar63":
> . . . Washington DC knows very well how to hide and disguised their corruption thru lobbying elites . . .

> From "onelifelive":
> We are not on top of this list because we call it "LOBBYING", "FAVORS", "GIFTS", "CORPORATE SPONSORSHIP", "PACS", ETC. ETC.

What struck me in the case of SWIMNUT is that s/he and fellow readers were no longer buying this media performance. A website was engaging in an annual ritual of presenting these metrics without much context or reflection, something that looks and feels like news but really isn't and probably never was. In fact, the real news story can be found in the comments themselves. They show the chasm between corruption as measured, on the one hand, and corruption as experienced by Americans, who see something deeply amiss in their own land, not just in the far-flung and exotic. Wealth has been fast accumulating among the few, leaving the rest of us languishing with stagnant pay and rampant unemployment among the young.

How is it that ordinary people have an instinctual grasp of the real nature of corruption and the inequality that often results, while many experts are still wedded to the idea that corruption happens somewhere "out there"?

Witness the "Occupy" protests that began on Wall Street in 2011 and the "Tea Party" movement that helped grind the U.S. government to a halt in the fall of 2013. They may otherwise have little in common, but they share a resounding refrain: that the "system" is gamed by the powerful.

Research out in 2014 shows just how gamed it really is. Two political scientists looked at 1,779 policy issues hashed out from 1981 to 2002 and found that policies widely supported by economically elite Americans were adopted about forty-five percent of the time. If these same Americans indicated little support? Eighteen percent. They write: "The central point that emerges from our research is that economic elites and organized groups representing business interests have substantial independent impacts on U.S. government policy, while mass-based interest groups and average citizens have little or no independent influence."[2] Lest you blame the typically business-oriented Republicans, consider what one of the researchers said in an interview: "Both parties have to a large degree embraced a set of policies that reflect the needs, preferences and interests of the well to do."[3]

That the system is rigged resounds worldwide. There's a documented and striking loss of confidence in formal institutions, from governments, parliaments, and courts to banks and corporations, to the media.[4] Apparently, people feel that their public institutions and leaders now merit even less confidence than in the past.

The frustration and anger this breeds appear to be a major reason that middle-class people in democracies around the world—from Turkey and Greece to India, Brazil, Ukraine, and the United States—feel enraged and have taken to the streets. While protestors may have an intuitive sense of this loss, they may not realize that at its core is a modern-day form of corruption that is so far little understood. Their instincts are spot on, even if they don't quite grasp the ins and outs of what I call the new corruption.

Indeed, people the world over sense that unseen elites are at work, using forces beyond anyone's control. It seems almost conspiratorial, but it's far more complex and elusive than that; if only it could be so easily dismissed. We sense that something big has changed—and not for the better.

But what, exactly? Let's look at the old world versus the new. By "old," I mean within recent living memory.

- In the old world, high officials retired to a life of leisure or good works. Now, many turn themselves into one-man brands, with their public service a stepping-stone to lucrative, enmeshed business, government, philanthropic, and policy endeavors, leaving the public to wonder whose interests are being served.
- In the old world, players had more defined roles and agendas; now they are more apt to glide among them in an ill-defined blur.

- In the old world, you could point to the official or lobbyist or interest group wielding influence. Today, players and corporations can use nonprofit or "grassroots" organizations to press their case—but you'd never know it because, more than in the past, they don't need to disclose who writes the checks.
- In the old world, the long term was actually long. In the new world, whether in finance or media, short-term results are prized; actions and impact are measured in hours, minutes, or even micro-seconds.
- In the old world, the media were more focused on real news; now, "likes" and page views shape what becomes "news," and much airtime and Web space consists of mere "performances" to catch our attention and convince us that action is happening when it hardly is.
- In the old world, it was easier to locate a bureaucrat who was responsible for solving your problem. Today, you get trapped in an endless phone maze powered by technology, leaving less room to maneuver the outcome to your advantage.
- In the old world, we, the public, were not implicated. In the new world, we are complicit the moment we turn on our computers, hand over personal information, and "agree" to conditions that we say we have read but, of course, have not.
- In the old world, those who betrayed the public trust might be found with cash stashed in their freezer and end up in handcuffs. In the new world, no money passes hands, and no one lands in jail.
- In the old world, people recognized others' moral failings; now everyone can blame the "system."

Whether it's trying and failing to figure out whose fingerprints are on public-policy decisions, who is calling the economic shots, or whose dollars are funding various politicians, we are up against shadow influence that is difficult to discern and sometimes even anonymous. This isn't a conspiracy. As we'll see throughout the book, many policies that affect us all are no longer molded by conventional power elites, lobbyists, interest groups, or influencers that we can identify and therefore hold accountable. When we can't pinpoint who has the authority to fix the problem, then lobbying, bribery, or other traditional influencing mainstays don't work. Meanwhile, there are unregistered lobbyists, campaign financiers, and other shadow influencers who operate in and around government, business, nonprofits, and media. How can we decipher their actual agendas and tangle of roles? How can we know whom to trust, when "experts" besiege the Internet and airways, pronouncing on crucial public-policy issues and presenting themselves as impartial and objective, all the while concealing that they actually have a dog in the fight? In short, how can we have any modicum of trust in public institutions that seem to be so accountability-challenged?

Whether it's the behavior of public figures or the behavior of public institutions, the new corruption is anchored in unaccountability.[5] Unaccountability, as we shall see in the next chapter, is structured into the DNA of many of today's corporate and governmental organizations. It is an essential but incomplete condition for the new corruption—the violation of the public trust.

For the past several decades, I have been considering what happens to society when the public no longer trusts its institutions, leaders, and public figures—in places as diverse as communist states (where they seldom did) and Western democracies (where not long ago they did much more so). What happens when the accountability needed to sustain that trust is absent from our interactions with the organizations and functionaries on which we daily rely? Or with our relations with once-respected public figures?

I began my explorations in communist Poland in the 1980s and have continued them in the United States. Throughout my career as an anthropologist, I have seen it as my mission to explain the changing profile of power and influence, and how people both break and create new rules of the game.

Today I am not surprised that people are outraged. Privacy virtually everywhere is under siege, whether by faceless spymasters at the U.S. National Security Agency, through the likes of Google and Facebook, or by government and corporations in concert.[6] Outrage at government and public institutions on nearly every continent, especially since the global financial crisis of 2008, reflects the public's frustration. The economy continues to stagger with hardly anyone punished for rampant financial abuses. In this fraught environment, the absence of trust threatens to become a permanent feature of our civic life. Some of the chief culprits are even "failing up": bubble-wrapped from the adversity they helped create, they continue to land influential jobs despite their spectacular and well-publicized errors of judgment and often of ethics.

That's in part because they are conquering media, new and old. The powerful are performing and branding themselves and their preferred narratives on every conceivable digital and old media outlet, leaving satirists like Jon Stewart and Stephen Colbert more truth-tellers than the more sober media, something strongly reminiscent of my time in Eastern Europe under communism.

Meanwhile, the rest of us are exposed to the consequences of the culprits' misdeeds, with little recourse to challenge the practices that now govern our private information and public policy.

Betrayal of the public trust is at the core of age-old notions of corruption, such as those revealed in texts in the Bible and the Qur'an.[7] At the same time the most common, internationally sanctioned understanding of corruption today is "the abuse of public office for private gain," as propounded in the late 1990s and promoted around the globe by Transparency International, the World Bank, and other organizations.[8] Straightforward corruption such as bribery is still common and causes outcry in countries around the globe. Yet the older and, I believe, more currently relevant notions of betrayal of the public trust appear to be closer to the hearts of many protesters—and lie at the heart of the new corruption.

In the United States and many European countries, the new corruption may have surpassed the old. Across Europe, with entire economies devastated, signature Western banks colluded with feckless local leadership.

Look at the destruction and global ripple effects wrought by Standard & Poor's, which took cash to bestow AAA ratings on worthless investments in the mid-2000s.[9] Then there's Goldman Sachs, which pursued an express policy of placing its "alumni" in top government positions in the United States and around the world, like former Goldman managing director Mario Draghi, installed in 2011 as president of the European Central Bank. Goldman, along with other top U.S. banks, "helped" struggling European economies like Greece, Italy, and others hide their debt in the early 2000s and, according to the *New York Times*, was still "helping" avert the inevitable crash in late 2009.[10] Such collusion between Goldman and government leaders cannot help but fan the flames of public mistrust.

In still another case, known as the ABACUS deal, in 2007 Goldman devised investment vehicles for one client without disclosing to other clients—including pension funds, insurance companies, and foreign banks—that they were being set up to lose billions. Notably, this was a case in which regulators actually did try to accuse the company of outright fraud. Yet the matter was settled in 2010. Why? In the eyes of many observers at the time, the government didn't have a strong case. But in 2014, a retiring U.S. Securities and Exchange Commission trial lawyer let loose at his going-away party. James Kidney, who'd been with the SEC for decades, was apparently one lawyer gunning for more charges against executives.[11] He lost the internal fight, but his parting shot was memorable. Kidney told colleagues and well-wishers that the SEC is "an agency that polices the broken windows on the street level and rarely goes to the penthouse floors. On the rare occasions when enforcement does go to the penthouse, good manners are paramount. Tough enforcement, risky enforcement, is subject to extensive negotiation and weakening."[12]

Another parting shot came from a Goldman Sachs vice president. He described the violation of the public's and client's trust, exposing inside practices in the *New York Times* on the day he resigned in 2012. Here he sums up his belief that the firm violates the public's (in this case, its clients') trust: "I don't know of any illegal behavior, but will people push the envelope and pitch lucrative and complicated products to clients even if they are not the simplest investments or the ones most directly aligned with the client's goals? Absolutely. Every day, in fact."[13]

Still, we ceremonially attack practitioners of the old corruption. The media (TV, in particular) often cling to narrower definitions of corruption to mean simple bribery and outright fraud. They dish out, and we eat up, the images of former high-flyers handcuffed and perp-walked. In America, these include former Illinois governor Rod Blagojevich, super-lobbyist "Casino Jack" Abramoff, and Bernie Madoff, architect of the largest Ponzi scheme in history. The media had its role to play in the performance. It used all the visual symbols to cue the viewer: here is corruption, the governor with the absurd hair and endless blather, appearing for any TV audience he could find; the hulking figure with the signature black fedora and trench coat; the disgraced investor's Italian velveteen slippers monogrammed in gold embroidery.

Blagojevich, Abramoff, and Madoff may have become symbols, but they are sideshows. Those who practice the new corruption and help create deep and lasting inequalities don't typically land in jail. As for Madoff and his ilk, we can count their victims, they clearly broke the law, and they were prosecuted for it. They are likely to be defined as corrupt; the others rarely are, if ever. But the *consequences* of their actions pale by comparison to the shenanigans of the rating agencies, the Wall Street "wizards" who helped bring down the global economy, and all manner of lobbyists, including those on the vanguard who simply choose not to register formally as lobbyists, when they are quite obviously still wielding influence that we can't see or trace. They will continue to have a far greater impact on our health, habitat, and pocketbooks, and on the execution of America's wars.

Does that make any sense? Have the practitioners of the new corruption not violated the public trust? Isn't that corruption at its most basic?

—⁓—

The rub is that the system works to catch old-style corruption, but it doesn't work for the new corruption.

Where, for example, is the sanction or even the shame for the highfliers who leave public office and take on inscrutable roles of influence within the corporate world or the international relations game? Think, for instance, of former Prime Minister Tony Blair, who, soon after leaving office, used his prestige to create a highly lucrative influence brand that's been dubbed "Blair Inc.," what the *Telegraph* describes as a "confusing mix of business, politics and philanthropy that is administered by a complex system of companies." Blair has advised a Wall Street bank, a European insurer, the government of Kazakhstan (among others), and even Libya's brutal dictator Muammar Gaddafi.[14] While counseling Gaddafi at the same time that JPMorgan Chase was seeking deals from Libya, Blair additionally served as an official peace envoy to the Middle East.[15] At the very least, these overlapping roles are more than murky, if not suspicious. Blair mixes formal and informal roles—and, as I'll discuss shortly, informality can create a giant black hole of accountability.

Or what about former Obama budget director Peter Orszag? In 2010, he left Washington for an executive job at Citigroup, one of the very companies that needed and received government help after the financial crackup of 2008. One of his three titles there is Chairman of the Public Sector Group, which smacks of a stealth lobbying department.

Orszag is not accused of wrongdoing. He is a model of *"structural rather than personal* corruption," as journalist James Fallows commented in *The Atlantic.* "The idea that someone would help plan, advocate, and carry out an economic policy that played such a crucial role in the survival of a financial institution—and then, less than two years after his Administration took office, would take a job that (a) exemplifies the growing disparities the Administration says it's trying to correct and (b) *unavoidably* will call on knowledge and contacts Orszag developed while in recent public service—this says something bad about what is taken for granted in American public life." These kinds of high-level migrations, Fallows observed, "pile up in the background to create a broad American sense that politics is rigged, and opportunity too."[16]

Meanwhile, these players not only challenge accountability—they have helped to create vast inequalities in income and wealth and will long reap the benefits of the policies and the political climate they have abetted. When their policy influence leads to real-world trauma for what has become known colloquially as the 99 percent, these power brokers don't generally slink into obscurity: they continue demanding high-profile rewards, and often get them.

Given all this, it's clear that we must pay heed to the new corruption—which helped spark the outrage that has fueled today's far-flung protest movements. In the new corruption, no envelope is passed under the table. No laws are clearly broken. Indeed, the players we meet in this book are far too subtle and sophisticated for the bribe-dispensing or even conventional lobbying of yesteryear. They are difficult to monitor and to hold to account precisely because their "corruption" is elusive, hard to detect—and legal.

But don't they violate the public trust—or get close to doing so? And aren't their actions often more damaging to society than the old-fashioned bribe?

Yet many people and even corruption scholars, influenced by the agenda of what has been called the "anti-corruption industry," have not thought about it in those terms. Following the Cold War, the World Bank, and NGOs such as Transparency International of corruption-ranking fame, powered the industry in a worldwide anti-corruption campaign. That industry has favored targeting what is now called "need" corruption—people managing an impossible system—over "greed" corruption—people gaming the system.[17] That industry has played a significant role (even if not quite knowingly) in this obfuscation, as we shall see in Chapter 4. Meanwhile, it is telling that systemic violation of the public trust—the emblem of the new corruption—today resonates with protesters worldwide. Recall the insistence of SWIMNUT and his or her fellow commenters that the United States should occupy a high place in corruption rankings. They don't need experts to tell them that they are subject to a corruption that bears little resemblance to the petty bribes that flourish far away. That's because ordinary people are grappling with the grim consequences of the well-entrenched new corruption. The elites who helped entrench it scarcely face such costs. No wonder many elite experts don't even recognize that a problem exists.

The financial arena is rife with lapses in accountability and even clearcut violations of the public trust. But a stunning discovery of my research is that unaccountability invades practically every area of public life. Later we'll see how stealth influence can quite literally involve life-and-death matters when the pharmaceutical industry and physicians intersect. We'll see it, too, in cases of unregistered, under-the-radar operatives carrying the water for less-than-savory foreign entities. And it rears its head in once-respected institutions—government, business, the military, and academia, among others.

In all these realms, not only is unaccountability a problem: the public trust is under siege.

TRUTH UNHINGED

How did that happen? For one thing, many of the old pillars of truth have gone wobbly.

Signature institutions such as media and finance have lost the ability to themselves judge the truth, much less to be accurate purveyors of it. The *Washington Post*, the paper that toppled a president (Richard Nixon), now casts a very faint shadow, bought recently by a tech billionaire, Amazon's Jeff Bezos. Jamie Dimon and JPMorgan Chase, which came out of the 2008 financial crisis with a better reputation than many of its peers, has had that reputation battered by the "London Whale" trading fiasco.

The almost willful lack of clarity about the value of the financial instruments and complex derivatives being held or traded was at the core of the 2008 collapse—and reportedly continues today. And the real-world impact of exotic or opaque deal-making is wholly removed from the way traders are compensated, encouraging them to push the limits and "innovate."

Recall the expression "Let's listen to what the market says." Markets were said to function as harbingers of truth and barometers of the state of the world. That was back when banks still knew, more or less, what holdings they had, and traders knew the value of what they were trading. Information was, and is, of course, never as perfect as the economic orthodoxy had it. But with the proliferation of obscure financial instruments, prices have become much more disconnected from reality. Markets convey a lot less truth about the intrinsic value of what they are selling than they did just a few years ago, and this disconnect now underpins the financial system.[18]

The "rational" models of risk—such as the computer-generated ones we'll explore later—that have taken hold, and the titanic faith placed in them at the expense of on-the-ground analysis, have abetted the disconnect not only from the people supposedly served by them but also from reality. Former trader and sociologist of finance Vincent Antonin Lepinay, who spent nearly two years studying derivatives in a French bank, writes that "the bank itself did not always assess properly its risks and costs. Only after having launched these innovative products did it try to devise ways of counting them and measuring their costs." Moreover, both clients and investors were kept in the dark about the bank's "secret and opaque strategies," and there was no mechanism in place by which investors owning shares could monitor its strategies.[19]

Anthropologist of finance and political economy Alexandra Ouroussoff agrees. She spent several years studying rating agencies (such as Moody's,

Standard & Poor's, and Fitch) from the inside in the years leading up to the 2008 financial crisis. She argues that this dominant new (unspoken) model—which has come into being since the 1980s—posits, incredibly, that profits can be made without taking risks. This is distinct from previous conceptions of capitalist profit-making, where risk was intrinsic to competition.[20] As a result, corporate executives massage their numbers much more frequently to conform to what she calls the "rationalist model" compelled by rating agencies. As one executive told Ouroussoff, "We used to lie twenty per cent of the time. Now it's eighty per cent."[21]

With finance barely understandable even to many practitioners, we can't count on the media to explain it clearly. That landscape has been flattened by the Internet. As we shall see in Chapter 5, the standing of the media, whether old or new, as an accurate purveyor of truth has also been undermined. The Internet age has both ravaged the ranks of journalism and inundated us with "information" that is questionable in accuracy and obscured in sponsorship. We seem to increasingly accept "facts" that feel right, especially as social media have given us like-minded "friends" to agree with those facts. Back in 2005, comedian Stephen Colbert first dubbed this phenomenon "truthiness"—the *feeling* that something is true, and the idea that if enough people believe something, it actually becomes true.

Truthiness requires the active participation of the listener, and, as with offering up our personal information on Facebook, or affirming that we have read the details when signing on to a new software package or computer system, truthiness depends on our participation. Truth is the listener's choice. We tune in to those "experts" and commentators whose facts are compatible with our worldviews and, not surprisingly, get "truthi-news," as Colbert calls it. As we, the listeners, actively buy into truthi-news, the media, too—whether right-leaning or left—loses its bearings. Truth that is disconnected from core institutions provides the perfect breeding ground for the new corruption.

COMPROMISED LEADERS

What of the leaders of democratic society who, theoretically, could help guide us out of this conundrum? Those who once displayed integrity now personify a mixed bag of intentions. Heads of once-admired institutions hand us even more reason for the lack of public confidence.

In the old world, at least in many democratic nations, public service was a good in its own right and an endeavor that earned one social respect and status. It was not merely a rung on the ladder to big money. Today, former heads of state don't confine themselves to the golf course or philanthropy. Many take on opaque roles of influence—and they no longer command the respect they once did.

Take, for instance, those in charge of the "free world." In the old world—before the last couple of decades—it would have been unthinkable for the leader of one sovereign state to buy the leader of another, especially Germany, the third-largest industrialized democracy. In the new world, Gerhard Schroeder, while chancellor, agreed to a pipeline deal with Gazprom, the Russian energy giant that commands a quarter of the world's natural gas reserves and represents a murky mix of state and private power. The pipeline was highly controversial in both Western and Eastern Europe, and Germany paid a political price for the deal.[22] But the deal went through, and Gazprom, within a matter of months, nominated Schroeder to a highly paid position as head of the shareholders' committee for the Gazprom-controlled pipeline.[23]

No wonder his successor, Angela Merkel, was reportedly furious in the spring of 2014 when Schroeder defended Vladimir Putin's aggression in Ukraine. Could anyone trust the former leader's intentions, considering that his current lucrative role depends on Russia's goodwill?[24]

Neither Schroeder nor Tony Blair is alone in his adoption of multiple opaque international roles. Since leaving office, President Bill Clinton, in addition to establishing the Clinton Foundation and its Global Initiative, has served as a paid adviser to a global private equity and consulting firm called Teneo (among other business ventures). His close aide Douglas Band reportedly recruited donors to be Teneo clients. As the *New York Times* put it, "Some Clinton aides and foundation employees began to wonder where the foundation ended and Teneo began."[25] Such overlapping roles lead one to wonder whose interests are at heart and stand to undermine the integrity of the good work that the foundation might do.

What appears to be new with Clinton and Blair is the melding of business, philanthropic, and potentially policy portfolios. When the boundaries among them are nonexistent or shift conveniently, we have to question where accountability lies.[26]

A different kind of president has been leveraging considerable power as well. Universities, once prized for adding to the public good, are also yielding to this lucrative brand of blurring. In the old world, members of the Ivy League and other institutions of higher learning cherished their reputations for scholarly impartiality. In the new world, ivory towers can often seem more like influence generators, with scholars marketing their supposed impartiality as a selling point outside the academy, something I'll examine in depth in Chapter 8.

Perhaps the scholars are taking their cues from those at the top of their institutions, college and university presidents. In 2010, the *New York Times* examined what it called the "Academic-Industrial Complex"—namely, the vast numbers of university presidents serving on corporate boards, lending their prestige for a tidy fee even when they have little expertise to add. The list included the then-president of Brown University, Ruth Simmons, who served on the board of Goldman Sachs in the years leading up to the financial crisis, earning more than a quarter million dollars a year.[27] As one critic assessed, some of these presidents were brought on *because* they had no expertise in the relevant subject and couldn't ask tough questions.[28]

Nearly all of these players will say they are doing good and possess unique expertise. Some may be, and many do. Whatever the case, they risk abrogating responsibility to more than one institution.

And, whatever the case, it is reasonable for us to ask: Where is the genuine leadership? In the old world, prestige was earned by excellent performance and working one's way up the ranks. Today, enduring social respect may be giving way to momentary popularity.

Case in point: General David Petraeus, whose skillful cultivation of the media helped catapult his career to the stratosphere of stars and celebrity. He was widely lauded for his war-strategy acumen.[29] His charm offensive with the media earned him glowing coverage across it, from glitzy publications like *Vanity Fair* to sober musings in *Foreign Policy*.[30] That was, of course, until the exposure of a personal affair with his biographer forced him to relinquish his position as CIA director. Only then did the mainstream media begin to question his aggressive nurturing of them, his taste for lavish parties and sycophants seeking their own publicity. And, crucially for the public interest, only then did his war strategy undergo serious scrutiny by the mainstream media, now belatedly questioning whether tactics that appeared to "work" in Iraq made sense for Afghanistan.

Celebrities are still celebrities, though, even when they stumble or fall. Within a year of his resignation, ostensibly with both his personal and professional reputations battered, Petraeus went to work in the private equity firm Kohlberg Kravis Roberts, in a newly created "KKR Global Institute" (note the impartial, scholarly-sounding name).[31] He also weighed numerous university offers. Not only did he "fail up," he is teaching (at least by example) others how to do the same, having landed additional jobs mentoring ROTC members at the University of Southern California and serving as a visiting professor at Macaulay Honors College at CUNY.

Supporters credit Petraeus for fresh thinking and shaking up a lumbering military bureaucracy. Still, it's reasonable for us to ask: What does his intense focus on burnishing his own image augur for the public interest? When people at the top use their positions to launch their own platforms to accrete brand recognition or personal wealth, at the possible expense of an organization that has entrusted its mission to them, does this not kindle public *distrust* in these same entities?

And yet, this is also a statement about society. What is one to make of the supposedly disgraced General Petraeus and his post-scandal career? Why would a private equity firm want to employ a retired general, especially one whose much-vaunted acumen had been called into question? According to *Forbes* contributor and author George Anders, Petraeus was recruited to lend intellectual prestige to the KKR "brand" in the "thought leadership" business.[32]

Is this truly the kind of leadership we need?

IN (UNACCOUNTABLE) NETWORKS WE TRUST

While players like Petraeus bask in the limelight, many public-policy influencers sidestep the media spotlight and regulatory scrutiny. In arenas from finance to foreign policy, policymaking gravity has been shifting away from the old hubs. Formal procedures, hierarchies, and bureaucracies that have stood the test of time are giving way to trust-based informal social networks and ad hoc organizations. Losing ground are formal and legal modes of operating within and across organizations. Losing ground, too, are formal policymaking bodies altogether. Gaining ground is informality. Today's informal, under-the-radar way of doing business is not illegal, of course. It also is by no means necessarily corrupt and may even be, in some cases, the only way business can be accomplished. Nonetheless, it is unaccountable and lacks democratic oversight.

This modern-day informal, yet power-charged, policymaking comes in several forms.

One form is when officials in government agencies who are also members of a power clique—an influential, close-knit network—exclude other officials from participating in crucial public-policy decisions—that is, colleagues who are outside the informal network but who should be included because of their expertise and job descriptions. Yet, at the same time, these new-style officials bring in members of their power clique who occupy private roles.

Let's look, for instance, at a Washington-Wall Street clique that established just who was included—and excluded—from a policy that would have a huge impact on the global economy—and would bear significant responsibility for the global financial crisis: decision-making in the Clinton administration about the regulation of exotic derivatives trading. An example of exclusion is Brooksley Born, in the late 1990s chair of the Commodity Futures Trading Commission. She stood well outside the Wall Street-Washington power clique that believed generally in financial "innovation" and specifically in blocking a proposed regulation of a new kind of exotic derivative that she thought (correctly, as we now can't deny) was dangerous. One would think that running the CFTC—which had played a role in regulating early derivatives but also had created a wide loophole prior to her tenure—would give one some formal power.

By many accounts, Born did not like to be pushed around and, when pushed, tended to dig in her heels. In one particularly notable episode that began in early 1998, she stood up against the clique, which was led by Federal Reserve Chairman Alan Greenspan, Treasury Secretary Robert Rubin, his deputy Lawrence Summers, and Securities and Exchange

Commission Chairman Arthur Levitt, Jr.[33] Their advocacy of both unregulated derivatives and a repeal of the Glass-Steagall Act in 1999 would have a devastating effect on the global economy (though it would take years for many people to catch on). Banks, liberated from Depression-era restrictions on the kinds of activities they could engage in, were able to accelerate an already frenetic era of creating and trading in toxic derivatives.[34]

But, despite Born's apparent best efforts, the informal power of the clique overwhelmed hers.

Born may have lost that battle, but she continued to fight the clique, hoping the collapse months later of the hedge fund Long Term Capital Management (with not one but two Nobel laureate economists as the company's braintrust) could serve as a wake-up call on the risk of unregulated derivatives.[35] She reported that risk to the House Banking Committee—one of at least seventeen times she testified before Congress. Her warnings fell on deaf ears. In 1999, she returned to her old law firm before retiring to advocacy and overseeing pro bono work at the firm.

And the four members of the clique that stonewalled her? Each went on to take a role at a Wall Street firm, bank, private equity firm, or hedge fund that made bundles on . . . unregulated derivatives. The explosion of "innovation" scarcely benefited those beyond Wall Street, Washington, or other bastions of privilege.

The modern-day power clique, composed of members in official and private roles, not only circumnavigates should-be included officials and standard processes; it also works through unconventional venues. Let's look at how another power clique dodged military procedure, working through a new Washington think tank to shape war policy. This clique, the so-called COINdinistas, played a key role in making, executing, and justifying the post-9/11 military policy that shaped the more recent years of the wars in Afghanistan and Iraq. A collection of generals, influential military reporters, scholars, defense contractors, and think-tankers coalesced around an idea known as Counterinsurgency, or COIN. General David Petraeus, about whom we heard earlier, helped write the book on COIN (the Army and Marine Corps Counterinsurgency Field Manual, issued in 2006), which promotes deep engagement with local populations as a way to counteract terrorism.[36]

To pursue the COIN strategy, Petraeus and a handful of other top leaders did an end run around the bureaucracy, using as a vehicle a think tank called the Center for a New American Security (CNAS).[37] Deploying their own across the media, they swayed public and policymaker opinion to their side. By sidelining the bureaucracy and enlisting the media to help, they won the fight and left their colleagues with little choice but to walk with them. Later, we'll explore this story as a case study in how new-style think tanks wield influence.

Modern-day power brokers are, increasingly, using outside organizations to push through their policy agendas. These entities don't have the strictures or transparency demanded in formal government venues, not to mention the input of democratically elected lawmakers. In transnational governing, informality appears to be the ascendant MO. While power rested more in visible and rule-bound bodies in the old world, today small informal gatherings and associations are gaining global influence. Some scholars have argued that the more transnational and multi-pronged the activity, the less likely governing is to rely on traditional forms of regulation and supervision. Private actors assume a growing role.[38]

A case in point is the Group of Thirty, the Consultative Group on International Economic & Monetary Affairs. Stuart Mackintosh, its executive director, tells me that the body is "a cross between an internal think tank and a very exclusive club" whose members have "multiple, overlapping associations . . . with one another."[39] Political scientist Eleni Tsingou, who studied the group, describes it in strikingly similar terms, as a "part think tank, part interest group, and part club" of "actors who write the rules."[40] Its list of members reads like a Who's Who of those who help shape the global economy.[41] "We don't make policy," says Mackintosh, "but you can see our recommendations ending up in policy."[42]

One example of this is the hugely consequential issue of derivatives trading and accounting of them. The G30's study group and report on derivatives in the early 1990s helped solidify the standards for "best practices." Tsingou and other analysts suggest that the group was closely aligned with the would-be regulated (banks) and furthered policy that closely matches their interests and biases. Here's Tsingou on the composition of the derivatives study group and its "landmark" work:[43]

All the "right" people from the private sector (technical experts, users and dealers of the instruments and representatives of the major Wall Street financial institutions) volunteered time and money and Derivatives: Practices and Principles (Global Derivatives Study Group, 1993) became another landmark in the G-30's history. The group had firmly established itself as an organisation of experts, capable of providing authoritative proposals on the "nuts and bolts" of the financial system.

Gillian Tett, social anthropologist and *Financial Times* journalist, forms a parallel view. The derivative study group's report served as a kind of preemptive strike on government intervention, she reports in *Fool's Gold*:[44]

On July 21, 1993, the long-awaited G30 report was finally unveiled. . . . If the report could show that the industry already had a credible internal code of conduct, there should be less need for bureaucrats to impose rules.

The G30 writers, Tett suggests, wanted a pragmatic, serious, and comprehensive guide, with the side benefit of getting in front of government interference. At the time of its release, the *New York Times* described the report this way:[45]

A group of leading financial experts gave a relatively clean bill of health yesterday to the rapidly growing set of financial products called derivatives that some have suggested make the global financial system vulnerable to a widespread crisis.

The late Dennis Weatherstone, the man who chaired the steering committee overseeing the derivatives project that produced the 1993 report, wasn't just an expert—he was a banker who ran JP Morgan. The banks, of course, didn't want increased regulation on their new and emerging profit centers. The report included recommendations on how banks could best account for derivatives. But, as Tett writes:[46]

Equally important was what the G30 report did *not* say. The tome did not suggest the government should intervene in the market, in any way. Nor did it drop any hint that the derivatives world might benefit from a centralized clearing system . . . , providing a valuable barometer of activity that signaled signs of trouble.

Of course, this laissez-faire approach would allow derivatives to lay dynamite throughout the global financial system.[47]

The G30's influence also extends to promoting a key computer-generated tool that is now blamed for encouraging risky bets by banks. JP Morgan is viewed as having invented these tools, and Morgan's then-chief, recall, led the effort on the derivatives project.[48]

Mackintosh, who has served as the G30's executive director since 2006, said that the G30 has had a "big impact" on the Dodd-Frank regulations passed in the wake of the financial crisis. "If you read the action plans agreed to by the G20 [the official organization of the major economies' finance ministers] in April of '09 in London, you can see the [same] language. It's almost a direct lift [from the G30] and that's not coincidental. That's a good example of how we work—almost as a think tank—but most think tanks are not as influential."[49]

Evaluating the efficacy of G30 recommendations is beyond the purview of this book. What is within our purview, though, is its modus operandi and model of influencing. The space it occupies between formal and informal, public and private, is clearly the key to its influence. "What makes it effective," Mackintosh observes, "is that it has a spot between public and private. . . . We issue recommendations that neither the public or private sector could promulgate on their own," he says.[50] Of course, it is in that chasm that accountability stumbles.

Mackintosh told me that he is impressed by how movers and shakers in world finance are willing to give their limited time to work with the G30.[51] So what do members get out of the experience? The club–think tank atmosphere feeds and bolsters their individual and collective capital. In Tsingou's words, it "increases their shared prestige, defends their conception of honourable behavior."[52] And this further promotes the effectiveness of the group and the acceptability of the space it occupies: a sort of "rule-free zone" with increasing legitimacy. This space, of course, is beyond our accountability.

We've seen how close-knit, preexisting networks of influential players bridging state and private organizations can intentionally exclude the inconvenient (for them) participation of policymakers in government who do not belong to their network (the Rubin-Summers circle excluding Born). We've seen how informal networks, operating unconventionally through think tanks and the media and circumventing military procedure, can drive interest and consensus in a certain direction about the conduct of war (the COINdinistas). And we've seen how high-prestige, powerful players can increase their weight, both individually and collectively, while creating an influence-wielding venue that will outlast any individual members (the Group of Thirty). While not necessarily unethical, and while sometimes resulting in policy decisions that can be deemed to be in the public interest, all these groups are virtually beyond the authority of elected leaders and democratic processes. And most of these decisionmaking episodes could have benefited from including expertise outside their own networks; some decisions caused huge harm because they didn't. If a broader group of voices and robust media oversight had been there to hold players accountable, perhaps the painful consequences of some of these episodes could have been mitigated, or even averted.

And yet the question remains: How to institutionalize the needed voices and oversight? How to get those outsiders in?

—m—

What has happened to move the center of policymaking gravity away from formal organizations and toward epicenters of players and networks that circle in, around, and also away from the organizations?

What has happened is a sea change, and it has ushered in the new unaccountability. And unaccountability, as I said earlier, is a necessary—though not complete—precondition for the new corruption.

Several transformational developments over the past few decades have broken down barriers and allowed power brokers to hold more sway. They include the privatization, deregulation, and governmental "reform" fervor of the West that began to take hold in the United States and the United Kingdom in the early 1980s; the end of the Cold War a decade later, dispersing global authority and opening up sparsely governed arenas; and the rise of the Internet and digital technology soon after that.[53] For better, as well as for worse, these developments, both on their own and through their interactions, have created myriad new opportunities for individuals, networks, ad hoc groups, companies, and nongovernmental organizations, be they private contractors carrying out functions heretofore mostly performed by governments; transnational networks laundering money or promoting human rights; currency traders conducting instant global transactions; or denizens of the Web gracing us hourly with their opinions.

This sea change has altered how we interact with corporate and government organizations (unidentifiable bureaucrats who know too much about us while we know precious little about them); instituted formulaic ways of dealing with the customer (the Mobius phone loop); helped to disconnect institutional trust from value (derivatives trading); produced power brokers who are *in* organizations but not *of* them; and served up leaders who give us ample reason for the decline of the public trust (certain former heads of the democratic world).

This sea change has even reconfigured what constitutes government. In the old world, government meetings were mainly made up of government officials. In the new world, a very real question is: Who is the government? Today, contractors, consulting firms, think-tankers, and quasi-official bodies daily stand in for it, in the process composing a more dispersed and fragmented governing system. In the United States, for instance, three quarters of the people working for the federal government actually now work directly for private companies, sometimes with a lot of influence and often with little oversight—but always focused first on the bottom line, not the public interest.[54] Contractors (think Edward Snowden) run intelligence operations, control crucial databases, screen airport security and law-enforcement officials, choose and oversee other contractors, and draft official documents.[55] And there's been an increase in the numbers and influence of think tanks and quasi-official bodies like government advisory boards.[56]

The sea change has also diversified and obscured the missions of both official and private organizations. In the old world, the military fought wars, think tanks published policy reports, and media investigated and reported the news. Boundaries were clearer and organizational missions more narrowly focused. As we shall see in Chapter 9, today, campaign fund-raising groups pose as nonprofits or grassroots organizations.[57] Chapter 7 shows think tanks acting as news outlets.[58] News outlets and even military units function like entertainment companies. Navy SEALS, the same armed force that killed Osama bin Laden, co-produce a film with Hollywood in which the SEALS play themselves.

Businesses, too, are stretching into areas far beyond their traditional reach, not to mention beyond the reach of regulation, oversight, and accountability. Several large banks have become traders in commodities like aluminum, activity enabled by lax oversight.[59] Goldman Sachs, Morgan Stanley, and JPMorgan Chase have conducted commercial activities that include power production, port management, oil drilling and distribution, and uranium mining.[60] In 2011, the *New York Times* reported, "an internal Goldman memo suggested that speculation by investors accounted for about a third of the price of a barrel of oil."[61]

The sea change has meant that an octane-charged flexibility is the key to getting ahead. The new era is all about "flex," responding to the opportunity of the moment and bending in whatever way serves a player's interests best. The era's most successful actors are adept at ambiguity, line-blurring, reinventing, self-regulating, adapting, and branding, all the while pushing the limits of acceptability.

Flexibility is so much a part of the modus operandi of today's top power brokers that I coined this term to describe them: flexian.[62]

An archetypal flexian is Lawrence Summers, who we will examine in greater depth later in the book. As one of his friends said about him in 2013, "[Summers has] been going about his life just on the basis of 'who knows what's going to come next?' and just sort of maximizing his experiences, given the opportunities in front of him."[63] He has certainly "maximized experiences" over the decades, to the point where it is hard to even enumerate the number of roles he has taken on. Here is a partial list: economist; deputy Treasury Secretary under Clinton; president of Harvard; Treasury Secretary (also under Clinton); sought-after public speaker; op-ed writer; think-tanker; senior economic adviser to the Obama White House;

university professor at Harvard (the highest academic rank); adviser to a vast assemblage of Wall Street and corporate outfits, including hedge funds, a trading floor operator, an asset manager, a venture capital firm, and big banks such as Citigroup.

Many of us perform multiple professional roles. But when they mesh in ways that disguise our true agendas or contradict the public agendas we purport to serve, defying accountability and transparency, therein lies the potential for violation of the public trust.

As Harvard's president, Larry Summers did consulting work for a hedge fund from 2004 to 2006. He then used the founders of the hedge fund as part of an "informal brain trust" that he tapped when taking on the top economic advisory role in the Obama White House. Summers also uses the media to brand himself as an impartial guardian of sound public policy. In writing an opinion piece in the *Washington Post* in 2013, he was described as "a professor and past president at Harvard. He was Treasury secretary from 1999 to 2001 and economic adviser to President Obama from 2009 through 2010." How is the public to know that the vast majority of his current income is derived from Wall Street and corporate gigs?[64]

The sea change requires that we alter how we make sense of the world. In this brave new world, which I make sense of as an anthropologist, the players themselves often are the pillars of power. They perform multiple and sometimes overlapping roles across government, business, think-tank, and media organizations, and it's sometimes difficult to tell where one organization or role ends and the other begins. Influence is vested not so much in organizations but in players who operate in and around them and connect them through their multiple roles and informal networks. Their very power stems from their ability to connect the dots—to blend and blur official and private boundaries—and from their flexibility and ability to fudge boundaries.

In other words, the very power of these power brokers stems from their ability to be unaccountable.

Whatever its virtues (and there are many), flexibility must be considered a chief culprit in today's unaccountability and hence the new corruption. Flexibility offers deniability, enabling power brokers to hide, obscure, and wriggle out of responsibility for actions in one role, saying they were operating in the capacity of another. Unaccountability thrives when responsibility can be denied.

Meanwhile, we, the people, buy into this agility. We seem easily impressed by the peripatetic pundits and policy missionaries we see on TV, as well as the highfliers who float in and out of officialdom, and we don't tend to look beyond their public presentations and personas. The "private" and the informal—players, networks, and solutions—seem more authentic, even as they may be supported, sponsored, or spawned by government or industry or other organizations. When we fail to look under the surface and are so readily seduced, we do nothing to slow—in fact, we *advance*—the march to unaccountability.

CALLING OUT THE NEW CORRUPTION

I return to the question I began with: What happens to society when trust, and the accountability needed to sustain that trust, is drained from the institutions, leaders, and the governmental and corporate organizations on which we depend? When Goldman Sachs settled the ABACUS case with the U.S. government, a well-known political gossip site ran this trenchant headline: "BREAKING—Goldman Did Not Break Any of Those Laws It Wrote."[65]

Of course, the use of the word "BREAKING" is part of the joke. Few were surprised that the U.S. government couldn't prosecute the case with the current laws on the books. As the writer puts it in darkly comic fashion, it's all part of the "new normal."

This new normal is a far cry from the bureaucrat who took a bribe or who served his personal interests at the expense of the client and the public good; *that* corruption was the pathology of the system. That corruption clearly broke the rules, was against the law, and could be held to account. But as I've shown, corruption must now be understood differently because the system has undergone a sea change, and, as we'll see in the next chapter, unaccountability is structured into it.

Now too, corruption must be understood differently because unaccountability allows the corruption of the new players to be far more indirect and difficult to detect. They flex and shift roles to suit their needs of the moment. They create organizations that morph as their needs change.

Now too, corruption must be understood differently because unaccountability has also emasculated the old ways of detecting, deterring, and punishing corruption. In the process, too, one of society's mechanisms for exercising social control—shame—has fallen away. The players' brazenness shows how widely their activities are tolerated, even accepted or admired.

Ethics have been reduced to individual choice, as political scientist Susan Strange famously noted as early as the 1990s.[66] The only real control is social pressure exerted by the trust network.

But when the pressure is merely that of the networks of today's informal power brokers, there will be the opposite effect. Far from bringing shame or sanction, the pressure they exert on and for each other instead enables them to "fail up."

This will not do.

We need to reinvent shame. It must take its place in civic life again. Shame, of course, emanates from the inside. But today's protesters, seeking to bypass the system and the institutions it comprises, consider themselves outsiders. Society runs the risk of producing a permanent class of outsiders.

That is one reason we need to redefine corruption as violation of the public trust and not just as simple bribery or illegal behavior. Reconceptualizing corruption as violation of the public trust moves us toward reestablishing the broken connection between people on the ground on the one hand and official and public institutions on the other.

As I learned in communist and post-communist eastern Europe, when people don't trust the system, they create workarounds to get reliable information, obtain what they need, and maneuver the daily economy and bureaucracy. And the system that's created by everyone working around obstacles leads people to see themselves as outsiders, *even as they participate in, and are daily co-opted into, their own survival by the workaround system they collectively created*. What is happening today is that the systems in place are (inadvertently) generating outsiders en masse (think the huge percentage of unemployed Greek youth). And these outsiders, understandably, have scant faith in the system.

The irony is that placing our faith in individuals instead of institutions mirrors the same impulse that produced the problem: the bypassing and disrespect of the system now practiced by the top players. When people have faith only in the personal or private realm, as we'll explore next, that creates a systemic problem for democratic society. When the public realm and public institutions have become so discredited that people trust only others who can be marketed to them as "private," there is little hope for the vital rebuilding of public institutions—and the public trust. Society gets reduced to bypassing and disrespecting these institutions, just the way many top power brokers do now.

In Eastern Europe during late communism, I witnessed a pervasive feeling of helplessness, fatalism, and gallows humor. Now I am seeing it here in the supposedly much more transparent West. "We" who are the victims of (and sometime collaborators in) all of this exhibit wide mood swings, oscillating between, as cultural analyst John Clarke tells me, "outraged (intermittently), complacent (much of the time), resigned (also much of the time) and cynical."[67]

Yet if trust in public institutions is to be reclaimed, mustn't we call out the violation of the public trust—the new corruption?

CHAPTER 2

Unaccountability, Structured

The cornerstone of the new corruption is unaccountability. It is structured into the workings of modern-day government and corporate organizations in ways that wouldn't have been possible before the waning years of the twentieth century. It pervades everything from bureaucracies and banks to even the way computers interact with us. Unaccountability means that the system has an unprecedented ability to get to us, while we can scarcely get to it.

Take, for a small example, my own odyssey in trying to clear my credit record with the Bank of America. My twenty-plus hours on the phone with no fewer than twenty Bank of America representatives illustrates how many organizations now immunize (while often enriching) those at the top, even as accountability disappears into a puzzling maze. No doubt those who tried to "help" me followed their prescribed checklist—amounting to a pantomime performance of accountability. Incredibly, even more than I had experienced decades before in Eastern Europe, the system was simply structured to defeat me.

My effort began when a mortgage lender told me that my otherwise stellar credit history—which I had hoped would win me a favorable interest rate—was severely damaged because of an overdue Bank of America credit card balance of which I was completely unaware. When I'd cancelled—or thought I'd cancelled—my card, Bank of America told me I had a zero balance. I had a cancellation number and the ID number of the customer service representative I had talked with to prove it. Straightening things out would be easy, I thought.

Not so fast. I proceeded from Derrick and Deena in customer service in southern California to John, a customer service supervisor, to Felipe in the privacy source department in _____ (he was not authorized to say) to Carolyn in the credit department (a totally different phone number) to Adam in credit protection (Omaha) to Elsa in the credit department (or was it card services?) in Georgia to Julia in external customer relations to Delia in the escalations department to Sophia, also in escalations (the name of which alone tells you something), and Carol in credit analysis in Ohio. Back to customer services (Dan) and then Heather in card services, Kenton in the credit department, Susan in online banking and deposits in South Carolina and—sandwiched somewhere in there—Jim, a manager at a call center.

My journey, and an entire notepad scribbled with notes and names and dates to prove it, transported me back to an unlikely place: communist Poland under martial law in the early 1980s. I recalled six hours I'd spent on hold one afternoon, waiting to place an international call. Was I now up against the same kind of behemoth? The sense of helplessness, the gut-wrenching frustration and mounting anger—it sure felt the same. I couldn't help but wonder about the fates of so many others whose situations were more dire than my own.

Exasperated, I tried to fix my problem the old-fashioned way. Hoping to appeal face-to-face to a physically present person, look him in the eye, and establish a sense of trust just as I would have in the old Poland, I walked into a local Bank of America branch. I was greeted by Charles. We were joined by Bob, who called in Ronald, the bank manager. All were sympathetic and eager to assist. But what could they do? Only get on the phone and call into . . . the same phone tree. Shrugging their shoulders, they apologized for their ineffectuality.

Even Bank of America's CEO claims to be helpless. At a 2012 share-holder meeting, Brian Moynihan faced protests and outrage for years of shoddy lending and unresponsive service as people struggle to refinance their mortgages. Moynihan's response: "You can call us, and we will figure it out." He urged people to try a toll-free number, "eliciting laughter," as Bloomberg News reported.[1]

Feeling victimized by bureaucracy is something we've all experienced, especially in recent years. (My point is not to single out Bank of America, or any other institution. The people I talked with tried to help, but they were constrained by their own system.) I was reminded of the exasperation that often typified encounters with the state-owned economy and bureaucracy in Eastern Bloc countries when one was trying to obtain scarce gasoline or meat or curtains or a favorable place in a years-long queue for a state-owned apartment or a passport to travel abroad. And yet, upon reflection, it seems to me that the systems prevailing today in the West and beyond are, in some ways, even harder to navigate than the ones I lived with and studied in communist Poland as an anthropologist in training.

Even under communism, with its quintessentially big, bad bureaucracy, many citizens found a way out, albeit far from an optimal one. The surest way to secure essential, yet formally hard to get, goods and services was to work through trusted family and friends, calling up favors in a long chain of reciprocal obligations. The key to success was *informal information*: knowing—or being able to find out through informal networks—whom to approach and how and where to intervene. Success elicited, in the psyche, both *shame* in lowering oneself to less-than-honest and sometimes even humiliating behavior and *pride* in one's ingenuity in having beaten the system. But in today's corporate and government bureaucracy, the human psyche is scarcely part of the equation. For how would we even know *whom* to approach to exchange a favor with or to butter up? I certainly couldn't crack the Bank of America goliath, although my problem was eventually resolved after I pointedly explained to customer-service representatives the similarities between the old Eastern Bloc and Bank of America bureaucracies. One representative, unsettled by that comparison, went to herculean lengths to locate someone in the company maze who could tackle the problem.

What does my run-in with an all-too-common bureaucratic morass have to do with unaccountability? My story (and surely you have at least one, too) aptly illustrates an insidious reorganization of power that has occurred with such startling speed over the past several decades that most of us have barely paused to consider the implications.

But we must.

First up, government and corporate organizations. Whatever bureaucracy we're trying to navigate or is impinging on our lives, we're constantly hitting a brick wall. From organization to organization, this technology-driven, partly outsourced, too-big-to-fail structure is more difficult to deal with than the bureaucracy of old. The problem is not simply inefficiency or bad management. Such impenetrable organization means that it's almost impossible to put your finger on, ultimately, who is responsible or account-able for what—if anyone is. This sets up the perfect environment for the new corruption.

Citizens in supposedly transparent democracies—no conspiracy needed—are now subject to unaccountable organizations and institutions in a way I haven't witnessed since Solidarity leader Lech Wałęsa was still an outlaw activist. Under communism, the reasons for the public's lack of trust were clear: the system delivered only minimally in economies where shortages were the norm; to live a more than marginal life in material terms required finagling.[2] But my experience with communist bureaucracy is that it was easier to maneuver than a Bank of America–type bureaucracy.

THE BUCK STOPS . . . NOWHERE

The erosion of the public trust goes to the very core of society: our corpo-rate and governmental organizations. Many are structured, in effect, to be unaccountable and to discourage the public trust.

Take my encounter with Bank of America. Did I mention that the charge that wreaked such havoc was a $13.69 bill and that it was for a *credit protec-tion plan*? That is, the package I had purchased to alert me to any problems with my credit actually upended it.

This new unaccountability is born of the interaction of several factors over several decades, notably new information technologies and checklist-type "accountability" systems, with developments like contracting out and outsourcing also playing a part. The result is a greater disconnect among "silos"—units or milieus in the same organization or structure. My Bank of America story, while relatively benign, encapsulates the dynamics of many such organizations.

What has been called "structured unaccountability" pervades the modern-day organization.[3] That organization is 180 degrees removed from the formal bureaucracy famously described by German sociologist Max Weber at the beginning of the twentieth century. Weber's bureaucracy is *legal*—it follows the rule of law; *rational*—the organization has goals that it attempts to realize; and *impersonal*—a client's ability to achieve a goal doesn't depend on his or her personal relationship with a bureaucrat in it.[4] Weber's bureaucracy could be mapped; but try mapping a Bank of America-type structure. The esteemed sociologist was, of course, charting the *ideal* organization. Bureaucracy in the real world often falls short; a disjuncture looms between its prescribed principles and actual practices, as studies the world over show.[5]

Yet today, interactions of the digital age have disconnected the bureaucrat from the client in ways Weber couldn't have imagined. The new-world bureaucracy is organized into discrete information universes with essential bits of information separated from each other, treading in a sea of digital routines. Employees are trained to know only what's in their own tiny silo. In the Bank of America example, Carol in Ohio in the so-called credit analysis department had never heard of the cancellation numbers or station numbers that I had been assigned by another Bank of America unit. The information given by one division may be flat wrong according to another, which may not even be authorized to communicate beyond its bounds. So one unit can send you a letter but isn't authorized to dispatch it to another division in the same company. The larger picture of institutional knowledge and memory is obscured, if not obliterated.

Both bureaucrat and client sit in the dark, at the mercy of new information technologies that live in an accountability-free no-man's-land that no one can totally manage. Where is the accountability in the automated phone tree, the customer chat line, and other inventions that take on a life of their own?

The result of these silo-ized units awash in bits and bytes is that my local Bank of America branch and Carol in Ohio likely know less about who in their organization can solve my problem than the communist bureaucrats

I encountered idling away in organizations very far from Weber's ideal. Carol and my local branch manager, while eager to help, are even smaller cogs in the wheel and less able to assist than their equivalents under a pre-digital communist system.

I, the client, have far less room to creatively maneuver—to interact to my advantage—in this digital netherworld. And when an actual person in a bureaucracy, albeit one on the phone, is eventually pinned down, s/he is primarily responsible to the checklist, not to the client/customer, as was the case with Weber's bureaucracy, however differently it may work in practice as compared to its own theory of itself. Weber's bureaucrat was responsible for solving the client's problem, following through with letters, meetings, court appearances, or other procedures. By contrast, Carol in Ohio is no doubt evaluated (and promoted) not by whether she actually solves customers' problems but by whether she completes the prescribed checklist and says the right things in the right way to me and others who course through her call center.

This is not Carol's fault. The very means of assessing accountability—of judging whether someone is doing a good job—is to blame. As practiced nowadays, "accountability" is more about ticking off the boxes on a checklist of things to do and say than about solving a problem. So Carol performs for the checklist. Her job depends on it. To be favorably appraised by her bosses, she must *showcase* accountability, which may well diverge from actually achieving it.

This was not the case in the old world when a local prospective home buyer met face to face with a bank manager to secure a mortgage. Nor was it the case when, having faced the bureaucrat, the customer could point a finger at his incompetence, arrogance, or corruption. Today, a "kind of a silent moral coup has stripped the customer of his/her individuality altogether," as an analyst of bureaucracy has observed.[6]

Most of us have found ourselves in the grip of this twenty-first-century organizational behemoth at one time or another, whether battling an insurance company over a disputed claim or a bank over an uncommitted offense. But this unaccountable structure has proliferated far beyond the customer call center, with far more deleterious consequences.

Take, for example, the financial system. Think of the housing bubble in the United States in the 2000s that helped precipitate the 2008 financial crisis. Under the assumption that home prices would continue to rise and thereby alleviate the risk of bad loans, mortgage loans were packaged and repackaged, with the value unknown, as traders reaped gains for every slice and dice, passing on damaged goods, no matter the consequences for the client individually and the public generally. Vast amounts of wealth were concentrated among Wall Street practitioners and high-flying investors while disaster awaited millions of others.

A number of scholars and analysts argue that such silo-ization writ large, use of jargon to obscure, and splintering of information facilitated the meltdown. Anthropologist Gillian Tett of the *Financial Times* interviewed bankers across financial capitals to try to make sense of how exotic derivatives evolved and proliferated.[7] She elaborates on Wall Street "tribes" within a single firm, and how the derivatives tribe came to dominate:[8]

> Groups such as Citi or Merrill appear to have developed a more hierarchical pattern, in which the different business lines have existed like warring tribes, answerable only to the chief. Moreover, the most profitable tribe has invariably wielded the most power—and thus was untouchable and inscrutable to everyone else. Hence the fact that, in this tribal culture, nobody reined in the excesses. . . .

Information did not flow freely between divisions or among banks, Tett observed. Analysts in one unit often knew less than she did about what was happening in other units of the same bank.[9]

Making a parallel point, William White, chairman of the Economic and Development Review Committee at the Organization for Economic Cooperation and Development in Paris, highlights "the complexity of operations and the interrelationships among firms." One of the pre-crisis convictions of regulators and overseers upended by the crisis, he reflects, was the "belief that regulators, traditionally focused on the good health of individual institutions, actually had a good understanding of the health of the system as a whole."[10] Apparently, they did not.

Functionaries in such complex organizations, be they traders in complicated financial instruments or employees or contractors working in customer service, are incentivized to have a stake only in their own little cubicles, not in the larger outcome for the client or the public. The term "structured unaccountability" was coined by a team of sociologists to capture this very disconnect. After the collapse of Lehman Brothers, the iconic Wall Street firm that fell in the autumn of 2008, signaling the global financial crisis, the sociologists interviewed dozens of Swiss, German, and Austrian bankers (managers and employees from different departments and at different levels), who described how the industry had changed. It used to be that bankers were responsible for a borrower's ability to pay back a loan. There came a point in the early part of this century, though, when they were no longer responsible for the results of their lending, only for doing deals—as many as possible.[11] Bonuses were generally granted according to the volume of deals made, not necessarily the consequences of any given deal. True accountability was structured out of the equation.[12]

Who is at fault? The answer is hardly satisfying. We tend to take on the ethics of our silos and professions, with their success becoming our focus, rather than the client/customer—or, more holistically, the larger results of our actions. Tett writes:[13]

> I know it's very fashionable to think the bankers were trying to hoodwink the world. And yes, there probably were some bankers being greedy—maybe mad or evil too—but I think the vast majority of bankers were not any of these things. They wanted to get on and do their job and they simply didn't have much incentive to challenge the system.

Like Bank of America's Carol et al., rewarded for completing the checklist (sans a bigger picture), many on Wall Street and in corporate America have been rewarded for their short-term investment gains, or the volume of their deals, regardless of the deal or trade's actual long-term merits or its effect on the parties to the deal, the firm, or the broader society or economy.[14] Indeed, this was Goldman Sachs's defense when hauled before Congress in 2010. Having shorted their own clients, "Goldman representatives accounted for themselves in the hearing not as advisers to clients, but as 'market makers'; essentially as traders among traders," writes anthropologist of finance

Caitlin Zaloom. The problem for ordinary people is that these self-styled "market makers" have their own "moral apparatus, sets of responsibilities, and ideas of virtuous action."[15] The client is scarcely part of this picture.

Removed from the client, this new-style answerability often displaces old-fashioned professional ethics, as several scholars have shown.[16] It is a poor substitute for both having a broad sense of what needs to be done and taking responsibility for doing it.

Technology, The Decider

Technology and automation have played a role in both creating Frankenstein financial instruments and in fostering unaccountability in still other ways. Complex derivatives, collateralized debt, and anything termed "exotic" would have been nearly impossible to generate and proliferate without computer technology doing the slicing, dicing, collating, and near-instantaneous transfer of information.

In removing the human dimension and the accountability it can provide, the computer models used in the financial industry (while promising to minimize risk) may actually have *introduced* risk into the system, some analysts argue.[17] As Tett writes, the "opaque and complex" tools bankers used, and the very way they "disbursed risk across the system," actually increased risk.[18] The so-called Value at Risk (VaR) proprietary models were devised to assess risk within a financial organization and came into wide use to help satisfy regulatory regimes.[19] VaR was the preferred risk measure adopted by the so-called quants (short for quantitative), mathematicians and other pedigreed number-crunchers who held sway in the decade leading up to the financial crisis. As the smartest guys in the room, quants believed that they could accurately predict risk; but as we know now, this was one test they flunked. As the *New York Times* puts it, "VaR's great appeal, and its great selling point to people who do not happen to be quants, is that it expresses risk as a single number, a dollar figure, no less." But hedge fund billionaire David Einhorn summed up VaR as ". . . relatively useless as a risk-management tool and potentially catastrophic when its use creates a false sense of security among senior managers and watchdogs. This is like an air bag that works all the time, except when you have a car accident."[20] The 2008 crash was the car accident.[21]

Since 2008, some critics have argued that letting the banks use their own proprietary models caused them to underestimate risk and shut out the more subjective assessments based on experience and "gut." In fact, one firm averted some of the problems that plagued others by putting human agency back into the equation. The company asked top managers in 2007 how things "felt." Their gut said "danger," and the firm, Goldman Sachs, began pulling back on risky securities.[22] By contrast, despite calls to rein in VaR, faulty VaR models are blamed in part for JPMorgan Chase's multi-billion-dollar loss in 2012 (thanks to the trader nicknamed the London Whale).[23]

The decisionmakers in this unaccountable system have their reasons and rationalizations, often cloaked in the silo-speak or lingo of their own bailiwicks. Indeed, in this era of unmatched complexity and ever-permuting technologies, the worlds of high finance and other such realms are too difficult for us lay people to understand; the experts will take care of it for us then. While both were invented by (and ostensibly for) humans, you wouldn't know that from the insiders. Tett describes bankers at an exclusive conference thusly:[24]

> The way they talked about credit was to emphasize the numbers and to quite deliberately exclude any mention of social interaction from the debate and discussion. In the first couple of days I sat there, they almost never mentioned the human borrower who was at the end of that securitization chain. They were also very exclusive. There was a sense that "we alone have mastery over this knowledge."

This "complexity narrative," as one anthropologist of finance calls it,[25]

> [is one] that empowers the [bankers and their lobbyists] who can say, "listen Congress, listen policymakers, we're the ones who know what's going on. So just back off. There's no way you can understand unless you have a degree in advanced math or advanced physics."

Damning evidence of this kind of hubris can be seen in a statement to Congress in 1998—when the derivatives time bomb might have been defused—from then-deputy Treasury Secretary Lawrence Summers. He clearly internalized the idea that the Wall Street pros knew best:[26]

> . . . the parties to these kinds of contract are largely sophisticated financial institutions that would appear to be eminently capable of protecting themselves from fraud and counterparty insolvencies.

I spoke in 2014 with Sony Kapoor, a finance think-tanker and adviser to governments and global institutions. He talked about the "technocratic competence idea" that reigns supreme. This can be seen here in Summers insisting that only the parties being regulated (banks), and those like himself who have direct experience with the regulated, are the ones "eminently capable" of doing the regulating.[27]

Players like Summers no doubt believe they have unique information, expertise, and the personal integrity to act on our behalf, even when their actions leave accountability in the dust. But with such players obviously not worthy of our trust, we, the public, know not where to turn.

Deniability

Unaccountability can thrive wherever responsibility can be denied. When lines of authority are clear; when players wear one hat, not ten; when systems are less complex and have fewer silos, it is much harder for those involved to insist "It wasn't me" when things go wrong. But none of those conditions exist any longer. We are dealing with systems that are complex on a mind-boggling scale. As William White, who observed the unfolding of the financial crisis up close, put it to me: "Almost by definition, those contributing to [complex systems] can claim the failings of others are to blame."[28]

Accountability is at risk wherever deniability is built into the system. Computer models make it easier to deflect blame when those models fail to mitigate risk, as they did spectacularly in 2008. They take a large degree of human agency out of the all-important assessments of how much risk a firm is actually taking. And who is responsible here? It's certainly easier to say "the computer model was wrong" than "I was wrong." Human agency and moral thinking have been crowded out by technology.

Deniability is built in to the system in still other ways. Today's endless delegation to contractors and subcontractors, and to people whose status as inside or outside the system is unclear, is custom-made for deniability.[29] Accountability rules for government contractors are typically more lenient than for those employed directly by government. Yet outsourcing is a sizable part of how the U.S. government (and many other governments at many levels) gets its work done.[30]

"Accountability" primarily to the volume of deals or to the checklist invites deception. High-finance bankers and even Carol in Ohio cannot be totally straight about the limits of their ability to answer to the client, even as they most likely have never given much thought to it. Neither is the investment banker always forthcoming about what s/he knows about the quality of the investment s/he is selling. Unlike the (anti-) sales clerks and bureaucrats of the communist era, who were often the antithesis of customer-friendly and sometimes even aggressively hostile, today's functionaries are trained to appear to please and placate the customer even when they know they cannot help or when the financial package they are selling may do harm. The brash, or even bullying, attitude I witnessed under communism is, in effect, more honest. Deception, whether conscious on the part of the deceivers or not, can't help but foment public distrust.

We have trouble wrapping our heads around this new unaccountability because Carol and others working in these organizations are not bad people and cannot be perceived as corrupt. But the system in which they operate, incredibly, is set up to be even less accountable than the byzantine communist bureaucracy of 1980s Poland.

This ubiquitous unaccountability, despite our supposed age of "transparency," turns on the elusive origins of authority. It's virtually impossible to identify the levers of authority or figure out where and how to intervene. The absence of responsible parties can lead to untruths that take on a life of their own. Without our knowledge or consent, the system can erroneously relegate us to the category of poor credit risk, debtor, or deadbeat—any of which could ruin our chance for a better mortgage or the ability to keep our house or even a much-needed job, and all of which could be resolved if the organization were set up to be accountable.[31] Does this state of affairs encourage trust in governmental and corporate organizations in what's supposed to be the world's model democracy?

Because it is difficult, if not impossible, to challenge the insidious system, only the ethics or judgment of a few "bad apples" are questioned (think, for example, Fabrice Tourre of Goldman Sachs, a.k.a. "Fabulous Fab," the rare Wall Street employee who the SEC found liable for securities fraud). But it shouldn't be so difficult. Structured unaccountability has the potential to warp our lives and generate inequalities in ways both small and very, very big. Because Wall Street is still trading opaque, vastly complex financial instruments in a system mired in structured unaccountability, no one can really know, in a holistic sense, where the financial TNT has been planted, just waiting for detonation.

Unaccountability and Runaway Information

As we await the next explosion, twenty-first-century corporate and government organizations challenge accountability in an even broader way. They are constantly morphing their purposes, often far beneath the public radar—taking on totally different missions from those they advertise. While these are set up to look like we, the consumers/customers/clients, are empowered, the weight of their power is stacked against us.

The lifeblood of many organizations is now in information. Though a key purpose of a Bank of America is, supposedly, to answer to the client, "customer service" has evolved, at least in large part, into a means for getting the client's personal information to use for direct advertising or market research—or even to sell to other companies or governments. Many government, corporate, and even campaign organizations have become secret services, gathering tons of information about us, often under the pretext that they're working for us: keeping us in touch with friends (Facebook); giving us "points" when we make credit card purchases (card companies); "connecting" with a preferred political candidate; and even finding information for us (Google searches that prompt specific ads showing some of what they know about our lives). While harnessing the information we freely give up, Google, Facebook, Verizon, and other companies may dispute willing collaboration with government agencies. But the point is, how would we know if it weren't for the Edward Snowdens of this world?[32]

We want to be in the know, minute to minute, with our whole panoply of interests; but the implicit deal we make (with the devil?) is that powerful algorithms will amass an easily exploitable profile that might shock us with its specificity and invasiveness. At least one that *should* shock us.

Meanwhile, no matter how many revelations come to light, it's never going to be clear who holds that information or what uses it is being put to—or could be put to—because, as I have said, authority in these organizations (and the wider systems in which they operate) is often hard to pin down or is even completely unknown to nearly everyone, even within the organization. There's no real way of learning the truth in real time unless we are deep inside it. We, the public, can't possibly compete with the organization, either in terms of knowledge about its operations or the specific data amassed.

And amassing they are. As the industry and intelligence of data-mining have risen, corporate and government organizations have joined forces. You can see it in the synergy between espionage agencies and the technology companies of Silicon Valley.[33] The move of Max Kelly, the chief security officer for Facebook, to the NSA in 2010, for instance, "underscores the increasingly deep connections between Silicon Valley and the agency and the degree to which they are now in the same business," the *New York Times* noted. The NSA may be concerned with intelligence and Silicon Valley with profit, but they "both hunt for ways to collect, analyze and exploit large pools of data about millions of Americans."[34]

Informality and Unaccountability

Silicon Valley and the tech sector, of course, excel at DIY (do-it-yourself)—from Uber cars to Airbnb to crowd-sourced venture capital. Their focus on private solutions to public problems largely leaves accountability behind. As a *New Yorker* article titled "Bay Watched: How San Francisco's New Entrepreneurial Culture is Changing the Country" details, twenty-something "cool kids" at the business-digital cutting edge are merging moneymaking with new-age-style social purpose. (HBO this year debuted a trenchant satire show, *Silicon Valley*, depicting this unusual blend of capitalist and tech-powered idealism.) These new entrepreneurs are overtaking Wall

Streeters as the model of success.[35] They project being relaxed, casual—and informal—and also no doubt believe they are doing the right thing and that they have the expertise and the answers to big questions.

Informality has become the fashion of the moment on all kinds of levels, and you will see these loose ad hoc arrangements throughout the book. It runs the gamut from how you can now get a ride to the airport all the way to how war strategy is devised. I saw firsthand that informality was what enabled people under communism to survive, and there seem to be some parallels with twenty-first-century America. As I've said above, in 1980s Poland, the most ingenious eked out a livable life with creative dealmaking. Flash forward to today in the West. With an economy under severe stress, the most creative players have innovated, using technology to set up ventures like Airbnb, Task Rabbit, and Uber, where people can rent out their private resources—houses, labor, cars. This has brought part-time work and extra cash for those who use it, much as I saw in East Bloc Poland when regular people leveraged any tiny asset or resource they might have. The ones who've made out best, of course, are often the elite who own or invest in these burgeoning companies.

What's more, informality is often found now—and even prized—among elites in policymaking and in ways that might be born of stress as well. As government becomes increasingly privatized, expertise is lacking when big public-policy decisions must be made. Players pull trusted friends in during a crisis (case in point: the financial bailout) or when life-and-death decisions must be made (another case: whether to stage a military "surge" in Afghanistan) and when making other policy choices.

So what's wrong with informality? It is not in itself wrong, and surely it even has some clear benefits. But there is one thing that informality makes nearly impossible: accountability. If an informal group is involved in deciding policy, how do we know that the people chosen represent the variety of voices needed for vigorous debate? We certainly have plenty of examples, as you will see, of voices very much excluded from high-stakes debate. If the "cool kids" chosen to participate aren't formally public servants, do they have the same ethics and disclosure rules? Usually not.

Sony Kapoor, that finance think-tanker who has been in and around the financial discussions taking place, told me that, in a crisis, there is the feeling among players that there is simply not enough time to amass the twenty people who should be in the room, and accountability becomes an afterthought. With regard to the 2008 financial crisis and bailout, Kapoor said: "[There was] next to no information on what central banks knew, what they thought the risks were. . . . Everyone was given the benefit of the doubt after the fact. . . . If it were any other part of government, there would have to be due diligence."

Aside from emergencies, he made it clear that finance people often speak of a tradeoff between "efficiency" and "accountability." The attitude is "We're the experts; we don't have the time." Kapoor suggests there really are no outside perspectives because, quite simply, there are no outsiders: "Those who might have authority or information or wherewithal . . . are in one way or another a part of the system."[36] Indeed, if the players are assembling themselves informally, it's not all that astonishing that they choose like-minded individuals with similar agendas not necessarily in the public interest.

Informal arrangements can be expedient and efficient. But accountability is almost inevitably sidelined, whether it's in policymaking as seen in the financial bailout—or in what's been dubbed the "sharing economy" emerging from Silicon Valley.

What about harm, liability, and risk when an Uber car crashes or an Airbnb house catches fire?[37] The idea that all public problems have a desirable ad hoc private solution is, to say the least, reality-challenged.

Also reality-challenged is the hotly debated idea that more information unleashed by the digital revolution has made the world more transparent. Ironically, the control of information now seems weighted in favor of the entities and authorities (many of them corporate or private) that collect and use it for purposes mostly hidden from public view.

This can hardly inspire the public trust.

WE, THE COLLABORATORS

And yet, unsettling as this may be, I must raise this question: What about our own complicity? We may be the victims, but we are also collaborators. The first thing we do when signing on to a new computer system or program is to lie—that we have read all the legalese and caveats, and that we

45

agree to them. But I would bet that very few people read the fine print (the companies monitoring our computers can probably tell us definitively), and those who do are seen as nerds or paranoids. We download and "agree" to the terms of use of software and such because we want to have them and realize that if we don't click "agree," we're not going to get what we want. We disregard the privacy notice that comes with our credit-card bill and bank statement because, even though we know that information will be collected and used in ways we might not like, we need the credit card and the checking account.

Most of us play by these new informal rules because not doing so would relegate us to far more hassled—if not downright unworkable—lives. I can't help but be reminded that likewise, to avoid marginal lives under the communism I witnessed, most people opted to skirt the broken formal system by fudging and finagling under the table to get what they needed. And while both cases involve deception, communist-schooled psyches are much more conscious of their own participation in this frequent practice. Should our not-quite-aware complicity in our own self-delusion concern us?

At the least, it should give us pause.

And so should the intermarriage of spies and Silicon Valley techies and what that portends. The communist experience is instructive. Communist publics were much more savvy than others about what happens to society when a massive machine is unleashed that can monitor and control people. Nearly everyone, at least under late Soviet and Eastern Bloc communism, knew full well that their systems were not designed to adequately fulfill citizens' material needs and civic desires. Moreover, surveillance was in your face, subtlety nowhere in sight. When Romanians went to the authorities to register their typewriters each year, not only did they have no choice but to comply, but there could be no doubt that the purpose was to keep tabs on them. In that system, too, authority could be anonymous, but the intention was much clearer. (It is no accident that many of my Polish, Russian, and other eastern European acquaintances, recalling communism, have declined to join Facebook. They know all too well where the tools of such a surveillance bonanza can lead and how information gleaned from it can be used.) And today's authorities don't even have to steal our address books or strip-search or interrogate us directly; we willingly connect with our "friends" on Facebook, often divulging how we know them, along with myriad other details—and on a daily basis.

When core institutions are structured to be unaccountable and to flout the public trust, and when the trust between bureaucrat and client is broken, is this not a setup for pervasive violation of the public trust—the new corruption? And what are we to make of—and do about—the fact that, just as I witnessed under a communist system, we, the citizens, however powerless and in however small a way, are complicit in our own violation?

Our collaboration may be largely passive. It is nonetheless collaboration.

And have we not allowed ourselves to be seduced? As William White, again reflecting on what went wrong that led to the financial crisis, argues:[38]

> All of the parties who contributed to the crisis (borrowers, lenders, regulators, central banks, academics and politicians) were each seduced by various influences into believing different things that were not true. Moreover, since seduction normally involves more than one party, the relationships between these various parties also contributed to their having "no eye to see and no ear to hear."

—⁂—

Do you recall what happened when I walked into a Bank of America branch, hoping my problem would be solved?

Nothing.

When the old means of restitution no longer work, and it is impossible to hold responsible parties to account, that is a sure sign that the system has moved on.

Just as many of us are defeated by the system at least some of the time, the most agile players among us know how to exploit it and take charge. We will see in the next chapter how some of those who do so violate our trust and fully engage in the new corruption.

CHAPTER 3

Inside the New Corruption

We are told this is an age of transparency. And yet the business of influencing appears to be getting less, not more, transparent. Before we look at the world of influencing, though, let's first consider a setting that is ultra-transparent. In the community of fewer than two thousand in which I grew up, the proverbial six degrees of separation are more like one or two. You can't help but play multiple roles in a small town: a teenager babysits for her next-door neighbor's kids whose father is also her schoolteacher and a colleague of her father's and whose mother is also her Sunday school teacher. Is there potential for nepotism and corruption? Yes. But at the same time, everybody knows what everybody else is doing and it's difficult to hide. In communities like this, agendas, roles, relationships, and sponsors are pretty clear.

When it comes to today's top power brokers, this model is only partly accurate. Roles overlap and decisions get made with the same kind of small-town incestuousness—but, to the outside world, there's little of the transparency of such a community.

Consider the examples of the following players who entered into a consequential policy debate affecting the global economy, airline security, and the American healthcare system, respectively. Each had information, along with experience and contacts, that they had amassed from their previous high-ranking roles in government or business—or, as is typical, both.

- Dan Jester, "retired" from Goldman Sachs, was brought in by Treasury Secretary and ex–Goldman Sachs chief Henry Paulson to assist in the 2008 financial bailout. He was hired as a "contractor," not a government employee, and thus was not required to disclose his financial holdings and was subject to far fewer rules. The *New York Times* notes that Jester seemed "to have had his finger in every pie: rescuing Fannie Mae and Freddie Mac, the Lehman Brothers bankruptcy, the A.I.G. calamity, the decisions to bail out Citigroup, G.M. and Chrysler, and the creation of the Troubled Asset Relief Program. Jester also tried to negotiate deals for Lehman with both Bank of America and Barclays." By all accounts, he served as Paulson's de facto envoy in these high-stakes gatherings.[1]

    Whose interests was Jester representing during those meetings that would affect the entire global economy? We'll never know, since he was accountable to no one other than Paulson. We can never know for sure that Jester wasn't just helping an old friend and the global economy through a grave crisis. And we will probably never know what role he played in securing the bailout terms that seemed to favor the interests of Goldman. The *New York Times* noted that Jester, not surprisingly, had holdings in the company. The *Times* also called him one of the "mystery men" of the financial crisis. And he is likely to remain so. He claimed to have "followed an ethics plan," but we'll have to take his word on that.[2]

- Former Senate Majority Leader Tom Daschle helped shape President Obama's signature legislation, healthcare reform, even while he was consulting for healthcare firms. His nomination to be Obama's Secretary of Health and Human Services was derailed in 2009 after a brief scandal over unpaid taxes. But Daschle was already assuming a much less visible, yet influential, profile in healthcare reform before and after his withdrawal. Not long after leaving the Senate in 2005, he became a consultant to a private equity firm;[3] joined a prominent Washington law and lobbying firm, Alston & Bird, advising various insurance and health companies, including UnitedHealth, though never registering as a lobbyist;[4] served at a think tank that received funding from a pharmaceutical company;[5] sat on a General Electric advisory board that devised loan incentives for rural doctors to buy the company's software;[6] and became a sought-after speechmaker at many healthcare outfits that might stand to gain from his access and prestige.[7] He quickly evolved into a K-Street powerhouse in the healthcare business, moving from Alston & Bird to DLA Piper in 2009.[8] He advised the White House and met with President Obama, Vice President Biden, and Senate Majority Leader Harry Reid to strategize on the Affordable Care Act, now popularly known as Obamacare.[9] All this while simultaneously working with the healthcare industry on the application of new information technologies, among other matters.[10]

What was Daschle's agenda? On whose behalf was he working in his meetings with the president and on Capitol Hill? Perhaps the more important question is: How can we, the public, ever know? Daschle has lobbied so flagrantly, without registering, that his evasion technique has been described as the Daschle Loophole.[11] Unaccountability, anyone?

- More recently, as the United States was considering military intervention in Syria, a strong voice appeared in the *Wall Street Journal* trying to allay fears that a U.S. air strike would simply aid rebel jihadists.[12] Elizabeth O'Bagy's August 2013 piece originally called her a senior analyst for the Institute for the Study of War. She had already been making her case in the media and to dozens of congressional offices, as well as to universities and think tanks.[13] But this op-ed propelled her farther than all her other advocacy. Soon she was appearing on media outlets as disparate as Fox News and NPR's *Morning Edition*.[14] Both Secretary of State John Kerry and Senator John McCain cited her work during congressional hearings in their push to intervene in Syria, with McCain always pointedly calling her *Dr.* O'Bagy.[15]

O'Bagy's sudden rise to prominence took a turn, however, when her perhaps more relevant role was more directly identified. She apparently had a contract with a pro-rebel group, the Syrian Emergency Task Force, which itself has contracts with the U.S. and U.K. governments to aid the Syrian opposition.[16] She had disclosed this role in some outlets, but it went unmentioned in the *Wall Street Journal* editorial. (O'Bagy was then also outed for lying about whether she had a Ph.D. from Georgetown University.) While she was fired from the Institute for the Study of War (for having misrepresented her credentials), for a brief, but significant, moment in a major debate, O'Bagy appeared frequently as an impartial expert when she was everything but. Disclosure was selective, and it appears that media outlets failed to examine her agenda carefully enough.[17] Before this information came to light, how would we have known that we were being directed to a certain viewpoint? We, the public, had no way to sort this out because we didn't know there *was* something to sort out. In the spirit of the era, O'Bagy rebounded fast, taking a job with Senator McCain.[18]

Such novel power brokers have ushered in a whole new world of challenge as they shape, make, or pronounce on public decisions. Whether through op-eds, appearances as "experts" on television, radio, or the Internet, or in advisory capacities to public figures, they and those who promote them or put them on the air lead us to believe that they are acting in the public interest. But their feet are planted firmly in another set of (private) interests. And these official and private agendas intermesh in ways that make it impossible for us to know in a time frame that matters, if ever, what they are up to and whose agendas they serve.

The information system doesn't work for us in the way it might have in the past. There was a time not so very long ago, at least in large swaths of the Western world, that we could have more confidence than we can now in the objectivity of the experts who advised government and pronounced on issues of vital importance. Roles of influencers and power brokers were better defined and more stable—like the banker, the minister, or the county official in my American Midwestern home community. That was before the sea change charted earlier in the book upended so many staples of society—from investigative reporting, to our interactions with Bank of America–like institutions, to the very core of what constitutes a bank, a think tank, or a media organization, to who carries out the work of government (officials or contractors?) and who is accountable for it.

The new-style influencers exude a shadow air in that their agendas or sponsors are obscured (Daschle and O'Bagy), or their titles do not comport with their outsize roles (Jester). In either case, we, the public, can't quite know who or what is behind their influencing activities. We cannot say, since most of us are not privy to the venues they inhabit. We do not have the benefit of the face-to-face contact that one would need with the banker or minister or county official that would allow us to get a feel for whether they can be trusted. Yet the decisions the high-flying new players make without our input affect our lives and livelihoods in ways beyond measure.

In short, we, the public, have little possibility of holding them to account. None of the activities I have described is illegal or subject to ethics regulations. The players are sufficiently novel and unconventional that they fly beneath the radar of many watchdog organizations whose missions are to monitor registered lobbyists, interest groups, and the like. They even escape the notice of many investigative journalists.

But even if such power brokers flunk the smell test, what has this to do with corruption? Where does a super-clever way of exerting influence end and a violation of the public trust—the new corruption—begin?

The age we're in has spawned a swarm of players to meet its needs. While most are unaccountable, not all, by any stretch, teeter on the edge of the new corruption. And only some tip over, violating the public trust.

Two kinds of all-out power brokers are by definition unaccountable and often abuse our trust. The modus operandi of these players, their sponsors, and their ways of organizing in and around all manner of entities (which we'll explore in depth in Part II), make them unaccountable. Some, like Humpty Dumpty, fall full-face into the new corruption.

There is no dearth of such power brokers. Some are household names like Summers, Rubin, and Daschle. But others that you may never have heard of are equally unaccountable, as are many whose names you know but whose machinations you may not be aware of. The front pages routinely offer up so many examples that in our featured column in The Huffington Post, co-author Linda Keenan and I have had a wealth of instances from which to draw (see, for example, our article profiling ten players from the last decade, including General Barry McCaffrey, Richard Perle of the "Neocon Core," and former German Chancellor Gerhard Schroeder).[19] These unaccountable players have shaped public policy, ranging from the decision to go to war in Iraq to the decision to run a direct gas pipeline from Russia to Germany.

To see just how this happens, let's first take a look at how such players—whom I call "shadow lobbyists" and "shadow elites"—evade accountability. The way they organize their roles, work in and around entities, and enlist sponsors—in short, their MO—enables them to accomplish this. The players themselves are the centerpiece of this chapter.

Whether the focus is the players themselves, or the entities and sponsors they engage with (the subject of Part II), today's dominant methods of wielding influence are less visible and more difficult to detect than, say, in the last half century. And this puts accountability on the line.

LOBBYING BY ANOTHER NAME

Shadow lobbyists, the simplest in terms of the modus operandi of the new breed of influencers, are a big part of the new corruption scene in the United States, Europe, and, by many accounts, beyond.[20] The enterprise of influencing appears to be getting increasingly informal.

In the United States, where a power broker once might have sought the title "lobbyist" to display his influence, today he is likely to take on an executive role with a title like "strategist" or "adviser" or "government affairs specialist." As a former president of the American League of Lobbyists (ALL), Paul A. Miller, observed, "'. . . there's a new way to lobby . . . and that includes PR consultants, grassroots consultants,' and many others working outside the disclosure rules."[21]

The enterprise of lobbying has changed so much that the ALL decided to drop the word "Lobbyist" from its name in favor of the more innocuous "Association of Government Relations Professionals."[22] "We suggest

'Congress Plus',' quipped the editorial board of the *New York Times* in response, citing the employment in the lobbying industry of "more than 400 former members of the Senate and House, plus former congressional staff members estimated in one study to total 5,400 people over a recent 10-year period."[23] The lobbyists themselves said that the term was too narrow to encompass their current activities. As ALL (or AGRP) president Monte Ward said in a letter to members:[24]

> Through surveys and research, we discovered that a majority of our membership no longer identified themselves as only "lobbyists." In fact, most of those surveyed stated that their responsibilities as a lobbyist encompassed just a fraction of their duties. While our organization was founded in 1979 to support the lobbying community, this industry has evolved dramatically over the years and now includes a variety of disciplines.

So what is the matter with lobbyists entering other arenas, or with changing the name of the association, as ALL did? Aren't these smart players, skilled as they are at claiming and gaming the system, just helping to evolve an up-to-the-minute way of doing business?

Yes, they are. And that up-to-the-minute way is designed to avoid accountability. Indeed, many top power brokers eschew the term "lobbyist" because it allows them to evade regulations that were put in place to prevent conflicts of loyalty and interest. Individuals who are paid to lobby the federal government are required, under a 2007 law (which strengthened and amended parts of a 1995 act), to register and file regular reports of their activities and funding. Like regular lobbyists who abide by the legal requirements of the venues in which they operate, shadow lobbyists are (generally paid) advocates who try to persuade legislators or relevant government officials to enact policies that will benefit a particular industry or group.

When shadow lobbyists don't register, they don't have to disclose their true agendas or sponsors.[25] Because we, the public, are in the dark, they can be much more effective. We didn't know, for instance, that O'Bagy might have had her own agenda while pronouncing on potential U.S. airstrikes in Syria. And these influencers often have more access to the citadels of power than those whose titles are clearly "lobbyist."

Shadow lobbyists are frequently former high government officials now connected to consulting firms, academia, the media, or think tanks; others might be one-timers, the way O'Bagy appears to have been. Still others are key players in corporate America or Wall Street. They peddle a policy, using the legitimacy or credibility gained in a current or former official role or affiliation. This aids the impression that the policy is in the public interest, even in situations where that case would be difficult to make.

As the *New York Times*, one of the few entities that has picked up on the ways of these influencers, writes: "They develop strategy and use their contacts to open doors and then leave the appointment-making to more junior people who are registered as lobbyists."[26] Jack Abramoff, who published a book about how the Big Boys operate, described the rules of the game thusly:[27]

> . . . they'll pick the phone up and they'll call their buddy, the senator, their old buddies, and they'll say, "Listen, I'm here at this law firm now. I can't lobby you, but my new partner, Jack, can lobby you. Can he come up and meet with you?"

While Abramoff himself went to prison for blatant acts of fraud, this kind of corruption, he underscores, remains fully legal and widely accepted.

It's so accepted, in fact, that shadow lobbyists may be overtaking registered ones, at least in the United States. Registered lobbyists are on the decline. Their number peaked in 2007 at 14,845 and fell to 9,434 in 2013.[28] In 2013, the *New York Times* reported "dramatic" drops at some of Washington's top lobbying firms. The well-known firm Barbour, Griffith and Rogers (also known as BGR Group) saw a thirty-eight-percent revenue falloff from 2007 to 2012; the firm QGA had a fifty-eight-percent decline over a similar time period.[29] The business of influence, though, is far from dead.

Shadow lobbyists also come from places that might seem far removed from political power centers: top universities. High-profile academics are particularly insidious. They are attractive to those who buy their services precisely because, ironically, it's the image of the neutral, incorruptible scholar that these academics sell to the public. But sometimes they are hardly so.

As we shall see in Chapter 8, economists have been especially active shadow lobbyists—and not only in America.[30] German economist and former European Central Bank official Otmar Issing penned an op-ed in the *Financial Times* to argue against a rescue package for Greece, while failing to mention that he was a Goldman Sachs adviser. This was flagged by a fellow economist, Simon Johnson, who questioned whether Issing might be "talking Goldman's book, whether he realizes it or not." He was suggesting the very real possibility that Goldman might indeed profit from Greece's failure, and that readers should at the very least know Issing's affiliation. Johnson also notes that globalization means there is no clear jurisdiction or body to investigate potential impropriety in a situation like this. "Welcome to the scary and essentially unsupervised world of international banking," he writes.[31]

Shadow lobbying knows no particular ideology or political party. Both the American liberal Howard Dean and the conservative Rudy Giuliani were paid to speak on behalf of an Iranian exile group engaged in an all-out effort to be taken off the U.S. list of foreign terrorist organizations.[32] These and other politicians have endorsed the exile group by speaking at its events for handsome fees—an activity that smacks of shadow lobbying.[33]

THE FOREIGN CONNECTION: "SHAME IS FOR SISSIES"

Some of the most sophisticated—some might say shameless—shadow lobbying in the United States is in the service of foreign governments. Lobbying on behalf of foreign governments, a kind of paid privatization of diplomacy, leaves little room for accountability. Yet today it is a huge business enlisting individuals of high renown.[34]

Foreign governments, of course, have sought to press their interests throughout American history. And some countries still do advocate through their embassies in the United States; that is, if they still have a powerful, well-staffed outpost that understands Washington. But "many, if not most" do not, according to John Newhouse of the think tank World Security Institute. Now countries of every variety—established, "emerging," and perhaps especially "rogue" regimes and dictators—routinely seek out those in the know who have privatized the channels of diplomacy. These players take the experience they gleaned through public service, join or create a firm, and then offer their privileged knowledge to foreign countries that want to trade cash for access. Here's Newhouse, writing in 2009 for *Foreign Affairs*:[35]

> . . . the U.S. government has become so complex that only insiders, such as former members of Congress or congressional staff members turned lobbyists, can navigate its confusing structure. The most well-connected individuals are likely to join one of the major hybrid law and lobbying firms, such as Patton Boggs, Akin Gump Strauss Hauer & Feld, or BGR Group. The subculture of public relations and law firms that do this kind of work reflects a steady decline and privatization of diplomacy—with an increasing impact on how the United States conducts its own foreign policy.

A partner "who focuses on international clients" in the firm Qorvis, about which we will hear more later, reported that foreign countries are relying more and more on PR, as opposed to traditional lobbying. He said that "People still see the value in traditional lobbying, but its [*sic*] not always the first stop now when you come to Washington, when it used to always be the first stop."[36]

Shadow lobbyists not only seek to sway policymakers; opinionmakers and the public are also key targets. This shadow lobbying can have a corrupting effect on foreign policy.

On paper, at least, lobbying on behalf of foreign powers would appear to be a strictly regulated affair. The Foreign Agents Registration Act, passed in 1938, was initially aimed at preventing Nazi agents from spreading propaganda. The Supreme Court described FARA this way five years later: "the general purpose of the legislation was to identify agents of foreign principals who might engage in subversive acts or in spreading foreign propaganda, and to require them to make public record of the nature of their employment."[37]

Lobbyists on behalf of foreign countries are required to register with the U.S. Department of Justice under FARA (excepting those who fall through several loopholes that I will describe shortly). Many, if not most, lobbyists working to promote foreign-country interests in the United States do, in fact, register; but they report their activities in ways that obscure their nature or full extent.

Even when the firms or organizations are registered and the actions disclosed, the public is often still largely uninformed about the full extent of their activities, especially as they become increasingly adept at manipulating Internet and social-media venues for propaganda purposes. Here are two brief examples of the unaccountability of shadow lobbying and its sometime role in suppressing the public interest.

- Turkey provides the first. Over the years, the country has amassed bipartisan lobbying power to fight a formal acknowledgement by the U.S. government of the early-twentieth-century Armenian genocide. In Turkey's corner (among other firms): International Advisors, Inc., founded by a prominent neoconservative and deputy undersecretary of defense for policy under President George W. Bush, Douglas Feith, with fellow top neocon Richard Perle serving as "adviser"; former Republican congressman Bob Livingston of the Livingston Group; and DLA Piper, one-time home of former House Majority Leader Richard Gephardt, who once supported the Armenian genocide resolution in Congress but later found the issue more complex, apparently, after his firm signed a reported $100,000-per-month contract with Turkey.[38] Among those at DLA Piper on the Turkey account were two top fundraisers for Hillary Clinton's 2008 presidential campaign.[39]

  Given Turkey's lobbying ammunition and the country's geopolitical importance, the U.S. recognition of genocide in Armenia has not moved forward. As U.S. senators, Clinton and Barack Obama both backed the genocide resolution, but the legislation has since gone nowhere. President Obama broke a promise to Armenian-Americans to publicly deem as genocide Turkey's actions nearly a century ago. In 2012, then–Secretary of State Clinton, the assumed front-runner for the 2016 Democratic presidential nomination, described the genocide recognition as "opening a door that is a very dangerous one to go through."[40]

- The use of informal envoys is another illustration. As Egypt began exploding in 2011, the Obama administration chose a special envoy who wasn't employed by the State Department to deliver a personal message to the embattled President Hosni Mubarak: former ambassador-turned-lawyer/lobbyist Frank Wisner. Wisner, of the firm Patton Boggs, returned from Egypt with such a pro-Mubarak statement that the Obama administration had to immediately distance itself from its appointed informal envoy.[41]

  Patton Boggs strongly denied that it or Wisner had any financial interest in propping up the Mubarak government and said that it had performed work in Egypt had been finished for years. But, however urgent such privatization of diplomatic expertise might seem in a given case, should it not give us pause as a practice? The State Department spokesman remarked: "We're aware of his employer. . . . And we felt that he was *uniquely positioned* to have the kind of conversation that we felt needed to be done in Egypt" [emphasis added]. Is it any surprise that Wisner went "off-script," or that Wisner's interests were questioned because he is a lobbyist?[42]

  As for those who *were* actively lobbying on behalf of Mubarak's government in the lead-up to the unrest, they included three top players: K-Street legend Tony Podesta, former congressman Toby Moffett, and, once again, Bob Livingston. According to the *New York Times*, they had a "joint, multimillion-dollar contract with Egypt. [They] met with dozens of lawmakers and helped stall a Senate bill [in 2010] that called on Egypt to curtail human rights abuses."[43]

These are but a few examples of a practice that in the past ranged from the simply rare to the inconceivable or even treasonous. In a crisis situation like that of Egypt, it's understandable that an administration might look to the players they know and trust, private or public. (And one could argue that at least Wisner had been a public servant, unlike Dan Jester, the banker friend Hank Paulson turned to when suddenly forced to bail out the financial system.) Be that as it may, and wherever one's sympathies (and the facts) lie with regard to Armenia/Turkey or Egypt, there is no question that the manner of influencing is beyond accountability.

These days, lobbying by foreign powers is so accepted as "business as usual" that foreign money even ends up in campaign coffers, according to the book *The Foreign Policy Auction*:[44]

> In a nutshell, here's how foreign money flows from a foreign government to US politicians: A foreign government signs a contract with a DC lobbying firm; the firm pays its lobbyists, at least partially, with that foreign money; then, lobbyists make campaign contributions or organize fundraisers with that money. In fact, I've found dozens of instances where foreign lobbyists made contributions to legislators on the exact same day they meet to discuss the needs of foreign governments. While this may look a lot like bribery to you and me, it's, unfortunately, perfectly legal.

And, at this point, this practice is also mostly respectable. The possible taint one might expect for those who engage in it seems to be minimal or short-lived. As the author of *The Foreign Policy Auction* puts it:[45]

> There is no arch-villain here, no dark lord, no one to unmask at the end of the show. There are only politicians seeking reelection, lobbyists seeking more revenue, and foreign governments competing for influence over the most influential government the world has ever known.

For decades, there *was* a sort of "dark lord," one of the best known lobbyists for "rogue" powers in particular, named Edward von Kloberg III (1942–2005). Words like "infamous" were constantly used to describe the flamboyant, cape-wearing von Kloberg, who had added the "von" for effect, deeming it more "distinguished." What really distinguished von Kloberg was that his Washington firm represented a slew of dictators starting in the early 1980s, including Iraq's Saddam Hussein, Nicolae Ceaușescu of Romania, Liberia's Samuel K. Doe, and Mobutu Sese Seko of Congo, formerly Zaire.

"Shame is for sissies" was one of von Kloberg's mottos. He claimed to have rejected only one client: Somali warlord Mohammed Farah Aidid.[46]

These days, though, many A-list lobbying and legal firms take business from unsavory regimes and undisputed dictators. But instead of admitting that they are brazen, like von Kloberg did, they tend to cast their activities in a benevolent light. Their frequent argument, as you'll see here and in later chapters, is that they are actually helping these regimes down the path to democracy. This rationalization emanates from the legal and lobbying firms, as well as the various public relations shops, including Burson-Marsteller and Weber Shandwick, that engage in "image management."[47]

The field abounds with similar claims, which may indeed be sincere, at least in some cases. As a member of the Washington Strategic Consulting Group recounts: "Our firm really said to leaders, 'This is what you need to do.' The whole idea was to encourage them to reform." In our shadow-elite age, such claims are not easy to evaluate. Even a former ambassador to Angola has said that the PR firm his host country used held more sway than he did.[48]

The Limits of Regulation

While lobbying is regulated, there is many a slip between cup and lip.

An agent who is registered with FARA is supposed to make detailed filings, not just of meetings with those who have influence, but of propaganda or public-relations work as well. A look at the Foreign Influence Tracker set up by the public-interest news outlet ProPublica and the Sunlight Foundation will show just how specific those filings can be.[49]

And yet there is always a lag between the propagandizing and filing. Once reporters are able to expose the foreign influence, the damage is likely already done, even if filings are timely and complete. It's unlikely that the public or policymaking community will take much notice retroactively. And it's nearly impossible if the filings are not timely or thorough.

For instance, a filing appeared in March 2013 that confirmed a paid propaganda campaign waged by the Malaysian government.[50] The goal was apparently to spread negative press through a range of mainstream American outlets against a pro-democracy figure, using ten opinion writers. But the filing came a bit late: the campaign dated back to 2008.

The foreign agent in this case, conservative pundit Joshua Trevino, maintained that he didn't know there was any database or that he needed to file at all.[51] That's likely because until President Obama took office, the enforcement of FARA had been lax, to say the least, and the law less well known. The Justice Department long favored "voluntary compliance"[52] and, in fact, very few have been successfully prosecuted for a FARA violation.[53]

With that track record, it is no surprise that filings can be haphazard. One fellow for Southeast Asia at the Council on Foreign Relations spoke to an unnamed lobbyist for a foreign country in 2010, who told him this: "I was so careful to document every phone call, every meeting, and then I found that some other people, they don't file at all. . . . Does anything happen to them? Not really."[54]

In part, that could be the result of massive loopholes. A big one involves the Lobbying Disclosure Act, which ostensibly monitors domestic lobbying and has far less stringent requirements than does FARA. If a lobbyist has multiple accounts and registers under the LDA, he then no longer needs to register as a foreign agent. Another loophole allows meetings to be held overseas; those don't fall under FARA's purview.[55] And one loophole in particular is being exploited amid the rise of—shall we say purposely—ill-defined influence or "nonprofit" groups.

One reporter describes it this way: "[A]s long as the entity is formally a nongovernmental organization and isn't funded by a government—a chamber of commerce, an advocacy group, or some other entity—the [FARA] law does not apply."[56] Her article cites the Brussels-based European Centre for a Modern Ukraine, suggesting that it is a front for the repressive (and now deposed) Ukrainian government. But because of the group's amorphous definition and ties to Ukraine's former leadership, two lobbying firms, the Podesta Group and Mercury/Clark & Weinstock, were reportedly able to represent it under the LDA. (One report said the lobbyists went "radio silent" after their client, Viktor Yanukovych, fled the country in February 2014.)[57]

The Obama administration did beef up FARA enforcement: firms in 2011 reported a big upswing in the number of audits coming from the Justice Department, with one lawyer describing the "wave" as beginning around 2009.[58]

The president may have known that enforcement was his only option, since his attempts to close loopholes during his brief tenure in the Senate were nonstarters. And some have argued that politicians have no appetite to really close these loopholes, because they are happy to accept campaign donations from the foreign (shadow) lobbying firmament. The list of politicians who've done just that now includes Obama himself.[59]

Of course, foreign lobbying has been going on for a very long time. But John Newhouse assesses that the co-opting of diplomacy by private interests is not an occasional problem, but now rather "a broad and deepening pattern of corrupt and corruptible members of Congress making self-serving deals with lobbyists working for foreign entities."[60]

Others argue that the traditional mode of influence—meetings with lawmakers, say—has given way to the newer, more creative forms of lobbying that can evade even the stronger requirements of the FARA law. Ken Silverstein, journalist and longtime foreign lobbying watchdog, writes:[61]

> One Washington lobbyist told me, "Access lobbying is dead. Congress is gridlocked so meetings on the Hill are useless. Now it's all about perception and molding public opinion. That's why so many lobby firms have become integrated, and do so much work on the P.R. side."

The Southeast Asia expert at the Council on Foreign Relations adds:[62]

> Such makeovers are the result of sophisticated campaigns. In the past, dictatorships simply used lobbyists to court the mostly below-the-radar support of American politicians. But in the post-9/11 world of 24/7 media coverage of every human rights crackdown in Kazakhstan or every whisper of Saudi Arabia funding extremists, authoritarians need a different strategy—an intensive, crisis-management approach to P.R. Like Angelina Jolie, who transformed her image from wild woman to paragon of charity, these dictators have rebranded themselves completely, using every avenue to promote their new images.

We'll look more at the whole enterprise of shadow lobbying for foreign governments elsewhere in the book. Specifically, in Chapter 5 we examine how firms that fall on the "dark" side of PR do their work. In Chapter 8 we observe up close how high-prestige academics use their seemingly neutral affiliations to (shadow) lobby on behalf of foreign entities.

FAILING UP AND COVERING UP

Like shadow lobbyists, shadow elites are decidedly insiders. While shadow lobbyists engage in one-off projects as solo operators (like O'Bagy on foreign policy), their close cousins, shadow elites, are more complex and highly flexible creatures.[63] Shadow elites are more difficult to decipher, working as they often do as part of a longtime trust network and coordinating their efforts to advance their mutual agendas as a self-propelling team.[64] Administrations come and go, but shadow elites are not the instruments of any particular administration, even as some of their members join them. Shadow-elite networks persist, spinning overlapping roles at the nexus of official and private power and creating a virtually closed loop that challenges accountability. They are less stable, less visible, and more global in reach than their powerbroker forebears. And they are a paradox in terms of political influence, as political scientist Simon Reich tells me: they are more amorphous and less transparent than conventional political lobbies, yet also more coherent and less accountable.[65]

One network that has certain key features of shadow-elite networks includes Lawrence Summers, whose legendary flexian machinations I touched upon in Chapter 1,[66] Wall Streeter and former Treasury Secretary Robert Rubin, and several others who have held key posts in the Clinton or Obama administrations or both (and some members who took part in George W. Bush's). Much has been written about these players in large part because they bear considerable responsibility for setting in motion a whole slew of changes regarding how government deals with financial institutions, the consequences of which we will be saddled with for years to come. My goal here is not to rehash the details of the network's activities, but to highlight their MO and show how its mode of influencing has helped make them so effective.

Shadow elites exhibit staying power through close-knit insider-ism. Roughly the same people keep coming up in different incarnations to accomplish their joint agenda(s).[67] Members of this Summers–Rubin circle who found their places on the Obama economic team—including Treasury Secretary Timothy Geithner and Budget Director Peter Orszag—are all connected to Rubin and each other in various configurations through tenure at either Goldman Sachs or Citigroup, the Clinton administration, and a think tank Rubin founded to promote his economic philosophy, the Hamilton Project.[68] The team members had so many connections to Rubin that "the White House now looks like a backstage party for an episode of Bob Rubin, This Is Your Life!" journalist Matt Taibbi quipped in late 2009.[69]

Such a circle's strongly held shared mindsets, even ideology, help them stick together and persist. They have unique expertise, they believe, and are licensed to use it. The Summers-Rubin set preached that containing inflation would be good for Wall Street and everyone, and that if Wall Street went gangbusters, so would America and the world. Even before Obama was sworn in, economist Robert Kuttner observed about the number of Rubin acolytes advising him: "What worries me is there is not one person in the senior group who is the outsider to this club. . . . Where is the diversity of opinion in this economic team?"[70]

It is not just a matter of group-think or of people from the same orientation or intellectual and experiential milieu gathering together. A network's ability to implement policy rests on much more: often, loyalty to it trumps formal practices, testing accountability to the public institution on whose behalf its members supposedly work and to us, the public. Shadow elites circumvent or informalize, actively excluding those officials who should be at the deciders' table were their job descriptions the determinant.

Consider Rubin and Summers in the Clinton administration. Rubin's history (his company, Goldman Sachs, perhaps Wall Street's most elite firm, had long donated more to Democratic candidates than Republican) fit nicely with Clinton, who wanted to put an end to the tax-and-spend liberal cliché in favor of a new kind of Democrat: fiscally conservative, and supportive of both business and the "free market."[71] Rubin and his deputy, Summers, surrounded themselves with fellow believers on Wall Street, as well as at the Federal Reserve, the Securities and Exchange Commission, think tanks, and economics departments at America's top universities. They were lionized by the old media, and the newly emergent TV business news outlets such as CNBC were their cheerleaders, complete with pom-poms.

Outsiders who tried to puncture the Rubin-Summers bubble found themselves shut out. Recall, for instance, the story of Brooksley Born, head of the Commodity Futures Trading Commission, who took on Summers, Rubin, Greenspan, and Levitt.[72] While excluding outsiders to the circle when standard practice would have included them, shadow elites work closely with others (such as bankers in this case) in their close-knit network—who are not, officially, their colleagues—to achieve their agendas. Witness how Rubin and Summers behaved toward Born: at one 1998 meeting, Rubin, according to a participant, famously said to Born: "You're not going to do anything [to regulate], right?"[73] Around the same time, Summers reportedly called Born and yelled: "I have 13 bankers in my office and they say if you go forward with this you will cause the worst financial crisis since World War II."[74] The very players Born wanted to regulate apparently had the deputy and soon-to-be Treasury Secretary (Summers) on speed-dial.

Fast-forward to the next decade and the Obama administration and we see the same MO—the exclusion of should-be included officials and the inclusion of individuals from the network. Take, for instance, Treasury Secretary Geithner. He tried to cut out Sheila Bair, who chaired the Federal Deposit Insurance Corporation (FDIC), whose mission is to safeguard depositors' accounts.[75] After she publicly dissented from Geithner's handling of Citigroup's bailout in 2008, the FDIC was confronted with a proposal that would shut the agency out of regulating banks that were deemed to pose a "systemic risk." That power, Geithner's Treasury suggested, should rest with the Federal Reserve. The *New Yorker* described it as relegating the FDIC to the role of "sidekick."[76] Bair left government in 2011 and wrote a memoir that accuses Geithner of being too close to Citigroup during the bailout.[77] As she said in a 2012 interview, "My sense was the market needed to have some accountability. The government came in and took all the risk . . . [and] no one learned a lesson."[78]

Geithner apparently even ignored President Obama, who, like Bair, had asked him to consider breaking up Citigroup, according to journalist Ron

Suskind's book *Confidence Men*. Geithner was dead set against the idea and followed his own agenda promoting the interests of top banks rather than his boss's wishes. Suskind calls Geithner's action a "fireable offense."[79] (Geithner, who has released his own account of the era, *Stress Test*, takes aim at the recommendations of Bair, as well as of Brooksley Born.[80]) Did his allegiance to Wall Street trump even his allegiance to Obama?[81]

Where do the loyalties of players like Geithner, Summers, and Rubin lie? Of course, they and their network fiercely argue that their ideas are good for the entire economy, while flouting both the competition of business and the accountability of government. They insist that their intentions are always the best. Yet with their feet so firmly planted in their own powerful network, it is reasonable to ask to what extent their interests converge with ours.

Another notable characteristic of shadow elites is that they "fail up." Summers's career epitomizes that principle, one that depends on flexian ways and means and on being part of a powerful trust-based network. One might think that with his track record both in government and as president of Harvard,[82] Summers would have been the last person under consideration in July 2013 as it emerged that he was a leading candidate to become chairman of the Federal Reserve, the single most powerful position in global finance. While he eventually withdrew his name from consideration amid criticism from a number of quarters, he was apparently within a hair's breadth of being named to the post by President Obama.

While failing up, members of shadow-elite networks also rewrite history. Rubin, after the fact, has tried to fudge the story of his opposition to derivatives regulation.[83] Summers is just as brazen, if not more so. He said in a speech that he wasn't convinced that financial "innovation" had caused the crisis, a convenient narrative if ever there was one.[84] (And a bit hard to square with what he'd said the previous year on PBS when asked if he had any responsibility for the crash. He contended that credit default swaps were "the center of the issue now," and this financial innovation "barely existed [during his tenure at Treasury].")[85] Interestingly, in that same interview, he used the words "mistakes," "error," or "failure" five times, pointing not at himself but squarely at Wall Street and corporate America.[86]

Given Rubin's and Summers's roles in helping foment economic crisis, their accounts of history are at best a radically incomplete telling of their roles and, at worst, deceptive in their revisionism. As the likes of Rubin and Summers fail up and cover up, meanwhile, we're the ones who feel the repercussions of the economic crisis. That is not all: while touting the virtues of the "free market," their set has helped facilitate exactly the opposite, markets that are intermeshed with the power and billions of the state. Much has been made of the failure of the "free market" in the financial calamity of the past few years, but what is free about a market that has been "regulated" by executives, insiders and lobbyists, not to mention shadow lobbyists and shadow elites? It is set up not just to vastly enrich insiders, but also to protect them from the consequences of failure that a true free market would demand. Within this closed culture, the ideals of the free market are espoused in repeated performances by insiders—but not upheld. This disconnect between how the system purports to work and how it actually does is stark—and reminiscent of communism.

And the public, once again, is left with little to trust.

THE LOCOMOTIVES: WITHHOLDING INFORMATION

A phenomenon like systemic decline in accountability may be easier to see on a much smaller canvas than the United States. Looking across the Atlantic, we encounter a similar shadow-elite network, dubbed the Locomotives, who brought Iceland's economy to its knees as the economic crisis was unfolding in 2008. With the largest banking collapse in history relative to the size of a country's economy, Iceland's leaders brought about sustained devastation from which the country is still reeling.[87] The group had its origins in the early 1970s, when students at the University of Iceland took control of a journal called *The Locomotive*. These young "free market" ideologues were attempting to bust the stranglehold that the country's traditional family-based elite—known as the Octopus—had over life and advancement in the country. Over the next few decades, they would succeed in pushing Iceland down a reform path of deregulation and privatization (dubbed by some "neo-liberalism"), that the United States under Ronald Reagan and the United Kingdom under Margaret Thatcher also were traversing.[88] But the so-called Locomotive Group's free-market fervor would lead Iceland to ruin. Ironically, but perhaps not surprisingly, the new interlocking, corrupt elite with a tight grip on power—that is, the network that they created—turned out to resemble the Octopus that they had infiltrated.

How did this happen?

David Oddsson and Geir Haarde, two of the original Locomotives, are key members of this group. Oddsson became prime minister of Iceland in 1991 and stayed in office until 2004, when the job went to his protégé Haarde, who had served as finance minister. During this time, fellow Locomotives fanned out across spheres of influence in business, law, academia, and the media, promoting the philosophies of Reagan and Thatcher. Oddsson, far from retiring in 2004, reappeared soon after stepping down—this time as head of the central bank. Oddsson and Haarde's friend Hannes Hólmsteinn Gissurarson, described as the "leading ideologist of Icelandic neoliberalism" by a scholar at the University of Iceland, was a ubiquitous voice in Icelandic media there to support them as well as their compatriots in business, law, and other spheres of influence.[89]

The Locomotives made sure that they and their allies occupied key roles in official and private venues that were essential to achieving the network's goals. During the Oddsson era, the Locomotives privatized the publicly owned industries, with themselves and their allies in crucial institutions, such as banks, and as prime beneficiaries. There were, of course, also spillover effects. As the banks exploded in size, Iceland took on a boom feel and moved from a fishing to a banking economy.[90] These policies of deregulation and privatization encouraged an incestuous intertwining of state and private power that is the essence of shadow-elite strength. On leaving office, cabinet ministers maintained the network's influence by taking on directorships and consultancies. As journalist Roger Boyes, who wrote a book on the subject, explains: "The state was divesting some of its economic power, through deregulation and privatization, yet it wanted to retain influence. How did it do so? Through networks that ensured the placement of like-minded people in the economic engine room."[91]

The Locomotives and their allies were effective in large part because they exerted control over information and its interpretation. Often that meant withholding crucial data from the public. With vital information in their exclusive hands, shadow elites can fashion it for public consumption and thereby control the message so the public doesn't know, literally, what it is missing. Until faced with the consequences, that is.

Claiming that their own central bank and commercial banks conducted superior research, in 2002 Oddsson shut down the government's National Economic Institute, known for its independent analysis, when it started to question Iceland's stability.[92] A chorus of independent scholars pushed another government agency, Statistics Iceland, to publish a more accurate calculation of the country's skyrocketing income inequality, according to two scholars who studied the case, Robert Wade and Silla Sigurgeirsdóttir. The agency continually dragged its feet. One last hope might have been an economics institute at the University of Iceland, but it was pushed to self-fund.[93] That meant that it sometimes became more of a researcher-for-hire; the wider-perspective papers that might have shown severe cracks in Iceland's economy went unwritten.

What *did* get written? One paper in 2006 was called "Financial Stability in Iceland," which prominent American economist Frederic Mishkin was paid $135,000 by the Icelandic Chamber of Commerce to co-author. (The fact that he was paid does not appear in the report, but rather in a 2007 disclosure after he joined the Federal Reserve as a governor. It's worth noting that he lists various other countries in which he also had lucrative consulting deals.)[94] The Chamber of Commerce also enlisted British economist Richard Portes. That body received a similarly positive assessment in 2007; he earned a reported £58,000.[95]

The shadow-elite MO suited the Locomotives perfectly. For a while, the Icelandic engine roared; but when it finally began sputtering in the mid to late 2000s, the Locomotives and their allies worked to suppress various outlets of independent economic research that ran counter to their narrative. Scholars Wade and Sigurgeirsdóttir explain that "[They] undertook an extreme 'privatization' of information, relying primarily on the research departments of the banks themselves for analysis of the economy and its prospects."[96]

When shadow elites get into trouble, they respond by switching positions with others in their network and enforcing an even tighter grip on information. Iceland's Oddsson and Haarde (and others) shifted ministerships with ease. At a lower level, the young economic talent made frictionless and lucrative moves from official to private venues: according to Wade and Sigurgeirsdóttir, "People joined the Central Bank or the FME [the government agency charged with overseeing the financial industry] with the aim of learning enough to cross the street [to join private banks] and double their salaries."[97]

The Locomotives kept the information and the decisionmaking to themselves. As worldwide economic collapse loomed larger, in October 2008, the Iceland Central Bank, led by Oddsson, decided to peg its currency, the króna, to the Euro, in a last-ditch attempt to prop it up even though Iceland at that point didn't remotely have the means to justify that artificially, fictitiously high rate. World markets caught on fast. In fact, one commentator described it as "probably . . . the shortest peg in history." The currency collapsed within hours.[98]

According to the two scholars, Oddsson consulted not even the central bank's chief economist, but rather his friend and protégé Haarde. This was much like the Summers-Rubin circle excluding the much-needed input of Brooksley Born and Sheila Bair.

With shadow elites, different rules apply to insiders and outsiders. Even though pegging the króna was short-lived, those insiders in the know would have had the opportunity to exchange their fast-depreciating currencies for stronger ones.[99] Outsiders, on the other hand, were left to suffer the consequences.

The resulting financial collapse outraged Icelanders, and Geir Haarde was their first and only major leader to face indictment for wrongdoing. But in the shadow-elite spirit, Haarde's "punishment" was a virtual slap on the wrist. Meanwhile, Oddsson installed himself in a media role that allowed him to brand the crisis—and deflect responsibility. That was possible because "Iceland's media has long been dominated by its financial elite," notes the *Telegraph*.[100] By September 2009, with the crisis still in full swing, Oddsson was a top editor at the leading Reykjavik daily, whence he orchestrated coverage of it. "It was roughly the equivalent," as Wade and Sigurgeirsdóttir recapped the words of one commentator, "of appointing Nixon editor of the *Washington Post* during Watergate."[101]

Could the law offer any accountability? It's difficult to prosecute activities that are legal. A special prosecutor brought in to look at these activities described facing suspects who "are not aware of when they crossed the line" and "defend their actions every step of the way."[102] Part of the difficulty in prosecuting bankers, he said, is that the law is often unclear on what constitutes a criminal offense in high finance. "Greed is not a crime," he noted. "But the question is: where does greed lead?" The prosecutor said it was often easy to show that bankers had violated their own internal rules for lending and other activities; but, "as in all cases involving theft or fraud, the most difficult thing is proving intent."[103]

By populating key posts and switching roles to cover their actions, containing information, and dissolving independent parts of government and the media, the Locomotives and their allies reveled in deniability. They steeped themselves in unaccountability *and* violation of the public trust.[104]

RESURRECTING SHAME

What is inherently wrong with the overlapping roles and incestuousness that are the MO of shadow elites and some of their kin? After all, such roles and networks can make a community like the one I grew up in vibrant and strong—and help explain why it can be, at one and the same time, insular and highly engaged with the world. This structure supports mobilization, whether for a community festival at home or relief efforts abroad. That is at least in part because firsthand information and interdependencies are mainstays of community life.

There is nothing inherently wrong with that. In my home community, there is a lot of (sometimes too much!) transparency. Here's the difference: as in any small community, when an acquaintance approaches you at a funeral expressing condolences at a relative's passing and you've already heard that the acquaintance sells life insurance on the side, you can discern his agenda pretty quickly—and make a decision to smile and nod or turn away. He may be all about maneuvering you somewhere else. But with shadow elites or shadow lobbyists, we don't know when or to what end we're being maneuvered. Simply put, the information system is woefully inadequate.

On a small scale, such interdependency of roles and relationships can be beneficial. But when applied to today's top power brokers, the model can lead to the violation of the public trust. Whereas in a small community it's easy to ferret out hidden agendas and to know whose word counts for what, no such system is available to the public when it comes to the players here described. They rely on the same kind of firsthand information exchange, but they guard it closely and block its release to the public. We are left without reliable means of knowing what shadow elites and shadow lobbyists are up to—be it their overlapping roles, dense relationships, or undisclosed sponsors and agendas—which would, of course, be the basis for our ability to make informed judgments.

The damage that shadow elites and shadow lobbyists can do is not just in their lack of transparency and the policies they put in place: the effects of their practices are wide-ranging and long-term. Inequality is a huge case in point: these players have been the virtual progenitors of wide disparities in income and wealth that also have helped them continue to receive excessive rewards, while the "99 percent" suffer real-world trauma.

Can these power brokers be curbed? If so, how?

Sadly, they face few institutional roadblocks as they leapfrog rules and borders. As we shall see in more detail in Chapter 5, focused on the media, one venue for checks and balances has been hobbled: journalism overall and investigative journalism in particular.

Is there anything we, the public, can do? For one thing, we can help resurrect shame. It used to be that players in need of reprimand could be more easily sanctioned by society for violating its trust. Today, shame seems to be an alien concept, especially to those who most need to feel it. But we do not have to accept the camouflage of track records à la Robert Rubin or Lawrence Summers.

In fact, the public is capable of being stirred. It appears that we may be starting to wise up to the shenanigans of these players. When the hue and cry over Summers's likely appointment as chair of the Federal Reserve got the attention of the media, those in power finally took note. That Summers withdrew his name highlights the critical importance of calling out the new corruption at every possible turn.

Perhaps this is a hopeful sign. If so, the public is ahead of the "anti-corruption industry." That enterprise, while targeting corruption around the world for two decades, and while drawing attention to the problem, may have actually made it *more* difficult to discern the new corruption.

Let's take a look at that industry.

CHAPTER 4

High Priests and the Gospel of Anti-Corruption

T he date was February 1999. The venue, a glitzy Washington hotel within spitting distance of the White House. The "Washington Conference on Corruption," organized by an array of U.S. and international agencies and associations to "explore the private sector's part in the war on corruption and to discuss strategies for the future," was billed as "the first of its kind."[1] A keynote speaker at the opening session: the Honorable Robert Rubin, Secretary of the U.S. Treasury and past co-chairman of Goldman Sachs. Just a week earlier, he and his deputy secretary, Larry Summers, along with Federal Reserve Chairman Alan Greenspan, were mugging triumphantly on the cover of *Time* magazine, hailed as the "Committee to Save the World."[2] At the conference, Rubin would lend his heft to one saving-the-world project: "anti-corruption in developing countries and emerging economies." He would be joined in this endeavor by "some of the world's foremost experts in the fight against corruption."

The cause had become "hot."[3] So much so that a busy Treasury Secretary, an anointed High Priest of high finance, would make time to dispense his wisdom to the 150 or so participants. According to the organizers, corruption is largely a matter of "crony capitalism, lack of transparency, [and] bribery." The conference's aims were not only to examine the role of the private sector in fighting corruption in poor and emerging economies, but to "generate a private sector action plan geared toward the 21st Century."[4] Adherents would help spread the gospel of enlightened capitalism. After all, what was good for business was good for the world.

The lineup, with stars like Rubin, as well as George Soros, the billionaire currency trader/philanthropist, was certain to attract an exclusive group of leaders in business, government, multilateral trade associations, and international development. Think power networking in the elevator and over coffee and lunch. The world's top business lobbies—such as the International Chamber of Commerce (ICC)—as well as the accounting and consulting giants PricewaterhouseCoopers and Deloitte & Touche were listed on the program, along with heavyweights from the United Nations, the Organization for Economic Cooperation and Development (OECD), and top government officials from the countries under discussion.

And who wouldn't want to join the party? Business, finance, and economics were riding high. Despite some market tremors overseas, the U.S. economy was roaring at full blast. Dot-com IPOs were all the rage, the coming crash not quite yet in sight, and Enron was making headlines as an audacious innovator, not yet revealed as the giant fraud that it had become.[5] Unemployment that month was a low 4.4 percent and would head even lower as the year went on.[6] Remarkably, inflation was staggeringly low as well.[7] Regulations on Wall Street were about to loosen up, and why not? Stock prices were spiraling ever upwards. Wall Street was going like gangbusters, so the conventional wisdom was that they could best police themselves.

In this heady atmosphere, the conference participants and their brethren in the business and investment community could crack the problem of corruption rearing its head in Africa, Latin America, Asia, and the former Soviet Union and Eastern Bloc; do good; and make these countries "out there" more hospitable to investment at the same time. The new corruption, the potentially much more harmful kind, did not even enter their thinking, even though Washington insiderism (as exemplified by the "Committee to Save the World") and Wall Street malfeasance were already thriving, only to reach their calamitous peak in 2008. In the Western mind of 1999, "crony capitalism" applied only to certain Asian countries (following the financial crisis that had swept the region beginning two years earlier) and perhaps some post-Soviet ones.

There were facts and indices to back this up. Some of the world's most publicly engaged economists, including at least one featured on the conference program, had devised metrics to make sense of corruption in terms of a single number or score. By 1999, Transparency International (TI), a nongovernmental organization created to "combat" corruption, one of the conference's "partner" organizations funded substantially by corporate donors, was in its fifth year of publicizing its Corruption Perceptions Index. That annual list measures corruption in countries around the world, as perceived by experts and business leaders.[8] In 1999, a typical year, Scandinavian and Western European countries ranked the highest, meaning the most "clean," with the United States not far behind. Economies like Indonesia, Nigeria, and Cameroon were at or close to the bottom.[9]

The Corruption Perceptions Index and a few other user-friendly ranking systems had been focusing public attention on corruption. Strange bedfellows—"driven activists, pressured institutions, and hard-nosed businessmen"—were coming together in a worldwide effort to put the issue on the public-policy map, as Steven Sampson, an anthropologist who both studies and consults on anti-corruption efforts around the globe, put it.[10] Anti-corruption programs were appearing as line items in the budgets of Western governments and multinational organizations. NGOs were setting up shop and foundations were joining the action. In fact, what has been called the "anti-corruption industry" was in full swing. The industry's "knowledge, people, money, and symbols" were showcased at the conference.[11] And the conference fee ($500 for advance registration and $650 for walk-ins—in today's dollars about $700 and $910, respectively) spoke volumes.

At the time of the conference, the anti-corruption agenda, its private-sector sponsors, and "free market" economics were in ascendancy. TI's corporate sponsors in this era included AIG, Arthur Andersen, Bank of America, Bechtel, Boeing, Bristol-Myers Squibb, Coopers & Lybrand (and, later, PriceWaterhouseCoopers), Deloitte & Touche, Enron Corporation, Exxon, Ford, General Electric Company, General Motors, IBM, KPMG, Lockheed Martin, Merck, Motorola, Raytheon, Shell, Texaco, Pfizer Pharmaceuticals, and Westinghouse.[12] Corporations, of course, don't sponsor efforts for nothing. Companies seeking access to new markets specifically, and eager to spread capitalism generally, could do both while looking like good corporate citizens in "combatting" the menace of corruption. Economists had reached a pinnacle of power, prestige, and pride, and several of them leading the anti-corruption charge were listed as speakers. All were bent on spreading the private-sector gospel—privatization and liberalization—using economic models that looked great on paper, even when they did not work out so well in the real world. At the same time, other economists, preaching the same sermon, were serving as handmaidens in the West for investment banks, regulatory institutions, and credit-rating agencies as these institutions engaged in some of the boldest violations of the public trust in history.

While turning a blind eye to ethically challenged activities in their own ranks, economists essentially dictated what corruption is. Their way of thinking was constructed to deal with what is now characterized as "need" corruption, which "builds on coercion and extortion," as two political analysts have defined it. There was little room for "greed" corruption, in which actors collude to advance their own agendas and which is more difficult to see.[13]

Moreover, the flawed analytic tools the economists crafted and sold us served to shove accountability under the rug. Their faulty metrics would point the finger in the opposite direction from themselves. Thus the First World banker trading in exotic derivatives and betting against his own clients would get a pass, with economists' political influence helping keep regulations at bay and thereby sanctioning the lack of sanction against these practices. Meanwhile, the mid- or low-level Nigerian or Ukrainian bureaucrat earning many times less than his Western counterpart is disparaged for taking bribes that feed his family. The new corruption right under the economists' noses—the bad actors soon to help unravel the world economy—was ignored. Their actions were often even embraced as financial "innovation." And many of them were welcomed, some quite literally so, into the halls of power in Washington.

However unaware of their blinders and however well-intentioned many of the economists and their acolytes might have been, this narrow view of corruption offered the perfect intellectual cover. And with corruption defined down, First-Worlders could feel good about their countries' favorable scores on corruption indices.

It would be another decade before the seeds of unaccountability sown by the likes of the Committee to Save the World would undeniably blossom in the West. But blossom they would, and bear bountiful and continuous bitter fruit for the world to swallow. Through it all, the new corruption flourished.

THE HIGH PRIESTS

Central bank leaders, predominantly economists, have been likened to Old Testament prophets and medieval priests for their near-unquestioned infallibility and power.[14] Still, boring, nerdy economists may not have seemed like good candidates for making corruption hot. But indeed they did. Economists plied their trade, the public-policy equivalent of sex toys: media-friendly numbers and headline-making ranking systems. They also bandied metaphors—yes, metaphors—which routinely seduce our unsuspecting selves and which are widespread in economics more generally. The metaphors encapsulated their theories and made them accessible. With the exception of the isolated scandal, corruption had pretty much just sat on the shelves of social scientists.[15] But now, these innovations were attracting attention to the topic and giving corruption a seat at the public-policy table.

Ranking schemes, notably TI's Corruption Perceptions Index, were the divining rods of the High Priests and a communications bonanza. The CPI was, in the words of the organization, "one of TI's most important tools in raising awareness for the problem of international corruption."[16] Indeed, as TI reported: "The 1996 Index generated headlines literally around the world. In Berlin we were besieged with telephone calls, in one day responding to interview requests from about thirty radio stations in four languages. Several of these were from international radio services."[17]

The CPI was easy to grasp. Johann Graf Lambsdorff, a German economist, had created this grading system. Executed, seemingly with military precision, through one simple number, in one fell swoop, it revealed who's most corrupt, who's least, who's somewhere in the middle—and who has moved up or down since last year. Just one number released each year, in the same vein as the monthly figures that track the rate of inflation or the number of jobs lost each month or the level of unemployment, would mark a country for the coming year and beyond.

Metrics made corruption easily digestible for busy reporters without the need to investigate a specific case or news story. A regularly updated, soundbite-ready ranking is, in the words of a TV business news producer during the 1990s, "an easy hook" for a simple story without much context.[18] Ivan Krastev, a Bulgarian-based political scientist who observed the anti-corruption industry as it revved up, argues that corruption-ranking indices generated essential momentum.[19] To amass resources and build a continuous cycle of mobilization, the movement had to attract the media. It had to create buzz and keep that buzz going. The annual CPI releases did just that. High-powered, attention-grabbing conferences also helped. Within a few years, policy circles spanning international financial institutions, Western governments, big business, NGOs, and Third World elites embraced the anti-corruption cause.

The High Priests were steeped in a theory that guided a lot of public-policy thinking and would skew understanding of corruption and how to curb it. The principal-agent theory, as it's called, is simple: there are two parties. One party (the principal) employs another party (the agent) to do a job for him. Let's say that the principal is a government and the agent is a bureaucrat. The agent is supposed to be working for the government and not in his own interest. If he thinks he can do better for himself by taking a bribe rather than working "clean" for the government, then, the theory goes, he'll take the bribe. As economist and corruption scholar Robert Klitgaard explains, "An agent will be corrupt when in her judgment her likely benefits from doing so outweigh the likely costs."[20] The challenge for the principal, then, is to devise incentives to ensure that she (the agent) will act in the best interest of her principal. This is the essence of the principal-agent theory in terms of corruption.[21]

It forms the High Priests' scripture on corruption and underpins many anti-corruption efforts.[22]

The public and the media didn't need to quite grasp the theory, because the High Priests—like anyone else, including me, trying to get a point across—explained it to their supplicants using metaphors. While policymakers routinely spoke of "combatting" corruption (a military metaphor), the High Priests are fond of medical metaphors. Thus corruption is an "illness" or a "disease [with] many . . . strains and mutations," as economist Klitgaard declared.[23] "*Pathologies* in the principal/agency relation are at the heart of the corrupt transaction [emphasis added]," as another economist, Susan Rose-Ackerman, wrote.[24] Such dramatic metaphors command our attention and are catnip to quote-hungry media outlets—ever more so in an age of 24/7 news cycles and multitasking attention deficits. They prod us to action: with failures of the system (like parts of the human body) being disorders that require redress, and corruption a disease, it follows that "skillful surgeons" can excise it, as Klitgaard claimed.[25] The economists, of course, signed up for the role of surgeon.

The High Priests were accustomed to this role. Since mid-century, economists had dominated the world's financial institutions such as the International Monetary Fund, the World Bank, and the OECD. Eminent players routinely bounced between the ivory tower and, say, the Federal Reserve or the U.S. Treasury.

The economists assumed even more power in the 1990s, after the "end of history" and with the "new world order" brought about by the collapse of the Soviet Union, as President George H. W. Bush declared.[26] In the exhilarating days of America's having "won" the Cold War, the icons of American capitalism and their true believers were on top of the world. Economists and Wall Street pundits gained outsized visibility and influence outside the ivory tower. The new cable-TV business channels offered them an outlet to promote their ideas, and they were gobbled up as gold. Economists of high repute, such as the late Nobel Laureate Gary Becker, whose musings on corruption had heretofore been confined to academic journals, now expounded on the issue in publications like *Business Week*.[27] American-style capitalism lifted all boats. It was thoroughly embosomed not just by its usual sponsors—Republicans—but now by Democrats too.

With America and its economy riding so high, and American hubris and can-do-ism at full throttle, economists became even more godlike.

The High-Priest economists were armed with the answers—liberalization and privatization—and renegades were swiftly sidelined. Economists and the then–Big Six accounting firms had been designated the prime arbiters of change, charged as they were with the once-in-a-lifetime mission of turning the formerly communist Soviet and Eastern Bloc region into capitalist states as the Cold War was winding down.[28] That was the very region where signature anti-corruption programs were launched just a few years later.

Thus economists also became the High Priests of anti-corruption, not simply of economics, finance, and business. By the mid-1990s, corruption overseas was making headlines and entering public consciousness in the United States and much of the West.[29] Wide swaths of the globe, including many barely governed spaces cut from the ruins of the Cold War, were now the playgrounds of "mafias" or elites, both homegrown and not, bent on extracting resources. With the U.S.-versus-the-U.S.S.R. meme now relegated to the history books, we looked for other ways to understand the "new world." For many in the West, certain place names were brand-new—from the "stans" like Kazakhstan, to Georgia and Azerbaijan, to Croatia, Bosnia, Serbia, and other states of the former Yugoslavia. Corruption helped fill the void of understanding left by the bygone battle of the two superpowers. A 1997 editorial in the *Wall Street Journal Europe* touting the work of TI spoke of "the global corruption hydra" as an especially "frustrating" target, "as enemies go."[30] Corruption helped frame our narrative of the new world, popping up in casual and cocktail conversation. It was a theme on which a winning doctoral thesis could be written and one that could launch a lucrative career as a consultant. And big business could wrap itself in the moral mantle of anti-corruption while, at the same time, easing entrée into new markets.

It was in this context that the anti-corruption industry led by the high-priest economists gathered such force.

INSTITUTIONAL ACCESSORIES

A brief detour to the geopolitics of the Cold War is required to make sense of how corruption (and anti-corruption) came to the fore. During that era, the West needed—and bought, through foreign aid—the loyalties of Third World dictators. These included such figures as Mobutu Sese Seko in what was then called Zaire, Ferdinand Marcos in the Philippines, Haile Selassie in Ethiopia, and Mohammed Zia Ul-Haq in Pakistan. Such tyrants often sported Swiss bank accounts (where they stashed some of their countries' aid-supplied GDP), chateaus on the French Riviera, and their own private jets to get there.

Meanwhile, in the ivory towers of the First World, scholars, notably economists and political scientists, were trying to make sense of the Third World.[31] Of course, the First World and the Second (the Soviet Union and its satellites) were already demarcated. Then there was the Third World, a notion that crystallized with the Cold War.[32] Economists, steeped in that notion (along with most everyone else), helped define the field of international economic development, while political scientists theorized about modernization (in short, an evolutionary view of a state's transition from "traditional" to "modern" society). Problems of corruption would figure in both disciplines.[33] At the time, scholars from both fields generally shared the view that corrupt behavior, as the Harvard political scientist Joseph S. Nye put it, "is likely to be more prominent in less developed countries because of a variety of conditions involved in their underdevelopment."[34] And twenty years later, economist Robert Klitgaard would similarly assess that "corruption is one of the foremost problems in the developing world."[35]

But is corruption good, or bad? That was the subject of debate. Some analysts postulated that corruption actually facilitated economic development.[36] Nye employed cost-benefit analysis to sort out whether corruption is beneficial or harmful.[37] He concluded that, with certain exceptions, "The costs of corruption . . . will exceed its benefits."[38]

Still, that cost would be way down the road and, meanwhile, the struggle for world domination between the two superpowers took center stage.

The Cold War came to a close. And, with it, so did the blanket tolerance for bald-faced corruption. Large-scale ripoff of aid, now more visible, became harder for Western taxpayers to swallow.[39] Dictators whom the West had valued for their anticommunist backing became less useful. "When their rule ended, they were then presented to the public as greedy, evil kleptocrats," as one observer put it. "These 'revelations' converged to feed the anticorruption cause."[40] Now the West could wash its hands of such leaders without risking the loss of essential allies. It could confront corruption.

In this climate, two organizations, both dominated by economists, breathed life into the anti-corruption cause: Transparency International, of CPI fame, based in Berlin; and the World Bank, the foremost global development agency, headquartered in Washington, D.C. With the largest presence in these institutions, economists poised themselves to draw attention to the issue of corruption, define the approach to it, and sponsor anti-corruption efforts worldwide.

If the anti-corruption effort was like "combat," the World Bank would supply the heavy artillery (read: resources), reconnaissance officials (read: diagnostic studies), and the boots on the ground (read: anti-corruption initiatives and training). The Bank's head would be the commander-in-chief. In 1996, Bank president James Wolfensohn issued the call to arms to "fight" corruption.[41] In a speech that has been routinely characterized as "seminal" and "landmark," he decried the "cancer of corruption" at the World Bank–International Monetary Fund annual meeting. That talk is even credited with mobilizing an international anti-corruption agenda.

With the Bank providing direction and resources, not only for action but also for research, economists were the best positioned to build a new body of corruption scholarship and to propel their discipline's frameworks into the corruption fight.[42] Both the most influential corruption scholars and the intellectual godfathers of anti-corruption were economists, and many of them were associated with the Bank.[43] Bank-sponsored economists were prime movers in shaping how corruption was conceptualized and studied, honing the theory to support it, and prescribing solutions.

A close partner in this mobilization was TI. Peter Eigen, a German economist who had co-founded TI in 1993, was a former World Bank official. Other TI movers and shakers had also made careers at the Bank.[44] Eigen and his co-creators were concerned about the corruption they had witnessed in Third World capitals. An equal, if not greater, concern was that American multinational companies were unfairly disadvantaged abroad by the 1977 U.S. Foreign Corrupt Practices Act, as some commentators contended, given that their competitors were not subject to prohibitions against bribing foreign officials embodied in the law.[45] In 1997, Eigen pronounced: "A large share of the corruption [in developing countries] is the explicit product of multinational corporations, headquartered in leading industrialised countries, using massive bribery and kick-backs to buy contracts in the developing world and the countries in transition." As I noted earlier, TI was (and continues to be) substantially supported by big business.[46] When confronting corruption turned into a public-policy imperative, TI's mission and targets evolved. All the while, it pursued a "full and productive partnership" with the Bank, in the words of TI's 1999 annual report.[47]

With the help of "a globalised elite discourse," as anthropologist Sampson describes it, anti-corruption efforts became institutionalized, as movements typically do if they last. And so it came to pass that a standardized "series of policies, regulations, initiatives, conventions, training courses, monitoring activities, and programs to enhance integrity and improve public administration" spread throughout the globe. This "elite discourse" is critical to the continued success of the industry.[48]

The High-Priest economists became the anointed arbiters of anti-corruption. The question was not so much what corruption was (more often than not, it was in the realm of "need" corruption), but where resources would be targeted and how an agenda would be put into action. The answers to all these questions would set up the disconnect between the anti-corruption enterprise on the one hand, and the new corruption and unaccountability that was gathering on the horizon on the other.

In the mid to late 1990s, I was a well-placed witness to see firsthand how these all-important questions would be answered, from Warsaw to Washington. As an anthropologist, I had lived and studied and was intermittently based in eastern Europe, where the World Bank debuted its first anti-corruption programs and where TI set up local chapters. I had witnessed Western aid advisers on the ground just a few years earlier—in the late 1980s and the early to mid 1990s—and observed both Collision and Collusion (the title of my book on the subject), as the West sent foreign aid and advisers to the region.[49] Now anti-corruption was joining that agenda. The same lineup of aid and development bodies, from the World Bank to Western aid agencies and governments, was pursuing anti-corruption efforts in the late 1990s in many of those same countries and more. As resources were earmarked and demand for expertise on the subject grew, a slew of Western and local consultants cropped up and were put on the case. The anti-corruption industry shifted into high gear.

Indeed, corruption was an issue in the region—from the physician accepting an under-the-table payment from a patient en route to the operating room (the "gift" was now often cash, unlike in communist times) to the informal "clans" that coalesced—as communism crumbled—to control the economy, energy, and natural resources. The breakdown of authoritarian command systems with nothing comparable to replace them had put up for grabs many spoils of (communist) state-owned industries and riches. In short, opportunities for corruption of all kinds abounded—and much of it.

In the late 1990s, I joined the ranks of scholars who did stints as corruption consultants for the World Bank. In addition to participating in a Bank-sponsored assessment of corruption in a particular eastern European country, I helped develop ideas for identifying potential entry points for anti-corruption initiatives for the region. Some Bank officials working on the ground there, I found, were very astute and attuned to local realities.[50] While well aware of, say, the newspaper editor-in-chief who tripled as a member of parliament and a political leader, the more typical focus of potential action seemed to be a low-paid customs official or a bureaucrat open to payments from businessmen in exchange for permits. Of course, the choice of focus is a delicate dance for the World Bank, which deals with governments, depends on their cooperation, and cannot willy-nilly pick at ruling elites without some governmental buy-in. Yet it was hard not to wince with irony when a Bank official, no doubt earning a robust six-figure salary, inquired about the possibility of moving customs officers around a country from border crossing to border crossing. That way, officers taking bribes to feed their families on otherwise paltry salaries could not collude with smugglers and border-crossers with whom they had become acquainted. And, of course, there I was myself, earning a reasonable consultant's fee yet struggling to come up with anti-corruption prescriptions in an environment where, among local people, the subject was scarcely broached in polite company.

Later, at the tail end of the 1990s and in the early 2000s, I was based in Washington, where government agencies, from the U.S. Treasury to the U.S. Department of Justice, embarked on international anti-corruption programs. I secured a perch in the Justice Department as a research fellow.

For me, the irony never quite abated. Fighting corruption came with unimpeachable motives—much like, say, the war on cancer or providing aid to needy children. But such areas are invariably difficult to assess clear-headedly. Often, the urgency and reality of need dwarfs unblinkered analysis of where the funds actually go, how and by whom they will be used, and the immediate and long-term impact—never straightforward—of that use.

Consider, for instance, my time at Justice as a member of a U.S.-Ukrainian working group. Part of our job was to select, for U.S. funding, research projects on organized crime and corruption to be conducted by Ukrainian scholars. Supporting good research is a good idea. But nearly all the people with access to the necessary information and contacts to apply for the funding belonged to one insider group or another, almost by definition. In my on-the-ground look at foreign aid to the region, I had seen how even tiny funds (by Western standards) entrusted to a few individuals in a resource-poor environment to, say, promote civil society or democracy, often entrenched the influence of those individuals and their close-knit circle, lending them further power and influence. In this case, the money might indeed support worthwhile research; it might also reinforce existing hierarchies.

And what of our financing research on the trafficking of women (often for prostitution) while we stayed in the best Ukrainian hotels? Did not our presence, and that of many delegations like ours, help to create the demand for the heavily made-up, hot-pants-and-stiletto-clad young ladies milling around the lobby in the dead of winter?

It was easy to call out—though not so simple to stop—traffickers involved in the enslavement of women, a problem the media loved to cover because it had a certain sensational appeal. It was easy to focus on mid- and small-fry customs officers. And yet, all the while, some of the most valuable resources on earth were being acquired in the least capitalistic, least democratic fashion—by insiders—sometimes not only with the High

Priests' blessings but even with the practical help of those within their profession. The more insidious, less visible, corruption was being obscured.

THE ANTI-CORRUPTION CREED

Ideas and ideology drove, and drive, anti-corruption efforts, just as they might any such mobilization. In this case, though, the evangelizers were the High Priests and they had the holy grail. "Ethics" was scarcely in the lexicon of the prevailing economics doctrine. Yet the economists were not in the least bit reticent about sermonizing.

Their way of thinking focused on "need" corruption, with "greed" corruption hardly in the picture, as we have seen. And the High Priests suffused anti-corruption efforts with several assumptions—not always stated, acknowledged, or conscious—that emanated almost entirely from their way of thinking. In brief, they are that corruption afflicts the Other, not us; that governments, not private sectors, are the primary problems; that "smaller" government is necessarily less corrupt than "bigger" government; that corruption is nearly synonymous with bribery; and that the essence of corruption can be conveyed in country-specific, single-number scores.

My point is not that these assumptions are necessarily wrong. My point also is not that corruption, as defined by economists and the Bank-and-TI establishment as pretty much "need" corruption, is not a problem. To the contrary, as I said earlier, it is a huge problem for those who face it in many parts of the globe. My point is that, in powering anti-corruption efforts, these assumptions focused scholarship and solutions so narrowly that, by definition, the new corruption and the massive unaccountability inherent in it were excluded. It is also that these assumptions (and the approaches they bred) obscured other forms of corruption as they began to emerge, for the approaches of the anti-corruption industry diverge a full 180 degrees from the realities of the new corruption with its built-in unaccountability.

The Patient Is the Other

The most important thing to know about any patient is that the patient is sick. In the language of economists and the anti-corruption industry, many Second and Third World countries were very sick. The entire enterprise embraced this underlying assumption.[51]

During the Cold War, there had been a lively intellectual debate about the benefits versus the harms of corruption, as I mentioned earlier. Some economists and political scientists had argued that corruption could have developmental benefits. But after the Cold War, "out" was debate about whether corruption is harmful. "In" was discussion about how to "cure" the "cancer" of corruption. Any mention of the potential benefits of corruption virtually disappeared from the economics literature,[52] apparently under the weight of the massive resources that had been made available to study the subject. As economist Lambsdorff reflected in 2006, years after the anti-corruption effort had burst forth, "Most economists . . . have become much less tolerant of corruption than their predecessors. Current research emphasizes the adverse welfare consequences of corruption."[53]

The essentially unified opinion among economists about the harms of corruption now was the same sermon preached by U.S.-based multinational businesses. American companies, arguably the strongest in the world, were eager to curb corruption *and* level the business playing field.[54]

The idea of corruption as bad for big business became an article of faith among economists and business leaders alike. In the anti-corruption world, as well as in big business and investment circles, the conventional wisdom had it that corruption, because it distorts the "free market," diverts resources to ineligible or unintended recipients, holds back economic development, and frustrates business goals.

The second crucial thing to know about this particular patient, as viewed by the economists, is that the patient is rarely us. The patient is the Other, whether an entire country, a government, or a bureaucrat. TI's 1997 annual report is telling. A chapter on "National Developments" devotes, in this order, seven pages to Africa; eight pages to the Americas, concentrating on Latin America (with the United States covered in less than a page and a half, reporting TI-USA's assistance to international anti-corruption efforts and standard setting); about seven pages to Asia; eight pages to Europe (with attention to Central and Eastern Europe and Russia, and then to Western Europe, mentioning the work of national TI chapters, as well as scandals involving the Belgian police and judiciary and Swiss banking's lack of transparency); and not quite two pages to the Pacific.[55] Of course, this idea that the patient is the Other is hardly surprising, given that the anti-corruption industry came on the heels of the Western push to reform and transform the former Soviet Union and Eastern Bloc. And the fact that the World Bank, the premier global development institution, was a chief leader of the anti-corruption charge could only reinforce corruption as belonging to those Others.[56] The Russian financial crisis of 1998, as well as the Asian one that erupted a year earlier (which was attributed to "crony capitalism"), intensified the "otherness" of corruption even more.

Just which corruption—and causes thereof—the economists chose as their focus helps explain why they couldn't see the new corruption in the making. While the new corruption crosses borders, the ranking systems of the anti-corruption industry generally imply that corruption is endemic to a specific country (recall TI's Corruption Perceptions Index).[57] Moreover, corruption emanates from the inside. Largely excluded are external influences, say, the impact of foreign-aid dollars on local politics, which, as I noted, can be all-important.[58]

But while players of the new corruption meld their official and private activities for maximum influence, the anti-corruption industry zoned in on governments, not on the whole latticework of power. In the economists' creed, corruption primarily afflicts governments, not private sectors.[59] Because the public sector is a fountain of corruption in this approach, minimizing it contains corruption. As Gary Becker advised in *Business Week*, "To Root Out Corruption, Boot Out Big Government."[60] Business is the salvation. Of course, this, and also the idea that markets are best left to self-regulate, were prevailing tenets in 1990s America about how to fix most everything. In this view, the state is evaluated according to how friendly it is to business, with corruption treated "as both effect and cause of incomplete, uneven, or ineffective economic liberalization," as Michael Johnston, a political scientist who studies corruption and efforts to counter it, has written.[61]

This perspective has been expressed in two distinct aid approaches, often undertaken in tandem. The first was to streamline government by reforming the bureaucracy or, say, shrinking opportunities for corruption by decreasing the number of bureaucracies that an entrepreneur needs to engage with to start a business. The second form of this containing-government approach was the push to privatize state-owned companies.[62]

The argument fit perfectly with the no-holds-barred, almost frenetic rush to privatization of the early to mid 1990s that I saw firsthand in Russia, underwritten by economists' ideology and Western resources.[63] This was little surprise, since the drive in the West to privatize and deregulate had been gathering steam since the Reagan era and now found staunch Democratic adherents in the Clinton White House. But when deployed unregulated, in lands where virtually everything had been owned by the state, such divestiture (whether underwritten by the West or not) was a virtual guarantor of corruption, sometimes on a colossal scale, as scholars and analysts documented as early as the 1990s.[64] Throughout the region, political-business networks with inside information routinely "grabitized"— that is, privatized—for themselves entire swaths of heretofore state enter-prises at fire-sale prices.[65]

By and for insiders, this privatization of priceless national goodies produced powerful oligarchs, "clans," and other informal ruling elites. It produced fan-tastic income inequalities. And it created countless opportunities for expanding unaccountability. In providing incentives to players to fuse state and private realms, privatization fostered the new corruption.[66] Such fusion and the prac-tices it invited would find their way back to the West.

News reports and scholarly works about these elites, as well as "mafias" and transnational organized crime groups, emanating from the former Soviet Union and Eastern Bloc, eventually attracted mainstream attention, including at the World Bank. Still, it wasn't until *after* many, if not most, of the privatization schemes in the region had been implemented that the High Priests began to make the connection between the rise of these groups and the thrust to privatize in the absence of legal and regulatory accountability.[67] To plenty of economists, state institutions mattered little beyond privatizing them.

Reducing Corruption to Bribery

While the High Priests were busy shrinking the states of their would-be supplicants, their colleagues in ivory-tower seminaries were conceptualizing corruption essentially as bribery and as illegal activity—that is, primarily as "need" corruption.

Economists treated corruption, in effect, as a synonym for bribery.[68] The World Bank's definition of corruption as "the abuse of public office for private gain" could be interpreted more broadly. But the working definition had it that most acts of corruption are committed by public-sector bureaucrats, with the typical act of corruption being a bribe—an illegal, one-off transaction in a single venue. The task of the analyst, as economist Rose-Ackerman writes, is "to isolate the incentives for paying and receiving bribes and to recommend policy responses based on that theory."[69] The concentration on bribery and single transactions also meant, as I laid out earlier, that the anti-corruption prescriptions tended to target the rank and file, not elite players.[70]

Economic models also focused on the individual, not the network, as the crux of the problem. The individual bureaucrat taking bribes was the guilty party. But what about the informal networks and groups that underwrote so much corruption across state and private venues? The emerging players of the new corruption who specialize in crossing boundaries—state and private, national, international—were not even a blip on the radar screen. Once again, the unaccountable won.

The Principal and the Agent

The problem is not only that the High-Priest economists were blinded by their own religion: the problem is also that they spent so much time with their own scriptures (read: economic models and econometrics) that many were barely familiar with the contexts in which they were intervening. They assumed all gardens to be the same and garden-variety bribery to be the key problem. Stunningly, their theoretical favorite, the principal-agent model, was often inaccurate when applied even to bribery—much like applying the theory of bacterial infections to treating a virus.

You will recall that the principal-agent theory, with the bureaucrat (agent) incentivized (or not) to do the job the government (principal) needs doing, assumes that the principal is an honest broker and that the only potential problem is ensuring the agent's reliability. But is that always, or even often, the case?[71] In an earlier era, were the principals—the governments of Mobutu, Marcos, Selassie, and Ul-Haq—honest brokers, needing only to make sure that government bureaucrats (the agents) did not take bribes?

The principal-agent theory is even less suited to make sense of the practitioners of the new corruption. It can only deal with "need," not "greed," corruption, which lacks clear principals.[72] It implies discrete acts, between two parties, with defined benefits (say, a corrupt lawmaker takes a bribe from a company in exchange for a favorable vote). Yet an influencer like former Senator Tom Daschle, who we discussed in Chapter 3, surely doesn't take bribes. But he has advised the president while working for companies that stand to benefit from the decisions made by the president. The principal-agent framework breaks down even more when one considers that relationships are multiple and moving, and organizational missions are blurred. Highfliers like Tony Blair or Bill Clinton, to use other examples, operate in perhaps a dozen different venues of influence during the same time frame. The fact that they have so many roles makes it impossible to determine at any time who is the principal and who is the agent. Although they have not been shown to be corrupt, their modus operandi makes transparency and accountability close to impossible.

In short, the principal-agent framework is seductive because of its clarity. But in the face of much, if not most, corruption—even that which is defined as bribery—its usefulness is limited.

Seducing with Numbers

Another core approach of the economists is that corruption is conducive to analysis through metrics and country-ranking schemes. A single score, the story lines imply, conveys the corruption of an entire country. Ordering countries by rank tells us how one compares to another. Yet like the VaR metric that we heard about earlier, such single numbers are seductive—and can be dangerously misleading.

Consider the following: in 2008, the United States had a corruption score on the Corruption Perceptions Index of 7.3 on a scale of 10, with 10 signifying clean government.[73] In 2009, its score improved slightly, to 7.5. In 2008 and 2009, the United States ranked 18 (tying with Japan and Belgium) and 19, respectively, out of 180 countries included in the measurement.[74] At the same time that America looked so respectable, some of its signature players were engaging in massive mortgage fraud, and Goldman Sachs was betting unknowing clients against others, setting up some to fail, in schemes that would help tank not only the U.S. economy but that of much of the world.[75]

Iceland, the economic devastation of which we discussed in Chapter 3, routinely ranked even cleaner than the United States. That nation scored 8.9 and 8.7 in 2008 and 2009, respectively, and ranked among the least corrupt countries with an overall rank of 8 out of 180 in 2009.[76] At the same time that TI's index showed that Iceland was practically corruption-free, its "Locomotives," devoted as they were to unfettered privatization and deregulation, were wreaking economic havoc. Iceland, which for years was controlled by a "ruling class, so small, so tightly bound by obligations, by blood and money" (as journalist Roger Boyes, who wrote a book on the subject, chronicles), routinely ranked very high despite the actions of those inbred elites that caused the country's economy to crater.[77]

In the same vein, Ireland, its scores and rankings between those of Iceland and the United States, improved its score from 7.7 in 2008 to 8 in 2009, despite a massive real estate and banking collapse.[78]

How can there be such a disconnect between these rankings and reality? Between the so-called experts' understanding of corruption, and that of so many people who, more and more, view corruption as violating their trust?

Let's look at what, exactly, these schemes consist of. While the Corruption Perceptions Index is often taken as an indicator of actual corruption, it does not claim to be that. Economist Lambsdorff, who developed the CPI, describes it as "a composite index based on a variety of different elite business surveys and expert panels."[79] This "poll of polls," as TI's 1997 annual report clarifies, is "an attempt to assess the level at which corruption is *perceived* by people working for multinational firms and institutions as impacting on commercial and social life" [emphasis added].[80]

Be that as it may, the CPI promises an accurate global view of corruption, at least to many—if not most—of its consumers. Such indices are assumed to transmit fact.[81] But these "facts"—that is, the numbers—are sometimes thrown together in an analytic jumble: tools that "measure very different things, despite having similar-sounding titles."[82] Hatched by corruption-index-happy economists and the like, the CPI conflates disparate sectors and processes to create one showcase number. Political scientist Ivan Krastev, who observed the anti-corruption industry on the ground in Bulgaria, blows apart the efficacy of such indices:[83]

What do we claim when we assert that [a] certain regime or certain period is more corrupt than [an]other? Do we claim that during this period the number of corrupt transactions has increased? Do we claim that the number of people involved in corrupt transactions has increased? Do we claim that corruption has reached the highest places of power? Do we claim that the social costs of corruption have increased? Do we claim that society as a whole is more tolerant to corruption, or do we claim these together?

Delving deeper, we should ask: What do we mean by corruption, and what are we measuring? The activities of a sector? Bureaucrats more generally? Elites? Black markets? Attitudes? Levels of trust?

Then there is the pesky issue of context. Indices are entirely stripped of it. The study of corruption is "portrayed as similar to the study of inflation," as Krastev writes.[84] Numbers are made to stand stark naked, on their own, and do things for which they are ill fit.

The emperor, too, has no clothes, because corruption is not like inflation. Inflation indices measure the value of a basket of goods during one short period. By contrast, corruption indices are charged with capturing the dynamics of an enormously diverse collection of people, motives, contexts, and systems in societies that often are dimly understood by the economists who devise the indices (and who nonetheless set up programs to change incentives). Yet it is stories (told by participants, observers, and their confreres) about corruption that convey the context in which it is embedded; that show us what it is and how it works in a given setting; and how it fits into the political, economic, and social web.

Meanwhile, the metrics have consequences. A country's ranking on the CPI and other indices like it is not just a thirty-second news story on the evening news: it can batter or better national reputations. It is used to benchmark developmental progress. TI itself has claimed that the CPI "influences the policies of major aid agencies and is a factor in the foreign investment decisions of multinational corporations." Aid agencies have told countries they need to improve their TI (or similar) scores to qualify for assistance.[85]

The Corruption Perceptions Index pioneered a trend. It was (and probably is) the best-known metric of its kind. It helped spawn not only a body of corruption literature and a (pseudo) science of comparison, but it also gave birth to an entire genus of ranking systems.[86] Indices generated by the World Bank and a plethora of NGOs, consulting firms, and think tanks sought to tweak it, improve on the idea, or simply, as one scholar put it, to "provide a particular agency or NGO with a 'signature' index to attract visibility and funds."[87] The "science" of comparison across countries was now possible and palatable to the public.[88] Soon to follow were annual rankings of countries according to their levels of "good governance," democracy, and even economic freedom.[89]

All this fits perfectly with a larger trend in international practices and institutions and among their globetrotting subscribers: up with numbers and down with words. A few years ago, numbers began to systematically replace words as a way of analyzing transnational governing developments and initiatives.[90] In "What Do Numbers Do in Transnational Governance?" two scholars show that "numbers increasingly complement if not displace linguistically articulated norms." Removed from their context, slipping agilely across international boundaries, and seductive in their simplicity, numbers take on mythical, even magical, powers. They provide an "illusion of transparency."[91] We are seduced, yet deceived.

The metaphors employed by the number crunchers are no less deceptive. Metaphors are colorful ways of explaining a position and a powerful communications tool, which is why they are ubiquitous in political and public discourse. They can help mobilize movements. But they come with built-in bias, hiding certain features of an issue while highlighting others.[92] When confused with analysis, as they often are, metaphors can obfuscate actual analysis.[93] They obscure more ambiguous and more insidious activities that can have far graver consequences.

Relying on metrics as a substitute for inquiry is not only a fetish of ivory tower, World Bank, and anti-corruption economists: the practice was—and is—rampant in the financial industry, among other arenas (like VaR in finance). Doing so gives their audiences—be they policymakers, the public, or fellow CEOs—a false sense of calm and control. But, of course, this is delusional and causes (yes, immeasurable) harm.

In short, these assumptions of the anti-corruption industry, along with the powerful imprimatur of the activist High Priests, has so dominated the world of anti-corruption that the new corruption has only recently begun to enter the imagination of the industry.

IRONY IN OVERDRIVE

While the diagnosticians and anti-corruption surgeons busied themselves with ranking systems and surveys and dispensing prescriptions, a new class of power (and money) brokers was on the rise. Many were far too savvy to break the law, even if stretching its limits. Their opportunities mushroomed with the mass privatization of state-owned wealth and the invention of novel global financial products enabled by new information technologies, among other developments.[94]

The straitjacketed thinking of the economists and their industry acolytes allowed them to get away with playing a double game. It even allowed some high-profile economists to be corruption experts while simultaneously engaging in the new corruption themselves. On the ground in eastern Europe, I had observed certain prominent Western consultants plying their influence as they moved among academia; Washington; and Warsaw, Moscow, Kiev, and the like. These budding flexians, as I call them, were adept at "representational juggling" as they performed multiple roles across multiple spaces with multiple sponsors, without fully disclosing them.[95] Those honing the new corruption while doubling as scholars of corruption and policy advisers especially caught my attention.

Harvard economist Andrei Shleifer illustrates the irony of the extremes to which some would go. At the same time Shleifer was "modeling" corruption in scholarly writings (and cited liberally by corruption scholars and in anti-corruption handbooks) and defining it essentially as bribery, he was a personal example of the new corruption.[96]

While leading Harvard's U.S. government-funded project to reform Russia's economy and helping craft the blueprint for the corruption-inducing privatization scheme launched in 1992, Shleifer also made personal investments in many of the same areas in which he was being paid to provide impartial advice—thereby allegedly defrauding the U.S. government, according to the U.S. government.[97] A chief Shleifer argument—that a shrinking state sector would necessarily help minimize corruption—would prove to be flat wrong. Later, writing for the prestigious *Foreign Affairs* about the Russian "reforms," he was identified simply as a Harvard professor—not someone who had helped design them. Of course, he declared them successful.[98] Neither the publication nor Shleifer himself revealed that, in fact, he was grading his own homework.[99]

All the while, the professor presented himself as an independent analyst, and the powers that be drank the Kool-Aid. He even delivered testimony before a congressional committee as a scholar on corruption.

Such players as Shleifer exemplify just how much our culture has changed—accepting without question exemplars of the new corruption in the same person as scholars of the old. And still their scholarship on corruption is taken on faith.

And what of the principal-agent theory that was supposed to explain corruption so well? At first glance, Shleifer (the agent), leading a signature U.S. government aid project, failed to serve his principal (the U.S. government). But on closer examination, powerful parts of the principal were complicit, to say the least. Shleifer secured aid funding to reform Russia's economy in the form of (highly unusual) noncompeted U.S. awards (with help from Larry Summers when he served as a high U.S. Treasury official in the Clinton administration). And was he the principal or the agent when he was covering his tracks in congressional testimony and *Foreign Affairs*?

The assumptions, approaches, and theories of the economists have clouded our vision to the point that they obscure the activities of the irony manufacturers, not to mention some of the biggest, baddest actors of the new corruption.

BACK-PEDDLING?

While not quite by conscious design, the assumptions and approaches of the economists and the anti-corruption industry weakened their eyesight—and set us up for the same.

Much like the Vatican, the High-Priest economists issued periodic reforms. In time, for instance, economists expanded the shrinking-government-to-fix-it notion to incorporate governance and institutions (which other social scientists had already been doing).[100] In 2006, several World

Bank economists expounded on the learning that had taken place over the previous decade: "Today there is widespread consensus among policymakers and academics that good governance and strong institutions lie at the core of economic development."[101]

Subsequent scholarship on corruption would broaden the views of some economists. In time, too, some of the High Priests went beyond their concentration on garden-variety corruption. By 2000, structural and institutional relationships, such as the concept of "state capture," defined in a World Bank publication as "the actions of individuals, groups, or firms both in the public and private sectors *to influence the formation* of laws, regulations, decrees, and other government policies to their own advantage . . ." [emphasis in original] was commanding more research attention.[102] The concept of state capture describes the illicit and non-transparent manipulation of state power to benefit private interests, whether of politicians or private sector firms.

As for Transparency International, despite over-focus on its media-friendly CPI, the organization has initiated some useful work on a much broader front. One example is its National Integrity Assessment, a questionnaire that assesses a country's institutional "pillars," including business and civil society, as well as the independence of its watchdog institutions. Deployed in many countries, the results of the surveys have sometimes drawn local attention to such issues and resulted in change.

Even though major (especially finance-related) corruption scandals in the developed world of the late 2000s may have tempered the idea of corruption as primarily an affliction of the Other, the idea lives on in the corruption literature.

While the economists did issue some Vatican-style reforms, they mostly did so only within their own narrow framework. Only a handful of renegades, such as the Nobel laureates Joseph Stiglitz and Paul Krugman, began speaking of the United States and "crony capitalism" in the same breath in the 2000s.[103] Thus corruption economists continue to perfect the metrics, much like an abused, spurned lover who desperately keeps coming back, seeking to mend the relationship. And the "globalised elite discourse" that Sampson describes "ensures that the issue [of corruption] remains on the agenda . . . *even if in revised or 'new improved' form*" [emphasis added].[104]

As the anti-corruption industry matured, corruption indices generally became more sophisticated. Eventually—a decade after Lambsdorff pioneered TI's Corruption Perceptions Index—critique of the metrics-as-analysis approach came from within the economics profession itself.[105] And, at this writing, the endeavor has come to embrace scholars from different disciplines and those with real-world experience in a variety of settings.[106]

Yet despite fresh ideas about what corruption is and does, corruption-ranking indices are still *de rigueur* in the industry, even if many inside have abandoned the creed and even if the faith placed in them far outstrips their analytic value. Much like under late communism, the ritual has to be preserved. As one scholar writes:[107]

> While it is widely recognized that performance indices in this area suffer from severe methodological problems regarding precision and reliability, they nevertheless seem to co-exist with a deep-seated belief in the powerful factuality of numbers, measurement and comparison, just as they play an important role as a reference point for standards and scripts for action.

More crucially and tellingly, the anti-corruption industry has kept and even expanded its PR tools—the CPI and other metrics—despite alarm from inside and out about their serious defects. The industry won't give them up, ostensibly because much media attention would dissolve without them. And that attention is a must for getting policy done, as explained in an article by a political scientist titled "The Power of Performance Indices in the Global Politics of Anti-Corruption."[108] The "performances" that are the release of the CPI have become an anticipated necessity, some scholars argue.[109] And, as we shall see in the next chapter, "performance" is not to be overlooked.

—⁓—

The economists' crusade and the strange bedfellows at the Washington conference were just a taste of what was to come in 2008—and with well-known global impact. While the economists loosed their hubris on much of the world when the United States was riding high, the fruits of that hubris were about to circle back. And while the public trust was being violated by members of their profession, they reduced complex realities to single numbers, applied ill-suited theories, and misled us with inaccurate metaphors. This is not to say that they were necessarily conscious of their own myopia or that they are personally to blame. It is to say that the rest of us need to be all the more attuned to the power and prowess of a religion whose High Priests have invited so much unaccountability.

Finally, it is to say that we need to learn to discern the performances of the High Priests and their ilk and to look underneath the surface of performances, be they numbers, players, or the media—the subject of the next chapter.

CHAPTER 5

Privatizing Media,
Performing "Truth"

I f you can't trust your pornography, what can you trust?

It may seem preposterous to open a chapter on the public trust in the media and Internet—and what this means for accountability—by linking the words "pornography" and "trust."

And yet a sea change in the porn business illuminates much about our culture, our flagging faith in public institutions, and our retreat to the private realm in search of truth—and what passes for both private and truth.

Porn stars, we know, are actors. But the quest for (true) reality runs so deep that it is seen even in pornography, that land of artificial desire and silicone dreams, where everything is, almost by definition, a performance. It used to be that porn came in a brown wrapper or in an "adult" shop peepshow or a video made in southern California, the center of the (American) industry. But that porn provider is being edged out by the housewife in Omaha who might appear headless, performing self-sex, in her own posted video. Or by live ladies for whom you might pay up, then chat with online.

In the past, there was little denial that porn stars were acting. In fact, an anthropologist who studies porn culture has discovered that these days, one of the most compelling selling points in online porn is that what you are seeing is "real," performed by supposed "amateurs."[1]

Apparently, we so crave authenticity that we look for it even in an entertainment genre that is, well, staged.

Nowadays, the Internet enables us to cut out the middleman and fully indulge our tastes in a customized fashion. The modus operandi is DIY—do it yourself—for both providers and consumers. Practically anyone can become an online mom-and-pop porn proprietor, and the options transcend borders with ease. In one sitting, you can skip from the Midwestern headless housewife and go to Yukiko the Asian dancer and then to clips of Natasha, the Ukrainian blonde who supposedly just turned eighteen. A search for the word "real" might bring up a dozen categories on an online porn site: "real couples," "real homemade," "real teenager," "real orgasm." If you want to get "really real," so to speak, you might pay a premium for a live chat or personalized show, but a huge amount of material is now entirely free. And you can watch in the privacy of your own home (your choices being recorded only by your Internet provider and the NSA, as far as we know). We have sent the traditional porn industry into a tailspin, but this is just the most sensational part of our media culture that has been upended by the Internet.[2]

The sea change in porn might seem to be of little consequence to those who don't indulge in it. And yet it pulls back the curtain on the personalization of the media and Internet and why today's top power brokers, clothed as they are, can operate willy-nilly beyond accountability—and get away with it. Unlike with other arenas like finance or health care or national-security policy, however, we, the public, can hardly make a convincing case that the sweeping changes in the media just happened without our complicity. We have been, and are, ever-more-active participants in sowing this unaccountability.

Moreover, the media and Internet spill back into and drive just about every arena of public life, building themselves into their very essence. That's why I devote an entire chapter to how changes brought about by the digital age have completely reconfigured the mass communication industry that is now not just media, but a new creature: media/Internet. That creature enables power brokers to operate beyond accountability in ways never before possible and amounts to a wholesale societal and cultural shift. While practically every organization is now a beacon of "transparency," including the NSA (see its website and peruse its "commitment" and "dedication" pages[3]), ironically, just where "information" comes from and what agendas might be behind it is often less transparent than ever before in living memory.

Think of this new world of media/Internet as a sort of privatization, or personalization. I don't mean consolidation of the media—that it has become more concentrated in the hands of fewer owners (although this, too, is a crucial recent change[4]). I mean rather how our ever-growing access to "information" (and entertainment) is billed as a more efficient way of getting something, a better deal for everyone, by eliminating layers of middlemen. But like the privatization in other areas that I've studied over the years, this privatization has grave consequences for accountability, especially now in the shadow-elite era. For in personalizing the media, we have depleted it of uniform standards, like, say, fact-checking, and eroded the capacity for accountability. Think about it: our online "likes" and those pages we choose to "follow" are personal choices. That, by definition, exempts them from public accountability.

All the while, our personal/private choices in the collective would seem to guide how the news is shaped—indeed, what even *becomes* news. Success is assessed instantaneously through the number of "likes" on a blog post, views of a Web page, hits on YouTube, or number of followers or retweets on Twitter. What is deemed newsworthy is modulated through our collective media choices. How can we even think of accountability in such a personalized system?

And yet, how can we not? We are at the mercy of our ignorance. If we do not pay heed, it will come back to haunt us in ways that affect our daily lives and livelihoods—in forms we may not yet even imagine.

LOOKS LIKE NEWS

The search for authenticity—and truth—is reminiscent to me (and other scholars) of late communism in the Soviet Union and Eastern Bloc. Given the different contexts, this may seem jarring, but bear with me. In the West, this search follows a period of upheaval in the media. Many Americans (and people more widely)—no matter their political stripe—feel intuitively that there is a stark disconnect between what they experience as reality and what the dominant news presents as reality.

Mainstream news comes across as not-quite-real; in fact, it comes across as performed by both the media presenters and the newsmakers they cover. That is why so many Americans look to fake news—comedians Jon Stewart and Stephen Colbert are cases in point—because they tell it more like it is than does the so-called news. In short, these performers are more authentic, more believable, and, ironically, no more performed than the evening news on any major network. (Colbert's enacting a caricatured conservative is intended to be understood as performance, while the newscaster is not.)

Anthropologists Dominic Boyer and Alexei Yurchak have observed this as well—and saw, as I did, a similarity between the public propaganda of late-communist societies and the mainstream media of today in the West. News messaging has become strikingly standardized and formulaic, despite the seemingly infinite choices of media outlets.[5]

Boyer and Yurchak cite the "endless figures, numbers, charts, soundbites, [and] talking points . . . repeated from network to network and from one context to the next."[6] While you might think that digital media could offer a quick escape from that echo chamber, these scholars see "an increased tendency toward imitation" by journalists strapped for time, which means that much of the "news" we see online features more of the same talking points. Stewart's *Daily Show* in particular revels in displaying this trend:[7]

> According to Stewart, a central function in much of U.S. news media has shifted from informing the public to performing what he calls, [*sic*] scripted "political theater." By this, he means that addressing important social and political issues[,] news media tends to use the language dominated by predictable, fixed, and repeated scripts and rhetoric, paying less attention to the discussion of substantive political issues and their meanings.[8]

The anthropologists also mention the equal-opportunity-offender program *South Park*, which, perhaps more than nearly any other current satire show, aims its daggers at pieties right, left, and center. It is a show in which, as Boyer and Yurchak say, "everything is corrupt, deformed and hypocritical" and, by the way, in 2014 drew at least a half million more viewers weekly than either the *Daily Show* or the *Colbert Report*.[9]

Of course, the media are conveying what newsmakers deliver, in what the scholars call an "insular . . . [and] professional performance culture."[10] Just as journalists are spread thin across so many venues, newsmakers themselves know that they have to present compelling "theater" just to get attention in a fractured news environment.

This performance culture seems to have caused regular people to turn to parody in search of something more authentic—something I saw in my years in Eastern Europe during late communism.[11] As we've said, the emerging distrust in the West of official news has also pushed citizens to a more personalized, "privatized" kind of content, taking their cues from family, friends, and like-minded "friends" and "followers" in social media.

How can this be? There is nothing in the democratic West like a centralized Politburo department of propaganda that must approve the news or orchestrate "newsworthiness." Boyer and Yurchak point to what we will examine in depth in this chapter: extraordinary changes that have upended the media business in the West, mostly because of the pressures brought to bear by the emergence of the Internet.[12]

Something that *looks like* news has now substantially replaced the real thing. This medium is a simulacrum of what it used to be, as French philosopher Jean Baudrillard (1929–2007) might have said. He argued that today's society is constructed around simulacra, which (then) become reality. Simulation produces real intuitive feelings, emotions, or symptoms in someone and blurs the difference between the "real" and the "imaginary." As we shall see, many websites (or newscasts) of corporations, think tanks, and even presidential candidates are designed to *resemble* news sites.

We want this simulacrum of the news (substituting for the real thing) to come to us via people with whom we are acquainted. Today we tend to trust only people we know (or *feel* we know or have a connection to). Tellingly, this recalls what I experienced under communism in 1980s Poland—where your closest friends and family were your bulwark against all-powerful authorities. Reliable institutional arbiters were few and far between. Virtually no one trusted official sources (and for good reason).

Today in the West we, too, increasingly eschew institutional arbiters in favor of ourselves and our own. Just like the consumer of porn who has rendered the central middleman redundant, we are assembling our news ourselves. This is possible because more and more people are getting all their news online, increasingly on the fly through smartphones and tablets. According to the Pew Research Center, a public-opinion-research think tank, "a majority of Americans" surveyed in the United States in 2012 got their daily news through digital means.[13] Online news consumption has surpassed radio and newspapers. In fact, in less than a decade it has more than doubled. In late 2013, the Pew Center found that sixty-four percent of Americans use Facebook, with half getting news there. That amounts to thirty percent of the general population; for YouTube it's about ten percent getting news there, and for Twitter eight percent.[14]

Thus we are increasingly self-assembling our media playlist—an app on our phone, a posting from a Facebook friend, an inspiring tweet or YouTube clip from an admired politician—all of them now "news" providers (or news editors, when they select stories and send them our way) alongside Uncle Gary's fly-fishing experience recounted at a family gathering, then "shared" for "friends" on social media. Squarely in the driver's seat, we believe we are in control.[15]

And feel we are in the know. *Feeling* that something is true (or not) is our (the listener's) choice, à la Colbert's "truthiness," which has a foothold in the media. Truthiness requires our (the listener's) active participation.

As we drive along, personalizing and participating in the media, we can communicate in real time with like-minded individuals around the world and find or even create our own club. Sharing seeming intimacy with strangers appears to provide enormous psychological payoff. And that "intimacy" becomes our primary "truth." The quest for "truth" and belonging then edges out the desire for objectivity.

In fact, those who advocate for old-fashioned objective news may be considered dinosaurs, or hopelessly naïve.[16] *Objectivity* has practically become a dirty word, no matter one's political leanings. Almost everyone has an agenda. The now-famous Glenn Greenwald, who helped break some of the most important stories of the new decade, including the leaks about the NSA by the contractor Edward Snowden, appears to consider himself a journalist/activist. As he told the *New York Times*: "All activists are not journalists, but all real journalists are activists."[17]

As we opt for belonging to a "community" over objective news, our worldviews are shaped in ways never before possible. We also sort ourselves into information silos, some of which could scarcely be more divergent from each other. And while these silos may not connect with each other—each silo is an entity unto itself—within the silo, individuals connect in every which way.

Add to this emerging norm of manufactured resemblance the necessity of "connecting"—part of the simulacra equation. We must *look like* we are connecting personally—not only with "friends" far and wide, but with (heretofore) public figures, now privatized to our personal likes. We want our news providers to connect with us *personally*—and "connect" they do, whether it is a Facebook friend who fancies him/herself a news authority or a respected print journalist who sends out links to his articles on Twitter and Facebook and also tweets about his/her "tastes" and divulges (carefully crafted) details about his/her personal life.

A small sample includes *New York Times* political reporter Nicholas Confessore (with nearly 45,000 Twitter followers), who alternates wonkish tweets about income inequality with zingers about the Super Bowl half-time show. Or his colleague in the media department David Carr (nearly 450,000 followers). Then there is Jeff Elder, technology reporter for the *Wall Street Journal* (101,000 followers) and Chris Cillizza, political reporter for the *Washington Post* (200,000 followers), whose feed he calls "The Fix." Cillizza has another Twitter feed (now largely inactive) called "The Hyper Fix." This hyper-Chris Cillizza feed directs newshounds back to his more work-oriented feed by saying "Follow him @the fix for a more mellow, but still personal feed."[18]

We want our leaders to connect with us personally too—to skip the guy in the middle and talk to us directly. We "like" President Obama's Facebook page, and get the message right from the horse's mouth, along with his fondness for jazz and classic films like *Casablanca*. While we know these exclusive communiqués are likely crafted by brand-polishing twenty-somethings, we put up with the genre because we crave displays of sincerity, not unlike in the new-style porn.

When we receive a message "From Michelle Obama" shortly before Thanksgiving 2013 saying "I want to talk to your family. From my family to yours, Janine," we know that the First Lady's "authenticity" is manufactured.

This "authenticity" may be transparent. But there is a lot of fake authenticity in the media that is much more difficult to see through. Many, if not most, of us lack the depth of experience to figure out what is fabricated and what is not. In the golden age of "transparency," there's a dearth of information about where the information comes from and what agendas might be behind it.

As we, both creators and consumers of news, concentrate on the simulacra—on news as performance rather than as content—we move farther away from living in the brick-and-mortar world and closer to the virtual one.

Yet this personalization and obsession with performance (as in acting) has a profound influence on what is deemed real and what policymakers act on. For even when something is not true—it is merely "truthy," as Colbert might say—when enough people believe or engage in it, this "truthiness" can and does have real and huge consequences in the real world. The prime example is the rush to war in Iraq after 9/11, based on the faulty assumption that there were weapons of mass destruction there—a decision based on "truthiness" (as well as classic propaganda) if there ever was one.

Meanwhile, we are surely missing out on key stories—stories that are not just stories but can tank our livelihoods, health, and security. We are lucky to know what we know about the NSA story. We know what we know (and we can have little idea what we don't know) only because of the whims of one leaker (Edward Snowden) who didn't trust traditional media and a few journalists (namely journalists Glenn Greenwald and Laura Poitras) who were dogged enough to pursue the story. One would have hoped that stories as crucial as the NSA spying and the machinations that led to the 2008 financial crisis could have been unearthed by a robust media before so much damage was done. And we are ill prepared to spot the next financial crisis.

But we have substantially ditched the objective middleman (read: journalists), substituting nonobjective performers for them, even as they might parade as objective. When was the last time Americans heard about the "Fourth Estate"—that free press so crucial to democratic civilization that was supposed to be a bulwark against the powerful? It used to be that we got our news from a reporter or news organization that stood between us and, say, a powerful politician or a cash-flush corporation. That reporter gathered and helped interpret the news. S/he belonged to a profession steeped in a public-sector ethos. And, despite the shortcomings of the media as in any profession (some bad apples, poor judgment, and occasional incompetence), there was at least some expectation that the journalist would investigate and report the story with some modicum of objectivity and mindfulness of the public interest.

Instead, today, we are faced with sorting through simulacra—from downright falsehoods to appearances that detract us from less-sexy realities. This is no easy feat. That is because, while the *objective* middleman is passé, there is no shortage of accountability-challenged middlemen to take their place.

Short-Term Performing: Exploiting Television

The emphasis on performing, as in theater, has become *au courant* in the public sphere, as cultural analysts have shown, and as noted throughout this book.[19] Today's "professional performance culture," as Boyer and Yurchak call it, is reminiscent of the kind of performance that communist societies took to an art form.[20] But the pressure to make things look good right here and right now often results in the production of simulacra at the expense of truth and underlying realities—and we, unlike our communist forebears who became adept at reading between the lines, are short on the skills necessary to see through it.

Much of today's media reality began with the rise of 24-hour cable networks. This was a new stage on which power brokers of all sorts could now perform to many and varied audiences.

In the United States, one of the most damaging series of performances played out on the new financial news outlets, most notably CNBC.

In the 1990s, CEOs developed a laser-like focus on the stock price, in part because companies started paying them with stock options, which was supposed to align the interest of shareholders with that of the chief executive.

Now they were incentivized to gin up quarterly earnings for the short-term stock "pop." In well-choreographed performative routines, CEOs trumpeted their numbers to the media and investors, all to keep their stock prices high. With their shorter-term focus, CEOs sought to keep the stock price high at the right times, to make sure quarterly earnings "beat expectations," even when, internally, they didn't.[21] This increasing use of stock options gave "senior managers a strong incentive to mislead investors about the true condition of their companies," as *New Yorker* financial journalist John Cassidy found.[22] The result is that the wool was pulled over the eyes of the average investor—from minor accounting dodges or massaging of those quarterly results, to the massive fraud that took down Enron, Worldcom, Tyco, and other big companies in the late 1990s and early 2000s.

Changes in the media were a great enabler of truth-challenged performance. The new cable business-news channels, which thrived on excitement, gave executives a powerful platform to sell their version of corporate reality to average investors, according to a writer who worked in TV financial news during the dot-com era.[23]

Changes in the media, too, enabled—even exacerbated—the insider-outsider divide. Wall Street helped, deploying TV-ready, stock-touting "analysts" who seemed unbiased, even though ethical conflicts were unavoidable: their employers, investment firms, were actually getting business (and other insider perks) from those companies the analysts were often promoting.[24] Throughout the 1990s to the 2000s, there were cases of Wall Street analysts going on the air and talking up a stock while internally they were telling their people in the firm that the stocks were, in the words of one of the most infamous of them, "POS (pieces of shit)."

Here is how Henry Blodget, a well-known analyst, characterized two stocks publicly to unwitting potential buyers and shareholders, versus how he characterized them internally:[25]

> *On a dot-com called Lifeminders:*
> In Public: "We think [Lifeminders] presents an attractive investment."—12/21/00
> Internal: "I can't believe what a POS [piece of shit] that thing is."—12/04/00

On a dot-com called Infoseek:
In Public: Blodget rates it a Neutral to Accumulate—12/19/99
Internal: The stock is a ". . . dog . . ."—12/19/99

Blodget's many appearances on business-news channels were part of the elaborate performance expected of "star" analysts at that time.[26] Many analysts also played a role in so-called IPO "roadshows," when a new stock was pitched to investors.

With the focus squarely on the appearances of the moment, executives lulled the public into thinking things were rosy by putting up what was really a flimsy façade. The consequences, of course, are borne by "Main Street," not Wall Street. Main Street investors might have benefited short-term from inflated stock prices, but most didn't know when to sell, or even that they *should* sell, while many executives did.[27]

Wall Street analysts were eventually taken to task for their performances, but only after the damage was done. In 2003, top investment banks were forced by regulators to pay $1.4 billion in fines and to erect walls separating their banking departments from their analysts.[28]

And over on the general-news cable channels, another very insidious performance was (and still is) being staged. While there's been endless hand-wringing over political polarization and cheap opinion found on the cable channels, this trend deserves at least as much scrutiny: the use of pundits, analysts, or "experts"—often former high government officials—who now have a swirl of undisclosed or only partially revealed interests that the viewer knows nothing about. Many of these players are, in fact, shadow lobbyists or shadow elites.

That something smells bad has not been lost on us. A citizen-driven petition that went up on the White House website in March 2013 is telling. It asked the Obama administration to "require Congressmen & Senators to wear logos of their financial backers on their clothing, much like NASCAR drivers do." That suggestion could go even farther. As we saw earlier, often it is *former* politicians and government officials who hold sway. We see them on TV, and it would indeed be very illuminating if they wore sponsorship logos.[29]

One who could have used a logo might be former Homeland Security secretary Michael Chertoff. He took to the airwaves virtually nonstop in the weeks following the 2009 Christmas Day bombing attempt aboard a Northwest Airlines flight from Amsterdam to Detroit. He pushed for full-body scanners as a cure-all for lax airport security. His eponymous consulting firm represented the only company, Rapiscan Systems, to have initially qualified for the government contract to manufacture the scanners.[30] But the media outlets that used him as an expert failed to mention this fact.[31] And when the *New York Times* interviewed him on the subject, speaking to him twice, reporters did not inquire whether he had any financial interest in the matter.[32]

Indeed, nimble power brokers are all over the media. In 2010, *The Nation* conducted a four-month investigation and found one thing that bound together seemingly very different cable networks:[33]

> Since 2007 at least seventy-five registered lobbyists, public relations representatives and corporate officials—people paid by companies and trade groups to manage their public image and promote their financial and political interests—have appeared on MSNBC, Fox News, CNN, CNBC and Fox Business Network with no disclosure of the corporate interests that had paid them. Many have been regulars on more than one of the cable networks, turning in dozens—and in some cases hundreds—of appearances.

These power brokers (and the networks that put them on the air) are operating beyond accountability—without disclosing who they are shilling for.

The *Nation* article also makes another excellent and troubling point: that adding a role as a pundit can ease access to policymakers that the person might not get if he or she were just a registered lobbyist.

How did these pundit-"experts" become so popular so easily? Part of the answer lies in simple economics. With cable companies eager to squeeze more profit out of newsroom budgets, a programmer knows that talk is literally cheap, or at least far cheaper than reported stories. Stories created in-house might require a correspondent, a producer, a photographer, and an editor. Booking an "expert" or "pundit" requires none of that, aside from the phone calls, the logistics, and research for the anchor. This was true even before the Internet emerged, and a former producer at a top cable-news outlet in the late 1990s and early 2000s (who does not want his name used) describes the many challenges faced in ascertaining the agendas of guests, as well as the struggle to disclose their agendas.

> In listening to booker phone calls, and in viewing the research given to the anchor, there was not much attention paid to whether a former government official might now be eager to appear because they are shilling for a consultant group or company. In part, this was simply a new phenomenon. Guests didn't used to all have these vast professional portfolios they have now, or if they did, it wasn't quite known. And also, it was a stress-filled environment and it's hard to imagine having enough time to investigate a tangle of interests while also getting a show on the air. If there was a glaring conflict, a guest might be cancelled, but this was very rare. Even if a booker did emphasize that their guest might have a conflicting interest, that didn't mean that a disclosure always ended up on the air. A writer decides whether to put it in the copy the anchor reads. An anchor reads the research and decides whether it matters and is worth mentioning in the copy or the interview. A line producer or a technical director would have the choice to toggle among two different "fonts," or the titles of the guests [shown on the air]. Almost always, the default title used was "former government so-and-so," even if that had little to do with what the person was doing or representing in the here and now.

And that view came from a time before the Internet was king; these days, the old media is getting crushed by the new, as we'll explore in-depth shortly. It's no surprise, then, that cheap talking heads with hard-to-discern agendas are all over the airwaves.

The rise of the interview, typically at the expense of reported stories, has been quantified for one network. According to the 2012 Pew report:[34]

On CNN, the cable channel that has branded itself around deep reporting, produced story packages were cut nearly in half from 2007 to 2012. Across the three cable channels, coverage of live events during the day, which often require a crew and correspondent, fell 30% from 2007 to 2012 while interview segments, which tend to take fewer resources and can be scheduled in advance, were up 31%.

Under new leadership, CNN has cut packaged stories even further. According to one observer, the network:[35]

> has been placing more emphasis on live coverage of breaking events as well as documentaries, leaving less room for the creation of pre-taped video packages that had been more of a staple on the network.

Of course, such changes are by no means limited to CNN; they run the media gamut. That means that there's both a decline in reported stories (no doubt including some accountability journalism) and an easy opening for power brokers to help mold public opinion to their liking. There's even a side benefit of opting for interviews over reported stories: it removes some of the accountability. If a guest says something inaccurate, a news outlet can lay blame on the guest instead of its own in-house reporter.

While several of the networks have acknowledged the problem and attempted to modify some of their disclosure policies, the issues catalogued above are, minute by minute, buried under an avalanche of pressures, as *The Nation* found. Clearly, power brokers can easily take advantage and appear to be increasingly doing so. The former TV news producer quoted above believes that most reporters "want to do the right thing" but that the system just doesn't allow the time needed to really figure out a power broker's affiliations.

Producers also have to wrestle with the mushroom-like proliferation of amorphous political-influence groups. Getting to the bottom of who's responsible for something is a signature challenge of the shadow-elite era.

This has become even more difficult to discern in the United States since 2010, when *The Nation* conducted its investigation. The Supreme Court's *Citizens United* decision in January that year muddied the waters further by spawning a huge number of new political-influence groups.[36] Add to this the growing number of advocacy groups that parade as "think tanks" and with which power brokers now frequently affiliate. These entities also sometimes have murky sponsorship.

And PR firms take full advantage of all this. Qorvis, about which we will hear more shortly, executed a scheme in 2004 on behalf of a client, AIG, which claimed to know nothing of the plan. Qorvis had contacted a booking agency, hoping to find influential voices in finance that might be paid to criticize New York Attorney General Eliot Spitzer, who was probing the industry. According to *PR Week* and the *New York Times*, the e-mails mentioned a possible "$25,000 retainer, and $10,000 for opinion articles or TV appearances" for willing hands.[37]

An outlet as eminent as the *New York Times* may still have the wherewithal to get to the bottom of sponsorship in its reporting, but one can only imagine the struggle for a typically more harried and far less experienced television news team, whose daily job entails many other tasks beyond the actual reporting of a story or the vetting of a guest. It is easy to see why seasoned power brokers can so easily, and so frequently do, exploit the TV airwaves.

GUTTING ACCOUNTABILITY JOURNALISM

TV, like the entire old-media universe, is being slammed by the advent of the Internet. The entire field of journalism has been severely weakened by the emergence of cheap digital content.

What not long ago in the United States was a profession dominated by, say, a few dozen well-respected institutions (even though some may have had a partisan slant) has become atomized and fractured. The global rise of the Internet allowed a profusion of low-cost content to crowd out investigative reporting—not only at national levels, but at local ones as well. Ad revenue fell as the defection from print to Internet accelerated, and media companies began contracting. This trend predated the financial crisis of 2008, but when the economy detonated that year, layoffs in "old media"—television, newspapers, and magazines—exploded. There has been a steady hemorrhage of talent even at outlets with venerable histories.

Tellingly, the four reporters with sizable Twitter followings mentioned earlier have more followers than the entire daily print readership of the *New York Times*, which in 2013 stood at around 732,000.[38]

We should indeed be concerned about this bloodletting. The quality and integrity of traditional media still matters, even if it might seem that new media prevails. Even if consumers get their news through digital means, whatever device they use, they still tend to choose and share news stories that originate from mainstream or "legacy" outlets, according to the Pew Center's survey of 2012 news habits. But digital doesn't pay the newsroom bills, and these organizations are cracking at the seams.[39]

A related problem is that digital consumers can pick and choose what news they want to read and can ignore—even miss noticing—what might not be of interest to them but is nonetheless important. The old journalistic formula—who, what, where, when, why, and how (space permitting)—has yielded, at least on television news and sometimes in newspapers, to something far simpler: who and what. Where, when, and why take up too much space (or time) and, anyway, are presumed to be common knowledge because of social media. How is seldom covered anymore. It requires investigation, sourcing, fact-checking.

Just how dire is the state of American journalism, especially investigative reporting? Apparently it is a tragedy now worthy of farce. In 2012, on Jon Stewart's *Daily Show*, "correspondent" John Oliver set out to investigate the state of investigative journalism. He met reporter Kaj Larsen, a casualty of the near-abolition of CNN's investigative unit. Larsen, who had reported from various global hotspots and showed himself being waterboarded on television (the point of which was to describe what it felt like—that is, whether it was torture or not, the subject of huge debate at the time), is shown in a new job—a trainer at a Crossfit gym. But it is his second job that is most telling. Larsen is now pitching stories to a fake newsroom, as a consultant to the HBO drama *The Newsroom*.[40] This is, unfortunately, an apt commentary on journalism today.

The massive layoffs and shutdowns in journalism overall in just more than a decade are staggering. As the Pew Center recounts in its 2013 State of the Media Report:[41]

> Estimates for newspaper newsroom cutbacks in 2012 put the industry down 30% since its peak in 2000 and below 40,000 full-time professional employees for the first time since 1978 . . . *Time* . . . the only major print news weekly left standing, cut roughly 5% of its staff in early 2013 as a part of broader company layoffs.

A rebound is not expected. The Bureau of Labor Statistics assesses that the ranks could fall another 13 percent over the next decade.[42]

Some journalists have even been rendered obsolete by computers. The Pew Center notes in its 2012 report that "A growing list of media outlets, such as *Forbes*, use technology by a company called Narrative Science to produce content by way of algorithm, no human reporting necessary."[43] That means the company will use what they call "Artificial Intelligence" computer programs to amass and assess data, and take it a step further and actually create the narrative from the data. When you read something and think "a virtual robot could have written this," these days, you might actually be right.

Performing for the Public?

Consider one seemingly ready-made narrative that flourished after the selection of Mary Jo White in early 2013 to chair the U.S. Securities and Exchange Commission. In naming White, the Obama White House appeared to be blasting one very loud message—"we are getting tough on Wall Street." The descriptions usually affixed to the former U.S. prosecutor in New York are ones like these: relentless, hard-charging, gutsy. One *New York Times* editorial praised her record as "formidable" and lauded her "toughness, tenacity and aggressiveness."[44]

Who better to clean up Wall Street than the fearless dynamo barely five feet tall who pursued terrorists and mobster John Gotti? What she lacks in height, the narrative goes, she makes up for with chutzpah.

When the SEC in November 2013 secured a guilty plea in the insider trading case against hedge fund giant SAC Capital, one of White's predecessors, Arthur Levitt, Jr., called her a "rock star" in an interview with *Bloomberg News*:[45]

> This is real theater. This is David vs. Goliath. Little Mary Jo White takes on great big Stevie Cohen and not just for a day or a week or a month, but for years and her tenacity, her toughness has delivered what a great SEC chairman should deliver. It's an admission of guilt at long last that she has brought to the SEC, and it hasn't had that in 30 years.

On closer inspection, though, the fearsome "Little Mary Jo" narrative muddles somewhat, and we are fortunate that a handful of reporters still go beyond the simulacra. For one, when White joined the SEC, it was mostly her prosecutorial prowess that was trumpeted, with clips of the press conferences announcing indictments of people such as Omar Abdel-Rahman, the "Blind Sheikh." But there was little mention of her private-sector work—white-collar criminal defense and, yes, SEC cases at a law firm long favored by Wall Street, Debevoise & Plimpton—that netted her millions over several decades.[46] (The firm represented the insurance colossus AIG and "too big to fail" banks and investment firms, including Goldman Sachs. Her team helped former Bank of America CEO Kenneth Lewis and was hired by Morgan Stanley's board to help chairman John Mack.[47])

Defenders like former SEC chairman Levitt say that, since her appointment, she has proven that she can zealously prosecute and extract once-unheard-of admissions of guilt from several bad actors. Columbia University journalism professor and *New Yorker* staff writer Nicholas Lemann notes the effect White's efforts have been having: "During this run of cases, the S.E.C. was on the front pages almost every day. The news reinforced the perception that, under White, the S.E.C. had grown fangs."[48]

But, Lemann cautions, what if the fangs are needed elsewhere? He, for one, thinks that they are, notably in the fight over the nitty-gritty of the Dodd-Frank financial-reform legislation passed in 2010.[49] He explains:

> Enforcement is onstage, regulation is backstage. [L]ittle-noticed changes in laws and regulations were far more important in causing the 2008 crash than was law-breaking by the heads of the financial industry. The . . . industry is intensely engaged in trying to shape these [Dodd-Frank] rules, while the rest of the country has lost interest. The economy is in better shape. Prosecution is retrospective, and narratively riveting. Regulation is prospective, and boring and technical. It's entirely possible for the government to become a tougher prosecutor and a more lax regulator at the same time.

The Nation agrees with this assessment, zeroing in on the ". . . stealthy work of battalions of regulatory lawyers":[50]

> [A] kind of ground war has been going on for almost three years, with the regulators waging hand-to-hand combat to defend every clause and comma in Dodd-Frank, and the lawyers fighting to insert any loophole they can to protect their clients' extraordinary profits. . . . And if a regulator ever succeeds in publishing a rule . . . then brace yourself for . . . "Defcon 4": the bankers take the regulator to court, hiring the likes of Eugene Scalia [son of the Supreme Court Justice], who has carved out a lucrative niche blocking such rules on technicalities. . . . Three years after Dodd-Frank was passed, only 148 of the 398 rules requiring action by regulators have been finalized, and draft versions have yet to be submitted for half of the remainder.

Thus, White's performances serve to distract us from the important but less-"sexy" issue of regulation by providing a sense of progress on the financial-reform front. Sidetracked by appearances, we risk missing the fight over all-important rules changes.

Brain Drain and Strain

Puncturing the kind of narrative bubble that surround Mary Jo White and financial regulation more broadly is the crucial task of holding the powerful accountable. But there are fewer and fewer reporters to do the job.

The decline in investigative reporting in particular (not just in journalism overall) is harder to parse, in part because, as the *American Journalism Review* points out, plenty of investigative journalism happens within a particular beat.[51] For instance, the *Boston Globe*'s Bryan Bender is primarily a national security journalist, and yet he did an extensive investigation on retired generals and the influence they continue to brandish and profit from in their very active post-military careers. If he lost his job, would he be officially counted as a loss for investigative journalism? Perhaps not, but he should be. And there are many others like him.[52]

This brain drain has a pernicious effect on the public good, for reasons both obvious and more subtle. It's easy to see that the simple loss of manpower means that fewer reporters will be granted the extensive time needed for connecting the dots, sorting through the agendas of power brokers, and finding connections among them.

There's also the increasing strain on reporters who are now expected to "perform" across social-media platforms to generate more and more pageviews and eyeballs. As a result, according to a 2010 Pew report, journalists are ". . . focusing more time on disseminating information and somewhat less on gathering it, making news people more reactive and less proactive."[53]

Some journalists are plainly spread thin across these platforms. Others have created their own quasi-independent power centers. Some journalists and many opinion writers have established such large and engaged followings that they seem at this point almost like adjunct news outlets to the bigger mothership; it's hard to fathom that Nicholas Kristof, *New York Times* columnist, would lose much of his 600,000-strong Facebook readership were he to depart from the *Times*. This certainly has accountability implications. Journalists know they need to have a heavy social-media presence; when they get that presence, they have both their own power and that of the old-media institution that pays their salary. But if a journalist acts on behalf of some unknown interest while on social media, that old-media institution can always distance itself by insisting that it never has complete control of what journalists say on Twitter or Facebook.

By 2013, Pew's annual report was far more stark, describing how a "continued erosion of news reporting resources converged with growing opportunities for those in politics, government agencies, companies and others to take their messages directly to the public."[54] Some of their examples:[55]

> The government of Malaysia was recently discovered to have bankrolled propaganda that appeared in several major U.S. outlets under columnists' bylines. A number of news organizations, including The Associated Press, recently carried a fake press release about Google that came from a PR distribution site that promises clients it will reach "top media outlets." And recently, journalist David Cay Johnston, in writing about a pitch from one corporate marketer that included a "vacation reward" for running his stories, remarked, "Journalists get lots of pitches like this these days, which is partly a reflection of how the number of journalists has shriveled while the number of publicists has grown."

This combination of performance-driven personalized media and the decimation of traditional media means that power brokers can now spin their agendas with many fewer journalists standing in the way to challenge them. The new media platform has squeezed out the old gatekeepers and, at the same time, provided those in power with inexpensive and easily exploitable new venues to press their interests. And as journalists either leave the profession or broaden their professional mandate, they risk aiding or aping the very power brokers they might once have held to account.

THE JOURNALISM-TO-PR MIGRATION

That growth in publicity brings us to an often-overlooked area of the old media's implosion: Where do all the downsized journalists go? One unscientific survey of nearly six hundred self-described laid-off journalists found that just six percent of them remained in journalism, a profession that inculcates its practitioners with commitment to objective truth.[56] Of course, some journalists fall far short of this ideal, but the profession overall has a strong public-interest ethos that is supported at an institutional level at well-regarded outlets. This means that the loss of professional journalists—in absolute terms—is surely a loss to the public interest.

While former CNN reporter Larsen is now finding opportunity in Hollywood, many laid-off journalists find themselves aiding those with money and power, the very forces they might have helped keep in check as reporters. They end up on the other side of the press release—in public relations, what the chairwoman and chief executive of the Public Relations Society of America called in 2011 the "great journalism-to-PR migration."[57] ProPublica, a nonprofit journalism outlet, and the *Columbia Journalism Review*, the premier American magazine of journalism criticism, jointly reported on this migration in 2011 and found it worrisome, to say the least.

Reporter John Sullivan writes: "As PR becomes ascendant, private and government interests become more able to generate, filter, distort, and dominate the public debate, and to do so without the public knowing it."[58] He cites research in *The Death and Life of American Journalism*, which assessed labor statistics and found that in 1980, for every hundred thousand Americans, there were forty-five people in public relations and thirty-six journalists. By 2008, it was ninety PR people and twenty-five journalists. That gap has likely widened since 2008, amid further journalism layoffs.[59] And these statistics actually understate the divide between the persuaders and those who might hold them to account: that's because, as Sullivan points out, "those figures include only independent public relations agencies—they don't include PR people who work for big companies, lobbying outfits, advertising agencies, nonprofits, or government."[60]

The Strength of Simulacra

It is not just the ever-greater strength in numbers of the PR people as compared with journalists: it is the strength of simulacra à la Jean Baudrillard. In the digital age, the art of persuasion has become more subtle and difficult to detect. Some techniques have been employed and perfected for decades—ghost-writing, planting favorable stories, spin, fomenting doubt without outright denial.[61] But the shadow-elite digital age of blurred boundaries is new; so are en masse simulacra in the media/Internet that pervade virtually all arenas.

A classic example can be found at defense giant Raytheon, which hired investigative reporter Chris Hawley in 2012 just weeks after he won a Pulitzer Prize for Investigative Reporting. Here's how Hawley described his work at Raytheon, so-called "brand journalism," to a marketing strategist:[62]

> I'm helping to build a news operation. . . . We are working at Raytheon just like an AP beat to find interesting stories and tell the world about them in a way that engages. We have bureau chiefs in all of our four divisions. They have certain products that they want to talk about so we try to find new and interesting ways of exploring those stories. And we refine the story ideas, assign writers and we're doing a lot of training on editing and getting those stories out.

In other words, Hawley has become a promoter, specializing in media simulacra.

The same marketing strategist expounds on Hawley's editorial leadership and "checklist approach":[63]

> Chris has also taken on the role of establishing editorial guidelines for Raytheon and teaching staff about journalism. "We've tried to codify the writing and editing process," he says. "We've come up with a checklist approach to writing a web story that goes through everything from selecting if it's going to be a hard lead story or a soft lead story, right down to which scientific study should I pay attention to when I'm evaluating background information for an article."

As in many other walks of life, the checklist is now being applied to writing media stories, a subjective art.

A simulacrum is also being created in reverse: venerable journalistic brands have changed their models, to look like—well, not exactly like—traditional news outlets. *Forbes* allows "business leaders, entrepreneurs, book authors, academics and other topic experts" to expound on their website, as described in a report by Poynter.org. Note the corporatizing language used in the report to describe this "contributed content" model, by Forbes.com's chief product officer: "incentive-based, entrepreneurial journalism." This has the result of mixing content from current journalists, ex-journalists, and those who aren't journalists at all under the same century-old brand name.[64]

Former journalists are also seizing new opportunities in lobbying firms or advertising agencies. Case in point: ex-*Newsweek* White House correspondent Richard Wolffe in 2009 appeared on and even guest-hosted an MSNBC program while at the same time serving as a "senior strategist" for a corporate communications firm called Public Strategies. While he was eventually taken to task for this, he got away with it for several months.[65]

Journalists are also populating nonprofit and government organizations. Additionally, they are finding work at think tanks and advocacy groups (which may or may not be nonprofits), many of which have names with a grassroots feel that aren't quickly understood as influence groups. Even current journalists are taking roles with these groups and yet are expected to remain (and are often viewed as) objective news purveyors.

And herein lies a more subtle—but still pernicious—effect of journalism's economic decimation. With salaries pressed and future employment with established media outlets uncertain, working journalists *and* downsized journalists now often spread themselves professionally to augment their portfolios. These days, the idea that a journalist would operate in a single venue with a single standard of conduct seems as dated as an eight-track tape. The new influence groups mentioned above often can provide income and prestige-generating roles, as can academic appointments and speaking engagements. In this tangle of alliances and commitments to things that aren't clearly journalism, there is a stronger possibility that objectivity will be diluted and that hard questions will go unasked.

Many prominent journalists have gone on to serve particular agendas in a growing number of think tanks. Of course, reporters are always hungry for access. But with traditional newspapers in free fall, think tanks are able to entice many big names. National defense journalist Nathan Hodge, writing in 2010 for *Wired*'s Danger Room blog, identified a journalist/think-tank alliance and said it is widespread. Seeing it up close and personal in the national-security and defense realm, he explains the evolution this way:[66]

> The relationship between reporters and think tanks used to be, well, pretty simple. You called up defense expert X for a quote on, say, cost overruns on a stealth fighter jet, and if you were lucky, you'd get something lively. . . . Now . . . [p]rint is dying, newsrooms are shrinking and the media industry is generally in the toilet. Think tanks are starting to become full-time patrons of the news business, and they are bankrolling book projects, blogs and even war reporting. . . . [W]hat does this mean for journalism? When think tanks are often a revolving door for government service, what happens when reporters . . . become office-mates of past or future political appointees? How do you keep national security reporting from becoming an echo chamber of the Beltway policy elite? It's hard enough giving objective analysis of some policy maven's ideas, after you two have shared a few cocktails together. Now imagine how much tougher that becomes, when the policy maven is in the next cubicle over.

Ironically, less than six months later, Hodge's Danger Room colleague Noah Shachtman (now executive editor at the Daily Beast) announced that he was taking a position at the Brookings Institution, while maintaining his editorial presence at *Wired*. The venerable Brookings does have a good reputation for scholarly independence—even as it is watered down, under pressure as it is to put out constant product, like practically all think tanks these days. And to Shachtman's credit, he did acknowledge Hodge's earlier criticism of this very career move. But in trying to allay fears that he might lose objectivity, Shachtman doesn't quite succeed. "My Brookings bosses have assured me I'm allowed to tool on whoever I'd like at the Institution. They just want me to give that person the heads-up. Seems like a reasonable request." This raises the possibility that the target of the story, who could be, to use Hodge's formulation, "in the next cubicle," might be in a better position to spike the story. Shachtman also strenuously tried to make it clear that funders are well-removed from Brookings's research, stating in a blog post that "[a]ll a donor can do is give to the Institution's general fund" rather than a specific project or person. But now, in a corrected version, that line is struck through (but still readable).[67]

Clearly, the boundaries between journalism and PR have been so breached that the public's ability to know whom to trust has been seriously compromised.

THE WILD WEST DIGITAL TERRAIN

Think tanks aren't just hiring journalists. In the new digital terrain, some think tanks are beginning to look very much like news outlets themselves, attempting to adapt in an era where the limited attention span reigns supreme. This rearrangement is one of the countless variations of new forms of journalism and never-before-seen business models emerging from the ashes of the old media. Previously unknown players have leapt to the fore. While many experts praise the spirit of innovation and passion of many new media pioneers, the landscape is truly a Wild West in terms of transparency and accountability. Experts also warn that the creation of new "accountability journalism," the old investigative reporting in new format, at least for now, comes nowhere near to making up for the destruction of the old.

A former commissioner of the U.S. communications regulatory body, the Federal Communications Commission, was the sole dissenter on the 2011 merger of NBC Universal and Comcast (Comcast was the biggest video and residential Internet services provider in the United States at the time).[68] Described as "Mr. Public Citizen" by the *Seattle Times*, former FCC commissioner Michael Copps spoke late in 2012 with Bill Moyers of PBS:[69]

> The Internet has the potential for a new town square of democracy, paved with broadband bricks. But it's very, very far from being the reality. . . . The traditional media is a shell of its former self . . . really as hollowed out as [a] Midwestern steel mill, a rust belt steel mill. . . . [T]he new media—there's wonderful entrepreneurship and experimentation taking place in the new media, but there's no business plan to support

expensive investigative journalism. . . . You just wonder how many stories are going untold, how many of the powerful are being held completely unaccountable for what they did.

Activist/author Astra Taylor calls this new state of journalism "churnalism." In an interview, she described the term as "the intense pressure to produce and post and to be up-to-the-minute and how that ultimately becomes essential to financial survival for new media outlets."[70]

Philanthro-Journalism

This is not to say that some people aren't trying to revive investigative reporting in the form of the new accountability journalism. Consider "philanthro-journalism." It certainly sounds noble. Wealthy citizens and foundations, galvanized by the decline of the old media and investigative journalism, are stepping up to help fill the void. Many first-rate reporters are joining its ranks—and this book draws on sources such as ProPublica.

Glenn Greenwald, for instance, who helped break the Edward Snowden bombshell, has joined the ranks of philanthro-journalists. In 2014, Greenwald, along with other investigative journalists/activists, started an online outlet for "fearless, adversarial" journalism supported by a billionaire, eBay founder Pierre Omidyar.[71]

Greenwald is just the most recent and perhaps best known to make this move. By some estimates, more than a quarter billion dollars has flowed into this area over the past decade.[72] But "nonprofit" or "philanthropy" does not necessarily mean no "strings or baggage," as the *American Journalism Review* has outlined.[73]

Simplifying the issue a bit, one can think of it this way: In the old commercial-journalism model, an outlet is struggling to attract a vast readership or viewership to maintain subscription fees and high ad rates. But in nonprofit journalism, an outlet might be free to pursue accountability projects regardless of raw popularity because the readers, in effect, are not paying the bill.

But who is paying the bill, if not readers and advertisers?

In the case of ProPublica, probably the best known of the new nonprofit journalism outlets, the primary early benefactor was one liberal-minded couple: Herb and the late Marion Sandler, California banking billionaires. ProPublica, founded in 2008, has put out a slew of in-depth investigations spanning topics like "dark money" in campaign finance, fracking, the use of drones, and prosecutorial overreach. It was the first digital news outlet to win a Pulitzer Prize. But when the Sandlers themselves came under the investigative lens as the mortgage business exploded, they fought both *60 Minutes* and the *New York Times* strenuously. It appears that the Sandlers indeed were unfairly represented in many respects[74]; and yet what if they, or other patrons of philanthro-journalism, *had* deserved intense scrutiny? Would these nonprofit outlets vigorously report on the people underwriting their work?

A Slate writer was quick to raise doubts. Writing in 2009, he noted that "The nonprofit news business . . . is spreading like a midsummer algae bloom. . . . No matter how good the nonprofit operation is, it always ends up sustaining itself with handouts, and handouts come with conditions."[75]

How does this nonprofit journalism of handouts differ from the commercial media—say, Rupert Murdoch and his vast news empire—we might ask? Nonprofit journalism appears more "neutral." Yet, as we saw in earlier chapters, influence and funding are often obscured. Given the proliferation of nonprofits that range from pharmaceutical companies dressed up as patient-led advocacy organizations to energy companies parading as grassroots organizations, they can be much less transparent.

The Pew Center took up the issue in 2011. After an initial look at forty-six sites that fit the nonprofit model, representing news sites that skew both liberal and conservative, it found one key issue in common: a real lack of transparency about the true source of funding. "While they may have been forthcoming about who their direct funders were, often the funders themselves were much less clear about their own sources of income. This effectively made the first level of transparency incomplete and shielded the actual financing behind the news site. The chief funders listed for nearly two-thirds of the sites studied—twenty-eight in all—did not disclose where their money came from."[76]

The sites also tended to produce material that mirrored the ideology of their benefactors, despite presenting themselves as serving the civic-minded role that traditional media (warts and all) once held. One example involved an online news/advocacy outlet called the Fiscal Times, devoted to monitoring America's budget deficit. The Fiscal Times is backed by longtime deficit hawk and billionaire Pete Peterson, who founded the advocacy group Concord Coalition. In 2009, the *Washington Post* ran a story in partnership with this "news" outlet. The article argued that there was apparent growing support for action on the deficit, mentioning the Concord Coalition, while failing to mention that both the Fiscal Times and the Concord Coalition are funded by Peterson. (Interestingly, part of the *Washington Post's* defense of its omission when this came to light was that the two writers of the piece were "veteran" journalists, including one who had previously worked at the *Post*.[77] This is another case of the complications involved when old-school journalists find jobs at novel, boundary-defying outlets.)

It is telling that the biggest contributor to journalism among American foundations, the Knight Foundation—the philanthropic arm of the once powerful Knight-Ridder family news empire—has rolled with the times. Rather than focus on the loss of old-school journalism, Knight has wholeheartedly embraced the new model. In a paper called "From Journalism to Information: The Transformation of the Knight Foundation and News Innovation," a professor who studied Knight's involvement reported that "the Knight Foundation has sought to change journalism by renegotiating its boundaries. Namely, by downplaying its own historical emphasis on professionalism, the foundation has embraced openness to outside influence—that is, the wisdom of the crowd, citizen participation, and a broader definition of 'news.'"[78]

There are, however, genuine bright spots. Organizations and initiatives started by the investigative reporter Charles Lewis, and funded by an array of foundations, other institutional donors, and private donations, are among them. Since 1989, when Lewis founded the Center for Public Integrity, it has published hundreds of investigative works, many of them game-changers.[79] Lewis also founded the Center's International Consortium of Investigative Journalists (ICIJ), which became the "first global website devoted to international exposés," according to the *Encyclopedia of Journalism*.[80] In 2013, ICIJ boasted some 175 journalists in more than sixty countries, often collaborating across boundaries. That year, the

Consortium published a ground-breaking series of articles on offshore financial havens.[81]

The Center for Public Integrity, the first of Lewis's initiatives, was founded years before the stripping of investigative journalism. To an ordinary, or younger, reader, a worthy and well-established organization like the Center for Public Integrity might well (unfortunately) be lumped in with newer, murky philanthro-journalism enterprises.

While philanthro-journalism may be an obvious step in the United States, with its long tradition of charitable giving, it is by no means confined to America. Some of the earliest incarnations appeared in eastern Europe after the Cold War, with support from George Soros's Open Society foundation (about which we will hear more in Chapter 7), which sought to bring a free press to parts of the region that didn't have that tradition. In the present decade, philanthro-journalism has broadened its reach to include Britain and Australia, where, according to *The Economist*, "regulators and politicians have fretted about the decline of old-fashioned media without doing much about it."[82]

All in all, philanthro-journalism is a mixed bag. One journalist who attempted to study foundation-supported journalism came to this deadpan conclusion: "For the most part we have the foundations' own glossy reports to go upon."[83] Despite the troubling relationship with transparency, many entities, from think tanks to foundations, have decided that philanthro-journalism is the way to go. And they are not alone. But when it comes to the transparency on which accountability depends, there may be nearly as much peril as promise.

Digital Cowboys

The Netflix-made original series *House of Cards* that premiered in 2012 captures the zeitgeist of our era. The young, story-breaking, boundary-pushing reporter Zoe Barnes effectively gives up an old-media job for the edgy political site "Slugline." (She later persuades her established newsroom rival to ditch her own high-prestige perch for "Slugline" as well.) As the Barnes character says, "Everyone's a free agent, they write whatever they want, wherever they are. Most people write from their phones." Her new editor tells her "If eight minutes passes on anything,

I get bored. . . . In eight minutes, I could be bored with you." Speed is king and editing be damned. The new boss tells her "You don't have to send me things before you post. The goal here is for everyone to post things faster than I have a chance to read 'em. If you're satisfied with the article, just put it up."[84]

One might think, or hope, that Barnes's former employer would sneer disapprovingly. But the chic publisher knows she sits atop a dinosaur, telling the editor who once supervised Barnes "We don't need people who follow the rules; we need people with personality."

There's no shortage of personality in digital journalism; but rules, or standards? You'll need to look hard to find many of those. That's probably because seemingly endless permutations of new-media journalism now populate the Web. It would be impossible to catalog all of them, but here are some characteristic forms:

You have professionals striking out on their own, some former beat reporters who've created niche blogs that "go deep" in their field of interest. Others have "personality" or a "brand," like the popular blogger Andrew Sullivan, who left the Daily Beast and sought his own subscribers. Other high-profile journalists who've left the mothership of more traditional media include Ezra Klein, who generated considerable buzz with his WonkBlog at the *Washington Post*. He, along with Slate blogger Matthew Yglesias and colleagues from the *Post,* left in 2014 to a new venture for Vox Media.[85] Statistical whiz Nate Silver became a star for calling with near total accuracy the outcome of the 2012 midterm elections. Rather than digging in with the *New York Times*, which was licensing his FiveThirtyEight blog, he chose to move to the sports channel ESPN. While Silver's background in baseball statistics and predictions render his choice perhaps less radical than it might have been coming from other media people, it's worth noting that very few journalists in his situation would have made the same decision twenty years ago. Also noteworthy is Silver's metric success, a sign of the triumph of numbers over words discussed in the last chapter. Some critics say he has taken metrics too far and leaves analysis and creativity out of the picture. As *New York Times* columnist Paul Krugman commented, ". . . data never tell a story on their own."[86]

Digital technology has also allowed citizen journalism to flourish. The Pew Center examined the trend in the United States in 2010 and noted growth and creativity among citizen-journalists, particularly at the local level. At the national level, it was a "citizen-journalist" who captured one of the most controversial lines uttered by candidate Barack Obama in the 2008 presidential campaign, that some small-town voters might be "bitter; they cling to guns or religion."[87] And it was an amateur who in 2013 helped prove that chemical weapons had been used in Syria.[88]

Around the world, citizen-journalists (or just plain citizens) have been credited with sparking revolutions. Citizens were able to "evad[e] the censors in Iran and communicat[e] from the earthquake disaster zone in Haiti," according to Pew.[89] Citizen-journalists helped spread information through social media during the Arab Spring uprisings across the Middle East, as well as during the Occupy Wall Street protests.

But along with the reality of online communication often comes a fantasy. There is a propensity, particularly among the social-media–fetishizing young, to credit social media with what it is constitutionally incapable of: expunging memory and wiping history clean. Getting the message out and putting crowds in the streets do not, on their own, change the system or society. (Witness, for instance, the return of the generals in Egypt within just one short year of the democratic election that followed the Arab Spring.) Rah-rah social media too often goes hand in hand with a dangerous ahistorical clean-slate view of the world.

And so-called "pro-am" collaborations continue to spring up, with amateurs providing source materials or working in a more active way with the professionals who can use their outlet to widely disseminate the story or information. One example is the liberal activist site Alternet and its "Bubble Barons" project, which called on citizens to help build more complete profiles and trace the connections of sixty-seven selected billionaires.[90]

There are obvious benefits to more open participation in journalism through digital technology. Many believe that the old media have been corrupted by their proximity to power, and with good reason. A spectacular example is that of the *New York Times* reporter Judith Miller. A solid case has been made that Miller acted not as a journalist but as a bullhorn for a

George W. Bush administration bent on war with Iraq, and Miller eventually resigned.[91]

Regular people who don't derive their salary and status from access to newsmakers and power brokers may be more likely to challenge them. Amateurs also might be more likely to avoid the group-think and attachment to narrative that can happen within, say, the White House or Pentagon press corps. The blogosphere and, increasingly, Twitter users can serve as on-the-spot fact-checkers and truth-squadders.

But there are serious concerns with digital cowboys. Former beat reporters or ordinary citizens who create niche blogs are bound to be targeted by companies and interest groups related to that topic in hopes of getting their message out. Influence groups hire social-media specialists, and it can be hard to tell the difference between someone attempting to be objective and someone working an agenda. Certainly there is no uniform code of conduct among people putting out "information" or their own self-styled "news" in hopes of reaching the public. There's really no way to discern motive or source of funding, unless an individual decides to disclose them, and there's no institution enforcing ethics. In other words, accountability is not part of the latticework.

In dissing public institutions like the old media and opting for self-assemblage, we have seeded a muddled model. Consider Julian Assange, probably the best-known digital cowboy, and his document-revealing WikiLeaks. He encapsulates the promise of the age—and yet provides a case study in unaccountability and what can go awry with nontraditional "truth-seekers." Assange is a declared combatant in information warfare: a high-tech vigilante committed to radical transparency in governance. Several years before Edward Snowden leaked documents to Glenn Greenwald, Assange burst onto the scene in 2010 with his massive leak of Pentagon documents involving America's wars and sensitive diplomatic relations. He was immediately hailed by many on the left as journalism's savior. But while he demanded transparency from others, there was little or no transparency in his own practices at WikiLeaks. The *New Yorker* put it this way, well before Assange ran into legal trouble: "Soon enough, Assange must confront the paradox of his creation: the thing that he seems to detest most—power without accountability—is encoded in the site's DNA, and will only become more pronounced as WikiLeaks evolves into a real institution."[92]

It quickly became clear that there never was and perhaps never will be a "real institution." WikiLeaks is synonymous with one figure—Julian Assange—and Assange himself is deeply problematic. With the lack of an institution comes the lack of standards and principles according to which events are deemed newsworthy. In their absence, the choice of what documents to release becomes an idiosyncratic decision. Assange's dealings have been so contentious that the *New York Times* ran a critical profile of him, describing ". . . erratic and imperious behavior, and a nearly delusional grandeur" the same day it released a massive leak of Iraq war documents.[93] The *Times* also chose not to link to WikiLeaks's own site. It said this was not intended as a slight, but because it wasn't sure that Assange had taken care (or perhaps didn't have the expertise or knowledge) to redact enough names or other revealing details that could endanger lives.[94]

Assange, of course, embodies the full panoply of pros and cons of this new era of media/Internet. He has the passion and technical savvy that many, if not most, of the lumbering media giants lack. (And he does deserve some credit for helping foster the ambitions of Edward Snowden, who "broke the biggest story of the last five years," as one media analyst put it.) But objectivity and transparency are scarcely to be found in his operation, functioning as he does without standards of practice or clear lines of accountability. For instance, his "hactivism" is focused almost entirely on the United States and Western targets, not much on deserving places like China or Russia. And by turning WikiLeaks into a vanity project, he has failed to create an institution with a broad bench of support that could live on without him. His personal legal troubles have muddied the enterprise's ostensible ideals. So what might have been a group committed to more open government and policymaking has devolved into a cross between an international thriller, a scandal investigation (involving allegations of sexual abuse), and a study in grandiosity.

WHEN POWER BROKERS RUSH IN

Power brokers have ridden the tides of change created by the destruction of the old media and the rise of the media/Internet behemoth. Shadow elites, shadow lobbyists, and their fellows have simultaneously exploited both developments.

Colonizing the Internet

Consider this tweet:

> The IDF has begun a widespread campaign on terror sites & operatives in the #Gaza Strip, chief among them #Hamas & Islamic Jihad targets.
>
> —Israeli Defense Forces Twitter feed
> (@IDFSpokesperson), November 12, 2012

This was surely the first-ever war declared on Twitter—and likely not the last. In November 2012, Israel and Hamas used their respective Twitter feeds (@IDFSpokesperson and @AlqassamBrigade) to battle in real time for hearts and minds, while the actual blood-and-guts battle was being waged in Gaza. This was just the latest—and perhaps the most dramatic—case of powerful forces able to present their side, free of context and unimpeded by reporter-gatekeepers.

The pace of branding by powerful forces in digital and social media has evolved so fast that most of us barely have time to consider where the "information" cited comes from or the context in which it was crafted, let alone the implications. So much for the golden age of transparency.

A politician or influencer who *didn't* have a Twitter feed these days would be seen as a relic or an eccentric—if he even existed.

How might the digital media look these days if there had been no reduction in the old media? A former executive editor of the *Washington Post* speculates that the digital landscape would be mushrooming even if the old media were still intact. "There still would be growth in the ability of public relations people to directly reach the public," he assessed. "They are filling a space that has been created digitally."[95]

The digital age has lent new qualities and possibilities to branding and enabled it to push its message (and burnish its reputation) in ways never before possible, such as reputational rebranding and "search-engine optimization." Unlike the old microfiche, the digital record can be manipulated if you have enough cash.

Branding used to be confined to the corporate world. Now it is also used by political message-makers, aiming to create a look and feel that consumers identify with intuitively. False intimacy is the hallmark of the game. When power brokers (or their paid staff) tweet with emoticons or tell their "followers" that it's their kid's birthday, they're really selling their brand—and the narratives and "facts" attached to the brand.

Armed with more financial resources, power brokers can spread their self-serving messages easily by gaming search results on Internet searches. They can hire firms to engage in search-engine optimization, meaning their message will come up very high when people search their name or company. Getting good placement in what might look like so-called "organic search" is far more insidious than simply placing an ad that looks like, well, an ad.

Consider that, in the old days, an influence group might purchase a full-page newspaper ad. To a reader, it would be clear that this was put out by a group with an agenda. But it's much less clear if you, a citizen of today, are Googling something, and an influencer's message just happens to appear on the very top of the screen, or close to it.

While the Internet is frequently touted as democratizing, that enthusiasm should be tempered by the fact that what we see and read online is often manipulated by those with the cash and the power. Amid such lack of transparency, where can the accountability be?

DARK ARTS

It's not just that the new media create new openings: it's that PR operatives actively work the openings.

How does a state-of-the-art PR firm use novel tools and venues to launder, say, the reputation of a client, without the public suspecting that there might be anything amiss? As we saw in Chapter 3, shadow lobbyists working on behalf of foreign governments that seek to press their case in the United States focus their ingenuity on the media, thereby eliding problems of access to policymakers posed by legal and other restrictions.

Journalist Ken Silverstein pulled off a sting against two foreign lobbying shops in 2007 when he exposed company operatives intent on burnishing the image of Turkmenistan. According to Silverstein, they promised to ". . . plant opinion pieces in newspapers under the names of academics and think-tank experts they would recruit. They even offered to set up supposedly 'independent' media events in Washington that would promote Turkmenistan (the agenda and speakers would actually be determined by the lobbyists)."[96]

Two other PR firms—Washington-based Qorvis and U.K.-based Bell Pottinger—excel at laundering influence to make the system all but unaccountable. From gaming search results, to posting third-party blogs that appear independent, to setting up mouthpieces for dictators cloaked in benevolent-sounding organizations, all are designed to deceive. Of course, these are only two such firms in a much larger universe.

First, take Qorvis, founded in 2000 and staffed by some of Washington's finest who not only know the name of the game but have written its rules: a former member of the Bush White House communications team; several former journalists and veteran PR hands; a former senior Capitol Hill legislative assistant; a former top senatorial policy and communications adviser; and a former State Department official touted by *Washington Life* as one of D.C.'s most influential people under the age of forty.[97] Another Qorvis partner was the subject of an *Atlantic* piece that called him "the Jedi Master to television pundits" for training his clients on their TV appearances.[98] The *Atlantic* made only a cursory mention eight paragraphs in that Qorvis represents Saudi Arabia, side by side with the likes of Ringling Bros. and Barnum & Bailey, and Disney On Ice. Yet Qorvis represents some very unsavory regimes. And the Saudi Kingdom is just one of the questionable regimes Qorvis represents.

Qorvis itself makes a show on its website of listing the repressive governments on its client list as if the firm is transparent.[99] And, in an obvious simulacrum, the descriptions of what it does read more as if it were in the business of democracy-promotion than state-of-the-art spinning. Here's how the company describes its work for Bahrain, which began cracking down on opposition protestors in 2011:[100]

> Qorvis' ultimate responsibility is to assist Bahrain with the peaceful resolution of its domestic challenges and bringing

economic prosperity, development and stability for all citizens through positive and proactive communications.

Or Fiji, which has been the target of human-rights activists since the 2006 military coup:[101]

> The Government, under the leadership of Prime Minister Josaia Voreqe Bainimarama, is currently in the process of drafting a new constitution, one that will enable the country's first-ever truly democratic elections: one person, one vote, one value.

What Qorvis has done in both cases is to harness the supposedly democratizing power of the Internet to help whitewash the repressive activities of its cash-flush clients. More on that in a moment, but first let's take a look back at the beginnings of "rogue"-regime PR.

"The Saudis were the first to get this new era of P.R.," says the editor of the top trade magazine *O'Dwyer's Public Relations.*[102] Saudi nationals played an outsized role in the September 11, 2001 attack—fifteen out of nineteen hijackers were Saudis and, of course, bin Laden himself was part of a sprawling family with a construction business and close ties to the House of Saud. The Kingdom sought PR help after the attack, and one firm it turned to was Qorvis. The reported $14 million contract and an ensuing radio-ad campaign apparently led at least one partner to leave the firm.[103]

Qorvis took on other clients, sometimes in association with Bell Pottinger, including Mubarak's Egypt, Yemen and its then dictator Ali Abdullah Saleh, and Equatorial Guinea under despot Teodoro Obiang.[104] Equatorial Guinea is no longer listed as a Qorvis client, but Sri Lanka, Saudi Arabia, Fiji, and Bahrain still are.

Stealth programs, this time on behalf of the Bahrainis, include use of the Internet and social media. In one incident, Bahraini opposition protestor Maryam al-Khawaja appeared at the Oslo Freedom Forum to decry the alleged torture and disappearance of fellow activists. The president of the Human Rights Foundation described what happened next:[105]

Within minutes of Maryam's speech (streamed live online) the global Bahraini P.R. machine went into dramatic overdrive. A tightly organized ring of Twitter accounts began to unleash hundreds of tweets accusing Maryam of being an extremist, a liar, and a servant of Iran.

The president of the foundation pinned the blame on Qorvis. Journalist Tom Squitieri played a role: he penned three pro-government pieces in the Huffington Post over a nearly three-week period in 2011, noting vaguely that he was "working with the Bahrain government on media awareness."[106] There was no mention of Squitieri's employment by Qorvis. Salon pointed out that similar posts appeared on Squitieri's blog (which was active as of the end of 2013) on the Foreign Policy Association website. Links to these pieces could still be found on his Twitter feed as of May 2014 (again, no mention of his Qorvis connection). But now when you click on these links, they no longer work. Various other pro-Bahrain tweets were still visible as of that date.[107]

Squitieri's name also surfaced in an ugly spat between Qorvis and Wikipedia in 2013. According to the Daily Dot, which covers online communities:[108]

> Wikipedians accuse Qorvis of employing a small crew of sockpuppets—multiple accounts owned by the same user to deceptively orchestrate an editing bloc—to fan out across the free encyclopedia and attempt to whitewash the pages of its clients. . . . Wikipedia user "Sacoca" allegedly runs a string of five accounts that remove negative information and add PR fluff. . . . The Sacoca account is almost certainly run by Tom Squitieri. One of the alleged Sacoca sockpuppets, Harriet888 only edits the Qorvis page, adding information about current staff and awards and honors—and allegedly scrubbing it of any negative information, like hiding negative information about Bahrain. . . . This seems a strange obsession for someone to have, if they indeed have nothing to do with Qorvis.

A Qorvis partner later told the Daily Dot: "[Qorvis] employees may edit Wikipedia and they may not, but we have no corporate policy or interest in making this some kind of profit making venture."[109]

Qorvis's sometime collaborator, Bell Pottinger, also employs "all sorts of dark arts" (their words) on the Internet. These include editing Wikipedia entries deemed damaging; setting up third-party blogs that also appear independent and use words that would come up high in Google searches; and a general gaming of search results to ". . . drown out that negative content and make sure that you have positive content out there online."[110]

Because it operates in the United States, Qorvis is required to identify its foreign clients and certain activities to the Justice Department. And yet disclosure requirements hardly guarantee transparency. Are the documents filed with Justice a true disclosure, or only a *performance* of disclosure? Qorvis, and other firms like them, can perform the checklist and be done with it, following the letter of the law. Meanwhile, the time lag between activities and filing make disclosure and lobbying very hard for potential overseers or the public to parse.

When you look at Qorvis's Justice Department disclosures, you can see a continuous flow of press releases itemized and billed to Bahrain. An unnamed lobbyist tells Silverstein about a blizzard of such releases:

> Qorvis' releases are pure propaganda and it doesn't even bother flogging them to journalists. . . . They just trot the stuff out so there's something else to read on Google when one of their clients fucks up.

The Qorvis blizzard isn't about persuasion, Silverstein assesses: it is about plain old digital obfuscation:[111]

> Such releases are not aimed directly at public opinion so much as at Google and other search engines. A steady stream of press releases serves to push news stories lower in search engine returns; when it comes to Qorvis' clients, the news is almost invariably bad so burying it makes sense.

Qorvis has also used cyber-trickery in its work for Fiji. After spotting a piece in the Huffington Post written by the country's repressive military leader, a journalist noticed what she called an "exploding internet and social media presence" for Fiji that included what appeared to be "flogging" (fake blogging), tweeting, and another blizzard of press releases.[112]

Not everyone in the PR world has accepted this kind of business. In 2011, one unnamed former Qorvis insider said this to a Huffington Post writer: "I just have trouble working with despotic dictators killing their own people. . . . These scumbags will pay whatever you want."[113] It does raise the question: How do the employees of firms representing so-called "black hat" clients justify their work? Obviously some, like this former staffer, cannot.

Still, once again, the firms' first line of defense is the claim that they are enlightening their clients. One lobbyist told *Newsweek* that he helped "move the ball forward on human rights" when he was in charge of the Equatorial Guinea account for Cassidy & Associates, one of the firms that were the targets of the Silverstein sting.[114] This was the argument made many times by the organization, as well as by the high-flying players it (in most cases) hired to serve as stealth persuaders.

In any event, these PR campaigns are designed to obfuscate, confuse, and launder influence. How can we, the public, evaluate where the truth lies?

THE LIMITATIONS OF DIY

As methods often beyond our ken are at work, we are swayed by influence-laundering and downright deception subtly masquerading as something else. Meanwhile, as we assemble our own (sometimes "truthy") realities, we can scarcely compete with the onslaught because we can scarcely recognize it. Our act of choosing "Like" or "Share" may give us a feeling of control and even of taking action, a temporary boost of self-satisfaction, perhaps not unlike that of the headless housewife (of the do-it-yourself porn business) offering up her (heretofore) private moments.

And, with DIY all the rage and a cultural perennial—especially in the United States, the land of choice, can-do-ism, and conviction that every public-policy problem has a technological solution—it is easy to be over-confident in our own ease and ability to sort things out.[115] It is hard not to be swayed by the folks who pioneer noble experiments and exemplify the DIY cream of the media crop.

Take, for instance, Matthew Yglesias, previously of Slate, a blogger and sometime think-tanker. After Pew released its generally grim 2012 report, Yglesias took the opposite view: that we are in fact in the "glory days" of American journalism for consumers. Here's his tour of the bountiful offerings now just a click away:[116]

> You don't need to take my analysis of the Cyprus bank bailout crisis as the last word on the matter: You can quickly and easily find coverage from the *New York Times*, *Wall Street Journal*, *Financial Times*, and the *Economist*. Or if you don't want to see your Cyprus news filtered through an America/British lens, you can check out the take of distinguished Greek economist Yanis Varoufakis on his blog. Reuters created an interactive feature that lets you try out different formulae for making the Cypriot haircut work. A pseudonymous London-based fund manager using the name Paweł Morski has offered vital, deeply informed coverage on Twitter and his WordPress site. You can watch a Bloomberg TV interview on the situation with native Cypriot and former Federal Reserve adviser Athanasios Orphanides at your leisure.
>
> Best of all, today's media ecology lets you add *depth* and *context* to the news. Several sources on Twitter recommended to me a 2008 Perry Anderson article in the *London Review of Books* about the broader sweep of post-independence Cypriot history. Paul Krugman reminds us of the larger issue of small island nations serving as offshore banking hubs and the dilemmas this poses for global financial regulation. He also offers a link to a lengthy IMF report on Cyprus' economy.

This is great. But how many of us even know the outlets Yglesias references above, aside from, say, the *New York Times*, *Wall Street Journal*, *Financial Times*, and *Economist*? And what tiny percentage of any population has the time, let alone the savvy or wherewithal, to know where and how to look?

The average reader is just that—average. Moreover, Yglesias, a magna cum laude Harvard graduate in philosophy, has been writing since his days spent earning that degree. In his list above, he has chosen almost entirely legacy media sites where the standards are high; most of us who might Google a particular topic aren't necessarily familiar with these standards and might get one of the gamed results that power brokers pay to put front and center. Yet, as we have seen, more and more people are getting their news through their phone, on the fly, hardly the environment to offer much context. And when news comes from real friends or social-media "friends," it is they, not necessarily a professional like Yglesias, who are now your editors. Twitter feeds and Facebook pages of influence groups constantly post stories, typically with a quick slant attached. And people now often receive articles that have been aggregated; so even if the original article has the proper disclosures and disclaimers, those can easily get buried as they go through various "shares" and retweets, often given a new slant with each new share.

The fact is that most of us simply do not have the knowledge or the patience to sort through and select sources, nor do we know the quirks of each publication to mitigate being seduced by the above-mentioned gaming of the search system. Practitioners of the dark arts are, of course, trolling for ever-more-sophisticated digital, deceptive ways. They are set up for success: old media have been pounded to within an inch of their lives, and the new media/Internet, despite many noble experiments, are as yet ill equipped to deliver sufficient accountability journalism.

The idea of "churnalism" describes the pressures on the media, and yet I see a broader application: the focus on the short term, the performance, and the use of reductive metrics to measure complex phenomena can be seen in finance, government projects, regulation, think tanks, academia, you name it.

After all, power brokers from all these arenas have rushed in to colonize this cheap, exploitable medium without journalists blocking their way.

And us? We relish feeling in control, but how much of that control and participation is illusory? As we skip the objective middleman (the journalist), the PR person with an agenda, operating beyond our awareness, eagerly takes his place. Will we help move this trend even farther down the path of resembling late-communist messaging? Will we continue to be satisfied with the media telling us what we want to hear—reflecting ourselves back onto ourselves?

The danger is that the control bubble we've created, comfortable and cozy as it is, will burst as soon as reality confronts it. It is sure to be short-lived when we experience, firsthand and undeniably, the next manufactured war or the next financial crisis that we didn't see coming because our privatized/personalized media are unaccountable. Will we, collectively, act to avert this?

If we don't, any satisfaction the headless housewife might offer by way of distraction will be short-lived indeed.

PART II:

THE NEW CORRUPTION AT WORK

In Part I, we investigated the underpinnings of today's unaccountability. I laid out how the new corruption works, how it came to pass, and the foundation upon which it rests. We saw its chief protagonists in action.

In this part, we use perspectives from social anthropology to look at unaccountability from another angle, with ways of organizing influence as the point of departure. In the chapters that follow, we see the various and creative ways that unaccountability is organized—how different types of players, swirling in and around consulting firms, "think tanks," universities, "nonprofits," "grassroots" organizations, and other entities, construct and coordinate influence to sway policy and public opinion. In short, we see how huge swaths of our ecosystem are rendered unaccountable in today's world.

Seeing these patterns in action should help you spot similar examples in your own worlds.

CHAPTER 6

Spies, Company Men, and the Melded Company-State

O n June 5, 2013, the world woke up to what has been described—by the legend who leaked the Pentagon Papers forty years earlier, no less—as the most significant leak in U.S. history.[1] A man just twenty-nine years old who appeared even younger had handed over to the media a batch of bombshell National Security Agency documents detailing covert telephone and e-mail data collection of average citizens. And now he was on the run, a fugitive whose face was soon recognized by millions around the globe.

The first question was "Who is Edward Snowden?" The answer was that he was a system administrator for Booz Allen Hamilton Inc., a huge government contractor based just outside Washington, D.C. For many if not most Americans, the follow-up questions included these: What is Booz Allen? What's a contractor? How could it happen that a mere contractor could have such seemingly unlimited access to a treasure trove of highly sensitive and volatile classified materials?

A telling fact is that Snowden deliberately chose to work for Booz Allen—a private firm—for the express purpose of gaining access and then leaking American government secrets.[2] While he had worked at both the CIA and the NSA, Snowden surely knew that Booz Allen was now as much a part of the government as was the government itself.

As noted earlier, government and governing have undergone a sea change over the past several decades. It happened so quickly and, often, so invisibly—without revolution or public debate—that many Americans still don't know that a giant workforce has invaded their nation's capital—one that can undermine the public and national interest from the inside. The fact is that *most* of the work (upwards of three quarters) of the federal government today is performed not by government bureaucrats but by a vast off-the-books "shadow government"—people hired by the consulting firms, companies, nongovernmental organizations, and "Beltway Bandits" that occupy high-rise bastions in the Washington suburbs. This shadow government has mushroomed; just the cost of services sold to the government more than doubled after 9/11, from 2001 to 2008.[3] (In particular, the wary post–9/11 environment greatly expanded the intelligence and security realms of the government—and much, if not most, of this work is done by government contractors.)

Wherever they serve, the workforce invaders are not just cafeteria workers, printers, or gardeners. As we saw in Chapter 1, many perform core government functions such as running intelligence operations, choosing and overseeing other contractors, drafting official documents, and controlling homeland-security databases; this practice has become the rule rather than the exception.[4] The result is that many government functions are conducted, and many public priorities and decisions are driven, by private companies and players instead of government agencies and officials who are duty-bound to answer to citizens and sworn to uphold the national interest.[5]

In this blended atmosphere, new forms of governing are forged that fuse the power of the state with the agendas of companies that are formally "private" but whose business comes exclusively (or nearly so) from the "government" and that are, for all practical purposes, less-accountable subsidiaries of it. A fused system is neither truly one nor the other, lacking *both* the essential qualities of business (competition) and those of the government (accountability). Blurring these lines by definition challenges accountability. In the most extreme circumstances, accountability virtually goes out the window.

The window, for its part, has become opaque because transparency has gone AWOL too. We are in the "information age," right? Yet the amassing of information often does not benefit us, the public. The shadow government's rise is draining the government's "brain"—meaning its information, expertise, institutional memory, personnel, and practically everything that would enable government not only to know what's going on, but to oversee its contract employees.[6] Information that once was or should be in official hands is being privatized, ceded to government contractors at a time when government agencies have diminished capacity to monitor them, especially in real time.

And while government contractors like Booz Allen, SAIC, and Northrop Grumman are well known, some prefer anonymity. Case in point: Endgame Systems, founded in 2008 to ride the cyber defense tsunami.[7] "'We've been very careful not to have a public face on our company,'" wrote a former Endgame vice president to a business colleague. That e-mail surfaced in a WikiLeaks dump and is quoted here from what was reported by *Wired* magazine. The company's founder added: "'We don't ever want to see our name in a press release.'" As *Wired* commented, "Endgame is transparently antitransparent."[8] Its anonymity, of course, obscures what is being done in the name of the American people.

In this "antitransparent" company-state, many public priorities and decisions are driven by contractor companies instead of government officials and agencies that must answer to citizens, with officials only signing on the dotted line. In piles of reports from the Government Accountability Office (GAO, the watchdog agency of Congress), inspectors-general audits of agencies, and congressional testimony, investigators have asked whether government has the information, expertise, institutional memory, and personnel to manage contractors—or is it the other way around?[9] And who really sets policy—government, or contractors?

These questions are especially pressing when it comes to rapidly expanding portfolios, such as cyber security, a $30 billion annual government business, almost entirely in private hands. *Wired* calls this the "cyber-industrial complex."[10]

As you'll see from the various examples provided in this chapter, the interface between state and private, and the lack of accountability therein, runs the gamut. There are agencies that are so strapped for expertise and manpower that they contract with companies saddled with glaring conflicts, and provide little or no government monitoring. These firms are often filled with former government workers now earning higher salaries than they would or did with the government and effectively carrying out tasks that should be performed by the agencies themselves.

Aside from contracting, the company-state also encompasses agencies that have mixed mandates, directing them to promote the very industries they are supposed to be regulating. More to the point, businesses aren't just sidestepping or fighting regulators: their MO is to try to make *themselves* the de facto regulators of their own activities. As in the case of BP and the oil spill it caused, which we'll explore later, this can have catastrophic results.

Then there are arenas that have evolved into seamless operations in which government work and core functions are totally meshed with companies (and other "private" entities) in nearly indistinguishable forms. In these cases, "accountability" and the "public interest" seem as anachronistic as the vocabulary of the charmed past.

Consider, for example, Booz Allen.

THE SHADOW INTELLIGENCE COMMUNITY

Booz Allen has been called the "shadow IC (intelligence community)" (by a former CIA deputy director) and "the world's most profitable spy organization."[11] With the Carlyle Group (a prominent private equity firm) its majority owner, Booz has been at the forefront of the mass explosion of intelligence, "homeland security," and military contracting-out that followed 9/11.[12] In 2008, the company was ranked the "No. 1 Consulting Company by Federal Revenue and a Top 10 contractor for Department of Homeland Security headquarters."[13] With some seventy percent of the U.S. intelligence budget now outsourced, Booz Allen's operating profits have soared in recent years.[14] The company now boasts an annual revenue of nearly $5.8 billion, upwards of half of which derives from U.S. intelligence and military agencies and nearly all of which is from government contracts.[15] Keep in mind that in the case of a contractor, their revenue is actually your taxpayer dollars. In the past few years, Booz Allen's profit margins have grown much faster than the company's sales would indicate, suggesting that, at least in this aspect of the company-state partnership, the company has the upper hand.[16]

Based in McLean, Virginia, the consulting giant employs some 24,500 people, the majority in the Washington area.[17] Its clients range from the Department of Homeland Security to the Department of Defense and the U.S. Army, to the Internal Revenue Service and the Department of Health and Human Services.

While Edward Snowden was (briefly) part of the Booz rank-and-file, earning $122,000 a year, the Booz Allen leadership is a case study in how melding state and private power can create a black hole of accountability.[18]

The DNI-Booz Fuse

Let's consider the relationship that's emerged between Booz Allen and the nation's top intelligence official—the Director of National Intelligence (DNI), the position created after 9/11 to integrate what were then deemed dangerously fractured operations of the intelligence community. The DNI heads the Office of the Director of National Intelligence (ODNI), leading and overseeing the work of the U.S. government's sixteen intelligence agencies and reporting directly to the president.

In 2007, for the first time in the sixty-year life of the intelligence community, a government contractor was appointed to head it.[19] When President Bill Clinton's former NSA director, Vice Admiral (Ret.) John Michael "Mike" McConnell, was named DNI after a decade as vice president at Booz Allen, he was asked what it was like to be back in government. In a telling statement, he unabashedly said to the *New York Times* that his work as a (Booz Allen) consultant "has allowed me to stay focused on national security and intelligence communities as a strategist and as a consultant. Therefore, in many respects, I never left [government]."[20]

Indeed.

McConnell is not just spinning through the proverbial revolving door. It's almost as if the door has disappeared completely. As journalist Glenn Greenwald noted in 2010, several years before he helped break the Snowden revelations:[21]

It isn't that people like Mike McConnell move from public office to the private sector and back again. That implies more separation than really exists. At this point, it's more accurate to view the U.S. Government and these huge industry interests as one gigantic, amalgamated, inseparable entity—with a public division and a private one. When someone like McConnell goes from a top private sector position to a top government post in the same field, it's more like an intra-corporate re-assignment than it is changing employers. When McConnell serves as DNI, he's simply in one division of this entity and when he's at Booz Allen, he's in another, but it's all serving the same entity.

"Same entity," yes. But players earn very different pay depending on their role. When McConnell wears his public hat, he earns less than $250,000 a year; when he puts on his private hat at Booz Allen, that salary jumps at least tenfold. Clearly, that time in public service pays off.[22]

McConnell has swooped back and forth in swift succession, with one or more roles shoring up his own power and influence, as well as those of his associates, in the next. From 2005 to 2007, while at Booz Allen, he chaired the Intelligence and National Security Alliance (INSA). That industry association later cited its mission as:[23]

> [providing] the intelligence and national security communities with a non-partisan catalyst for public-private partnerships which identify, develop and promote creative solutions through access to committed experts in and out of government.

With one hundred and fifty corporate members and several hundred individual ones, including many former senior intelligence officials and influential academics, INSA's championing of public-private partnerships promotes the move toward the privatization of intelligence and serves CIA and NSA contractors.[24]

The prevailing national feeling of the post–9/11 period, of course, was fear and, on the government's part, the need to protect the populace. McConnell was well placed at the time. In late 2002, he deployed his government connections to secure business for Booz Allen,[25] as well as to help ramp up a vast "surveillance state," according to Shane Harris, author of *The Watchers: The Rise of America's Surveillance State*. McConnell helped Admiral John Poindexter, then working in the Pentagon for the Defense Advanced Research Projects Agency (DARPA), to sell and set up the Orwellian, reportedly short-lived, "Total Information Awareness" surveillance program:[26]

> . . . McConnell was prepared to provide "top cover" by talking to senior members [of Congress] and committee staff about TIA. . . . [He] could broach the subject of surveillance laws and regulations with far more credibility and less drama than Poindexter. He had enjoyed an impeccable Navy career, and his name counted for a lot in Washington, particularly among senior members of the Bush administration. He could clear Poindexter's path. . . . But McConnell didn't want to stop there. He told Poindexter that he should award Booz the entire TIA contract, letting the company effectively take over the research, testing, and construction of the prototype, a soup-to-nuts arrangement.

McConnell had to settle for a smaller role, a contract of around $8 million, which would still tap into his government connections: as Harris puts it, "Booz . . . would get TIA out of the lab and into the hands of government users . . . McConnell would spread it around. His connections, and those of his company, would pay off after all."[27]

Indeed they did. In 2007, as mentioned, he was tapped as DNI. The issue was not whether, but when, McConnell would return to DNI, according to Harris.[28] As Harris tells it, McConnell worried that his "ability" (read: power) as DNI would be "limited." His concerns were abated when he realized he would be surrounded by allies, including "longtime friend" retired Air Force Lieutenant General James R. Clapper, Jr., who also had worked at Booz Allen and who later hired the contractor while he was the head of the National Geospatial-Intelligence Agency: "The proverbial stars had aligned," writes Harris. "[Then-Defense Secretary Robert] Gates at the Pentagon, ready to help. Clapper coming back [as Gates's intelligence chief]. [Retired Air Force General Michael] Hayden, a former NSA director and a friend now in charge at the CIA." Harris reports that McConnell spoke with both Clapper and Gates to ensure their support of himself and his goals.[29]

Glenn Greenwald, in his 2010 takedown, took aim at McConnell for his activities as DNI, calling him "a perfect symbol for the legalized corruption that dominates Washington" and detailing his efforts to grow intelligence outsourcing:[30]

> As Bush's DNI, McConnell dramatically expanded the extent to which intelligence functions were outsourced to the same private industry that he long represented. Worse, he became the leading spokesman for demanding full immunity for lawbreaking telecoms for their participation in Bush's illegal NSA programs—in other words, he exploited "national security" claims and his position as DNI to win the dismissal of lawsuits against the very lawbreaking industry he represented as INSA Chairman, including, almost certainly, Booz Allen itself. Having exploited his position as DNI to lavishly reward and protect the private intelligence industry, he then returns to its loving arms to receive from them lavish personal rewards of his own.[31]

McConnell was DNI for only two years before leaving for . . . Booz Allen in 2009 "to lead the firm's Intelligence business," states the company's website, as an executive vice president. Two years later, he was promoted to his current position as Booz Allen's vice chairman.[32]

And just who was deemed most suited to take over as DNI from McConnell? Why, McConnell's friend and Booz Allen stalwart, James R. Clapper. His career path mirrors that of McConnell's. After "retiring" from the military in 1995, Clapper worked at Booz Allen and the government contractor SRA International until 9/11, when he returned to government as head of the National Geospatial-Intelligence Agency.[33] Journalist Ken Dilanian, who has connected some of the dots of Clapper's many and lucrative private-sector postings, details his moves after leaving that government perch in 2006:[34]

> Four months after James R. Clapper left his federal job as head of the National Geospatial-Intelligence Agency in June 2006, he joined the boards of three government contractors, two of which had been doing business with his agency while he was there. . . . In October 2006 he was hired full-time by DFI International, which was trying to boost its consulting with intelligence agencies. In April 2007, when he returned to public service as the chief of the Pentagon's intelligence programs, DFI paid him a $50,000 bonus on his way out the door, according to his financial disclosure statement. Five months later, DFI landed a contract to advise Clapper's Pentagon office, though company officials do not recall collecting any revenue from the deal.

Let me point out that the selection of contractors in certain areas is made complex by the notable consolidation of defense companies in recent years and by the fact that, in certain areas of contract "competition," there can *be* little competition because very few companies meet the specific requirements of a given contract. Still, how can the public feel confident that Clapper's office made that choice of contractor for the right reasons? A former DFI official didn't exactly inspire faith in his recollection of the facts when he told Dilanian "I am almost positive we never saw a dime of work out of this." The White House insisted Clapper wasn't directly involved in selecting DFI, and, as is often the case, cited his decades in the military as a sort of all-purpose defense of his integrity.[35]

Looking at this case involving DFI shouldn't detract us from the larger picture of Clapper, McConnell, and their allies and their broader push to enhance both their own power and their promotion of contractors to carry out sensitive intelligence work. Like McConnell, Clapper, after five years of working in the contractor world, agitated for enlarging the outsourcing of intelligence. As journalist Tim Shorrock, author of *Spies for Hire: The Secret World of Intelligence Outsourcing*, wrote in the *New York Times*:[36]

> In 2000, thanks in part to an advisory committee led by James R. Clapper Jr. . . . the N.S.A. decided to shift away from its in-house development strategy and outsource on a huge scale. The N.S.A.'s headquarters began filling with contractors working for Booz Allen and hundreds of other companies.

And in 2010 confirmation hearings before the Senate Intelligence Committee, Clapper expressed goals similar to McConnell's. He signaled that he would seek to shore up the clout of the DNI and "push the envelope" to deepen the authority of the intelligence head.[37]

Although the Office of the DNI technically oversees all U.S. intelligence agencies, its budget and control are restricted, and concerns about a lack of DNI power have surfaced since the position's inception. A stronger ODNI would be a good thing, some argued. During the hearings, Clapper characterized the surge in contractors as "in some ways a testimony to the ingenuity, innovation and capability of our contractor base."[38] While he said this to the Senate committee, it seems to me that his intended message, and the one most likely understood throughout the intelligence world, is that Clapper planned to consolidate power in the DNI and use his influence to grant contracts and decide on intelligence matters, in and out of government.

I am not arguing that McConnell or Clapper or their fellows are bad or unethical people. And they and their allies will no doubt say they are honorable men who can self-police, as was implied with the White House brandishing Clapper's decades of military service in his defense. I am arguing that the system in which they are playing—indeed which they are helping to create—hardly has the public interest at the forefront.

Indeed, the accountability—and security—void is vast. When information supposedly of and for government is in private hands, the information, and the power that goes with it, is at risk of being used to serve private agendas, with corporate and private players influencing policy to suit those agendas.[39]

Budgets are also at risk. There is little evidence that shadow government is a more efficient use of taxpayer dollars, and some evidence that it is not. Case in point: in 2003, Booz Allen landed a $2 million contract to assist the new Homeland Security department, a tab which had exploded to $30 million a year later, and then to $73 million a year after that. Two of those contracts were "no bid," that is, no competition involved.[40]

Failing to see the problems, or perhaps willfully ignoring them, politicians perpetrate a scam on Americans that only causes the government—the shadow one—to get bigger and bigger and to deplete traditional government of its lifeblood. The mantra of "small government," like motherhood and apple pie, has fostered flat-out deception. In an ostensible effort to restrict the size of government, caps have been put on how many civil servants government can hire. But regular Joe still wants his tax refund on time, his prescription drugs proven effective and sound, and his homeland safe. To surmount this impossible situation, both Democratic and Republican administrations have turned increasingly to contractors. Because contractors aren't counted as part of the federal workforce per se, it looks like government is much smaller than it actually is. This is a farce, like the Potemkin village constructed to make the ruler or the foreigner think that things are rosy. Meanwhile, the budget for government goes up and up, and with it the fortunes of the companies that do the government's work.

Meanwhile, too, contractors, of course, are not subject to the same rules as civil servants; contractor executives, unlike government leaders, are seldom dragged before congressional committees for hostile questioning when their activities come under fire. We have no easily verifiable way to know how they are actually performing. The only undisputed winners are the contractors themselves.

Surely Mike McConnell is one of the winners. At Booz Allen, McConnell was hired to head up the company's cyber portfolio, which included a "cyber-solutions network" that connected nine facilities.[41] Not surprisingly, he has been one of the leading voices warning about emerging cyber-threats, penning a piece about it in the *Washington Post* in 2010. But little did he imagine that a cyber-attack of a different sort would come from within his own ranks at Booz Allen, from leaker Edward Snowden.[42]

After Snowden's revelations, McConnell's associate, DNI Clapper, found himself grilled by members of the Senate Select Committee on Intelligence on what Snowden had unleashed. Clapper was asked by Senator Ron Wyden whether "any type of data at all on millions or hundreds of millions of Americans" had been collected by the agency. "No, sir," was Clapper's response. "Not wittingly."[43]

Senators were astounded by Clapper's answer, and a half dozen congressmen later accused him of "lying under oath" and called on President Obama to fire him.[44]

He didn't. And the fact that a one-time community organizer (Obama) has ensured the continued power of this Booz Allen set, even the expansion of it, indicates something of the deeply entrenched, unaccountable system that we, the public (and by no means only the *American* public), are up against. Booz Allen operatives have created a self-perpetuating machine, exerting long-term, strategic control and influence. Their leaders embody the company-state—the height of unaccountability to the public.

SHADOW GENERALS

You might have noticed that the two main players discussed above—James Clapper and Mike McConnell—are military men, a "retired" lieutenant general and a "retired" vice admiral.[45] While both are in their seventies, they are quite *au courant* in the conduct of their post-military professional careers.

President Dwight D. Eisenhower was, of course, prophetic when he warned, more than fifty years ago, about the "grave implications" of what he dubbed the military-industrial complex. But even he might be astounded by how the complex has mushroomed since his farewell speech of January 17, 1961, and the role that many esteemed retired generals and other high-ranking officers now play in it.

The military has held public service over personal achievement as its core value. This value now seems at risk in the highest ranks of the U.S. armed forces. Many top players now appear focused on turning themselves into one-man defense-industry moguls, some of them angling for personal rewards even before official retirement. Of course, they retire at a comparatively young age. Still healthy and productive, many want to use the expertise they have acquired over a lifetime and stay in the game. And now, more than ever, given the ballooning of government contracting, incentives are in place for these people to be lured to the private sector for substantially more money—even when performing essentially the same duties as in the government. This sets up a relatively new and accountability-challenging phenomenon.

Times have clearly changed. Senator Jack Reed—a West Point graduate—said this to Bryan Bender of the *Boston Globe:*[46]

> When I was an officer in the 1970s, most general officers went off to some sunny place and retired. . . . Now the definition of success . . . is to move on and become successful in the business world.

But the business world, as Julia Pfaff, who has served in the military and as executive director of the National Military Family Association, and who now works at George Mason University, tells me, "has a very different core value, one which comes in direct conflict with the long held military value of public service over personal gain." Thus these senior officials "find themselves balancing public service and private-sector profits," she observes.[47] What is the impact? "Many of those who succeed in business feel conflicted. Yet when they fail to question the harm to the public good (while touting their military service) they risk nurturing cynicism to the institution they love. This leads to a decline in loyalty [to the institution] from the inside."[48] This seismic culture shift mirrors the decline in trust in formal institutions from the outside—that is, of the public—as I detailed in Chapter 1.

In contrast to twenty-five or so years ago, when most senior officers retired to "some sunny place," today most of them no longer predominantly do so. A ground-breaking 2010 study by Bender for the *Boston Globe*, which amassed a database of 750 retired generals and admirals (which my Mapping Shadow Influence Project has enlarged), looks at the post-retirement careers of these former public servants. Over several decades, these retired senior officers went mostly from actual retirement—that is, they stopped working when they retired from military service—to mostly continued "service."[49] Today, very active "retirements" are commonplace: the retirees pursue a multi-pronged strategy that affords them money and influence. Some act as advisers in military agencies while serving simultaneously as paid consultants to defense and intelligence contractors. Others work as consultants to these contractors or sit on their boards,[50] while also sitting on government advisory boards that afford them crucial insider information and access.[51] Still others launch start-ups.

Amplifying their influence, such generals are also in hot demand as media analysts. And according to a 2008 *New York Times* report, "[m]ost of the analysts have ties to military contractors vested in the very war policies they are asked to assess on air."[52] Journalist David Barstow painted an indelible portrait in the *Times* of retired four-star Army General Barry McCaffrey, his swirl of defense-consulting activities, and his success in promoting his interests on television: Barstow called it "One Man's Military-Industrial-Media Complex."[53]

Lest one think the "rent-a-general" phenomenon, as Bender puts it, is winding down, his *Globe* investigation shows that this longtime trend has been accelerating:[54]

> From 2004 through 2008, 80 percent of retiring three- and four-star officers went to work as consultants or defense executives. . . . That compares with less than 50 percent who followed that path a decade earlier, from 1994 to 1998. . . . In 2007, thirty-four out of 39 three- and four-star generals and admirals who retired . . . are now working in defense roles— nearly 90 percent.

Not only do these generals and admirals profit from their years of privileged access to vital information and connections, they are also afforded deference because of their service and those stars. This deference tends to continue after retirement, according to the *Globe* investigation, with generals often treated in advisory meetings as if they still held official roles.[55]

As noted, generals and admirals and other senior military officers typically retire at a relatively young age, and it's understandable that many want to continue working.[56] But the form this work takes often gives them the opportunity to flout the public trust—and many do so, however unwittingly. They can easily convince themselves that they are continuing to "serve," using their information and skills for the public good while being handsomely compensated. What they may not realize or choose to ignore is the corrupting influence of their migration.

They aren't sneaking around. Reporting (from the *Globe*, the *Times*, *USA Today*, and others) finds that the Pentagon either ignores their behavior, accepts that this is how business is done these days, or, at times, actively encourages it. And while the retired officers' new ventures are no secret, we, the public, have no way of knowing specifically where accountability is being breached. As they put the information gleaned in their government roles to use in their new roles, they can do so in a way that makes it very difficult for us, the public, to know whether they are more concerned about their own and their companies' financial interests or ours, let alone whether they are pushing a self-serving lucrative project that may even compromise national interests.

Consider the process of vetting defense projects, which should be, at least in theory, unimpeachable. First and foremost, countless lives are on the line. Second, these projects carry staggering price tags, and they can last for decades. Such investment of taxpayer dollars and time means that the process of allocating these precious public resources should be as fair and free of corruption as possible. That is hardly the system now in place.

Given the astronomical money involved in weapons systems and other big-ticket defense projects, there's plenty of lobbying to go around. And while conventional lobbying, say, of Congress by defense companies is still paramount, today's full-service influence effort embraces shadow lobbying, including sometimes by rent-a-generals. In its investigation of retired officers, the *Globe* reported on two decisions—whether to keep buying Humvees, and whether to make a new surveillance helicopter.

With regard to the first, the vehicles' manufacturer, AM General, enlisted three retired generals to make sure the Army kept buying new Humvees rather than fixing up old ones. Retired Army General Jack Keane spoke with a top-ranking Army official and helped persuade Congress; but, as is common these days, he did not register as a lobbyist. Devoting less than twenty percent of his time to such activity, he need not register; and after all, as he said, "he only helps clients reach the right decisionmakers in the Pentagon or on Capitol Hill," the *Globe* reports.[57]

Two other retired generals used by AM General in the late 2000s had deep ties to defense acquisitions from their time in the Army: one had been in charge of buying ground-combat vehicles, including the Humvee; the other had been chief of the Army Materiel Command, which is effectively in charge of buying everything. As we saw with the top intelligence officers, these men were performing work similar to what they had done in the Army—choosing equipment—except now the people paying them, well, were the ones actually making the equipment.[58]

In 2010, the Army decided to keep buying Humvees.

The other case is that of an unmanned surveillance helicopter called the Fire Scout that Northrop Grumman hoped to sell to the Army. But before the Army could buy the helicopters, it needed to know how it would use them and whether it wanted them. To help the Army make its determination, Bender notes, Northrop Grumman engaged the longtime "rent-a-general outfit" Burdeshaw Associates Ltd. That move would serve the company well. Burdeshaw not only opened doors to key Pentagon officials, but they also drafted an official government procurement document, "concept of operation," which detailed the functioning of the helicopter and its purpose. This document provided the justification the Army required to develop the weapon system.[59] Presumably, like a good marketer, Burdeshaw also included the needs of Northrop Grumman in the "concept of operation," which potentially would give Northrop an edge in any competitive bid.[60] The Army accepted the idea for the weapon system and subsequently placed an initial order with Northrop for eight Fire Scouts, at a cost to taxpayers of more than $100 million.

The rent-a-general trend remains alive and well. A subsequent investigation by the watchdog group Citizens for Responsibility and Ethics found that seventy percent of the 108 three- and four-star newly retired generals and admirals they tracked ended up at defense contractors or as consultants. They found, too, that some were still advising the Pentagon while working for contractors.[61]

Senior Military Mentors

Retired senior officers often argue that they can police themselves. Their expertise, aura of rectitude, and decades in military service foster this belief. They can also argue that they have the crucial expertise needed to make these enormous decisions, and that, once they retire, the military is depleted of that expertise.

So, in an ostensible effort to regain some of that know-how, the military set up a "Senior Military Mentor" program.[62] What could sound more innocuous?

The mentors, retired officers, were enlisted to advise their former colleagues in defense agencies, as a 2009 *USA Today* exposé details.[63] It's one of those ideas that might seem sensible at first glance. Only on closer inspection are the potential conflicts of interest revealed: eighty percent of the retired officers were also working in some capacity for defense contractors, advising on military services even as they were consulting for companies seeking to sell military products, and these same officers might also have financial ties to the company peddling the services.[64]

Since the mentors were part-timers, they were not subject to the same rules as full-time federal employees. The selection of mentors, the identity of their defense clients, and the mentors' pay levels were beyond government and public scrutiny. While contributing their invaluable experience, these officers also gleaned invaluable inside information. It is hard to imagine that they erased what they learned as mentors when they worked as defense industry executives or consultants, and vice versa. But imagine trying to figure out if important information had made its way back to those defense contractors, or how to trace possible influence in what to buy. *USA Today* makes it clear that it was no easy task even ascertaining from the military the average hourly rate these generals were earning. (As much as $440 an hour, many times what they would earn in active duty.)[65]

The scrutiny from the paper did prompt change. In April 2010, Defense Secretary Robert Gates ordered that mentors convert to so-called Highly Qualified Experts—government employees who initially were allowed to disclose their financial interests only to ethics officers, but within months, due to the paper's focus on the issue, were required to publicly disclose. Apparently not even the former had gone over well with them. According to a Defense Department Inspector General report, the vast majority of retired generals and other senior officials wouldn't convert (that is, disclose their ties, even internally) and quit.[66] In November 2011, *USA Today* reported that "The Pentagon's use of retired generals and admirals as paid advisers has virtually ceased."[67] As reporter Tom Vanden Brook told me, "These guys were unwilling to have their corporate ties open to public scrutiny."[68]

It's hard to imagine that those who devised the mentors program weren't aware of the obvious ethical, security, and financial concerns. Everyone in the military knows what many ex-military officials are doing nowadays. So it's worth noting that the name chosen sounds so wholesome, even evoking a spirit of volunteerism. Of course, unlike volunteers, the mentors were paid hundreds of dollars an hour.

As we have seen throughout this book, innocuous- or generic-sounding names connected to powerful people and groups often deserve our attention. That is because, as is the case here, such names can cover for accountability holes.

Ethically Challenged?

Are all these retired senior officers gunning for personal profit at the expense of the public good?

It's likely not that simple.

We should not reduce their choices solely to self-interest. They are responding to what their peers do and to the ethics of their community. The vast majority likely have not considered these ethical questions or the unaccountability inherent in the overlapping roles that they craft for themselves. Any suggestion of ethical taint is likely to evince a reaction along the lines of "I've been in the military for forty years. Don't you think I know right from wrong?" In fact, one will find several iterations of these defenses offered by the generals and admirals interviewed by Bender. "You spend 35 years in an ethical place," said one. "You don't leave that at the door."[69]

The pattern has changed drastically in just a few decades. I asked several retired senior officers why so many of their peers continue military/intelligence work after retiring. Air Force Colonel Randall Gressang, who performed such work (via professional-services contracts to defense agencies) for eighteen-plus years after retiring, told me this: "They see more [of their peers] do it and the monetary rewards are potentially much greater."[70]

Some of these retired officers seem to think that we should just take it as a given that they will behave with the utmost integrity. Bender reports:[71]

> The generals who navigate these ethical minefields said they are capable of managing potential conflicts without oversight.

. . . "You have to have a firewall in your head," said industry consultant and former Vice Admiral Justin D. McCarthy.

But it's entirely reasonable for the public—and, in fact, should be our duty—to see this differently. With all due respect to the vice admiral and his cohorts, public accountability would demand that the "firewall" be on paper for all of us to see. And while it seems anachronistic, one would hope and expect that whatever roles and relationships these generals accept do not undermine the integrity of the institution and the public interest. I suspect that a certain five-star general named Eisenhower might agree.

And yet someone like Mike McConnell apparently sees nothing wrong with "having never left government" while at Booz Allen. In fact, he would probably think we are naïve fools for even perceiving a problem.

As you'll see next, powerful players who don't have any stars or medals also try to make the claim that they can regulate themselves. Again, former government officials are paid top dollar to carry out activities that one would expect to be the domain of the government, and that are accountability-challenged.

SHADOW REGULATORS

Professional services outsourced by government have typically encompassed such activities as information-gathering, analysis, administration of programs, and core functions mentioned earlier, such as managing intelligence operations. Now government is also, remarkably, contracting out regulatory power and, in the process, diluting it.

What, exactly, is Promontory Financial Group? A single *American Banker* profile used these varying phrases to describe it: ". . . sort of ex-regulator omnibus," "shadow network between banks and regulators," "an auxiliary . . . private-sector regulator." Or, if you really want a head-scratcher: "a kind of arbitrage and interlocution between regulators and banks."[72] No matter which description one chooses, there is no doubt that Promontory illustrates some of the perils that come with outsourcing government duties and even informal authority to private entities.

A private consultant to Bank of America, Morgan Stanley, Wells Fargo, PNC, Allied Irish, and the Vatican, among others (and with fifteen offices that span the globe from Toronto to Tokyo, Denver to Dubai, Singapore, San Francisco, and Sydney, and, of course, Washington, D.C.), Promontory is hired by these and other top financial firms to manage a crisis, or to navigate the thicket of new regulations meant to rein in some of the banks' now infamous investment "innovations."[73]

Who can provide the best advice on the thinking and doings of regulators? Former regulators, of course. Almost two thirds of Promontory's approximately 170 senior executives have been employed by agencies charged with monitoring the financial industry, according to the *New York Times*.[74] No surprise, as the firm was founded by Eugene Ludwig, who, under President Bill Clinton (a friend from both Oxford and Yale Law School), headed the U.S. Treasury's Office of the Comptroller of the Currency (OCC), charged with supervising national banks. Its advisory board is another heavy-hitting list that includes two former SEC chairmen, Mary Schapiro and Arthur Levitt, Jr., and former Federal Reserve Vice Chair Alan Blinder.[75] With these ex-regulators on board, Promontory can advance the interests of its banker clients: using very recent government experience with regulations under consideration, helping defang the implementation of the Dodd-Frank legislation passed after the 2008 financial crisis, and (shadow)-lobbying former regulatory colleagues to do so.[76]

Since opening its doors in 2001, Promontory has evolved alongside the big changes in financial regulation around that time. The Sarbanes-Oxley Act, aimed at preventing corporate malfeasance following the spectacular accounting frauds of Enron, Worldcom, and other companies, was passed in 2002. Wall Street firms played their own role in abetting these crimes.

But the real trouble that was to percolate over the next decade emanated from Wall Street and was perfectly legal and largely unregulated: exotic derivatives. (Ironically, back in 1994, as comptroller, Ludwig himself had warned about the dangers of such derivatives.)[77]

After derivatives detonated in 2008, Wall Street poured huge amounts of money into blocking financial reform. When the Dodd-Frank legislation eventually did pass in 2010, the new game became implementation—or, as some analysts might call it, obstruction. As we mentioned in the previous chapter, the truly important fight is not so much in the headline-grabbing prosecutions we've seen over the past few years, which are sometimes high on performing for the public and low on results that matter: rather, it's what's happening inside the dense fine print of Dodd-Frank, with some of the top lawyers in the United States haggling over details, sometimes not even for substantive reasons but simply to thwart implementation.

Enter Promontory. Even with the extraordinary attempts to delay and obstruct, firms still know they have a lot of new rules to contend with, and Promontory, by its own description, wants to be their consigliere: "for every well-run company the right balance between risk and reward is always critical. Today, unprecedented changes and obligations make doing so more challenging than ever before. Promontory can help you achieve and maintain the right balance."[78]

Its clients might get the "right balance," but what about the public? With entangled allegiances and shifting roles as the firm bends with the whims of its clients (at times even standing in for regulators as overseers and auditors), accountability to the public strikes the wrong balance.

Promontory has served as sort of a proxy for government auditors, "a firm brimming with former regulators who can hold sway with old colleagues or stand in for them altogether," as the *Washington Post* put it.

These ex-regulators are now paid by those they audit.

Promontory also acts as an unconventional lobbying outfit, intervening with regulators on behalf of its clients. Founder Ludwig insists that he and his people are committed to the health of the financial system, not just its bottom line: "We are here to implement what the government wants done," he told the *Post*. "People who come here [to work] have high integrity and want to help institutions do the right thing in the aide [*sic*] of financial stability."[79]

One can sense, as with the retired military officers, that Ludwig is pained to be quizzed on his integrity and indeed, by many accounts, he is well regarded and well liked in both state and private sectors.

But the way his company operates—its emerging role as a shadow regulator, buffering its clients from regulation through shadow lobbying, while also availing itself of privileged regulatory knowledge, deserves our inspection.

I'll look at the question of lobbying first.

Shadow Lobbying?

Despite being filled with well-versed and well-placed ex-regulators, Promontory insists that its people do not lobby their former employers. That doesn't quite square with some accounts. One area that Promontory has weighed in on, according to *Time*, is the Volcker Rule designed to rein in risky trading by U.S. banks (and named for the former Federal Reserve chief who champions it).[80] The chief counsel at the OCC until 2012, Julie Williams, tells *Time* that she recalls taking at least several meetings with Ludwig (or other Promontory representatives) about the Rule during the rulemaking process.[81]

Williams left OCC to join Promontory in 2013. Her replacement at the OCC? Amy Friend, a managing director at Promontory. The *New York Times* described this as a sort of "Freaky Friday"-style body-swapping job switch.[82] *Time* adds that Friend recused herself from Volcker Rule matters when joining OCC, suggesting that Promontory was indeed at least somewhat involved when financial firms and regulators were hashing over the much-disputed rule.

Indeed, the *New York Times*, analyzing data from a nonprofit that studied the issue, found in 2013 that although Promontory hadn't been a registered lobbyist for four years, "the firm's executives have met with regulators at least 10 times in the last two years on thorny issues like the . . . Volcker Rule."[83]

Promontory insisted to the *Times* that meetings do not necessarily constitute "lobbying." Ludwig himself made this argument to *American Banker*, saying "We do the opposite of influencing government. We try to influence the private sector in terms of what the government wants it to do."[84]

Regulation Sleuthing

Promontory has helped pioneer another accountability-challenged influence practice: anticipating regulation with the benefit of fresh insider knowledge. An unnamed source who watched the process in action said this to *American Banker:* "Law firms have been doing . . . mock hearings for clients for decades. . . . Promontory does that on the regulatory side. [Ludwig] was the first to come up with that model."[85]

There are at least two problems with this practice. First, Promontory almost certainly has access to knowledge from the inside surrounding regulation garnered through recent work experience. Since the firm is packed with ex-regulators, there is the strong possibility that banks are getting such information, which by rights should stay in government hands. (The banks aren't paying a reported four figures an hour for nothing.)

And clearly the company and its clients value the freshest insight. The *American Banker* profile notes that Promontory "even has half a dozen former staffers from the Consumer Financial Protection Bureau, which is not even three years old yet."[86]

Second, hiring a firm like Promontory surely encourages banks to continue to strategize in every possible way to remain within the letter of the law while still developing new, legal, but potentially risky profit-making "innovations." We know by now what fully legal financial innovations ended up being for the global economy in 2008: a wrecking ball.

Shadow Oversight

In Promontory's role as a shadow regulator, we see how authority, even that of the government, gets dispersed. It is mobile, to say the least.

The government has diluted its own authority and muddied the regulatory waters by calling on firms like Promontory. This has both informal and formal variants.

The first and most common (informal) variant appears to be that when banks hire Promontory, that act carries informal weight which they can throw around to demonstrate that they are supposedly in compliance. An unnamed lawyer, one apparently working for Promontory, said this to *American Banker:*[87]

> If the regulators are saying jump on your right foot for 10 miles, we'll tell you 20 miles. . . . And once you've done it, we'll tell the regulators that you "get it," and you will pay us well for repairing your regulatory relationship.

This surely encourages the industry to believe that it can continue to self-regulate, a fiction that has for years been embraced by the financial world, especially if banks hire a kind of "fixer" with sterling government connections.

With regard to the second variant—the formal outsourcing of authority—sometimes the government itself mandates that banks use Promontory (or a firm like it) to do some of the financial oversight that would seem to be the province of the government itself.

This has led to some very big accountability problems.

First, there is the now-bankrupt firm MF Global, headed by Jon Corzine, formerly of Goldman Sachs, the U.S. Senate, and the New Jersey governorship.

MF Global was starting to show up on the regulatory radar years before it finally imploded. In a 2008 settlement over a trading scandal with the Commodity Futures Trading Commission, charged with regulating derivatives, MF Global had to agree to hire Promontory—which is, remember, a *private consulting firm*, not a regulator—to ensure that it was complying with the government's edicts. Two years later, Promontory lent MF Global its approval, saying "Promontory has witnessed a remarkable turn-around . . . in terms of leadership and culture since our original review[.]"[88] Not remarkable enough, clearly, since less than six months later, MF Global would collapse in spectacular fashion after making nearly a billion dollars in "improper" transfers from customer accounts in a desperate bid to cover trading losses, a striking departure from custom. In June 2013, regulators slapped a civil complaint against Corzine, the CEO, for failure to properly supervise. Did MF Global receive a positive report because it was paying the authors? Of course Promontory says no, but we have no real way to verify.

Perhaps an even bigger failure of public accountability can be seen in the now-defunct Independent Foreclosure Review. After investigating more than a dozen mortgage servicers, including Bank of America, the government created the Independent Foreclosure Review, a vehicle through which offenders would review their files and offer some relief to homeowners drowning in mortgage debt. The banks were told to bring on government-approved "independent consultants"—Promontory and others—to help determine how much homeowners should be offered in relief. The Huffington Post described this as "one of the most ambitious and costly auditing projects in U.S. history."[89]

After a year, the banks had handed over $1.5 billion, by some estimates, *but not to the homeowners.* That money went to Promontory and the other firms, with Promontory alone earning nearly a billion. Promontory, in other words, reaped the lion's share of the reward. Aside from the exorbitant amount spent on consultants and not on the homeowners they had been ordered to help, questions quickly arose: Were the consultants truly independent from the banks that were paying them?

ProPublica, the nonprofit investigative news service, found that the Independent Foreclosure Review might not be independent enough and that Promontory may have simply been rubber-stamping what the banks wanted it to rubber-stamp. A small army of contractors hired by Bank of America apparently had even taken the lead in the supposed review, not Promontory:[90] ProPublica, which obtained some internal documents and e-mails from Bank of America, concluded: "As for Promontory's role in making the final determination, a Bank of America employee said the widespread understanding among bank staff working on the review was that 'it's only a matter of double-checking.'"[91]

Promontory, of course, strongly denied that it was a pawn of the bank; but months later, the Huffington Post also investigated and found that at least some contractors hired by Bank of America were doing the "substantive, evaluative review work," with Promontory taking charge more fully only after its role had been criticized.

And those Bank of America contractors reportedly knew they were supposed to look the other way when they saw things in the documents that might offer homeowners justification for greater relief. As one employee remarked, "We knew what we were looking at. . . . But we were told under threat of losing our jobs to not report what we saw."[92]

In January 2013, the government pulled the plug on the program and substituted a $9.3 billion payout to be split among the more than four million homeowners eligible for relief under the program.[93]

At a congressional hearing following the debacle, called "Outsourcing Accountability? Examining the Role of Independent Consultants," Senator Sherrod Brown said this:[94]

> At the [Office of the Comptroller of the Currency] alone, nearly one-third of their legal actions since 2008 have required banks to hire an outside consultant to review their actions and

to propose solutions. Because most consulting firms are private companies, there's little transparency about their business model to either the public or to Congress, leaving us to wonder about financial incentives, leaving us to wonder about business relationships. Recently we've heard about consultants hired at regulators' request to find and to fix illegal activity. In these few high-profile cases, they either missed serious problems or gave the banks a free pass.

When pressed by Brown, the head of the OCC said quite plainly: "[I]ndependent consultants have subject matter expertise that the bank does not."[95] Or the regulator itself, clearly.

The OCC is reportedly exploring ways to strengthen its standards when it comes to hiring private consultants like Promontory, to ensure that the firms chosen are both independent enough and up to the task. But a more fundamental problem is at work. As the *Washington Post* observes:[96]

> Accounting firms, like PricewaterhouseCoopers and Ernst & Young, with consulting practices adhere to professional standards set by the American Institute of Certified Public Accountants. Pure consulting shops, however, operate with no formal regulatory oversight.

Clearly, ambiguity of identity lends Promontory cover and aids escape from monitoring.

Meanwhile, affected homeowners began receiving $300 or $500 checks in the spring of 2013, some of which bounced.[97] There's even a Facebook page "liked" by more than a thousand people called Independent Foreclosure Review Victims. In June 2013, that page decided that the homeowners should all go in on Powerball (lottery) tickets, believing that they might have better luck winning the lottery than in winning timely relief from banks deemed by the government as bad actors.

Where is the sense of responsibility toward us, the public? At least one regulatory expert thinks the public was never part of the equation. Sheila Bair, former chair of the FDIC, made this withering assessment: "It [the

Independent Foreclosure Review and the use of consulting firms] was designed to generate fees for consultants, not to help homeowners."[98]

The problems highlighted by Promontory are fundamental and familiar: it is neither fish nor fowl. It isn't a registered lobbyist or an accounting firm or a government regulator. With no fixed identity, it can flex to suit the occasion. Ambiguity, blurred boundaries, and the enigma that is Promontory serve it and its clients' purposes splendidly.

The public, not so much.

MIXED MANDATES

Contracting out, to varying degrees, has created a shadow government populated by ex-officials, richly compensated by taxpayer-supported contractors, and operating with far less oversight and far more conflicts. In short, built-in unaccountability is the essence of today's company-state.

Still another path to the company-state doesn't involve contracting out. It arises instead from the mixed mandate of the agency doing the regulating: part of a stated mission might be to regulate a certain industry, and yet another part might involve promoting the business of that very industry. With cross-purposes built into its mission and operations, ambiguity and deniability are the order of the day.

The U.S. Department of Agriculture and its promotion of the cheese industry, made all the more incongruous by First Lady Michelle Obama's war on childhood obesity, star in one example. According to the *New York Times*, the Agriculture Department instituted Dairy Management Inc. in 1995 as a nonprofit "marketing creation" to promote the consumption of dairy products.

A few years later, Dairy Management Inc. strategized with the Domino's Pizza chain to make a pizza line with forty percent more cheese; commissioned a study on consumers it dubbed "cheese snacking fanatics"; and heralded 2002 as the "Summer of Cheese," resulting in the use of more than a hundred million pounds of extra cheese.[99]

While Dairy Management looks and acts like an industry trade group, the fact that it is a project of the Agriculture Department means, as the *Times* reports, that Dairy Management's[100]

. . . annual budget . . . is largely financed by a government-mandated fee on the dairy industry. [T]he Agriculture Department . . . approves its marketing campaigns and major contracts and periodically reports to Congress on its work.

The *Times* adds that "Although by law the Secretary of Agriculture approves Dairy Management's contracts and advertising campaigns, the organization . . . has become a full-blown company. . . ."[101] Its longtime chief executive earns three times what the Agriculture Secretary earns. Not bad for a supposed nonprofit.

How does the ambiguity serve Dairy Management? In this case, the fact that the government supports the dairy industry (among other agricultural industries) helps insulate leadership from the charge that government obstructs private business. But when asked about Dairy Management's role, the Agriculture Department was able to emphasize to the *Times* the looseness of its connection:[102]

[T]he department said that dairy promotion was intended to bolster farmers and rural economies, and that its oversight left Dairy Management's board with "significant independence" in deciding how best to support those interests.

Dairy Management can also use the government's imprimatur as a shield when it needs to. When the entity's billing of dairy foods as a diet aid was challenged as false, writes the *Times*, "government lawyers defended it, saying the Agriculture Department 'reviewed, approved and continually oversaw' the effort."[103]

As we can see, such flex-ability to play different sides lends deniability. Good, perhaps, for government PR, but not so good for accountability to the public.

Far from the world of dairy products is another agency with a conflicted mission: the Minerals Management Service, the U.S. oil-drilling "regulator" that came under scrutiny after BP's massive oil spill in the Gulf of Mexico, the worst environmental disaster in American history. It took the death of eleven workers and the spilling of nearly five million barrels of oil for the media to take notice.

Was the MMS an arm of the industry, or was it a government regulator? You be the judge of this description, from the *Wall Street Journal*:[104]

> It is supposed to be a watchdog that halts drilling when it spots unsafe behavior. But it is also supposed . . . to generate government revenue from drilling on government lands. . . . Of MMS's fiscal 2010 budget of $342 million, nearly half comes from the oil industry.

No surprise, then, that the MMS had essentially rubber-stamped BP's plan to explore the Deepwater Horizon well lease. According to its plan, the risk of an oil spill was minimal and "no mitigation measures other than those required by regulation and BP policy will be employed to avoid, diminish or eliminate potential impacts on environmental resources," according to the *Washington Post*.[105] Should there be a spill, damage to fish, birds, and marine mammals would be minimal, the plan had it. MMS also granted BP's lease a "categorical exclusion" from environmental-impact analysis by the National Environmental Policy Act—just eleven days prior to the oil-rig explosion.[106]

A *Wall Street Journal* investigation found that the MMS:[107]

- doesn't write or implement most safety regulations, having gradually shifted such responsibilities to the oil industry itself for more than a decade;
- said that offshore drilling is so complicated that only industry can really regulate itself;
- let the industry devise its own solutions to problems;
- let a trade group take over the role of telling companies what training was necessary for workers involved in keeping wells from gushing out of control.

In its defense, the agency "pointed to a 1996 law that encouraged federal agencies to 'benefit from the expertise of the private sector' by adopting industry standards."[108]

A few government officials and investigators did try to extract increased oversight of BP long before the massive spill. One EPA official a few years earlier threatened to "debar" BP from government contracts if it didn't submit to tougher regulation.[109]

Such entreaties fell on deaf ears. It is no coincidence, perhaps, that a high-wattage roster of Washington power brokers who had served on government advisory boards and panels was deployed by BP to burnish the company's image well before the spill. Some were reportedly paid $120,000 a year to . . . "advise." These include former Democratic Senate majority leader Tom Daschle; two former Republican senators, the late Warren Rudman and Alan Simpson; Bush EPA administrator Christine Todd Whitman; Clinton deputy attorney general Jamie Gorelick; Leon Panetta, before he became President Obama's CIA director; and former Democratic Senate majority leader George Mitchell (now Penn State's Athletic Integrity Leader).[110]

BP took some of its high-powered advisory board members on a helicopter ride out to the Gulf of Mexico to "demonstrate safeguards." Whitman told *Newsweek:* "We got a sense they were really committed to ensuring they got it right."[111]

In 2010, following the disaster, the Obama White House moved to split MMS's oversight and revenue functions and to increase resources to tip the power back toward the regulators. Thus the "MMS" is no more—in name, that is. It is now two entities: the Bureau of Ocean Energy Management (BOEM) and the Bureau of Safety and Environmental Enforcement (BSEE).[112]

But no matter the labels, it's hard to see how the government can easily reverse what seems to be a virtual takeover by the industry it is supposed to regulate—a meshing of state and private power, with the state getting the short end of the stick.

—⚏—

The rise of the company-state has brought an explosion of unaccountability replete with entities and players who can easily wriggle out of responsibility. Following Edward Snowden's leaks, security within organizations (including government contractors) has become the new craze. It may be that a big—even the biggest—risk comes from within. But the first place to look is players at the top—and the company-state they power. When they are, by the structure in which they operate, most invested in their own agendas and not that of the public or the nations they supposedly serve, our wallets and possibly our security are compromised.

In the next chapters we'll see how the same signs of unaccountability we examined with regard to government and the companies and players swirling in and around it—overlapping roles, moving boundaries, and performing for the public, among others—are invading organizations we thought we understood. We'll see how the way in which enterprises these days are organized—from think tanks, academic expertise, "grassroots" entities, and political endeavors—sows antitransparency and unaccountability. And these enterprises move and shake policies through means of influencing that we may be only dimly aware of, if at all.

CHAPTER 7

Thought Leaders and Think-Tankers

T
hey've long been called "universities without students." Unfortunately, the more accurate name these days for many of the nearly
seven thousand think tanks around the world might be "power
centers without accountability."[1]

"Power centers"? What happened to the long-term policy studies produced by think tanks for consumption by government, political and policy
wonks, or anyone with a shelf? The ongoing work of experts on welfare, or
social security, or foreign policy? In the United States, we might think of
stodgy establishments like the Brookings Institution, the American Enterprise Institute, the Heritage Foundation, or the Cato Institute—each with
its own particular ideological slant and corner office space for out-of-office
politicians. In the United Kingdom, we might think of Chatham House.

While these institutions flourished during the Cold War, the number of
think tanks worldwide has risen so fast and furiously since the end of the
Cold War that we are prompted to ask whether there is really that much
more thinking going on.[2] By at least one estimate, the United States alone
has upwards of 1,900 of these public-policy research organizations today—a

figure that's more than doubled since 1980.[3] Considering the large number of organizations that look like think tanks these days, that figure actually may be far higher.[4]

It isn't just the sheer number of think tanks that's exploded. So have their scope and ambitions. A new species has been born that, while it might still be called a think tank, is a simulacrum of its earlier version.

Today, many think tanks have become partisan fighters, armed with rapid-response teams and quickly assembled reports. One think-tank veteran, Steve Clemons, even back in 2003, went so far as to speak of "The Corruption of Think Tanks" in an essay he penned. Then the vice president of the New America Foundation, Clemons wrote about "the development of an underground, or 'second,' economy of political influence" where funders of think tanks "increasingly expect policy achievements that contribute to their bottom line." Think tanks, Clemons added, "are less and less committed to genuine inquiry designed to stimulate enlightened policy decisions and more and more oriented to deepening the well-worn grooves of a paralyzed debate, frozen in place by the contending power of potential winners and losers with armies of lobbyists at their heels."[5]

The old think tanks, by contrast, were more scholarly and almost patrician. They did have ideological bents, but their members shared a kind of wonkiness that could transcend differences. Most important, the old think tanks' time frame was long rather than short. They conducted multiyear studies, and not necessarily in response to the mood of the moment or for immediate media impact. They produced reports that sometimes gained traction and became mighty policies. Think, for instance, of the work of the Brookings Institution on the federal budget. In the early 1970s, Brookings began publishing *Setting National Priorities*. This series of studies, along with additional analyses of federal spending, played a role in Brookings's call for the establishment of the Congressional Budget Office. In 1975, the CBO was born, and its first director was Alice Rivlin, a Brookings economist.[6]

The archetypal new-style think tank is hardly stodgy. It prizes performance in the short term: quick reaction to events, media-timed and -friendly reports, and minute-to-minute messaging. It prizes "impact" and metrics to show to donors and the world. Its stars create buzz on social media and TV and organize invitation-only conferences of power brokers. It may act like an advocacy organization, and, even more than in the past, it may express naked ideology.

Not only is the time horizon of this new-style outfit shorter than its older-style counterpart: many of today's most successful think tanks have only been around for a few years. The most successful think tank is not just dynamic and up to the minute: it is *creating* the minute.

Meanwhile, the old think tanks are struggling to catch up and merely sustain themselves. A longtime scholar at Brookings, for example, tells me that he and his colleagues are now asked to respond to more press inquiries. Just as with journalists, they are encouraged to use Facebook and Twitter.

The blurred boundaries of the shadow elite era are written all over the new-style think tank. Its playground is an environment where boundaries are porous and the organizational missions of government, business, media, and—yes—think tanks are unfixed and morphing. It's the same environment where who is a journalist, an expert, a businessman, or a philanthropist, as we've shown throughout these pages, is stretched and manipulated as convenience serves.

Think tanks are, by definition, ambiguous and have a hybrid quality, as sociologist Thomas Medvetz shows in his *Think Tanks in America*. It is no accident, then, that think tanks have mushroomed in the era of blurred boundaries—because they are themselves a product of a blur, rendering them especially in tune with our age. While the appeal of think tanks has always depended on their proximity to different arenas—politics, academia, business, and the media—and their placement in a space that smudges the lines,[7] the smudging has grown both quantitatively and qualitatively. As I have illustrated, ambiguity is the very key to the success of shadow elites, lending them deniability. The ambiguity exhibited by think tanks likewise is not an accident, Medvetz argues:[8]

> By combining elements of more established sources of public knowledge—universities, government agencies, businesses, and the media—think tanks exert a tremendous amount of

influence on the way citizens and lawmakers perceive the work, unbound by the more clearly defined roles of those other institutions.

The success of think-tankers in this new world hinges on moving among roles in these arenas—scholar, policy adviser, media contributor, entrepreneur, consultant. It depends not only on quick study, but on connecting and forging networks, on conferences and cross-pollination among politics, business, and media. Medvetz documents the fact that formal contacts among think tanks rose significantly beginning in the 1990s, with conferences and publications often sponsored jointly. Similarly oriented think tanks tend to congregate in the same geographical areas of Washington, D.C.,[9] or even share adjoining office space.

"In" are media-dazzling events; passé are the lengthy studies that used to be the pride and hallmark of a think tank. As another scholar who studies them, political scientist Don Abelson, writes:[10]

> What has changed over the past few decades is how deeply invested think-tanks have become in the marketplace of ideas. They are more politically savvy, more technologically sophisticated and better equipped to compete with the thousands of organizations in the United States jostling to leave an indelible mark on key policy initiatives. . . . This is what convinced the Heritage Foundation that it should specialize in what has come to be known as quick-response policy research. Several think-tanks and universities have adopted the language of corporations, and, in doing so, devote much of their time to discussing metrics and performance indicators. In the era of corporatization, numbers matter.

Here we see the corporatizing values of fast turnaround and "measurable" results. Those include: number of followers or friends on Facebook or Twitter, times a think-tank scholar has testified before Congress, website views or downloaded research, and—the one that seems most notable to me—number of think-tankers placed in government jobs.

Heritage, an expressly conservative think tank founded more than forty years ago, has gone high-octane under the recent leadership of Tea Party player and former senator Jim DeMint, who, as Bryan Bender of the *Boston Globe* points out, presided over a nine-city Defund Obamacare Town Hall Tour in 2013. His predecessor as president at Heritage made over a million dollars; DeMint's net worth before joining Heritage stood at around $65,000.[11] It looks like a lucrative career move for DeMint. Here's Bender:[12]

> Not long ago, Washington's think tanks constituted a rarefied world of policy-minded scholars supported by healthy endowments and quietly sought solutions to some of the nation's biggest challenges. But now Congress and the executive branch are served a limitless feast of supposedly independent research from hundreds of nonprofit institutions that are pursuing fiercely partisan agendas and are funded by undisclosed corporations, wealthy individuals, or both.

Where does the appeal of think tanks emanate from? Fundamental to their influence is the ability to trade on a neutral, academic veneer. But also fundamental is the much greater importance of connecting. This chapter, then, looks into the coordinated strategies of various think tanks whose inhabitants move agilely through government, consulting, media, and business roles and who sometimes are more interested in promoting particular agendas than the more scholarly policy research of the past. And, like the company-state and corporations featured in the last chapter, they sometimes stand in for the state in forging policy initiatives and public programs.

In the United States, this is by no means just a Republican-dominated trend, as we will see with players who are generally Democrats affiliated with the defense-strategy think tank Center for a New American Security (CNAS). (Though, as you will see, conservatives do appear to be more adept at creating networks of think tanks.)

Nor is it by any stretch solely an American phenomenon, as we'll see in various examples later in the chapter.

Before examining some examples of the archetypal of the new-style think tank, let me say that I spent several years as a senior fellow of the New America Foundation, a "post-partisan" Washington-based think tank, while writing my last book, *Shadow Elite*. (The New America Foundation is funded largely by foundations; government; technology companies, including Facebook, Netflix, Google, and Microsoft; private donors, including Google's Eric Schmidt; and a few other businesses.) Let me also say that not all think tanks conform in all—or even necessarily most—aspects of the archetypes I lay out here to illustrate how what are called *think tanks* can skirt or evade accountability. All, however, are subject to the pressures of our shadow-elite era.

OWN-A-TANK ADVOCACY

Just what is Third Way, less than a decade old? On the face of it, it is a self-proclaimed centrist think tank, founded by Wall Streeters, telecom veterans, and former Clintonites, with members of Congress as honorary co-chairs.[13] It was named "2013 North American Think Tank of the Year" by the British monthly *Prospect*. But like many other new-style think tanks, it seems like a vehicle for wealthy people to launder ideologically charged influence into difficult-to-trace advocacy.

A recent fight between the organization and Senator Elizabeth Warren, a fierce crusader for financial reform, ended up illuminating the issue of think-tank disclosure (namely, the lack thereof). Her demand for transparency goes to the heart of the problem with think tanks and unaccountable influence.

It began on December 2, 2013, when Third Way's president and senior vice president for policy wrote a *Wall Street Journal* op-ed warning that "nothing could be more disastrous" for Democrats than to embrace the kind of populism advocated by Senator Warren and the mayor-elect of New York, Bill de Blasio.[14]

Warren fired back just two days later with a letter sent to the CEOs of America's top banks, urging them to voluntarily disclose any financial contributions they make to think tanks:[15]

Policy makers need access to objective, quality research. . . . [P]rivate think tanks are well suited to provide this research

> . . . but for it to be valuable, such research and analysis must be truly independent. If the information provided by think tanks is little more than another form of corporate lobbying, then policymakers should be made aware of the difference.

In a way, this was a bit of a proxy fight, targeting banks directly. But perhaps it was a worthy one, because it unleashed more scrutiny on just who funds Third Way—and what agendas might lie behind it.

A senior vice president of Third Way eventually acknowledged that a "majority" of its funding comes from its board of trustees, and a majority of the trustees come from the financial industry.[16] *The Nation*, poking around Third Way's annual report, found a half-million-dollar donation from Peck, Madigan, Jones & Stewart, "a corporate lobbying firm that represents Deutsche Bank, Intel, the Business Roundtable, Amgen, AT&T, the International Swaps & Derivatives Association, MasterCard, New York Life Insurance, [pharmaceutical trade group] PhRMA and the US Chamber of Commerce, among others."[17]

The magazine also notes a $50,000 donation from healthcare giant Humana, which Humana reports as "non-deductible lobbying." In a later article, *The Nation* adds telecom giant Qualcomm, whose $25,000 donation is filed in the annual report under the rubric of "trade associations."[18]

Third Way has caused ripples in both the financial and healthcare industries since its formation; in 2009, a draft memo arguing against the so-called public option for healthcare reform became public, with the Huffington Post noting that one of the authors was a former Blue Cross-Blue Shield consultant and another "a former corporate attorney with Hogan and Hartson, a Washington-based law firm and top healthcare industry lobby shop."[19]

A year earlier, Truthout reported that Third Way was advising Jay Rockefeller, who was then chairman of the Senate Intelligence Committee, on "messaging" when it came to pushing for retroactive immunity for telecom executives who cooperated with the government's warrantless spying in the years after 9/11.[20]

Among the reported Third Way trustees at that time with connections to the telecom industry was Reynold Levy, a former AT&T executive. Truthout flags four others who also have telecom ties. That might explain why the organization was intent on defending Senator Rockefeller in the *New York Times* back in 2007 against criticism that he was taking donations from telecom executives seeking immunity. The *Times* describes Third Way as a "moderate Democratic policy group that has supported immunity for the phone carriers," but fails to mention the group's own connections to telecom executives and companies.[21]

So much for transparency and accountability.

Another of the think tank's areas of interest is recasting entitlement reform as something progressives should care about. This shouldn't be surprising, given that a Third Way co-founder is said to be an "acolyte" of longtime austerity hawk and billionaire Pete Peterson.[22]

So what is new about Third Way? While a think tank with an ideological agenda may be old-hat, the lack of transparency in Third Way's operations and media outputs, the amount of big money these days sloshing around looking to be translated into political action, and the freshly pressed dress with the sheen of neutrality that then appears on the runway, all together form a new fashion.

THE THINK TANK-INDUSTRY-GOVERNMENT-MEDIA NEXUS

How is war strategy "sold" these days? The Vietnam War was essentially sold to the establishment and the public by a small circle inside the Pentagon, including Defense Secretary Robert McNamara. The Pentagon Papers, leaked from within the bureaucracy, did much to buttress the public's gathering disenchantment. But in the shadow-elite age, war plans have been sold by celebrity generals who are melded with media and think tanks supported by defense contractors. The target of our disenchantment, if we are disenchanted, is thus removed from us, the public, several steps farther.

It might seem incongruous to see the words "think tank" and "hot" in the same sentence. But it is fair to say that for the crucial years in the latter half of the 2000s, the Center for a New American Security was indeed hot. In 2009, the *Washington Post* described it as the "It" think tank for its sphere of influence in military policy.[23]

But what does that mean, exactly? Typically, it means that the think tank is having real influence on public policy. Because it is a think tank, and—in this case—a very new one, it is hard, if not impossible, to truly capture its reach.

CNAS was founded in 2007 by Kurt M. Campbell, who focused on international relations and security in top positions in government and the military (in addition to business endeavors, another think tank, and a column for the *Financial Times*), and Michèle A. Flournoy, who worked for the Department of Defense before affiliating herself with a university, a consulting group, and another think tank. Campbell and Flournoy defined the mission of CNAS as promoting "strong, pragmatic and principled national security and defense policies" as an alternative to the failed ideological approaches of the outgoing Bush administration.[24] Delivering the opening keynote for the think tank was then-Senator Hillary Rodham Clinton, who had her eye (and apparently still does) on the White House.

Around this time, the idea of Counterinsurgency, or COIN, was becoming ascendant in military circles. Terms often associated with firmly held ideologies or evangelical religions were bandied about. *Rolling Stone* called it the "new gospel of the Pentagon brass."[25] Those who supported COIN were "COINdinistas," "adherents," "disciples," "believers," with "zeal." Their chief "prophet" or "guru" was General David Petraeus, then carrying out the so-called surge of forces in Iraq.[26] That surge incorporated COIN principles: emphasizing intensive local engagement. As one observer put it (again, note the religious imagery), "[t]he holy trinity of modern counterinsurgency is clear, hold, and build."[27]

The use of the language of religion to describe its leaders and acolytes, reminiscent of the exalted stature of the economic High Priests we discussed earlier, may signal intense devotion to the cause, worship of the leader, and close relations among believers.

Writing in the *American Conservative*, a COIN critic cast a skeptical view of the 2009 CNAS annual meeting:[28]

> [S]eeking to establish muscular national-security credentials ahead of the presidential election, CNAS's founders Michele Flournoy and Kurt Campbell made the savvy decision to position Petraeus's expanding counterinsurgency (COIN) ideal in their own evolving agenda. It was a marriage of convenience. Petraeus's patrons in the Republican Party

were on the way out, and Democrats were looking to retool their neoliberal interventionism, latent since the Clinton administration, into a sort of Counterinsurgency 2.0. The result was on full display as Petraeus broke down current operations in Iraq, Afghanistan, and Pakistan: a "whole of government" or "full spectrum" approach, led by the U.S. military, requiring untold financial resources, more weapons in theater, and more boots on the ground to "protect populations," turn around institutions, and train security forces. As one panelist said, "a long-term commitment" to the region. Nods of approval. A standing ovation. Why not? For every soul in the room who truly believes this is the "pragmatic and principled approach," there was surely another for whom the Long War means guaranteed employment, flush contracts, justified research, more trips to Capitol Hill. A reason for being.

Okay, harsh words from someone disposed against CNAS. But what is important to examine—and what should raise our accountability hackles—is how the Eisenhower-era military-industrial complex has morphed, proliferated, and dispersed across institutions to birth a more-difficult-to-crack beast, one replete with moving parts and swimming in informality. To better understand this, let's look at some specifics.

Defense Companies, Funding Support for War?

I begin with an important piece, albeit the one you'll likely find least surprising: the donor portfolio of CNAS.

Many defense giants and associated consultancies can be found on CNAS's funders page: Boeing, BAE Systems, Booz Allen, Bechtel, DynCorp International, Lockheed Martin, General Dynamics, Raytheon, and several oil giants.[29] *The Nation* pointed out in 2010 that "[CNAS also] generates income from research contracts with the Pentagon and intelligence agencies."[30] And military contractors deeply involved in the wars in Iraq and Afghanistan also appear, like Aegis Defence Services, and KBR, which used to be part of Halliburton. In a 2009 piece by CNAS president

John Nagl and senior fellow Richard Fontaine, they basically say that no one should be surprised by the presence of government contractors as part of the ongoing Afghan campaign. While the piece includes the thorny issues of managing forces driven by profit motive and not chain of command, they make it clear that contractors are here to stay and state that "not a single mission in Iraq or Afghanistan has failed because of contractor non-performance."[31] What is not noted in the article, however, is that CNAS gets support from companies like Aegis Defence Services and KBR. Does the donor portfolio of CNAS drive its policy? Of course, that is likely too strongly put and think-tankers would deny it, but the donor list invites questions.

That said, it would be short-sighted to ascribe some simple profit motive or quid pro quo to those perched at CNAS (and there's no evidence to suggest that there was any such quid pro quo). Like many think-tankers, they seemed most intent on amassing influence, relevance, and contacts—and getting their message in the media. Even as Barack Obama took the White House rather than Hillary Clinton, COIN doctrine and CNAS flourished. The media, always hungry for a fresh narrative, found one and ran with it. The year CNAS set up shop, co-founder Flournoy was profiled in the *New York Observer* under the headline "Hot Policy Wonks for the Democrats: The New Realists."[32]

Flowing among Think Tank and DOD and State

The think tank would serve as their launching pad. Less than two years later, Flournoy was tapped to serve on the Obama transition team and then tapped again as Under Secretary of Defense for Policy of the United States.[33]

Reporting on the transition in 2008, the *Wall Street Journal* noted that CNAS had emerged as a veritable defense and diplomatic "farm team for the incoming Obama administration."[34]

Political scientist Abelson uses the term "holding tanks" to signal that the government now relies on think tanks (not only CNAS) to provide the "institutional memory" and expertise it now lacks, owing to massive outsourcing.[35]

Three members of the CNAS board of advisers found prominent roles in the Obama administration: Wendy Sherman as Under Secretary of

State for Political Affairs; Susan Rice as U.S. Ambassador to the United Nations, and later National Security Adviser; and James Steinberg, Deputy Secretary of State.

Former Clinton White House Chief of Staff John Podesta, then on the CNAS board of directors, helped run the Obama transition team.

CNAS promoted other appointments in a July 2009 press release:[36]

> The Center for a New American Security . . . is pleased to announce that its President, Dr. John Nagl, and Senior Fellow, Robert Kaplan, have been named members of the Defense Policy Board (DPB) by Secretary of Defense Robert Gates. Nagl and Kaplan join a distinguished group of experts, including CNAS' founding Chairman William Perry, current CNAS Chairman Richard Danzig, and members of the CNAS Board of Advisers Wendy Sherman and Sarah Sewall.

At least one member of Congress found this wholesale flight from brand-new think tank to the high ranks of government troubling: Senator Jim Webb said this at CNAS co-founder Campbell's confirmation hearings after President Obama nominated him as Assistant Secretary of State for East Asian and Pacific Affairs:[37]

> The question really revolves around the creation of the Center for a New American Security in '07 being heavily funded by defense contractors in government contracts. And then from staff notes, former CNAS employees then migrating into the president's administration, and whether there are appropriate firewalls between the formation of that. This isn't the same situation as, I know you would appreciate, as a Heritage or an AEI or a Brookings that had been in existence, for a long period of time, and had resident scholars. The viewpoint here is that it was created just before an election cycle, with these contracts moving into it, and then so many of the principals or employees moving into the administration.

Campbell's nomination was confirmed.

And the think tank–government migration wasn't just one way: in 2008, CNAS hired COIN adherent David Kilcullen, who'd been advising General Petraeus in Iraq.[38]

The concern Webb voiced about the think–tank-industry-government-media nexus is not the only area that raises questions; so does the COIN policy itself. But the MO, not its efficacy, is my focus. The conventional wisdom had it that COIN (along with a "surge" of forces) "worked" in Iraq. But given the adulatory coverage of COIN and Petraeus in the general press, buoyed by this nexus, it remains to be seen whether alternatives for policy toward Afghanistan received enough attention.[39]

Enlisting Journalistic Firepower

The nexus encompassed a crucial component not featured in Eisenhower's military-industrial complex: the media. The COIN idea had to be sold to policymakers and the public. And here, in true shadow-elite style, we see the conflation of roles and agendas, and the challenges to impartial reporting and accountability.

We just mentioned Robert Kaplan joining the Defense Policy Board. Kaplan, however, did not come from a policymaking background; he is a journalist, a prolific author, and a longtime foreign correspondent for the *Atlantic*. Kaplan was part of the other indispensable piece of the CNAS strategy for gaining influence: harnessing media power, both in old-fashioned media and new. As one blogger joked, "CNAS Whale Swallows National-Security Journalists Whole."[40]

CNAS's then-CEO Nathaniel Fick, while not a reporter, is a telegenic presence. He took part early on in both the Iraq and Afghanistan wars as a Marine Corps infantry officer and then went on to become an author and, at one time, an on-air CBS News national-security consultant.[41] (Interestingly, Fick is now CEO of Endgame, the cyber-defense company seeking to avoid the public eye.)

Among the CNAS writers-in-residence were well-known defense and intelligence print reporters: Eric Schmitt, Thom Shanker, David Sanger, David Cloud, Greg Jaffe, and perhaps most notably Tom Ricks. They worked at various times, sometimes with overlapping tenures, at the

Washington Post, the *Wall Street Journal, Foreign Policy,* and the *New York Times,* among other outlets, each one either winning or serving on a team that won a Pulitzer Prize.[42]

Why does this impressive roster potentially undermine accountability? Of course, journalists are always hungry for access, and with newspapers in free fall it's no wonder that CNAS was able to entice so many prominent names. But at least three of the reporters named above continued reporting or blogging in traditional media outlets while at the same time affiliating with CNAS and writing books that would then be reviewed in . . . all those traditional newspapers or affiliated sites, often by like-minded COIN supporters.[43]

Some of the reporters affiliated with CNAS have taken on full-fledged government roles. One of them, David Cloud, went on to serve as special assistant to the U.S. Ambassador to Afghanistan in Kabul during 2009, before returning to journalism at the *Chicago Tribune*'s Washington bureau.[44]

How can we trust the efficacy of information from sources, however astute, whose journalistic missions are potentially compromised by their conflation of roles and support from the very parties promoting policies about which they are reporting?

Flouting the Chain of Command

The shadow-elite age is also characterized by sidestepping bureaucracy and the practice of informality. When Major General Michael Flynn, then the top intelligence officer in Afghanistan, wanted to deliver a blistering report in 2009 on the state of intelligence-gathering in the country, he did so through CNAS rather than through any official channel where it might have been buried. He enlisted the help of a former colleague of Tom Ricks—*Wall Street Journal* reporter Marine Capt. Matt Pottinger—as a co-author, who then used CNAS to release the bombshell report.[45]

Take it from Flynn's boss, General Stanley McChrystal, who said of Flynn once: "He never asks, 'Why can't we do this?' He just busts down walls."[46] He wasn't kidding. Not only did Flynn—at least in appearance—flout the military chain of command, but the think tank's president acknowledged that ". . . it was an irregular way to disseminate an idea for a serving officer."[47]

This highly unconventional release sparked many questions: Was the release privately vetted, as some reporters suggest, by McChrystal, the top U.S. and allied commander? There was this one from *Politico*: "More headaches for CNAS co-founder Michèle Flournoy, now under secretary of defense for policy, about whether her influential think tank is back-channeling the generals and COIN mafia outside of the chain of command?"[48]

While Flynn had informal relations with these think-tankers, who might have some role in making or shaping policy, they answer to no one. They are not under the same expectations and authority that a member of the military would be.

That flareup with Flynn didn't deter CNAS or its old-media stalwarts; they also—wisely—didn't neglect the new media.

Tom Ricks maintains a blog on *Foreign Policy*'s website called "The Best Defense," which at one point included a special feature he called "Travels with Paula." The writer of these guest posts was the soon-to-be famous Paula Broadwell, "knocking around Afghanistan, checking out operations, and visiting some West Point buddies," as Ricks described her.[49] Ricks would later give Broadwell an endorsement "blurb" for the glowing biography she wrote about her apparent boyfriend General Petraeus, saying: "*All In* feels at times like we are sitting at his side in Afghanistan, reading his e-mails over his shoulder."[50]

Selling the Surge

CNAS was a prime mover in pushing a COIN-style surge in Afghanistan. It hosted a blog described by one writer as "the go-to [one] for the COIN set," written by a former Army Ranger and young Middle East scholar named Andrew Exum.[51] Exum was part of a group of think-tankers (CNAS and others) invited to travel to Afghanistan with General Stanley McChrystal in 2009 as part of a "strategic assessment team." He and other think-tankers beyond CNAS filled the media echo chamber.[52]

In fall 2009, Exum released a report from CNAS in which he defined the "best-case scenario" to be one in which ". . . the United States and its allies agree to a fully resourced campaign to provide security for key population centers and continue to develop effective security forces," though it probably wasn't the most likely scenario.[53] Exum appeared on PBS's *Frontline*, lavishing praise on McChrystal and Petraeus, calling them "our best and brightest commanders."[54]

Defense correspondent Nathan Hodge, in an article describing how the surge was sold, named think-tankers (other than those like Exum affiliated with CNAS) who provided their support via the media. Several of the reports featuring these think-tankers didn't disclose their involvement in strategy-making or traveling with General McChrystal.[55]

Exum that fall faced criticism after reviewing (and panning) a book critical of McChrystal while failing to mention that he, Exum, had been a very recent adviser and travel companion of the general's.[56] Exum's defense was a real head-scratcher: he insisted that the *Washington Post* book editors had to know that he had been part of the assessment team because it had been covered, well, on the front page of the *Post* itself. The burden, he was saying, was on the *Post* to police all of that, though they pointed out that their contract calls for writers to police themselves for even the appearance of conflict of interest. This could have been a rookie error: Exum is young and perhaps was unaware that newspaper departments don't always know every detail of reporting in other departments, even if it's on the front page.[57]

Exum, as we have seen, is far from alone. When quizzed about conflict of interest, many powerful players insist that unless you have the goods to back up a conflict-of-interest question, you shouldn't even float it. They use this all-purpose line: good intentions, as perceived by the players themselves, trump everything and should inoculate them from inquiry.

The fact remains that for those inside the bubble, developing near or outright friendships with the people they cover, good faith deserves to be questioned. Often we are unaware of how much our conflicts dictate our judgment. As journalist Hodge astutely observes:[58]

> This is how the Beltway consensus is built: not through some crude pay-for-play but through the subtle reinforcement of conventional

wisdom. If the experience of Iraq taught us anything, though, it's that reporters need to maintain an adversarial relationship with the people who are helping to craft policy.

The journalistic gloves didn't really come off on the COINdinistas until Petraeus's affair of the heart was revealed, which happened after a groundswell of criticism in Washington military and policy circles holding that COIN was failing in Afghanistan. Media outlets began to see that the true seduction had been of the media itself: according to *Boston Globe* columnist Joan Vennochi,[59]

> [The media are in] deep mourning over the passing of Petraeus from fawned-over military genius to disgraced ex-CIA director. As they dish the latest Petraeus dirt, TV anchors and commentators shake their heads sadly over the affair that brought down the man who always answered their e-mail.

The New Yorker's Jon Lee Anderson: "He was an exceptional military officer, and he helped steer a turnaround in what had been a hopeless, bloody mess of a war in Iraq. But his lionization by admiring and opportunistic politicians and fawning journalists and biographers—such as Paula Broadwell, the woman he was involved with—has been craven and boundless."[60]

What warrants our attention is not the sensation of the Petraeus-Broadwell saga, but the blooming of a much more complex beast—in this case, the think–tank–industry–government–media nexus. These institutions have undergone seismic changes, with porous and blurred boundaries. The constellation they form is largely beyond our accountability.

The nexus is clearly alive and well. Soon after Petraeus's outing, the COINdinistas recognized that even if COIN might have "worked" in Iraq, budget realities were not going to support the expensive vision of decades of engagement in Afghanistan.[61] As they look for the next hot issues, the players continue to amass and reward the best and brightest among young thinkers in defense and related areas.[62]

—⁂—

CNAS does not appear to be part of a broader network of like-minded organizations, but that was not the case for the Republican defense establishment that preceded it.

Beginning in the 1980s, proponents of the "Star Wars" Strategic Defense Initiative set up or mobilized several pressure organizations to influence the opinion of decisionmakers, helping to keep missile defense alive after the end of the Cold War. And think tanks, along with so-called "letterhead organizations," helped buttress the dozen or so players I call the Neocon Core, who helped push the U.S. to war in Iraq in 2003.[63]

The Neocon Core used a web of interlocking memberships in these think tanks to help generate buzz and give the veneer of scholarly disinterest and neutrality to policy pronouncements that in reality were serving the ideological interests of the players agitating for war.[64] And it went farther than that. Their experts, true neoconservative believers affiliated with their think tanks, were brought in to populate secret offices in the Pentagon. These offices were set up to supplant the government's intelligence-gathering and analysis with their own version of the Iraq threat, a version that served the neoconservative goal of invading Iraq, but was at odds with much other intelligence gathered and did not reflect the facts on the ground.[65]

Next we'll look at how social networks that surge and coalesce around think tanks amid a governing and policy vacuum—the ruins of communism—can wield influence beyond accountability, for better as well as for worse.

ERSATZ GOVERNING?

The supreme case involves George Soros, the Hungarian-American billionaire, hedge-fund magnate, and global philanthropist. Having headed the most successful hedge fund in history for thirty years until 2000, Soros embodies "almost mythical status as a market player, influencer, and commentator," as Paul Stubbs, a sociologist long based in Zagreb, Croatia, who has seen Soros's operations up close, puts it.[66] Through his web of Open Society Institutes and Foundations, beginning in the early 1990s, Soros has supported an important and unusual series of entities, first in Central and Eastern Europe, and later with near global reach.

And while most of them are not, strictly speaking, think tanks, some have served as a springboard for elite networks—sometimes shadow elites—to make policy and to set up organizations explicitly called think tanks. Toward that end, in recent years, Soros created a Think Tank Fund that provides institutional backing to certain think tanks and supports specific programs.[67]

Soros's projects have contributed immeasurably to the region—from fostering intellectual capital to specific programs benefiting thousands of people. Still, the Soros Empire, as it has been called, provides a case study in how politics (and society) can be fashioned, and even de facto governing accomplished, through entities whose MO and networks exhibit informality, flexibility, and ad-hoc-ery—offering up certain challenges to accountability.

Stubbs, upon whose research and writing this section is drawn, casts a critical eye on the enterprise, as do several other scholar-observers here referenced.[68] And I, myself, encountered Soros-originated institutes and foundations through my many years based in Poland and my studies of foreign aid to Central and Eastern Europe.

First, some background. Soros ventured into philanthropy beginning in the late 1970s. His initial substantial commitment was to back dissident groups in communist Eastern Europe during the 1980s. He helped bankroll the NGO Helsinki Watch (later Human Rights Watch) and also funded projects such as universities' purchase of photocopy machines so they could circulate literature outside state control.[69] When the Berlin Wall fell, Soros launched the Open Society Institute (OSI), with offices in both New York and Budapest. In 1993, national Open Society Foundations were set up in most post-communist countries of Central and Eastern Europe, and in the former Soviet Union soon afterwards.

Soros's broad vision was "to promote open societies by shaping national and international policies with knowledge and expertise," as political scientist Diane Stone has written.[70] (The "open society" concept comes from the philosopher Karl Popper, his onetime professor.) His foundations and their networks have sought to advance progressive social agendas—promoting democracy, human rights, and civil society—with initiatives ranging from supporting independent media to the rights of women, gays, and Roma.

But what, exactly, is the Soros Empire?[71] It is neither fish nor fowl, exhibiting some of the characteristics usually associated with transnational expertized networks, global public-policy networks, transnational advocacy networks, and international knowledge networks, as Stone, who was affiliated with a Hungarian Soros-sponsored university and has investigated policy networks and philanthropy, has written.[72]

In this blurred space, Soros entities are marked by flexible identities, fuzzy boundaries, and insider-ism. Soros, seen by some critics as "far too pragmatic to care about details," as observer Călin Dan put it, has consistently relied on an inner circle of trusted advisers to identify key individuals in each country.[73] And these individuals, supplied by Soros with money, office space, and practical help, have been afforded "considerable autonomy" to set up shop in their countries, as Stubbs writes. He notes that,[74]

> in an essay on the role of the Foundation in Croatia, Slavica Singer, a founding Board Member, is quoted as suggesting Soros introduced a "jazz-structure" mode of function, based on considerable local improvisation, allowing the Foundation to escape from bureaucratization and work effectively in a rapidly changing environment.

Soros's overarching goal was to bolster the creation of a new policy elite opposed to both communism and nationalism. His distrust of bureaucracy and formal procedures, and his endorsement of risk-taking, have meant that innovative and experimental programs could be quickly implemented. "Nothing is settled in his environment," says Dan, such that "his change of initiatives can be seen as part of a general strategy which uses chaotic motion in order to reach creative solutions."[75]

This MO, employed in an environment of those already practiced in bureaucratic workarounds, has spawned perhaps the ultimate informality. Sociologist Kim Lane Scheppele, who, like Stone, worked for a Hungarian Soros-sponsored university, observes that "Things change suddenly, without warning, and everyone simply has to adjust."[76]

It is no secret that Soros institutes and foundations in a given country are almost always associated with a particular elite network that has its fingers in many pies (politics, business, intellectual pursuits, philanthropy)—a network usually well known locally and for which people might even have a nickname. And it is no secret, as Stubbs puts it, that the influence of the network is "compounded by the ample resources available to foundations, compared, for example, to public universities and even some governments." "In some countries," he writes,[77]

> such as Serbia under Milošević, the Open Society Institute elite was, in many respects, a state elite in waiting. In other countries, certain charismatic individuals used their Soros role to enact a kind of anti-political politics.

Such network-based, and often exclusive, operations have faced criticism, even as some of their projects succeed in genuine outreach. Stubbs assesses, for instance, that while purporting to promote democracy and progressive causes and while trumpeting expertise and professionalism, the network is, "above all, highly elitist" and often appears "to favor people whose connections outstrip their qualifications."[78] Scheppele adds: "The network operates in a more imperial fashion, without democratic processes or the security of expectations that the rule of law brings for those who actually work there."[79]

What do these informal, ad-hoc operations of chosen elites produce? Stubbs describes[80]

> . . . a generation of emerging flexians working in and expanding fluid, and unaccountable, spaces of power. Despite these flexians' roles in advocating for democracy, human rights and civil society in transitional settings, . . . the forms in which these advocacy initiatives are expressed may serve to erode the very developments they purport to promote. Above all, their emphasis on informal relationships, interpersonal connections, and network power reinforces and reproduces, albeit in a completely different context, a communist legacy in which "who"

one knows is more important than "what" one knows. The players created by these cash-flush operations could hardly be more relevant when it comes to influencing and even governing.

Some of these elite players form think tanks and some of these organizations appear to operate not so very differently from new-style think tanks elsewhere. As Stubbs told me:[81]

> The very idea that there was something else—a fourth form (not state, government, or civil society but think tanks)—was introduced into the region by Soros in the late 1990s/early 2000s. This coincided with the need to go beyond the big picture, the grand narrative of social change, and Soros's turn to the nuts and bolts of policy. This move gave the Soros elite another "in"—and means of having an impact in unaccountable ways.

Stubbs, who has observed the think-tank scene up close in Croatia, cites the case of the Croatia Legal Centre. "Its Soros elite worked very closely with the government," he says, "but was not directly part of it. Policy creation was outsourced, blurring the boundaries between where government begins and ends."[82]

In short, the Soros network has helped forge new spaces of governing where informality and the primacy of the network trump democratic process. And even when good works are done and we support the people or particular policies pursued, the fact is that there's little room in such spaces for accountability to the public.

Next, we'll look at another model of influencing with think tanks as the focal point: networks of entities set up by like-minded, ideologically driven networks of players. These think tanks focus on issues ranging from climate change to spreading free-market ideology.

LAUNDERING INFLUENCE FOR A CAUSE

Climate-change deniers have brought organizing around their agenda to a high art. A report by the environmental activist organization Greenpeace describes a "secret plan" forged in 1998:[83]

[A] small group sat down together at the American Petroleum Institute . . . to draw up a communications plan to challenge climate science. The group included representatives from Exxon, Chevron, [coal burner] Southern Company . . . and people from a number of the front groups and conservative think tanks that are still campaigning against climate science today, including the George C. Marshall Institute, Frontiers of Freedom, The Advancement of Sound Science Coalition and the Committee for a Constructive Tomorrow. . . . The plan they drew up proposed: "a national media relations program to inform the media about uncertainties in climate science; to generate national, regional and local media on the scientific uncertainties and thereby educate and inform the public, stimulating them to raise questions with policymakers."

Since then, scholars and reporters have been trying to understand these organizations and their sponsors. It isn't easy. What we do know is that the "Merchants of Doubt"—so-called contrarian scientists and their allies, as historians of science Naomi Oreskes and Erik Conway call them (also the title of their 2010 book)—have built "informal networks of action and influence, based heavily on personal contacts" and driven by ideology. These influencers exert their power across a wide range of life-and-death debates over science and public-health policy, everything from tobacco and acid rain to the ozone hole, DDT, and, especially important in recent years, global warming. "Contrarian" scientists Frederick Seitz, William Nierenberg, and Robert Jastrow co-founded the George C. Marshall Institute, which the watchdog group Source Watch describes as a "non-profit" powered by oil and gas money. This "think tank" coordinates with more established ones that share their views to undermine research findings that they see as overly alarmist. Of course, they promote not only their own ideological bias but also the interests of their energy-industry patrons.[84]

The climate-denialist movement is a vast one, but we will confine ourselves here to think-tank involvement. Media Matters, a nonprofit information and research center, has a useful compilation of their activities:[85]

- On the Manhattan Institute: "Media outlets have turned to the Manhattan Institute's Robert Bryce at least 39 times this year to comment on energy issues without disclosing that the Manhattan Institute is partly funded by oil interests."[86]
- On the Heritage Foundation: It maintains a database with a staggering number of "experts" that busy reporters could call on— not necessarily scientists by any means—apparently willing and able to talk about climate change.[87]
- On the Cato Institute: Patrick Michaels, an actual climate scientist, a contrarian, puts out an op-ed at least once a month for outlets such as *Forbes*, the *Washington Times*, the *National Review*, and others.[88]
- On the Heartland Institute: It holds an annual conference for denialists and features lawyer James Taylor, who has appeared on Fox News and in *Forbes*.[89]
- On the American Enterprise Institute: Media Matters flags a 2007 report from the *Guardian* showing that AEI was offering scientists and economists $10,000 and travel expenses to sow doubt in a big climate-change report from the Intergovernmental Panel on Climate Change issued that year.[90]

Denialist books spiked in 2007, speculate environmental sociologist Riley Dunlap and political scientist Peter Jacques, because of both the release of that report and the Al Gore documentary *An Inconvenient Truth*. They maintain that many of these books originated in some pivotal way from these allied think tanks and point out why books carry influence well beyond the actual reader:[91]

> [The authors] are interviewed on TV and radio, quoted by newspaper columnists and cited by sympathetic politicians and corporate figures. Their books are frequently carried by major bookstore chains, where they are seen (even if not purchased) by a wide segment of the public, [and] many receive enormous publicity on [conservative think-tank] websites and from conservative and skeptical bloggers.

Dunlap and Jacques studied the credentials and provenance of more than a hundred climate-denial books and found that seventy-two percent had a "verifiable link" to a think tank; at least ninety percent had no peer review in the conventional academic sense; and fewer than forty percent were written or edited by people with relevant scientific credentials. This "allow[ed] authors or editors to recycle scientifically unfounded claims that are then amplified by the conservative movement, media, and political elites."[92]

These think tanks have helped create what the scholars call an "alternate academia," and it's one that has become more vast and harder to trace, as DIY amateurs have gotten involved as well. Interestingly, they suggest that the involvement of a few real scientists drew out a "wide range" of those writing about a subject for which they had little or no credibility. Many of these armchair "climatologists" have expounded in their own self-published books. (Of course, self-publishing has also become more acceptable in recent years.)

Have such think tanks and the coordinated strategies of climate-change deniers had the impact they desired? They appear to be at least one factor in swaying public opinion (though this would be difficult, if not impossible, to prove definitively). Gallup polls show that the number of Americans who thought the risk of global warming was exaggerated stood at around 34 percent in 2006. By 2010? Some 48 percent. Over the past four years, that number has come down to a still-high 42 percent.[93]

Dunlap and Jacques also note the "diffusion" of think-tank–powered denialism crossing borders: "vigorous denial campaigns have developed in the United Kingdom, Canada, and Australia, and to a lesser degree in a number of other nations."[94]

If you think it's hard to figure out the credentials of those discussing climate change, just try figuring out how to account for the enterprises' funding.

A 2013 study by professor of sociology and environmental science Robert Brulle found that ninety-one climate-denial organizations took in nearly $900 million, but only $64 million came from "identifiable foundation support." He notes "evidence of a trend toward concealing the sources of . . . funding through the use of donor-directed philanthropies." The climate-change–denial agenda is being hyped through a range of organizations—conservative foundations and think tanks, trade associations, and advocacy groups with robust ties to friendly politicians and media outlets—that often obscure the source and sponsorship of the "information."[95]

A modus operandi similar to the climate deniers can be found at the Atlas Economic Research Foundation, which has been described as "the Johnny Appleseed of anti-regulation groups."[96] Its focus is germinating "free-market" think tanks outside the United States. Sociologist Karin Fischer and political scientist Dieter Plehwe studied the Atlas network, which has aimed to stem a so-called "Pink Tide" of populism, or socialism, from pushing across Latin America:[97]

> Over time, the Atlas Economic Research Foundation has become a central node in the transmission of funds, personnel and other resources in the transnational flow of neoliberal ideas and policies. . . . Membership of the Atlas network has been growing fast since the 1980s. The Atlas global directory currently comprises of [sic] 448 institutions worldwide. It is most important to realize that the various think tanks listed are not stand alone operations. Due to the embeddedness of each of the organizations in a comprehensive network, the total is larger than the sum of the individual parts.

Alejandro Chafuen, who describes himself as covering "think tanks, scholars and champions of innovation," quotes these same scholars in a blog posting for *Forbes*. Titled "Think Tanks and the Power of Networks," his posting champions the effectiveness of Atlas and other such think-tank networks in reaching their goals. Only by clicking on his full bio does the reader learn that he has been "president of Atlas Economic Research Foundation since 1991."[98]

So much for full disclosure and accountability.

—⚹—

What should we make of the new species of think tanks? While the new-style think tank, like the old, draws on a neutral, scholarly imprimatur, it marches to a different drummer than in the past. Enmeshed in the think–tank-industry-government-media nexus, these outfits push the boundaries to the limit and accountability, too, in the process.

In the next chapter, we look at the world of academic institutions, which play perhaps even more impressively on that supposed scholarly neutrality—and further challenge accountability.

CHAPTER 8

Professors, Physicians, and Prestige for Hire

We, the public, may have little faith left in formal institutions, but in prestige we still have some trust, even as what that social marker comprises may change. High-prestige institutions of higher learning still command respect and accrete prestige to those affiliated with them. And, like the new-style think tanks we saw in the last chapter, so the hallowed halls of academe, under many of the same pressures and sea changes, have bred new-style entities and messengers. And, like the new-style think tanks, it is the image of the impartial, incorruptible scholar or researcher that is bought and sold and that enables that scholar or researcher—who may be anything but impartial—to be so effective. In this chapter, we see again how fuzzy boundaries, titles, and definitions enable deniability; make it difficult to get to the bottom of who is behind what; and challenge accountability.

First we'll look at professors in the political and social sciences for whom the label "shadow lobbyist" would better characterize some of their activities; their efforts have been solicited and crafted by a consulting firm. Next we'll look at the High Priests—specifically, economics and finance professors—who, using their "we-are-the-experts" mantra to exclude others and shield themselves, employ their most prestigious roles (read: named professorships) to persuade the public, all the while masking their agendas and roles in the financial arena. These trailblazers, incidentally, were the first to show me how shadow elites and shadow lobbyists operate. Then we'll check out so-called Key Opinion Leaders, high-status physicians or researchers in the medical/healthcare arena. Finally we'll turn to academic institutions themselves, which, increasingly reliant on titans of industry for funding, dress up corporate and billionaires' goals with a scholarly blessing.

None of this bodes well for accountability. Instead, it bodes ill, because the scholars' activities are light years more effective—and insidious—than the antics of any celebrity, as we shall see. And it especially bodes ill because we scarcely even know it's going on.

PRESTIGE PROFESSORS, SHADOW LOBBYING?

Have former basketball star Dennis Rodman's visits to North Korea convinced us that Kim Jong Un, of mass starvation, concentration camp, and execution fame, is reforming? Or that he is somehow becoming a good guy?[1] I don't think so. We may not be persuaded by the likes of Rodman, but we are routinely swayed by the writings and appearances of certain elite academics who participate, either actively or unwittingly, in "reputational laundering" on behalf of unsavory regimes. And while Rodman's "basketball diplomacy" has been subject to intense media scrutiny, not so these academics, who, trading on their prestige, air their favorable assessments of the regimes' progress, without also airing that they receive pay or perks from them, albeit indirectly.

Without paying much attention, I—like many others, no doubt—developed during the mid-2000s a somewhat more favorable image of Libyan dictator Muammar Gaddafi's regime. Unbeknownst to me or the public at the time, this was most likely the result of a campaign by a Cambridge, Massachusetts–based consulting firm, Monitor Group. The firm contracted with the Libyan regime between 2006 and 2008 and engineered a sweeping effort to influence public opinion regarding Gaddafi's Libya.[2]

Using illustrious academics, public intellectuals from both sides of the Atlantic, and former government officials, the campaign burnished the leader's image. Monitor, however, was not registered as a lobbyist for Libya, as any American organization lobbying on behalf of a foreign government is required to do.[3] For this non-lobbying, Monitor commanded a retainer of three quarters of a million dollars per quarter.[4]

The Monitor Group—now Monitor Deloitte after its purchase by Deloitte in 2012—from its inception has capitalized on its proximity and connections to the world's most prestigious university. The firm was founded in 1983 by a handful of entrepreneurs connected to Harvard Business School, including one of its best-known professors, Michael Porter.[5] The *Boston Globe* describes young HBS graduates eager to capitalize on "both Porter's reputation and the Harvard 'brand'" at a time that branding wasn't yet *au courant*. Like the other new-style entities we've described throughout this book, Monitor seemed to avoid clear definitions, titles, and boundaries.[6] A couple of those in control boasted that the firm was "less formal" and had "very little structural hierarchy."[7] And it was so secretive about its clients that even many within it didn't know who all the clients were. As one 2001 profile of the company states,[8]

> Even in the buttoned-down world of consulting, Monitor Group is notable for eschewing the traditional corporate stratification. Instead of having a cadre of vice presidents and corporate spokespeople, Monitor defines people in a different way. In addition to having "thought leaders" in its continuing education division, Monitor University, the group also employs a "chief knowledge officer," who works in marketing. . . . [Monitor] has such a hyper-confidentiality policy about not identifying clients that their names are not even mentioned in-house. Instead, Monitor consultants use acronyms when discussing clients so that others within the firm cannot figure out who the client is.

That secrecy and lack of definition seem to have provided some convenient cover when, in 2009, news trickled out through documents obtained by a Libyan opposition group detailing Monitor's lucrative contract with the ruling regime.[9] But it wasn't until 2011, when Gaddafi began violently quelling the Libyan uprising, that anyone took much notice.

The documents show that Monitor sent hand-picked "thought leaders" to Libya to lend its client prestige. They also show that even though its elaborate plan looked, at best, like high-class whitewashing, and at worst, like straight-up lobbying, Monitor eschewed the label of "lobbying organization."[10] Indeed, the title of one of Monitor's status reports makes it clear that the trips to Libya were part of a "Project to Enhance the Profile of Libya and Muammar Qadhafi." To further this mission, the firm promised to[11]

> . . . provide operational support for publication of positive articles on Libya in these publications. For example: *Wall Street Journal, New York Times, Washington Post, Economist, International Herald Tribune, Financial Times, Weekly Standard, National Interest, Public Interest, Foreign Affairs*, etc.

Such articles required authoritative authors. Monitor, according to a self-described "action plan," aimed to[12]

> . . . identify relevant policy-makers and influencers, politicians (both Democratic and Republican), government officials, thought-leaders and academics and journalists. These individuals will be of the highest caliber in their respective professions and circle of influence.

Monitor was evidently successful in its efforts. The public intellectuals it enlisted included former Harvard Kennedy School dean Joseph Nye; political scientist Robert Putnam, best known for his book *Bowling Alone*; Princeton historian Bernard Lewis; famed *End of History* author Francis Fukuyama; political theorist and democracy advocate Benjamin Barber; and MIT Media Lab director Nicholas Negroponte, among others.[13]

Gaddafi's reputation benefited from the credibility the academics brought with them, the articles about their visits some of them wrote upon returning from Libya, and debriefings allegedly given to U.S. government officials.

Bernard Lewis is promoted in Monitor's documents as having access to the "entire" Israeli embassy; Negroponte is valued in part because his brother, John Negroponte, was then Deputy Secretary of State.[14]

Joseph Nye wrote an article in the *New Republic* about meeting Gaddafi and the possibility that he might be evolving into a more enlightened leader; the article does not say Nye was paid a fee by Monitor Group.[15] Princeton professor Andrew Moravcsik penned a piece for *Newsweek* called "A Rogue Reforms," with no mention of Monitor.[16] Benjamin Barber wrote a similar piece in the *Washington Post*, also with no disclosure.[17] The documents boast that Barber "writes frequently for *Harper's Magazine, The New York Times, The Washington Post, The Atlantic*, and many other scholarly and popular publications[.]"

Not all were academics. I can't say I was surprised to see Richard Perle's name in the documents. A former assistant secretary of defense under President Ronald Reagan, Perle has long surfaced at the epicenter of a head-spinning array of business deals, consulting roles, and neoconservative ideological initiatives, consistently courting and yet skirting charges of conflict of interest. Perle's name alone is his calling card: he had unimpeded access to the highest levels of power in the Bush White House. The documents state that he "made two visits to Libya (22-24 March and 23-25 July 2006) and met with Gaddafy on both occasions. He briefed Vice President Dick Cheney on his visits to Libya."[18]

The British sociologist Anthony Giddens, a well-known public intellectual, also visited Libya twice and published an article following each visit, making no mention of the Monitor Group. In the second piece, in the *Guardian*, Giddens asks whether "real progress [is] possible only when Gaddafy leaves the scene? I tend to think the opposite. If he is sincere in wanting change, as I think he is, he could play a role in muting conflict that might otherwise arise as modernisation takes hold."[19]

The Monitor case illustrates how the reputation of the impartial scholar can be leveraged for possibly less-than-reputable purposes. But it also shows something more. When accused of being involved in an unseemly practice, academics can also quite plausibly insist that they had a genuine interest in scholarship or improving international relations or the betterment of society. Indeed, as I and many other academics do when abroad, many of them delivered public lectures during their trips. I, myself, might find the offer of a trip to Libya enticing (I'm an anthropologist, after all). Still, it would seem wise to think seriously about how one's credibility might be used when being *hosted* by a leader like Gaddafi and paid by a consulting firm tasked with doing it's-not-clear-what for such a regime.

Backtracking?

And yet the case is laced with ambiguity. When these academics were forced to explain their involvement in the PR program (and not all did), it wasn't entirely clear what the Monitor Group had told its "thought leaders," or even that all of them were compensated. Nicholas Negroponte, for instance, says he wasn't paid a consulting fee or travel expenses, and "proudly" viewed his visit as an academic, diplomatic, and humanitarian opportunity.[20] Joseph Nye said he was paid, but also viewed the trip as enriching his academic research. His *New Republic* article wasn't explicit about that fee; in responding to criticism, Nye said that editors had revised the second sentence of his disclosure. The original read:[21]

> I was in Libya at the invitation of a former Harvard colleague who works for the Monitor Group, a consulting company which has undertaken to help Libya open itself to the global economy. Part of that process is meeting with a variety of Western experts whom Monitor hires as consultants.

Even if the second sentence had been published as written, it's not at all clear that readers would grasp that Monitor had paid Nye. Also note the way he presents Monitor's agenda, as helping "Libya open itself," which, of course, sounds better than "rehabilitating the reputation of a notoriously violent dictator."

And surely this may have been how Monitor sold the academics on its project: when the firm put out a statement, it insisted that it had lofty goals, such as trying to help Libya in ". . . accelerating modernization and increased openness. . . ."[22]

Benjamin Barber also came out swinging in his own defense and (presumably unintentionally) offers some credence to critics of freelancing intellectuals. In one interview with *Foreign Policy*, he ponders the "old question that goes back to Machiavelli" of whether thinkers should engage with power: "My answer is that each person has to make their own decision."[23] In another defense to *The Nation*, he insisted that he was genuinely interested in fostering democracy in Libya and was never swayed by money, or told to write anything at Monitor's urging, adding: ". . . it is not who pays you that is important, but whether they are paying you to do what you do, or you are doing what they want you to do because they are paying you."[24] Barber also suggests that if you have a longtime reputation for integrity, you should be trusted to regulate yourself.

Barber indeed has a point. The shadow-elite age of representational juggling and focus on performance is also an age of ambiguous ethics. People who try to take action, even—perhaps especially—positive action across venues, find themselves making judgments (and, often, uneasy compromises) amid an ethical minefield. I know more than one of the scholars named above and do not believe they are bad people. Still, on the face of it, this sort of activity raises questions. And while self-regulation is essential, is that the only answer? Should not one's peer group and outside community (the public, that is) be concerned? After all, we are the consumers of such seemingly independent assessments by big-name scholars.

If the various "thought leaders" believed they were engaged in something wholesome, it's worth noting that at least one wasn't fooled. Danielle Pletka of the American Enterprise Institute was invited, and declined. Her reasoning:[25]

> I did not have any desire to aid and abet Gaddafi's P.R. effort. It was clear that was what was intended—the person from the Monitor Group spent quite a lot of time on the phone telling me all about how Libya had changed for the better and how they wanted the world to see them. That's P.R. in my book.

Robert Putnam, who met with Gaddafi, says that he declined a second trip, saying "by then I had concluded that the whole exercise was a public-relations stunt."[26]

The fact remains that top intellectuals found it necessary to engage in rhetorical jujitsu to explain their (perhaps inadvertent) role in a propaganda program. They expressed very little regret, not to mention shame. And yet is it not their professional obligation as analysts of politics and society to suss out the settings in which they choose to operate and anticipate the consequences of their actions? Meanwhile we, the consumers of media, were misled by their actions. Was our trust not violated?

And yet the activities of these academics can hardly compare to some of the compromised practices that have been taken to an art form by the High Priests of economics and finance.

HIGH PRIESTS, SHADOW LOBBYING

While the opportunities for, say, historians and political scientists to make money outside the academy are comparatively rare, the same cannot be said for those whose expertise is in economics or finance. For some time, these scholars have plied their trade outside academe as consultants with, say, the International Monetary Fund, or as experts testifying before governmental and policy bodies, such as parliamentary or U.S. congressional committees. At the high end, they have taken up stints in key public or governmental bodies like central banks (such as the Federal Reserve Board) and treasury departments, or with entities like the National Bureau of Economic Research (a prestigious outfit with which many American Nobel laureates in economics have been affiliated) or in leadership positions in academic associations and on editorial boards of journals.

But today, in our age of proliferating roles, representational juggling, and the prestige of big bucks, these High Priests also lend their services to companies and consulting firms.

At the same time, with greater effect than in the past due to the sea changes in the media (described in Chapter 5), these luminaries can help shape public opinion as never before through their op-ed pieces, TV and radio appearances, and public testimony. They interpret for us, the laity, what is happening in that impenetrably technical world of economics/finance, banking on our inability to understand without their help. And yet, while performing in their capacity as professors and prized experts, they can champion a particular policy or industry in the media or in testimony, without divulging that the policy benefits the industry for which they consult.

That is by no means all. While serving in key governmental and public roles, the High Priests act as gatekeepers for what information gets released to the public, who within their ranks gets promoted, what ideas get aired, and whose wisdom is the received of the day. We, the public, again are left to wonder whether they are proffering opinions gleaned from impartial research that are in the public's interest, or rather those that might serve their own.

Sadly for us, as these players—notably, many at the high end of their discipline—traverse university, disciplinary, governmental and public, corporate, and media roles, many become shadow-elite or shadow-lobbyist exemplars, serving the interests of their fellows and firms before ours.

Back in early 2011, a reader commented on the website of the *New York Times*, responding to an article on whether economists needed a code of ethics: "An ethical code for economists? That's a bit like adopting a chastity vow at the Bunny Ranch."[27]

This comment is striking, and not just because it manages to put "economists" and "Bunny Ranch" in the same sentence: it shows the stark disillusionment many were feeling toward some in the profession who had presented themselves as impartial when dispensing economic advice, even when they may well have a personal interest at stake.

In the wake of the 2008 financial meltdown, academic economists are still called upon to expound on financial reform. Some top economists continue to pronounce on the economy and how to fix it, completely white-washing their roles in screwing it up in the first place.

In 2010, Reuters examined nearly one hundred testimonies, mostly involving financial regulation, delivered by academics to the House Financial Services Committee and the Senate Banking Committee from late 2008 through early 2010. Among those they tracked who appeared before Congress while the most sweeping changes in financial regulation since the Great Depression were being debated:[28]

- A Harvard law school professor who doesn't mention his role on the board of a Wall Street firm.

- A professor of economics at Ohio State University who mentioned three affiliations, all ones that bolster his image as impartial scholar, but not the four financial-firm board directorships.
- A professor of finance at Louisiana State University. He described himself as the "Louisiana Bankers' Association professor of finance," but didn't mention his directorship at an economic consulting firm.
- A University of Pennsylvania Wharton Business School professor of real estate, who didn't mention consulting work for a real estate giant and GE Financial.
- A University of Chicago Booth School of Business professor who discloses that he is a consultant for a big bank trade association, but only in a footnote in his written remarks.

These professors are far from alone.

A few months before the Reuters report, Gerald Epstein and Jessica Carrick-Hagenbarth of the University of Massachusetts–Amherst released their study of the professional activities—outside the university—of academic economists. (While many economists work for financial firms, including those who helped devise the many faulty models we discussed earlier in these pages that measure risk, and they have been the subject of some criticism, much less has been aimed at the activities of academic economists who primarily identify as professors.[29]) Epstein and Carrick-Hagenbarth examined the activities of nineteen mostly "prestigious academic financial economists"[30] who were linked to both public and international institutions and who belonged to two groups that "put forth proposals on financial reform."[31] They investigated the economists' connections to both public and private financial institutions. Some not only consult for, or serve on, the boards of these private firms; they own or co-own them. The report declined to name their names because there are so many others like them, and the authors felt it would be unfair.

What the scholars found was not exactly surprising. Out of these nineteen prominent economists—all of whom gave "expert" advice to the media and public about financial reform—the "vast majority of the time, [they] did not identify [financial] affiliations and possible conflicts of interest." This was also true when the economists published their work in academic journals.[32] For elite economists, agility in affiliations may be the norm, not the exception. In addition to an academic post, having some attachment to a big public body like the IMF, the World Bank, or a Federal Reserve Bank can garner them prestige and benefits. An association with a private firm may bring additional standing, not to mention money.[33]

> [The accompanying table] depicts the evident flexibility of moving from academic to public to private sector work for these elite economists. . . . The fact that well over half the economists we evaluated have positions with private financial firms shows how commonplace it is. . . . It is plain that the purely academic financial economist in our survey is a rare species indeed.

A Code of Ethics?

Epstein and Carrick-Hagenbarth lay some blame on journalists for not asking about or investigating possible conflicts. But they emphasize that it's the economists themselves who really need a code of ethics.[34]

> . . . economists should disclose relevant sources of financial support and relevant personal or professional relationships that may have the appearance or potential for a conflict of interest in public speeches and writing, as well as in academic publications. . . . First, some may argue that this code would be redundant since many academic economists are already working under a . . . policy as put forth by their respective universities. But these codes primarily proscribe conduct that would conflict with the interests of their universities and do not address potential conflicts with respect to the broader public or government. Moreover, many economists are not academic economists and they too should be held to uniform standards of professional conduct.
>
> Second, some economists may believe that listing their paid positions on their CVs and/or biographies constitutes a sufficient act of disclosure. However, we do not think this

is sufficient disclosure. Our proposed code would require economists to disclose all relevant potential conflicts of interest in all relevant situations, particularly in academic articles, general media pieces, speeches and testimonies.

It's interesting to note that while other fields of practice, such as medicine and law (but also journalism, engineering, and accounting, along with other academic disciplines such as anthropology and sociology), have long had codes of ethics, not so economics.[35]

What happened to the proposed code of ethics? While some seventeen thousand economists belong to the American Economic Association (AEA), the code attracted fewer than three hundred signatories.

Nonetheless, the UMass-Amherst scholars' work, the Reuters investigation, and the documentary *Inside Job*, which exposed freelancing academic economists-for-hire, all came out around the same time. When *Inside Job* won the Oscar in 2011, this brought a renewed burst of outrage and exposure to the problem.

The AEA was persuaded to act. New rules were adopted in 2012 requiring its members to disclose potential conflicts of interest in the AEA's journals, including any "close relative or partner" of the author. An author who has received at least $10,000 from any "interested" party must be identified, defined as anyone with "financial, ideological, or political stake" related to the article. Paid or unpaid roles with corporations or nonprofits are also to be disclosed.[36]

As for public speech, like op-eds, TV appearances, or government testimony, the AEA merely "urges" the same disclosure.[37] The AEA code also does not cover the array of academics found in business schools, including the ones mentioned above such as a professor of finance or a professor of real estate. The general reader might have heard that economists had adopted a new code, but few will appreciate the difference between a finance professor and an economics professor.

And, as the *New York Times* found in 2013, those kinds of academics are still spinning, this time on behalf of those who didn't want the government to put curbs on speculators in the commodity business, and who deny that speculators are driving up consumer prices.[38]

[I]nterviews with dozens of academics and traders, and a review of hundreds of emails and other documents involving two highly visible professors in the commodities field . . . show how major players on Wall Street and elsewhere have been aggressive in underwriting and promoting academic work.

When questioned by a reader of his blog whether he was objective, the *Times* reports, one of the academics responded, "Uhm, no, dipstick."[39]

It's interesting that this professor responds contemptuously to a patently fair question. In his case, he directs a management institute at his school that has received money from companies involved in speculation. His defense is that he would have believed in speculation regardless of the money, as if the idea that money can incentivize behavior is an absurd one. Consider the irony that this denial of money-based motivation is coming from a *professor of finance.*

A small dose of public shaming—finally—got some reaction in the form of a code of ethics for economists. But the money and status from outside activities are so desirable and the patterns are so well entrenched that it remains to be seen if the new code will have an effect.

Epstein says it will take "five years or so" to know if the code will help "set norms of behavior that colleagues, the press, students and citizens can help hold economists to account."[40]

Indeed, new, *practiced* standards of conduct are needed.

KOLS, SHADOW LOBBYING

The loss of faith in formal institutions is even more immediate to us, the public, when it comes to medicine and our own health care. When we go to a physician, we expect that professional to offer impartial advice and to act in our best interest. Our physicians, too, no doubt subscribe to the Hippocratic Oath and believe they are doing well by us. But some of our faith may be overblown. It turns out that some of their professional opinions may be influenced, often unbeknownst to them, by members of their professional community who the pharmaceutical and medical device industries call Key Opinion Leaders, or KOLs.[41] Typically these experts are high-status physicians or medical researchers who sport impressive credentials and are affiliated with top medical schools, journals, and professional associations.

KOLs are paid or perked for their trouble: they often garner more in consulting fees from the industry than from their academic institutions;[42] they can attract honoraria for travel and speaking fees.[43] And yet it is their image as neutral, incorruptible scientists that lends them weight.[44] The job of these opinion leaders is to convince their fellow professionals that a particular company's product is the most efficacious.[45] They are chosen for their authority among their peers and effectiveness in disseminating the message to their community. "The KOL is a combination of celebrity spokesperson, neighborhood gossip, and the popular kid in high school," observes Carl Elliott, a professor at the Center for Bioethics at the University of Minnesota who wrote a book on the subject.[46]

And comes straight from the shadow-elite playbook: KOLs owe their success in the game in no small measure to flexible identities and fuzzy boundaries. As in the other arenas we've looked into, these qualities are essential to their influence and ability to deny that their industry ties have any bearing on their professional opinions.[47] The academic physician who sits on the editorial board of a major journal or a medical specialty association can act as a gatekeeper for what gets discussed and published in his field, and we have no way of knowing whose interests are being represented. Your physician hears the talk, reads the journal, reviews the literature, all the while listening to the "authority"—that KOL—in a particular field.

KOLs have proliferated since the end of the Cold War, possibly worldwide. Their use is well documented in the United States, the United Kingdom, Central and Eastern Europe, and Latin America.[48] If publication in an industry journal is any indication, their ranks have grown rapidly over the past decade-plus.[49] From 2000 to 2010, "the number of articles in . . . *Pharmaceutical Executive* that mention 'opinion leader' roughly tripled," explains Sergio Sismondo, who studies the intersections of philosophy and sociology of science and has written about these experts.[50] Another indication of the increasing use of KOLs is the rise of new businesses that "recruit, train, and manage" them, Elliott says.[51]

KOLs and the big pharmaceutical and medical-device companies that underwrite them can have an outsized impact, especially in places where the compensation of physicians, researchers, and government officials is much lower than, say, in the United States and Western Europe. Sociologist Piotr Ozierański, who conducted more than two hundred interviews on the subject in Poland, points to the comparatively huge impact of KOL networks coursing through the Ministry of Health and other government entities, parliamentary bodies, medical professional associations, and the media. These opinion leaders managed to get a particular vaccine mandated and paid for by the Ministry of Health—a windfall for the pharmaceutical company that produced it—despite solid scientific evidence that the drug was ineffective.[52]

Framing the Discussion

Wherever they operate, KOLs help define what medical treatments and concerns we should pay attention to. KOLs—typically those focused on research—can frame the very discussion, establishing what issues and opinions are accepted with regard to certain drugs and diseases, says Sismondo.[53] Elliott expounds:[54]

> The reason [KOLs] are so important is their role in managing the discourse around a given product. Equal parts scientific study, commercial hype, and academic buzz, this discourse will begin years before a drug or device is brought onto the market, and will usually continue at least until the patent expires. If a company can manage the discourse effectively, it can establish the desperate need for its drug, spin clinical-trial results to its advantage, downplay the side effects of a drug, neutralize its critics, and play up the drug's off-label uses. . . .[55] Virtually all physicians are on the receiving end of this communication, but only a relatively few deliver it. If the industry can influence those few, then it can also influence the rest.

Researcher KOLs not only sway opinion about the efficacy of a drug to treat a condition; they also influence the very fact of defining that condition as an illness. A case in point is researcher KOLs in the United States working on female sexual dysfunction. According to Sismondo, they[56]

. . . acted as mediators between pharmaceutical companies, the FDA, physicians, and potential consumers.[57] They held industry-sponsored workshops and wrote position papers that solidified female sexual dysfunction as an illness, thereby positioning themselves as the very experts to whom the FDA would turn for advice on drug submissions and to whom the media would turn for interviews and information.

Leading, Under Cover

KOLs often operate as intermediaries between government agencies, the medical community, and the public. In Argentina, multinational drug companies have enlisted opinion leaders to help forge alliances. They participate in seminars and symposia, pen "scientific literature" for circulation, and act "something like a brand spokesman," says anthropologist Andrew Lakoff.[58]

Still, these opinion leaders do not explicitly and openly endorse specific drugs, "at least not in ways that are too obvious," Elliott writes. Their ways are subtle and varied, and their views are disseminated[59]

> . . . sometimes by word of mouth, but more often by quasi-academic activities, such as grand-rounds lectures, sponsored symposia, or articles in medical journals (which may be ghostwritten by hired medical writers).

KOLs can be (unpaid) authors of manuscripts that are "ghost-managed."[60] Here's Sismondo:

> These are manuscripts for which pharmaceutical companies control or shape multiple steps in the research, analysis, writing, and publication. Pharmaceutical companies not only fund clinical trials, they also routinely design and shape them, typically employing contract research organizations to run those trials. By combining and splitting datasets, the companies propose multiple manuscripts derived from a study or group of studies. Hired medical writers produce first drafts and edit papers, which publication planners expertly shepherd

through the publication process. Because of the commercial importance of having the right sort of author and of keeping companies' interests in the background, KOLs serve as the nominal authors of manuscripts. It can then appear as if respected independent researchers, rather than coordinated corporate teams, led the research and analysis. KOL authorship increases the perceived credibility of an article while hiding key features of the research process. For example, even though an array of employees and contractors—company statisticians and researchers, reviewers from multiple departments, medical writers, and publication planners—often contribute more to the research and the articles than the nominal authors do, they are only rarely acknowledged in journal publications.

Made for Deniability

As in the other arenas we've explored, appearances are vital; the *performance* of independence and impartiality is integral to players' success. The same is true with KOLs. Both the industry and the opinion leader himself must maintain the patina of independence. Elliott observes that, for pharmaceutical companies, it's "just as important . . . that a KOL is, at least in theory, independent" as are his status and credentials.[61] Of course, these opinion leaders' flexible identities do not augur well for impartiality. Yet, at the same time, *displaying* independence is the key to their influence and deniability.

In other work, Ozierański and co-author sociologist Lawrence King point to several dimensions of this issue, showing how informality and deniability are plaited into the process, especially in the field of drug reimbursement. They note that relying on KOLs may be necessary for drug companies that lack personal ties to policymakers and therefore are unable to push their products through direct lobbying. They further observe that using KOLs to endorse products is a convenient way of building a buffer between a drug company and decisionmakers, thus structuring in deniability. This is especially important in relation to contentious issues, as it minimizes the likelihood that the company will be caught red-handed. (The authors cite an example of a drug company using a PR agency which in turn uses its own KOLs.[62]) Finally, generating pressure through KOLs reduces the need to use formal channels, say, to provide hard evidence for the efficacy and safety of a drug or medical product. Those, of course, would be subject to accountability mechanisms. In other words, it is far more convenient to use a KOL as a messenger than to make a formal offer that potentially could be scrutinized.[63] Informality is the handmaiden of deniability.

The Limits of Transparency

Transparency is widely seen as a panacea for rooting out corruption and ensuring accountability. But is it? Transparency relies on the idea that making activities visible will deter them from happening in the first place. Yet even when the facts are clear and known, transparency can be of limited use.

As with American economists who are now subject to a non-binding code of ethics, whether transparency has any effect remains to be seen. In 2010, the U.S. Congress enacted the Physician Payment Sunshine Act, which requires "drug and device companies to disclose payments to doctors and teaching hospitals to the Department of Health and Human Services."[64] The legislation followed Senate investigations that "targeted prominent academic physicians at Harvard, Stanford, Emory, Wisconsin, and Minnesota, among other universities."[65]

The Sunshine Act was implemented in 2013, and the government is slated to launch its own searchable website. Before that, ProPublica had set up a searchable database using information from voluntary disclosures;[66] from its website anyone with a computer can look up their physician to see if he or she has received pharmaceutical or medical-device dollars.[67]

What has been the result so far? The passage of the legislation may have forced companies to issue public reports on payments to physicians. ProPublica reported in 2014 that many top pharmaceutical companies had drastically cut their budgets for physician speaking engagements ahead of the disclosure rules taking effect.[68] ProPublica suggests several possibilities for the pullback. One explanation relates to companies' cyclical needs: drug patents were expiring and doctors are needed more for speaking at the beginning of a new drug's life cycle. Another possibility is that the latest crop of approved drugs were specialty drugs that didn't necessarily require many physicians to rally on their behalf. And yes, a third reason could be that the threat of disclosure is taking them out of the game.

It's too early to fully assess this, of course. But there are indications that disclosure might be more of a performance, without having the intended effect. According to Elliott,[69]

> Disclosure of conflicts is widely seen as a "win-win" solution to the KOL problem. Doctors get to keep accepting industry money; the drug companies get to keep giving it; and anyone else who might be affected can be reassured by the knowledge that the transactions are no longer secret.

What has happened to shame? As Ozierański explains: "It's difficult to name and shame such high-status professionals because even if it's clear that they have been involved in ethically dubious activities, they enjoy so much peer support and prestige."[70]

With sanctions less than effective, the upshot is that accountability to the public is weakened by the use of KOLs. Trading on the reputation of the impartial scientist can't help but violate the public trust. As Sismondo argues,[71]

> . . . we should be addressing the larger issue of the "institutional corruption"[72] of medicine; namely, that the pharmaceutical industry has a disproportionate influence on medical opinion, which weakens medicine's ability to promote individual and public health in ways that are independent of the industry.

UNIVERSITIES, LENDING LEGITIMACY

Shame and institutional sanction are sometimes in short supply in the home base of the academic—the university itself. Many universities now have institutes or think-tank–like entities that engage in shadow lobbying and, in the process, help support academics. These entities can use the university's impartial image to make a policy or a cause look like a scholarly conclusion, often downplaying or disguising the source of their funding.

One such place that has faced criticism is the Mercatus Center at my own university, George Mason. As the *Wall Street Journal* put it, "When it comes to business regulation in Washington, Mercatus, Latin for market, has become the most important think tank you've never heard of."[73]

The Charles Koch Foundation has donated some $30 million to George Mason; in Jane Mayer's investigation into Koch-funded political activities for the *New Yorker*, she writes this of Mercatus founder, former economics professor at George Mason, and current Koch Industries executive Richard Fink: "He said that grant-makers should use think tanks and political-action groups to convert intellectual raw materials into policy 'products.'"[74]

Mercatus puts out a lot of product. Of the nearly sixty people listed as scholars on its site, more than a third are professors, mostly at George Mason.[75] They regularly appear before Congress or federal agencies, not to mention the news media, sometimes identified as part of Mercatus, sometimes as professors, sometimes both.[76] While those they are addressing may know that Mercatus is backed by energy-industry billionaires who virulently oppose regulation, the public, by and large, does not. One Mercatus scholar recently drew the attention of *The Nation*, and not even for his Mercatus association. He testified before a congressional committee, with no mention that he serves as a "director of the Global Economics Group, a consulting business that boasts in a brochure that its experts have been hired by industry to influence the [Consumer Financial Protection Bureau] and other regulatory agencies."[77]

Another Mercatus scholar "testified before Congress on the costs of Dodd-Frank [and] . . . billed lobbying firm Greenberg Traurig (which represented the U.S. Chamber of Commerce and Nomura Holdings, among other firms) nearly $50,000 for his consulting work."[78] You won't find this on his Mercatus page, which notes that he is on leave to serve as the chief economist for the House Financial Services Committee.[79]

When a firm promises that its "experts" will "make strong cases to support desired outcomes," that sounds a lot like lobbying and nothing like scholarship. There's plenty of irony in scholars profiting as they attacked the Consumer Financial Protection Bureau, brainchild of Senator Elizabeth

Warren. That's because she studied the problem of "scholars for dollars" herself when she was *Professor* Warren.[80]

> In the bankruptcy area, data providers, such as the Credit Research Center located at Georgetown University, have taken money from the consumer credit industry to produce studies supporting the credit industry's political positions. In the case of the CRC, the studies bear the University logo, but the Center describes the data as "proprietary," belonging exclusively to the industry funders who decide what data are released and what data are held private.

That, of course, is anathema to academic norms of open research and publication.

As university budgets are strained and states reduce their contributions to public universities, pressure mounts for scholars, centers, and institutes to secure funding. University leaders and entire cadres of administrators are now deployed to beg for private and governmental dollars. Indeed, to have a better life at many universities, including my own—for instance, to secure summer salary, research assistance, travel funds—university entities and individual scholars need to raise money. At least some of that funding comes from corporations and other entities or individuals with advocacy agendas. As scholars are more for hire and universities succumb to the blending and blurring that have befallen other institutions, so do ethics blur.

—⟨⟨⟨—

As we have seen in this chapter, one ever-more-prevalent way to organize influence involves using and abusing the supposed impartiality of the scholar/economist/physician/researcher and the academy itself. Again and again we have observed that, when appearances are not what they purport to be, our trust is violated.

Yet another way to organize influence, as we shall soon see, is to use and abuse the image of grassroots and nongovernmental organizations.

CHAPTER 9

"Grassroots" and
Nonprofit Organizers

In what and whom do we trust? As we've seen throughout this book, our trust in formal institutions has been giving way to faith in the private domain: the blogger we feel we know; our friend who sends us articles to read, thereby acting as our editor; our participation in the "sharing economy." Disillusioned with formal institutions, we turn to private ones.

Our attraction to things "private" leaves us susceptible to efforts that *appear* private, as if they were coming from likeminded souls. We are so enamored of the we-can-do-this-together spirit that a lot of influence is organized to *appear* as if it were coming from a genuine community effort, that is, from the grass roots. We like it so much that those who want to influence us organize themselves under the rubric of nonprofit organizations—that is, private ones. We like it so much that politicians and their wealthy donors organize their efforts informally and to happen *outside* public institutions like political parties.

Perhaps the only people who like these "grassroots" efforts more than we do are their organizers, because the grassroots cachet is so effective in accomplishing their goal. That is, influencing us.

The use of what in common parlance are "fake grassroots" or "front groups" is not new by any means. But the advent of the Internet and social media, as well as the decline of investigative journalism, has made it far easier and cheaper to channel secret influence, propaganda, and money. These developments have also nurtured simulacra—things that suck us in because they *appear* to be something else but aren't. The digital age has sired a surge of "astroturfing," in which companies, politicians, and other organizations fake a grassroots campaign to get their message across, leading the public to believe there is a groundswell of support rather than a few self-interested sponsors. Astroturfing predates the Internet, but the Internet makes astroturfing easier than ever before.[1] The result of all this is that you can buy your morning coffee and more easily trace the source of the individual bean than it would be to trace the source of information that subtly influences your views on the most important public-policy issues of the day.

And influence such groups do, beyond the reach of accountability to us, the public.

The signposts for this form of influencing, straight from the shadow-elite playbook, should, by now, be familiar:

Tame or grassroots-sounding names, evoking citizens' advocacy or genuine DIY efforts. Organizations and efforts that are staged from the top—be they by one or a handful of billionaires or a tiny cadre around a president. Entities that morph their purposes as convenient for their puppet-masters. Organizations sponsored by companies or the super-rich to create an echo chamber and make it appear that there's a "there there" when there isn't. The use of big names or former top officials to give organizations heft. Sponsorship and funding sources that are indirect and almost impossible to track. In short, an enterprise whose influence is steeped in obscurity and lends itself to deniability.

In this chapter, I'll look at the use of "grassroots" groups and efforts employed by both corporations and self-interested individuals and networks, and amplified by digital means. I'll also look at how political parties and ideological billionaires use their own "nonprofit" groups, often supported by donors whose identity is in the shadows, to make you believe that it's your voice that matters, not theirs.

TOP-DOWN "GRASSROOTS"

In the United States, tobacco companies are perhaps the most accomplished corporate group when it comes to PR. In the 1950s, the industry perfected the state of the art through such techniques as placing ads, ghostwriting articles, courting media personnel and providing them with favorable copy, anticipating and countering unfavorable publicity, and mass circulation of favorable "news."[2]

As time went on, the industry also tried to create a supposed groundswell of grassroots involvement—in their case, to oppose the encroaching restrictions on smoking.

One document comes from R.J. Reynolds in 1987: "By year's end, 550 Smokers' Rights Groups will have been formed in 500 . . . of the 750 metro areas . . . (in all 50 states)." The document talks about grassroots opportunities in "areas now undeveloped (that is, minorities.)"[3]

Some "grassroots" groups like these are anything but, existing solely to promote one cause on behalf of a company or an individual investor.

Nowadays, many such groups are organized as 501(c)(4) "social welfare" nonprofits under the U.S. tax code, or 501(c)(3) "religious, educational" groups and, as such, are not required to disclose their sponsorship.[4] These are more formidable beasts than the "fake grassroots" and "front" groups of old.

Network of One

One group that received tobacco money is still around, boasting an eminently innocuous-sounding name, the Center for Consumer Freedom. It is a nonprofit enabler of soda-guzzling, junk-food–loving Americans everywhere.[5]

The Center was founded in 1996 by moneys from the tobacco and restaurant industries to thwart regulations on smoking. It has since moved on to fighting government restrictions on junk-food sales and genetically modified food.[6] An ad taken out in *Roll Call*, credited to the Center, presents an emaciated, apparently African child whom the nonprofit says needs "Food Not Propaganda."[7] It does not mention the agri-business or food giant presumably bankrolling the ad. We say *presumably* because as a nonprofit, the Center for Consumer Freedom, run by former food-industry lobbyist Richard Berman, doesn't have to report its donors.

From its "About" page:[8]

> Many of the companies and individuals who support the Center financially have indicated that they want anonymity as contributors. They are reasonably apprehensive about privacy and safety in light of the violence and other forms of aggression some activists have adopted as a "game plan" to impose their views, so we respect their wishes.

Note that the Center for Consumer Freedom, unlike many such groups, at least acknowledges there is an issue.

The Center's site is no-holds-barred: in one picture, New York City Mayor Michael Bloomberg, much loathed by food companies for his regulations aimed at junk food, appears as Nanny Bloomberg, dressed up in a lavender dress and scarf. There is nothing subtle about the message, though you won't find details on its sponsorship.[9]

Sponsorship is similarly obscure with some of the other five "nonprofits" started by Berman, according to the *New York Times*, all with "similarly innocuous names."[10] At first glance, Berman might seem like Jesus multiplying the five loaves of bread and two fish to make enough food for his disciples to serve the multitudes.

Except, in Berman's case, it's hard to find the disciples.

Shades of simulacra can be seen with his "Union Facts" website, which looks at quick glance like a workingman's paradise: happy, diverse faces are meant to signal "we care about labor." But really it's an anti-union operation; Berman's organization insists that it is only seeking more "transparency" for union leadership, not the rank and file.[11]

His other organizations' agendas run the gamut from fighting increases in the minimum wage to supporting decreases in blood-alcohol levels for drunk drivers. With "consumer freedom" as his mantra, Berman has tangled with nearly everyone, even Mothers Against Drunk Driving (MADD).

Berman eschews the term *lobbyist*. He apparently prefers *advocate*: according to a 2010 article in the *New York Times*, Berman's detractors allege that his[12]

. . . organizations are little more than moneymakers for his for-profit communications firm, Berman and Company. Last month, in what appears to be a new tactic by those critics, the Humane Society and MADD filed a complaint with the New York Commission on Public Integrity, charging that the American Beverage Institute and Berman and Company were in fact lobbying and had failed to register with the state as lobbyists.

It's hard to find the *non* in Berman's "nonprofits."

Big-Name Surrogacy

Other top-down "grassroots" groups sound positively praiseworthy, and this can make them even more seductive and insidious. Case in point: the Clean and Safe Energy Coalition. Who can argue, after all, with the need for safe and clean energy? For years CASEnergy Coalition has boasted as co-chairs former Environmental Protection Agency administrator and New Jersey governor Christine Todd Whitman; an original Greenpeace member-turned-PR consultant; and more recently, a former U.S. trade representative and one-time mayor of Dallas.[13]

CASEnergy Coalition is described on its website as a "national grassroots organization that supports the increased use of nuclear energy." You would be forgiven if you missed these four defining words in its "About" section: "Funded by the industry. . . ."[14]

As concerns about global warming have swelled, the search for cleaner (if not necessarily safer) power has meant that the nuclear industry has found a more sympathetic ear in corners of both the Republican and Democratic parties. A journalist who dug into CASEnergy Coalition in 2010 found that assisting that effort has been $600 million spent on lobbying over ten years, involving aggressive courting of both Democrats and labor unions.[15]

Not all of it is traditional lobbying.[16] The journalist reports that, to gain support,

[T]he industry, led by the [trade group] Nuclear Energy Institute, has created a network of allies who give speeches, quote one another approvingly and showcase one another on their Web sites. The effect is an echo chamber of support for nuclear power. While energy lobbies such as big oil and big coal have taken turns in the spotlight, big nuke flies largely under the radar. Alex Flint, the NEI's chief lobbyist, summed up the strategy last year at a luncheon with utility officials from Southeastern states: "Quiet." He likes to let surrogates make the case.

For the CASEnergy Coalition, a key "surrogate" is Whitman. Her tenure as a public servant is now serving her very well indeed. And it's hard to imagine that she or the former mayor of Dallas comes cheap.

You may recall that Whitman sat on BP's advisory board, along with a roster of other Washington highfliers. (And, after the BP spill in 2010, she wrote an op-ed urging that offshore drilling not be banned, without saying that she had served on a BP advisory board.) Whitman also seized the opportunity to pitch nuclear power, describing CASEnergy Coalition as "grassroots" and not "industry-funded."[17]

Whitman does list CASEnergy as a client on the home page of her own consulting firm, Whitman Strategy Group, but pity today's multitasking reader who tries to figure out that connection on, say, a mobile phone. Or the newspaper reader who comes across the various opinion pieces she writes without disclosing her industry ties.[18]

In 2013, Whitman co-authored a call to arms on the issue of regulating greenhouse-gas emissions in the *New York Times*; her op-ed does not point out that Whitman's clients might stand to benefit if another power industry is stymied by regulation.[19] In at least one report, Whitman is clearly identified as being funded by the nuclear power industry, which is useful for her; she can deny that she is hiding anything. But as PR Watch, a Project of the Center for Media and Democracy, found, "A Nexis news database search revealed that nearly two-thirds of news items that mentioned Christine Todd Whitman and nuclear power, from April 2006 to August 2007, failed to disclose her financial relationship with the industry."[20] And that's just one year's worth. One only needs to look at the number of more current articles she either writes or gets quoted in that make no clear disclosure of any kind. Some of it comes in the national press, but her writing appears in many local outlets as well.[21]

The CASEnergy Coalition site displays a jam-packed schedule of grassroots-style visits by its "members" across the country, and it's hard not to notice how many seem to involve minority communities. Photos of these events are displayed on its website and Twitter feed, making it look as if there's a wide range of regular people stepping up to support the growth of nuclear power.

But are they energized in large numbers? How can we know? It seems we should be dubious.

Pharma-Fed Patients

It's hard to think of a more emotionally charged subject for a PR campaign than one dealing with our own health and well-being, or that of those we care about.

Pharmaceutical and medical-device companies play on these vulnerabilities. They have been aggressive—and early adopters—in astroturfing through patient advocacy groups. This can be particularly difficult to deal with because getting to the bottom of people's and organizations' motives is tricky. Patient groups, of course, attract sufferers and many sincere advocates, regular people plagued with often-debilitating diseases or conditions and their families and friends. But they also attract money from pharmaceutical companies. These companies try to push their preferred drugs on prospective patients, encouraging them to seek a particular medication or diagnosis. These groups can also serve as conduits of money and influence in advocating for legislation favored by drug-makers, all under the guise of grassroots advocacy.

Key Opinion Leaders, which we discussed in the previous chapter, often act in concert with patient organizations, as several scholars have noted.[22] While I focus on the American context, the methods of influence here reviewed are also routinely employed in today's European context.

Shannon Brownlee, in her book *Overtreated: Why Too Much Medicine Is Making Us Sicker and Poorer*, discusses the astroturfing campaign waged by SmithKline in the late 1990s when it introduced the drug Paxil. To try to distinguish the drug from its competitors, SmithKline appeared to engage in "disease-mongering," in which pharmaceutical companies try to create new classes of disorders or wider diagnostic criteria and thereby generate a fresh market for a drug. SmithKline began promoting Paxil as a treatment for social anxiety, which, as a full-fledged psychiatric condition, Brownlee points out, is considered quite rare. The PR push included the full complement of "press releases" made to look like reported stories; pre-produced video and radio news releases; academics, experts, and carefully chosen sufferers; and ads with slogans like "Imagine being allergic to people." Without mentioning Paxil, the ads directed people to the "Social Anxiety Disorder Coalition," and their "member" groups, including the American Psychiatric Association, the Anxiety Disorders Association of America, and Freedom from Fear. Not advertised, of course, was its sponsorship. As Brownlee writes:[23]

> In reality, three of the psychiatric organizations listed . . . receive significant funding from SmithKline and other drugmakers. The fourth, the Social Anxiety Disorder Coalition, existed only temporarily in the New York offices of [PR firm] Cohn and Wolfe, which fielded all media calls for a few months after the ad campaign began.

SmithKline, of course, has hardly been the only firm to seed money into patient-advocacy groups. The industry's influence stretches far and wide.

In 2006, *New Scientist* magazine conducted an investigation of twenty-nine large patient-advocacy groups (ones with annual revenues of more than $100,000), as well as some "associated with bipolar disorder, restless leg syndrome and attention deficit hyperactivity disorder." The magazine chose these because they had previously been flagged by a medical journal for possible disease-mongering.[24] Only two out of the nearly thirty groups that *New Scientist* examined refused to accept drug-company money. About a quarter of the groups took more than twenty percent of their funds from drug companies, and these groups were concerned with relatively common conditions (that is, with a big market to be exploited) that require long-term medication.

What about when such groups get involved in policy-making? Several were especially active during the years leading up to the expansion of Medicare to include a prescription-drug benefit, passed in 2003. The pharmaceutical industry was concerned that the added benefit might include cost controls that would take a bite out of drug-company profits. To help make its case, it created the innocuous-sounding Citizens for Better Medicare. CBM spent about $65 million on issue ads during the 2000 election cycle in an effort to foil the drug benefit.[25]

We're not sure who the "citizens" were in Citizens for Better Medicare, but we do know that an elderly actress played "Flo," CBM's best-known "member." "Flo" appeared in commercials warning other seniors by declaring "I don't want big government in my medicine cabinet!"

Another CBM affiliate was United Seniors for America, which favored a subsidy for private prescription-drug coverage. According to the watchdog organization Public Citizen: "USA, which billed itself as having a '1.5 million activists network nationwide,' reported to the IRS that it received more than $20 million from a single donor in both 2002 and 2003, accounting for more than 75 percent of its revenue."[26]

Senator Charles Grassley in 2009 went after Big Pharma advocacy groups as part of a broader fight he began two years earlier against the influence game's impact on medical practice and policy. "These organizations have a lot of influence over public policy, and people rely on their leadership. . . . There's a strong case for disclosure and the accountability that results."[27]

He helped expose the funding sources behind the National Alliance on Mental Illness (NAMI). Described by the *New York Times* as "hugely influential in many state capitols," the organization had declined to reveal its donors.[28] The *Times* uncovered that roughly seventy-five percent of NAMI's funding over a two-year period came from the drug industry. This was an apparent surprise even to one of NAMI's own board members, a physician who said he was "shocked" by the level of industry funding, and resigned as a result. From the *Times*:[29]

> Documents obtained . . . show that drug makers have over the
> years given the mental health alliance—along with millions

of dollars in donations—direct advice about how to advocate forcefully for issues that affect industry profits. The documents show, for example, that the alliance's leaders . . . met with AstraZeneca sales executives on Dec. 16, 2003.

Slides from a presentation delivered by the salesmen show that the company urged the alliance to resist state efforts to limit access to mental health drugs.

"Solutions: Play Hard Ball," one slide was titled. "Hold policy makers accountable for their decisions in media and in election," it continued.

The alliance's own slides concluded by saying, "We appreciate AstraZeneca's strong support of NAMI."

Despite the shaming of NAMI (its website reports that in 2009 it began listing donations above $5,000), Grassley was unsatisfied with the state of disclosure from both patient-advocacy groups and professional medical societies that funnel influence through physicians, using lavish conferences and lucrative speaking and consulting jobs. These groups can have a big impact on the standards that get set, devices that are used or not, and decisions that can make or break the bottom line for medical manufacturers and drug companies.

In 2011, the senator demanded funding information from dozens of both kinds of groups, and as ProPublica reported, one professional society—the Heart Rhythm Society—turned out to be getting nearly half its money from the drug and device business.

More recently, Grassley and others have been targeting the explosive growth of opioid prescriptions, which many public-health experts believe has led to increasing addiction and overdosing, not just alleviating genuine pain. In 2012, he and Senator Max Baucus began investigating opioid makers and their connections to pain experts, including the American Pain Foundation, which shut down as the investigation got under way.[30] It was revealed that a full ninety percent of its funding came from opioid producers.

It's no doubt difficult for desperate activists to say no to drug companies bearing cash, especially in areas where there's a perceived dearth of government research. And, keep in mind, such donations become even more attractive to vulnerable patients and their supporters. But to most observers, that money is invisible, leaving the impression that patient advocacy groups and professional societies are run by the people they supposedly represent.

Grassroots Billionaires

Now we turn to a case where regular people and even political representatives find themselves in the crossfire between a hedge-fund billionaire betting against a company and the controversial company trying to sustain itself. Both the billionaire and the company have spawned "grassroots" campaigns to create the appearance of a swirl of consumer activity.

The company, Herbalife, which sells nutritional supplements, has been dogged for decades with suggestions that it is little more than a pyramid scheme. Indeed, Herbalife is a so-called multi-level marketing—or MLM—company that relies on recruiting more and more salespeople to stay afloat. But William Ackman's brazen crusade against the company has actually made it look like a victim.

In a presentation called "Who Wants to Be a Millionaire?" in December 2012, Ackman laid out for an audience of investors some of the reasons he believes Herbalife is a pyramid scheme.[31] But the most pertinent fact of the Ackman-versus-Herbalife story is that Ackman was making huge investment bets against Herbalife (which eventually totaled a billion dollars). At least in this respect, Ackman was being very public about his position.[32]

Ackman began, as some financial players do, pushing the government to investigate the company, which would likely cause the stock to fall and his bet to pay off.[33] He employed both digital-age-enabled "grassroots" strategies and traditional strategies (lobbyists) to achieve his goal. The bevy of lobbyists he hired succeeded in pushing both Representative Linda Sánchez and eventually Senator Edward Markey to call for an investigation. But it's his grassroots and behind-the-scenes campaign that I'm interested in here.

According to the *New York Times*, Ackman[34]

> . . . retained the Dewey Square Group . . . [a] firm that specializes in "grass-roots advocacy," to influence officials by

recruiting surrogates to speak out against Herbalife in emails, tweets, letters or rallies. . . . [L]obbyists and grass-roots organizers set up meetings with major consumer groups.

The focus was on Hispanics and other minorities who might have felt victimized by Herbalife. Through the Dewey Square Group, Ackman underwrote these "grassroots" efforts to the tune of $130,000.

Regulators and politicians began receiving letters from different groups. But the contents? They didn't differ much. The *New York Times* found that "All three of the letters from nonprofit groups demanding an investigation were identical—except they were signed by three different Hispanic community leaders, each on a different letterhead."[35]

Some "authors" had no memory of writing a letter. Some nonprofits said, perhaps genuinely or at least plausibly, that they were happy to get involved in rallies and letter-writing because they thought Herbalife was indeed hurting a vulnerable part of their constituency. Ackman, for his part, has been uncharacteristically quiet on the "grassroots" aspect of his advocacy, aside from putting out press releases saying that new nonprofits were coming out against Herbalife.[36]

While it's clear that the Internet was used to create an echo chamber, motives are not easily decipherable unless you know the backstory. There's a maze of websites attacking Herbalife, one of which is very explicit about its connection to Ackman, and others where the connection is less clear.[37] A Facebook page called the Anti-Herbalife Coalition has this post from December 9, 2012: "See the new anti-Herbalife site and SHARE. http://herbalife-scam.com/."[38] The Facebook poster's name pops up again elsewhere, as the web designer for the site http://www.isherbalifeapyramid.com.

The sites typically feature those who say they were victims of an alleged Herbalife pyramid scheme and encourage anyone with his/her own story to come forward. One of these videos, as the *Times* points out, was promoted by a New York nonprofit Hispanic advocacy group that received $10,000 from Ackman.[39]

One might think from reading thus far that Herbalife itself is a victim, but that is not necessarily the case. Herbalife has signed up its own army of high-wattage lobbyists; in fact, the company far outspent Ackman.[40] And a handful of Hispanic groups wrote their own letter—headed "Friends of Herbalife"—with no mention that five out of these seven nonprofits had reportedly received payment from Herbalife.[41] The jockeying for at least the appearance of "authentic" support from nonprofits actually—says the *Times*—created "a bidding war" between Ackman and Herbalife.[42]

It's worth noting, too, that Ackman's own interests and use of "grassroots" groups have perhaps muted deserved skepticism about a company like Herbalife, which appeals to the economically vulnerable. If Herbalife truly is a pyramid scheme or close to it, would anyone believe it now?

And the nonprofits that took money from Ackman or Herbalife have done themselves damage by not asking enough questions of either party.

One letter-writer interviewed by the *Times* heard a presentation *at church* by a former Clinton official well known in the Los Angeles African American community. Less known, apparently, was that she now works for the "grassroots" strategy firm hired by Ackman. Obviously distressed, the letter-writer told the paper, "Have I become an instrument in some billionaire's investment campaign?"[43]

In a word, yes.

"NONPROFIT" POLITICIANS

Thus far we have looked at the "grassroots" shenanigans of the food, beverage, and agribusiness industry; the nuclear-power industry; pharmaceutical and medical-device companies; and an individual hedge-fund billionaire. This is just a tiny sample of the financial and corporate players who have organized influence through faux-grassroots campaigns.

Now we turn to political parties who use "nonprofits" to both push their message unimpeded by reporters and to obscure donors with deep pockets.

You have likely heard about the 2013 scandal that rocked the Internal Revenue Service, the U.S. agency accused of inappropriately targeting certain groups that organize themselves as 501(c)(4) social welfare nonprofits, when they might be more accurately characterized as advocacy groups. Despite the focus on "conservative" groups, they are not the only ones that have rushed to create these nonprofit sinkholes of stealth influence; "liberal" groups have as well, even if they do appear to be playing a bit of catchup. These nonprofits (sometimes aligned with a Super PAC group) tend to cloak themselves in the aura of "grassroots support." The 501(c)(4)s, unlike Super PACs, have the huge benefit of not having to disclose their donors.

Public watchdogs made much of the 2010 Supreme Court ruling in the *Citizens United* case that fully legalized corporate donations to political campaigns, fearing they would skyrocket. And yet it hasn't happened. Nine months later, as the *New York Times* reported, "Corporations have so far mostly chosen not to take advantage of the *Citizens United* ruling to *directly* [emphasis added] sponsor campaign ads themselves."[44] In 2014, OpenSecrets.org analyzed it thusly:[45]

> Possibly wary of public backlash, publicly traded corporations have been less than eager to join in the outside spending game—at least openly. Perhaps aware that corporate spending on elections plays poorly with voters, only a handful of such corporations have made contributions to super PACs, including Chevron and Scotts Miracle-Gro. Privately held businesses, however, have not been so restrained; companies like Oxbow Carbon and Contran Corporation, which made direct contributions from their treasuries to conservative super PACs, were among 2012's biggest sources of outside money.

This is surely a sign of the value of invisibility in political contributing these days.

In Stealth We Stand

The operative word, of course, is *directly*.

Rather than exert influence openly, even when it is completely legal to do so, corporations and individual donors with deep pockets are apparently choosing to channel influence anonymously through 501(c)(4) groups. As one watchdog suggested, there actually is something worse than buying elections: it's when you don't even know who's buying the election.[46]

OpenSecrets.org assesses that *Citizens United* spawned nonprofit "dark money groups" that don't list their donors. It estimates that "Partly as a result [of the ruling], spending by organizations that do not disclose their donors has increased from less than $5.2 million in 2006 to well over $300 million in the 2012 election."[47] Who are these donors? "[H]ow much of that money came from corporate treasuries is unknown."[48]

Not only is their existence funded by we-don't-know-whom; these groups (as we saw above with the "grassroots" groups) declare that their primary purpose is the "promotion of social welfare," not partisan politics, and therefore they don't need to reveal their funding sources. The groups themselves, in shadow-elite fashion, add another layer of obfuscation with vague names that give no hint of politics or provenance.

The Koch brothers' group Americans for Prosperity and Crossroads GPS, brainchild of Republican strategist Karl Rove, are but two examples. The GPS in Crossroads GPS stands for "Grassroots Policy Strategies." That's right. "Grassroots Policy Strategies." The 65,000-odd people getting regular updates from Crossroads GPS's Facebook page are told that the group is a[49]

> . . . policy and grassroots advocacy organization committed to educating, equipping and mobilizing citizens to take action on the critical issues that will shape our nation's future.

From this description, you wouldn't know that Crossroads, along with sister organization American Crossroads (a 527 organization), became so influential during the 2012 election cycle that it was dubbed the Shadow RNC.[50]

Savvy political operators often pair a 527, which can now take unlimited donations but has to disclose its donors, with a sister 501(c)(4), which is subject to more restriction but has the huge advantage of nondisclosure. If all this sounds confusing, that is perhaps the point. Americans for Prosperity has nearly a million Facebook "likes" and many more state-affiliated Facebook pages with thousands of other "likes." There's no indication to its "friends" that the organization is one of many supported by the Koch brothers, whose business empire would stand to benefit from its anti-regulatory platform.[51]

In 2014, the *Washington Post*, along with the Center for Responsive Politics, provided a graphic of Koch-connected nonprofits and assorted "entities," which spent a whopping $400 million in 2012. They outspent the Shadow RNC and just about matched all the money raised by American unions, the voting and fundraising stronghold for Democrats.[52]

The Koch brothers are well known, having become a favorite whipping boy of the American left. But their nonprofit consortium involves quite a few other rich, like-minded donors whose names we would probably not recognize. And, of course, they'd like to keep it that way.[53]

Off-record donors enjoy influence with impunity. A controversial policy decision might be made, and the public would have no idea what questions to ask or even if they should ask them in the first place. Both the donor and the politician enjoy the benefits of deniability that come with anonymity. In short, information that not long ago was public is now firmly in a few private hands.

What do these 501(c)(4)s actually do? Aside from flooding the airwaves with thinly veiled attacks on political candidates under the guise of "issues," some of them engage in "dirty tricks," digital-style. In the process, the groups can deny both their partisan nature and their sponsors. And get away with it.

These "dirty tricks," or techniques, evolve along with the technology, creating new means of obfuscating the source of influence. Just to show how difficult such influence is to trace: it took two computer scientists at Wellesley College to identify a "Twitter bomb" tossed at Democrat Martha Coakley during her failed 2010 U.S. Senate run in Massachusetts.[54] They traced it to a low-profile group in Iowa, a 501(c)(4) nonprofit. That group, called the American Future Fund, was bankrolled by the Center to Protect Patient Rights, both of which can be found on the Koch influence graphic mentioned above.[55] This little-known group, which spent nearly $24 million in the 2012 election cycle, was outspent, as far as 501(c)(4)s go, only by Rove's Crossroads GPS.[56]

In sum, this *au courant* means of influence has double-blindness, disconnect, and deniability wrapped into it. We don't know who the sponsors are. The generic-, optimistic-, and often patriotic-sounding names of the groups provide few clues.

And we can only surmise the existence of a relationship between the donors and the politicians; we can't know for sure. For, to be legal, the relationship must be nonexistent—never mind that no one believes this.

In short, there is deniability at each level with each relationship: politicians can deny a tie to a group and its donors; and donors can deny funding it.

The double-blind means of organizing influence appears, in a few short years, already to have become a fixture of American politics. For their part,

Koch-allied outside groups are going large again in 2014. The *New York Times* reports that they are "spending up to 10 times as much as any major outside Democratic group so far." Their goal is to harness discontent with Obamacare and to translate that into a lasting distaste for "big government" of any kind.[57]

Organizing (and Re-Organizing) for America

The ideological goals of the Obama camp may be 180 degrees afield from the Koch brothers and their ilk, but the means of organizing influence is not. A pillar of top-down organizing from Obama's presidential beginnings has been OFA, originally Obama for America. Most recently, this novel organization decided in 2013 to become . . . you guessed it . . . a 501(c)(4). More on this latest incarnation shortly.

OFA has always proven to be eminently adaptable—changing its name (though not its acronym—that's the brand) with the circumstances and morphing from one mission to the next. But its unwavering constants are acting as the arm of the president and being a "grassroots" entity controlled from the top. This enduring, yet mutating, group relies on direct messaging and cutting out all manner of middlemen—be they journalists, political parties, or Congress.

As of this writing, OFA is on its third name. During the 2008 campaign, it was Obama for America, a campaign-organizing group that amassed an e-mail list of around 13 million people (now up to a reported 17 million), described in the *Washington Post* around that time by a Republican strategist as "no better asset in politics today": a direct, 24/7 digital communication line.[58]

That line has allowed Obama the ability to offer a steady stream of branding without reporters first getting a press release and then tempering or countering the spin. Here's a telling quote from Macon Phillips, the administration's new media director, during those early days: "Historically the media has been able to draw out a lot of information and characterize it for people. . . . And there's a growing appetite from people to do it themselves."[59]

The people doing the "characterizing," of course, are not the volunteers, but Obama spinmasters. That fact points to another notable advantage of this kind of setup to its influencers. Bill Kovach, chairman of the

Committee of Concerned Journalists, explains: "They're beginning to create their own journalism, their own description of events of the day, but it's not an independent voice making that description. . . ."[60]

After the election of Barack Obama in 2008, OFA became Organizing for America, an arm of the Democratic National Committee. This structure departs from past presidents who simply integrated their operations into the existing party apparatus. OFA continued to advocate and agitate among supporters on legislative priorities. Ari Melber, a journalist who studied the group, called it "the largest governance organizing effort by a national party in history," an unprecedented attempt to convert "a winning campaign's volunteer network into an organization devoted to enacting a national agenda."[61] The group asked its supporters to press Congress on specific political battles, notably health care, and later immigration reform[62] and gun control.

What happens, de facto, when a president has the ability to pitch people any time, day or night, about items on his agenda? To quote journalist Melber, who wrote a seventy-plus–page report on OFA's first post-election year:[63]

> Scholars, commentators and members of Congress have raised concerns about how presidents increasingly make appeals directly to the public, rather than working directly with the representative branch of government. Fortifying that model with a powerful, national whip operation [run by O.F.A., as opposed, say, to Congressional whips whose job it is to rally support among its members] could further undermine Congress' autonomy, in this narrative. Conservative critics of Obama have also argued that he would use his email lists to dominate Congress by conducting the presidency in "campaign mode."

All the while, OFA has kept a grassroots feel alive. There are the "personalized" e-mails that aim at an authentic touch, asking supporters, say, to sign the president's birthday card.

Obama's reelection campaign held its own convention coverage, streamed directly to those who turned over their e-mail addresses to the campaign, free of reporters or impartial analysis.

The result has been a novel organizing hybrid. The *New Republic* summed it up this way:[64]

> Obama's people ha[ve] created something both entirely new and entirely old: an Internet version of the top-down political machines . . . the difference (other than technology) was that this new machine would rely on ideological loyalty, not patronage.

Is the old patronage system giving way to new-style participation?[65] OFA encouraged the president's supporters to host house parties, perform public service, and engage in other social events that don't directly relate to a policy issue. The takeaway from many Obama supporters is that OFA was empowering the grassroots by helping to create a sense of civic-minded community. A more clear-eyed view is that OFA was trying to keep its army engaged and ready to assist in what really matters—the president's agenda—and also to fight the lethargy that sets in between elections, which was even more inevitable given the outsized expectations invested in Obama.

But amid the rhetoric of "yes we can," the "we" in control of OFA, according to reports, was always a very small, select group. Reports such as this trickled out: A mid-level employee who left OFA told me that decisions come squarely from the top down, while the organization tries to maintain the illusion of its grassroots members having a real voice. Another report quotes an activist complaining about "often secretive debate . . . among top campaign staff members."[66] The *Washington Post* notes that "Obama . . . is working to ensure [OFA] stays within the control of a small group who are charged with protecting the Obama brand."[67]

One volunteer said this to (journalist) Melber: "Seriously, I feel that OFA's main objective is to facilitate and maintain pseudo personal relationships with supporters in order to exploit them. . . . I think it's called relationship marketing."[68]

The very impressive turnout on Election Day 2012 may have been the result, in part, of OFA's success—namely its brand of Internet-driven organizing.

Organizing for Anonymity

What came next involved marketing to super donors. The "new" Organizing for Action in 2013 was reinvented as a 501(c)(4). Remember, these "social welfare" organizations don't have to disclose their donors. As the *New York Times* put it, "the . . . organization will rely heavily on a small number of deep-pocketed donors, not unlike the 'Super PACs' whose influence on political campaigns Mr. Obama once deplored."[69] It was to include tiers of influence—board of trustees, board of directors—that could be scaled by higher and higher levels of donations. The *Times* writes:[70]

> The 30-member board will include a 10-person council made up of "leaders in industry" committed to supporting the group's agenda. The organization is also creating a task force on policy, whose chairmen will be expected to raise at least $250,000 to finance advocacy work on specific issues. . . .

The president soon attended an OFA "founders' summit." The AP, which obtained a "save the date" packet for the event, described the entry price at $50,000 a head.[71] After a spate of criticism, the nondisclosure policy was changed. Jim Messina, Obama's 2012 campaign manager turned head of Organizing for Action, wrote in an op-ed that all donations over $250 would be disclosed quarterly and corporate donations wouldn't be accepted.[72]

Nonetheless, "OFA is an unprecedented organization," says Democracy 21, a group led by the venerable watchdog Fred Wertheimer, which spelled out some differences between today and yesteryear. For one, the old political parties are being sidestepped. In a blunt letter to the president, Democracy 21 writes in part:[73]

> No president has ever before helped create and been involved in this kind of privately-funded entity. While there have been a few instances where national political parties established section 501(c)(4) tax-exempt groups to help support their agendas, these groups were terminated relatively quickly. . . . In any event, these groups did not function as an arm of the presidency.

Large amounts provided to OFA create opportunities for individual donors and bundlers to buy corrupting influence over your administration's policies and decisions. At a minimum, large amounts provided to OFA create the appearance of such corrupting influence.

Later that year, when OFA did report its donors, one could see that just nineteen wealthy people had contributed fourteen percent of its total haul. They included hedge-fund titan David Shaw (of the firm D. E. Shaw), several heirs and heiresses, and some tech millionaires.[74]

Meanwhile, other Democratic operatives continued to build their own independent spending groups and 501(c)(4)s that, unlike OFA, would indeed keep their donors secret.

And a system of referrals came into play—a sort of "sharing economy" of donors' dark money. In 2014, longtime investigative reporter Michael Isikoff got ahold of e-mails showing a New Jersey businessman who wanted to attend an OFA event and was told by its fundraiser: "It's $25,000 per person . . . and for those that raise or write $100,000 there will be small clutch with the president."[75]

The donor wanted something other than a simple "clutch." He ended up meeting with White House officials about a personal legal dispute. But aside from the money-for-access angle, this story had an intriguing twist. The businessman's six-figure check didn't come from him: it was actually from a New Jersey physician who had applied for a pardon from his 1991 Medicare-fraud conviction.

OFA knew it couldn't take the "tainted" money; so what did they suggest? That it go to another liberal "nonprofit," one called America Votes, which, unlike OFA, isn't forced by its high profile to disclose its donors. And this isn't an isolated case. According to Isikoff, OFA officials have referred certain donors that might not pass the public's smell test to "other allied tax-exempt groups."[76]

The executive director of the Center for Responsive Politics, which tracks political contributions and spending, said to Isikoff: "What they have done here is create a shell game that I think gives the lie to the notion they are committed to transparency."[77]

As Isikoff sums it up:[78]

> Tracing the flow of the money is particularly challenging because many of the advocacy groups swapped funds back and forth. The tactic not only provides multiple layers of protection for the original donors but also allows the groups to claim they are spending the money on "social welfare" activities to qualify for 501(c)(4) tax-exempt status.

This kind of technique is hardly unique to OFA: the Koch network of nonprofits and entities has employed similar means.[79]

What will be OFA's next incarnation? One assumes that it will live on throughout the Obama presidency and maybe even into his *post*-presidency.

THE NONPROFIT-BUSINESS-PHILANTHROPY-POLICY NEXUS

That brings us to the nonprofit, philanthropic ventures of some former chief executives, most notably Bill Clinton and Tony Blair.

Former President George W. Bush has been ridiculed for one of his post-presidential passions, namely painting. There were the bathtub and shower scenes, myriad dogs and cats, and the special portrait for departing late-night host Jay Leno.

But two former chief executives have set a different model for post-leadership careers. Of course, they are baby boomers and retired relatively young from public office. Like many members of their generation, they want to remain involved and relevant. Still, their influence melds philanthropy, commerce, and sometimes foreign policy, creating a thicket of unaccountability.

First there's Clinton.

Since leaving office, in addition to establishing the Clinton Foundation and its nonprofit Global Initiative, Clinton has served as a paid adviser to a global private equity and consulting firm called Teneo (among other business ventures). Teneo, which formed in 2011, bills itself as "integrated counsel for a borderless world . . . focused on working exclusively with the CEOs and leaders of the world's largest companies, institutions and governments."[80]

You may recall that Clinton's close aide and Teneo co-founder Douglas Band reportedly recruited donors to be Teneo clients. The lines between the firm and the philanthropy became so blurred that, in the words of the *New York Times*, "Some Clinton aides and foundation employees began to wonder where the foundation ended and Teneo began."[81]

The Clinton Global Initiative, founded in 2005, had a new way of doing the business of philanthropy, which appeared to dovetail with the needs of corporate donors as well as, later, Teneo.

CGI would advise companies and other donors on how to dole out their money rather than take it and dole it out themselves. An annual meeting, with a five-figure entrance fee, was part of the deal, and would bring the powerful together to network and hash out global issues, Davos-style. CGI reportedly has secured commitments of at least $74 billion since its formation.

In a lengthy piece called "Scandal at Clinton Inc.," the *New Republic* magazine described what the various parties got out of the deal:[82]

> For corporations, attaching Clinton's brand to their social investments offered a major p.r. boost. As further incentive, they could hope for a kind word from Clinton the next time they landed in a sticky spot. "Coca-Cola or Dow or whoever would come to the president," explains a former White House colleague of Band's, "and say, 'We need your help on this.'" Negotiating these relationships, and the trade-offs they required, could involve some gray areas.

"Gray" is certainly one way to characterize this relationship of reciprocal expectations, as laid out in the magazine:[83]

> There was Canadian businessman Frank Giustra, who often made his luxury jet available to Clinton and Band. In 2005, Giustra and Clinton overlapped on a visit to Kazakhstan, and at a dinner, Clinton praised the country's autocratic ruler, Nursultan A. Nazarbayev. Days later, according to *The New York Times*, Giustra secured a huge uranium-mining deal in the

country. In early 2006, Giustra donated $31.3 million to the foundation, followed by another $100 million pledge. (He also "co-produced" Clinton's sixtieth birthday party in Toronto, which raised another $21 million.)

A few years after that, Band would strike out on his own, or perhaps it was just the *appearance* of going out on his own. Teneo was formed, and the Teneo-CGI meld has caused consternation among Clintonites—and no doubt with Hillary Clinton, who surely wants no fresh scandals to threaten her presidential ambitions. The crisscrossing and overlapping intensified. As some of Band's former White House colleagues have said, it is no surprise that a longtime Clinton acolyte would leverage these contacts when starting a business.

According to the *New Republic*:[84]

A number of key Teneo clients were also closely involved with Clinton's charitable work. One month before the Rockefeller Foundation presented Clinton with an award for philanthropy, it gave Teneo a $3.4 million contract to propose "tangible solutions to global problems." Another early client was Coca-Cola, which helped build the distribution system for medicine in Tanzania, Mozambique, and Ghana, for a CGI project. Band has served on Coca-Cola's international advisory board, and a former Coke CEO, Donald Keough, chairs the boutique investment bank Allen & Co., which holds a financial interest in Teneo. Other Teneo clients include the big hospital chain Tenet (which is a lead partner in the new Clinton Health Matters Initiative) and UBS Americas (which launched a Small Business Advisory Program with the foundation).

It was Teneo's work with the collapsed MF Global, then headed by former New Jersey senator, governor, and Goldman Sachs chief Jon Corzine, that eventually led Clinton to leave his paid advisory role. Teneo, by some estimates, was taking in $125,000 a month for . . . as one unnamed MF Global source told the *New York Post*, "I don't know what they did. . . . It was always unclear."[85]

Once again, celebrityhood, like the prestige of the scholars we saw in the last chapter, is used to carry the weight of credibility. "There's an undertow of transactionalism in the glittering annual dinners," as the *New Republic* puts it: "the fixation on celebrity, and a certain contingent of donors whose charitable contributions and business interests occupy an uncomfortable proximity."[86]

And what are we to make of a series of "donations" from Boeing to the U.S. government, as well as to several Clinton-related causes, starting a few years back?

Bill isn't the only Clinton who has harnessed the gravitas of high office. The *Washington Post* reported in April that in 2009, then-Secretary of State Hillary Clinton visited Russia just as Boeing was seeking a multi-billion-dollar deal. Boeing landed the sale, to the tune of $3.7 billion.

Boeing was apparently pleased with the State Department's promotional help: among the donations or assistance that came in from the aerospace giant: $2 million to the U.S. government for a troubled American pavilion project for the 2010 Shanghai Expo (a donation which the paper says sidestepped ethics rules); $900,000 to the Clinton Foundation, for Haiti relief; and then in 2014, a "Ready for Hillary" Super PAC fundraiser hosted by a top Boeing lobbyist and former aide to President Clinton.[87] Hillary Clinton, of course, would rightfully say that it's part of her job as secretary of state to promote American business abroad. But the *Post* notes that the Clinton Foundation has become a destination for corporate donations, which, should Mrs. Clinton run for president, will be an area of scrutiny—and deservedly so. And if she is elected president, it would make sense to probe her aerospace policy and ask whether it unduly favors Boeing.

The celebrity and gravitas of high office have also served former U.K. prime minister Tony Blair very well.

Blair, on the very day he resigned from office, picked up a new role: special envoy to the so-called Quartet on the Middle East, which is composed of the United States, the European Union, the United Nations, and Russia.

But that was hardly the only role he would assume. What the *Telegraph* dubs "Blair Inc." features a wide array:[88] there's the African Governance Initiative, the Tony Blair Faith Foundation, the Tony Blair Sports Foundation, and the initiative called Breaking the Climate Deadlock.[89] There's

Tony Blair Associates, which has advised the governments of Kuwait and Kazakhstan, among others. Blair can be seen in a Kazakh promotional clip called "In the Stirrups of Time," which the *New Republic* calls a "dreary, neo-Stalinist propaganda video."[90]

He became an adviser to insurance giant Zurich International and JPMorgan Chase, which has brought him many millions of dollars as well as intense scrutiny over visits to Libya, a few of them apparently paid for by Muammar Gaddafi. JPMorgan Chase was trying to broker a deal between the Libyans and a Russian oligarch (which eventually fell through). Blair has strongly insisted that he does not lobby on behalf of JPMorgan Chase. Let's assume, for a moment, that he is being entirely forthcoming. As the maker of a documentary on Blair wrote in the *Telegraph:*[91]

> Was Mr Blair in Libya—as the headed notepaper would suggest—to discuss Middle East peace with Gaddafi? Was he working on behalf of his Governance Initiative, which claims it "pioneers a new way of working with African countries"? Was he sounding out deals for JP Morgan, as the well-placed Telegraph source insists? Or was he there on behalf of his own very lucrative money-making concern, Tony Blair Associates (TBA), whose professed objective is to provide "strategic advice" on "political and economic trends and government reform"?
>
> This confusion of motive and identity follows Mr Blair almost everywhere he goes, as we found when researching our forthcoming Channel 4 Dispatches film, The Wonderful World of Tony Blair.

At the very least, JPMorgan Chase is going to use the Blair brand. They are paying Blair a seven-figure fee for it. As *The National Interest* notes, ". . . JPMorgan Chase apparently invoked his name during the negotiations" for the unsuccessful Libyan-Russian deal.[92] This is not unlike the way top lobbyists are able to evade the title of lobbyist: lower-level names get their phone calls answered because of the attachment to the more prestigious figure.

Adding to the Blair muddle: some of his "management companies" are organized as "liability partnership[s]," which means, so says the *Telegraph,* that Blair "does not have any legal obligation to publish accounts."[93] And, under British law, Blair can take money directly from governments with no disclosure.[94]

Again it is important for us to assess motive, because sometimes the belief that your goals are pure can blind a power broker to his own conflicts or potential for conflicts.

Blair insists that he is helping autocratic governments learn the ways of good governance (you have heard this argument before from those consorting with despots). His business ventures, he says, fuel the philanthropy and he's not in it for the money. As he stated: "I probably spend two-thirds of my time on pro-bono activity, I probably spend the biggest single chunk of my time on the Middle East peace process which I do unpaid."[95]

Blair's prime goal, it seems, is to remain relevant and in the game. Yet aren't his activities still problematic? These days, with power, money, politics, diplomacy, and even philanthropy inextricably bound, someone of the stature of a former U.K. prime minister, and current Mideast envoy, is going to be very hard to hold to account.

—⁂—

In what and whom do we trust?

Given the records of Clinton, Blair, and other such leaders, some of whose activities toy with accountability to the public, it's not surprising that they support our declining faith in formal institutions, which inclined us toward the private sphere in the first place.

But that inclination comes with a price: what we imagine to be "grassroots" entities and efforts, as we have seen, are sometimes just the opposite.

What can be done to counteract this mode of influencing and restore accountability to the public sphere? The good news is that the influence around these entities and efforts exhibits clear signposts and patterns, and we can learn to identify them.

In the next and final chapter, we shall consider how recognizing when the public trust is being violated can be used to spot and take on the new corruption.

PART III:

RESTORING THE PUBLIC TRUST

CHAPTER 10

What Is to Be Done?

F rom the outset, we must recognize that there is no going back to that seemingly safer, more predictable place—that place before the end of the Cold War and the advent of the digital age—where how things might unfold was more linear and the rules were more firmly entrenched.[1] Clearly, the new corruption, and the unaccountability that is its signature feature, have taken hold. What can be done in the shadow-elite era, the age of structured unaccountability of so many of our formal institutions, and of power brokers who "fail up"? In surpassing the old means of wielding influence—be they interest groups, registered lobbyists, bribery, or other means—today's premier power brokers have also surpassed the old ways of holding them to account.

What can be done when the old remedies, ranging from government auditing to public shaming, no longer work nearly as well as they once did?

Oddly, an episode in my life on a Sunday in the spring of 2013 may go part way to answering this question. I was standing in the front of a "security" line at Reagan National Airport in Washington, D.C., in advance of a flight to Florida for a conference. Clad in a favorite pink dress with my hair recently coiffed, I believed I looked the picture of unobtrusive innocence. My luggage had already gone through the baggage scanner and awaited my pickup on the other side. But there I was, waiting and waiting for the "pat-down" by a Transportation Security Administration officer, and still waiting. . . . Other passengers were sending their luggage through the machine and passing through the body scanner in short order. But there I stood, holding out for a "female assist." And waiting. . . .

I usually declined to go through the full-body scanner, not trusting that it was entirely safe, and all too aware that at least some were sold to the public and to the U.S. government in ways that defied some of the standards of accountability.

I had notified an officer, even before I got close to the front of the line, that I would opt for the pat-down, and he promised to find me a female assist. In navigating security, I had learned to be exceedingly polite—and patient. Now, at the front of the line, I inquired respectfully about every five minutes. I was (consistently) told that the staffing was short and I would just have to wait, and sometimes was even asked "What time is your flight?" If there was a sense of urgency among the TSA staff, I could not detect it.

Meanwhile, my flight departure time was approaching, other fliers were being processed through security, and I wanted to at least be able to grab a cup of coffee before boarding.

My polite entreaties obviously were not working.

Inwardly growing perturbed, but outwardly sporting a big smile, I burst forth with the first verse of "The Star Spangled Banner" at the top of my lungs. In full voice, and mustering up full stage presence like an opera singer, I gave it my all. The idea had just come to me that a headline TSA ARRESTS WOMAN FOR SINGING NATIONAL ANTHEM could be a little embarrassing for the powers that be. After all, singing "The Star Spangled Banner" could certainly be seen as a patriotic display, even as an endorsement of U.S. airport security procedures and the idea that they keep America safe.

What happened next? At first, all the officers looked around confusedly, trying to figure out where the singing was coming from. A loudspeaker, perhaps?

Then they spotted me, smiling and singing at full throttle well into the first verse. I was just about up to the "land of the free and home of the brave."

How long do you think it took them to find that elusive female assist?

I had barely finished the first verse before a TSA officer waved me through to my handler, who patted me down and sent me on my merry way. I got my coffee and made my flight.

For a few moments there, I felt empowered, though airport staff may have felt chagrined. Later I realized how proud I was of my success—of having beaten the system. It was like the pride I (and routinely many others) felt when they successfully maneuvered the challenges of everyday life in communist Eastern Europe in, say, getting that scarce item in a store through a relationship with the clerk. Pride is the antidote to succumbing to the humiliation that the system offers up.

What does this story tell us?

If I had screamed and yelled and expressed outrage, asked to see the big boss, threatened to file a complaint, or worse, the TSA would have known exactly how to react. They have procedures for that—well-honed methods for dealing with unruly behavior and disgruntled complainers. No doubt it is codified in their manuals and is a substantial part of their training.

My strategy worked precisely because my behavior was so far removed from the standard playbook that the officers were at a complete loss. *She is attracting puzzling attention, and it is awkward*, I can imagine them thinking. *How to deal with someone who is respectfully, yet unexpectedly, singing the U.S.A.'s national anthem? We must get her to stop. How to do that? Find that female assist, pronto.* Apparently, that was not a problem.

My (singing) strategy worked because it was out of place and didn't even come close to fitting into the confines of what the staff knew how to deal with. It worked because it diverged from the standard impersonal, formal way of operating. My behaving well outside the norm required the system's functionaries, too, to step outside their prescribed roles and find a unique way of reacting. The spectacle I had created demanded a *human* reaction—the same human reaction that has been lost in our age of structured unaccountability—replete with digitization of almost everything, silos, and a broken connection between bureaucrat and client, policymaker and voter.

The same connection that is lost in, say, the customer-service phone tree or the world of sliced-and-diced mortgages and exotic derivatives.

The old ways are no longer so effective, but such strategies as the one I resorted to in the airport can be.

My own small effort to get through an airport pales in comparison to the norm-busting strategies employed in cases much more consequential. Take, for instance, the so-called Yes Men whose slogan is "Sometimes it takes a lie to expose the truth."[2] They sought compensation for the thousands of victims killed and sickened by the 1984 Union Carbide chemical spill in Bhopal, India (a still-contaminated site), for which the company had disbursed only $470 million.[3] Posing as a spokesman for Dow Chemical (which had acquired Union Carbide) in an interview with the BBC on the twentieth anniversary of the disaster, a member of this enterprising duo said that Dow would assume full responsibility for the accident and pay $12 billion to the victims.[4] That hoax news required a response from the company. While an embarrassed Dow denied that it would do anything,[5] the spectacle "prompted the world media to put the debate over corporate responsibility in the news," as the *Washington Post* observed.[6]

Consider, too, the impact of fake news programs such as Stewart's *The Daily Show* and *The Colbert Report*. In the 2012 election cycle, and in the wake of the 2010 Supreme Court *Citizens United* ruling, Stephen Colbert's Super PAC, "Americans for a Better Tomorrow, Tomorrow," brought huge public attention to the unaccountability and lack of transparency of these political-influence groups.

Such hoaxing and posing "does not fit a common understanding of resistance or opposition," say anthropologists Dominic Boyer and Alexei Yurchak, who, like me, observed a similarity between the public propaganda of late-communist societies and the mainstream media of today in the West.[7] That is precisely why it works so well.

A successful norm-busting strategy draws public or media attention to an issue through a performance that is unconventional yet inoffensive, as well as puzzling, humorous, or dazzling. Ironically, it is imbued with qualities of shadow elites. The ambiguity surrounding the activity of hoaxers and posers and their agility in shifting roles and playing with the rules resembles that of shadow elites. In both cases, these qualities render the players effective—and unaccountable. Moreover, such strategy plays on the very performance culture that motivates regular people to turn to parody in search of something more authentic—and in the process, of course, is itself a performance. It must attract unusual attention and demand a response from its target and the public.

Still, however entertaining and successful such strategies may be, they are piecemeal, ad hoc, unsystematic, and thus severely limited in potential impact.

While not ethically challenged, these strategies, like those of the practitioners of the new corruption, also "innovate" beyond the bounds of law. Just as I broke the unwritten rules of how to behave in the airport security line (and just as there was no script for dealing with my behavior), so do practitioners of the new corruption operate beyond the bounds of legal violation.

And, let's not forget, while posing and hoaxes are public displays, they are *private* responses to broken public institutions. They cannot restore *public* accountability or trust. They are a workaround that highlights what is missing in society.

REUNITING ETHICS AND ACCOUNTABILITY

Before getting to some very specific remedies, let's look at the broader issues of what society must do to restore the public trust.

At the core of the rise of the unaccountable is the fundamental problem that ethics have become disconnected from the mores of a larger public or community and detached from the authority that states and international organizations, boards of directors, and even shareholders once supplied. Carol in Ohio, the Bank of America employee who appeared earlier in this book, performs for the "accountability" checklist, above answering to her clients. Through no fault of her own, the relationship between her and her clients has been severed.

Likewise, mortgages are sliced and diced and sold—all without consideration of the impact on the client, let alone the broader impact. "Innovative" bankers across Wall Street were stuck within the ethics and expectations of their silo, which valued short-term dealmaking more than long-term consequences. Yet they would not consider their activities corrupt. And retired generals who see no problem serving on both government advisory boards and defense-contractor boards surely believe this, too, because their silo—the military—has convinced them of their rectitude, expertise, and ability to self-regulate.

Were the generals or the exotic-derivatives traders to ask those outside their silo, at the diner or coffee shop, say, "Does my behavior pass the smell test," the answer might well be "no." They aren't asking that question of themselves nearly enough.

It's time that we ask again and again if there's any hope of holding the unaccountable to account. Why is that such a problem?

In recent decades, "accountability" has become associated with specific auditing practices in the United States, the United Kingdom, and elsewhere.[8] As checklist-type accountability practices ascended in the 1980s, *accountability* assumed a more mechanistic meaning, political scientist Melvin J. Dubnick has shown.[9] Such practices, whether applied to the state or private sector, disconnect accountability from much of what matters. Accountability is imposed from the outside—without the engagement of a "moral community"—a community "that shapes (and is shaped by) the expectations, rules, norms and values of social relationships," as Dubnick characterizes it. The resulting checklist accountability is removed from the internal ethics of a community—that very community or body that it is supposed to hold to account. Accountability gets reduced to a performance, a technocratic exercise without moral or ethical moorings.

The disconnect is not only from the outside. Auditing breaks things down into observable, isolated, and often quantifiable pieces and then scrutinizes the pieces—frequently with little or no regard for the whole. With essential parts separated from each other, knowledge, wisdom, and institutional memory are sidelined. We might ask how it can be that, in a society consumed with auditing virtually everything—from relationships to job performance to government programs—there have been so many failures of accountability in finance.

Promontory Financial, discussed in Chapter 6, surely went through many checklists of proper corporate governance with its client MF Global; MF Global was then able to demonstrate to the government that it had reformed with a laudatory report penned by Promontory. But it may have been just that—a demonstration—not so very different from a "performance." Promontory, acting as a paid, private stand-in for real government oversight, missed the broader picture of malfeasance that would explode within a matter of months.

Whether government, private, or some amalgam thereof, these parties are all constrained by walls around their compartments. Consider government auditors. Confined to silos and vertically structured laws and regulations, they cannot begin to effectively track the new power brokers, who work horizontally. In addition to limited jurisdiction, these auditors are not typically charged with tracing influence across organizations but rather with how governments spend taxpayers' money. Their methods hark back to an older world: one with clearer demarcation.

Accountability practices also evaluate individuals, not network or group actions. Groups are scarcely subject to investigation unless they fall under organized crime or terrorism, and even then it is typically individuals who can be held to account.

In today's world of shadow elites, shadow lobbyists, and their ilk, this will not do.

Beyond Checklist Accountability

Perhaps our most important task as a society is to reintegrate ethics and accountability. This is an essential undertaking, and one that will be hard to achieve.

The absence of moral community under today's checklist accountability shows how difficult it is for the players to be shamed, even when they can be named. Players we have met in this book—from the retired general who serves simultaneously as an adviser to a military agency and a consultant to a defense company pushing services to the agency, to the economist-scholar recommending lax regulation to a congressional committee without mentioning his Wall Street roles, to the high-status professor touting the "reforms" of a despot without mentioning that he is being paid by a PR firm—all try to inoculate themselves by claiming ignorance of the consequences of their actions. Of course, we can never quite know for sure what our activities will reap. But isn't it their—and our—professional obligation to anticipate the consequences of given actions and to read their implications?

Consider former U.S. Congressman and speaker of the House Newt Gingrich, who simply plowed ahead even when lambasted for serving as a handsomely paid "historian" for housing giant Freddie Mac in the decade leading up to the financial crisis. (He's currently enjoying a perch on the CNN program *Crossfire*.) Or the reporter who still calls himself a journalist even when a foreign, repressive regime is underwriting his salary as a well-paid lobbyist.

Often the players themselves seem only dimly aware of their own conflicts, as when Mike McConnell, then the Director of National Intelligence, suggested to a reporter, with apparently no reservations, that there was no real difference between his work for a private contractor (a lucrative business that paid him a huge salary) and his work for the government (on behalf of the public, that earned him a fraction of his Booz Allen salary). Is it that he has so accepted the intertwined nature of intelligence that he doesn't see the ethical tangles that are obvious to those of us who stand outside the system?

True accountability cannot be achieved merely by deploying a checklist. Helen Sutch, a longtime World Banker whose expertise on corruption of all kinds may be unparalleled, goes a step farther, suggesting that ticking the boxes "is a corruption risk in itself, because it implies that as long as the boxes are ticked, anything beyond that, if not explicitly forbidden, is okay. More broadly, it also discourages people from taking responsibility for the success of the whole activity."[10] The fact is that we need both accountability from the outside and trust on the inside.[11]

The traditional *accountability* had both connotations. So do many native terms into which the English word is translated. When I asked participants from China, Chile, Nepal, South Africa, Russia, and France, among other countries, at a 2003 workshop I organized in Poland to discuss how it is rendered into their languages and what it connotes, it became clear that the more recent meaning of *accountability* doesn't travel well. In French, Spanish, and other Romance languages, for example, *accountability* means responsibility.[12] This approach engages the moral community.

The damage wrought when a system is disconnected from moral community and practice is huge. A prominent Polish essayist just after World War II described an "excluded economy"—an entire informal system of off-the-books survival—that flourished under the weight of German occupation. "An economy morally excluded from the life of the nation has left behind calamitous psychosocial practices," he wrote. "Only now are we paying the price of the occupation."[13]

While this is an extreme example, far removed from the experience of most of us, I hope that the ethical disconnect that we have seen in this book is, by now, clear. Above all, ethics and accountability must be reintegrated. Today's crisis of formal institutions and of leadership makes this change all the more urgent. Thinking about corruption in terms of violating the public trust helps to clarify the issue.

STRATEGIES

Both law and ethics, as I wrote early in these pages, prove to be impotent counters to today's unaccountability. We must consider the long-term impact of both accountability legislation and the effectiveness of naming and shaming.

What of the first?

As we discussed earlier, it appears that an array of factors helped drive the American Economic Association to adopt a more stringent code of ethics in 2012 for thousands of economists. A study in 2010 of prominent economists not disclosing financial ties got some disapproving press. This came at the same time as an Oscar-winning documentary, complete with "ambush" interviews of academic economists who appeared to take money to deliver positive news about an economy that was about to collapse, namely Iceland. But has the idea that economists might be named and shamed for serving as scholars-for-hire or even just "consultants" struck fear into the hearts of economists with a swirl of undisclosed affiliations? Hardly. Are those economists without money-making and prestige-building roles concerned about guilt by association? It's doubtful.

Where is the social pressure of the community of economists? It's hard to detect. And yet, as I argue, if the pattern is to change, sanctions must also come from within.

As for Key Opinion Leader physicians, the passage of the Physician Payment Sunshine Act in the United States may force companies to issue public reports on payments to physicians. But as with economists, does this actually raise the specter of naming and shaming? ProPublica reported in

2014 that many top pharma companies had drastically cut their budgets for physician speaking engagements ahead of the disclosure rules taking effect.[14] While the threat of disclosure may have taken some physicians working in America out of the game, again, legislation and transparency alone—that is, naming—cannot suffice in the absence of the effectiveness of shaming.

The Limits of Law

Can law, and the enforcement of it, do all the work? Or even much of it?

The emergence of lobbyists who simply don't register should serve as a cautionary tale. The fate of several disclosure and ethics laws might be at play. There was the 1995 Lobbying Disclosure Act, which has many loopholes still exploited today. But it wasn't until around 2008 that the number of lobbyists mysteriously began a sharp decline. Political scientist Tim LaPira offers several reasons in a guest post for the transparency advocates at the Sunshine Foundation, including one I find interesting. He mentions the idea that after the passage of the Honest Leadership and Open Government Act of 2007 and President Obama's 2009 executive order putting more lobbying strictures on Executive Branch employees, players don't want to hurt their career prospects by wearing a Scarlet L for Lobbyist.[15]

In the end, LaPira believes that the Honest Leadership and Open Government Act is probably the most likely reason lobbyists have gone underground, seeing less risk in not registering than in registering. This shows a failure of enforcement, clearly. But he also emphasizes what I have throughout the book: that lobbying needs redefining to better encompass what it now really is. I would add that influence more broadly needs to be redefined to fit the contortions that power brokers are now making in flexing their muscles. So with both economists and physicians, we need to be on a sharp lookout for new behaviors that might be novel conduits of influence allowing players to evade the rules . . . and avoid being named and shamed.

In the beginning, as well as in the end, there is no substitute for society or what is sometimes called "civil society." I don't mean this in a lofty or over-arching way. We bring society alive when we connect with our communities beyond the silos of our own networks and professions to see our actions from a different perspective. We bring society alive when we cross-fertilize outside our usual networks. Many of the policy failures we have seen in this book lie with players and groups who are so embedded in their own tight-knit networks and mindsets that they not only ignore those outside their circles, they actively refuse them a place at the decider's table. Society is alive—and the public trust is possible—when outsiders have a seat.[16]

CORRUPTION AND RESTORING THE PUBLIC TRUST

Of course, corruption does not just afflict the Other, the benighted Third World country. The more elusive corruption is now very much a part of Western, highly developed countries that typically rank relatively low on corruption indices. In any case, the fixation on country-by-country ranking is itself misguided; today's power brokers, as we have said, are often global in reach and work in networks. To that end, the object of analysis should be the players themselves, their border-hopping allies, and the milieus in which they operate.[17]

And metrics aren't up to the task. Metrics might work if the focus on illegal acts—the single transaction in a single venue—made sense; but that, too, is outmoded. The prevailing definition of corruption, "the abuse of public office for private gain," is ready-made for the clarity of bribery but not for the ambiguity that swirls around today's influencers. They are more subtle in their dealings and have little need for blatantly illegal activities.

The old model might target a corrupt lawmaker receiving a bribe from a company to get favorable legislation enacted. That model breaks down in the new era, in which relationships are multiple and moving while organizational boundaries and missions are blurred.

And how does one account for corruption that might occur in the service of ideology? Certainly the actions of ideologically driven operatives would not fit neatly into a model that emphasizes transactions with clearly measurable benefits to the transgressors. Money is certainly not the sole motivation of the powerful.

It would seem that we should not just consider the activities of the players, but take a systematic look at their practices. The frenetic role-playing in and of itself doesn't make one corrupt, but the modus operandi does make accountability and transparency very difficult. A player who acts as a paid consultant in one venue, a pundit in another, and a professor in yet a third is not necessarily engaged in a "double strategy," but his consultancy and punditry activities can be at odds with his supposedly objective voice as a professor if he does not disclose the former.[18] And surely watchdogs will have their hands full trying to untangle all the activities at play.

In sum, to fully capture the new influence and the potential for corruption, metrics should take a back seat to patterns of operation and network configurations charted through analysis of the players' roles and networks. Shortly, I will describe this in greater detail.

Are They Corrupt?

Shadow elites, shadow lobbyists, and their fellow travelers may be unaccountable, with their "corruption" elusive. But are they, in fact, corrupt?

As we have seen, the bribe-taking bureaucrat or customs official is more likely to be defined as "corrupt" and punished, even as the consequences of his actions are nowhere near as egregious as, say, the financier who devised investment vehicles for selected clients to bet against the housing market without disclosing to other clients (pension funds, insurance companies, and foreign banks) that they were being set up to lose billions.

We redefined corruption as a violation of the public trust in Chapter 1, in broad sync with conceptualizations in texts such as the Qur'an and the Bible.[19] Political economist Lloyd J. Dumas elaborates:[20]

> The violation of the public trust for personal advantage (either for oneself or one's network) is the essence of corruption, whether it is the public trust of a government official or the trust implicit in a client-consultant relationship. For example, it is expected that the advice given and actions taken by medical doctors will be guided by what is best for the health and well-being of their patients, not by what course of treatment will maximize the doctors' income or satisfy their desire to try out experimental procedures that may bring them acclaim. In any relationship that conveys power and authority to one individual to act on behalf of others, or even to guide the behavior of

others, trust is central. That is one of the key reasons why the massive betrayal of clients' and the public's trust by rating agencies and top investment banks created such an earthquake.

According to Dumas, corruption "occurs whenever individuals use for their own personal agendas, the authority, power, or information that was given to them for the purpose of furthering the interests of others, to the detriment of those others."[21] I would add that the act need not be to the detriment of *those particular* others; the authority, power, or information could be used to the detriment of quite different others and still breach the public trust.

Of course, corruption as violation of the public trust cannot serve as a universal definition because, at least to some degree, the "public trust" itself is culturally defined. Still, seeing corruption as a violation of the public trust (recognizing, of course, that "public" is always defined indigenously, a term with variable meaning across time and place), upends the traditional approaches of the anticorruption industry and shines a spotlight on highflier power brokers whose activities are legal yet violate the public trust.[22]

Seeing corruption as a violation of the public trust can help clarify and call it out. But caution is warranted. Although the modus operandi of many of today's top power brokers renders them virtually unaccountable to government or corporate institutions and the public, it does not necessarily make them unethical or corrupt.

Why suggest reconceptualizing corruption at all? Because, clearly, the potential of shadow elites and shadow lobbyists for violating the public trust on a colossal scale is huge, with the possible consequences of their actions just as colossal.

READING THE WORLD IN THE AGE OF UNACCOUNTABILITY
So, what can we do?

There are ways for governmental and corporate authorities, journalists, and the public to take action that won't lead to an awkward airport encounter like mine.

We need to begin to connect the dots and challenge the unaccountable. As a result, we will be better equipped to assess the motives and message of the pundits, politicians, and consultants we encounter—whether in the media, social-networking outlets, town-hall meetings, or other venues— and to combat the new corruption.

First, citizens, those in the media, and those in government making public-policy decisions need to know how to spot a power broker who is spinning an agenda. As we noted in Chapter 5, we are increasingly getting news on our mobile devices, on the go. This seems like a particularly challenging environment in which to examine sources of information. One thing I'd encourage might be called "One Click More." As you are reading something that appears fishy, take one click more (likely you'll need more than one click, but at least one will get you started).

When you see a power broker pontificating on a topic, do you have a hard time figuring out who he is and who funds him? You might have had a clear idea of who he was a few years ago, say, when he was Homeland Security chief or secretary of the Treasury, but what is he now?

Here is an accountability red flag to watch out for: when someone is described as a *former* official, it is imperative to understand where they are *currently* and what stake they might now have in the topic at hand. You can take that one click more to a Wiki page and test yourself: could you sum up this person's career easily? Is the list of titles and affiliations daunting? If so, this doesn't mean this power broker is necessarily corrupt, but you should then know that he has a lot of irons in the fire. Even Wikis can be a bit misleading; they nearly all feature the public-service part of a résumé front and center, even if that service was years—even decades—ago. So make sure you scroll down to find the most current roles.

Another title to watch out for is "consultant." Many of us are consultants, yet the moniker can be a red flag. What is a consultant, exactly? Are there laws governing their activities? Do they have a clearly articulated code of ethics? Often the answers are no and no. I can tell you from my own experience that consultants can perform innumerable roles, and their agendas are often far from clear. Consultants are getting paid by someone; they are not getting paid to speak to a reporter or appear on television. So why are they doing so? Often it's because they have an agenda to push, their client's or their own.[23]

Consider carefully the title "expert." *Expert* can define any number of players. Michael Chertoff is likely an expert on terrorism, after his years as secretary of Homeland Security, but he is more currently a private consultant to the security business looking to sell its wares to the government. Former EPA head Christine Todd Whitman regularly expounds on energy issues in venues all over the United States, and yet she represents a variety of energy-company interests and has for years. Retired General Barry McCaffrey is an NBC News military analyst; but when he weighed in on the deteriorating situation in Iraq in June 2014, there was no mention on the *Nightly News* that he also runs a consulting firm.[24] An expert might also be an academic; if that's the case, it can be illuminating to Google the sources of his/her research funding. People from think tanks are often called experts. If that's the case, it's worth Googling whether the think tank is known as having a particular agenda and finding out who funds them.

Very often these days, corporations are part of the mix, even when the think tank has a very neutral, civic-friendly name. And with think-tank–like organizations popping up all over these days, it's also smart to consider how long a "think tank" has been around. Did it appear after *Citizens United* opened the door for unlimited and hard-to-trace political spending? If so, you might want to probe it a bit further. What is being called a think tank might actually be little more than a vehicle for secret political cash aimed at pushing an agenda. One glaring hint might be a website that has no area to detail "who funds us."

When you read about an important policy fight, like health care or whether to back a war, do you see names of people who might be described as "advisers," "backroom deal-makers," "rainmakers," or "right-hand man," but they don't seem to have an official role? Often the boundary between official and private activity is not clear. (See, for instance, the financial bailout, where it was sometimes hard to figure out who worked at Goldman Sachs and who worked at the Treasury Department. Or with issues of national security and intelligence, where the lines between "private" contractor Booz Allen and the Office of the Director of National Intelligence fade.) From the 2003 Iraq invasion to the financial bailout to Obamacare, each fight (and many more such fights) had players whose unofficial positions might have been described this way, and yet they will never be held to account because they were officially "informal."

Sadly, one must also place "philanthropist" in the category of red-flag titles. While many, if not most, appear in the media working to eliminate the scourges of poverty or war, there are now players, including Bill Clinton and especially Tony Blair, whose portfolios are so vast that they cannot be viewed as simple do-gooders. This skepticism should also be applied to little-known groups (like the think-tank–style groups) that call themselves philanthropies. They might be technically one of those so-called "social welfare" groups under the U.S. tax code, but once again they could be just a front for an agenda or "dark" campaign donations.

And of course, these days, it isn't just the Sunday-morning talk shows and the *New York Times* op-ed page driving agendas. One now needs cross-platform vigilance. E-mail, Facebook pages, Twitter feeds, you name it; if you get an unmediated stream from a person in power, a former official, you should remember that just because he trumpets his twentieth wedding anniversary in one post doesn't mean he won't try to sell you something in the next.

As you get your "information" and "news" across digital venues, it's also key to make sure you know the source—which these days isn't always easy—and to see the original piece as it was written. Stories nowadays, of course, are shared and retweeted with various colorations that more partisan "sharers" or self-interested power brokers might be adding. Sometimes these shadings are quite subtle—and you won't notice until you take one click more and see the original piece. Recall that in Chapter 5 we noted that much news is still originating from "old" media where there are still some standards; you might find that the conclusions reached by your powerful "sharer" aren't exactly borne out in the original piece. And sometimes you'll see that the original piece did not come from old media at all, but rather from a corporate entity trying to *look* like it's putting out news, or a think tank that's just a front for certain ideological warriors.

Watch out, too, for coordinated campaigns and networks of power brokers. (Also, groups that acquire nicknames—such as Rubinites, COINdinistas, Neocons, Locomotives—deserve more scrutiny.) Sometimes a group of officials and allied "talking heads" will descend in multiple venues spouting the same general message, perhaps best seen in the 2003 run-up to the Iraq war. Neoconservatives agitating for war began using alarming imagery in their rhetoric on all sorts of outlets, some warning that they didn't want "the smoking gun" to be "a mushroom cloud." (The speechwriter behind that rhetoric, Michael Gerson, went on to take an op-ed perch at the *Washington Post*.[25])

Keep a lookout, too, not just for formulaic and repeated language across media, but also for metaphors used to justify a course of action. As we saw in Chapter 4, they are commonly employed to sell public policies, and, while they pervade public debate, metaphors routinely highlight or hide the issue they are deployed to explain. What does a specific metaphor highlight? What does it hide?

And when it comes to spotting a coordinated group, like, say, the Locomotives who led Iceland to ruin, this is one of the cases where it does make sense to look backwards. Identifying them after the fact matters because they may well have moved on to another more current opportunity to exert stealth influence. Are the players with exclusive inside access and information also the very same people who were branding the information for the public? Were the players—"who is involved" in the action?—just as important as the action itself? Would the action never happen without the particular players?

After a big push like the Iraq invasion, those in the network often decamp to think tanks, universities, corporations, lobbying firms, and op-ed pages. They might review each other's books, or promote each other with a so-called blurb endorsement. You might see them trying to brand their actions in the previous fight as they gear up for the next opportunity. In the case of the Neoconservatives, some saw them moving on to Iran as the next threat to drum up in various venues. Deciphering these networks often requires not just experience, but also computing power, because of the amount of data and its complexity.

That is very much the case for shadow elites and shadow lobbyists. The object of analysis must be the players themselves, because their influence derives from their ability to blend and blur such boundaries as official and private, international and national.[26] Focusing on one or the other misses the point, since it loses the connection. Instead, the focus must be the players' roles, activities, and sponsors; their networks; and the organizations that they and their networks empower. How do these players and networks operate within and across borders and link to each other?[27]

No Magic Bullet, But Some Practical Measures

Those are some ideas about how to spot accountability-challenged power brokers; but how can we diminish their reach and impact?

First of all, no one person or institution can provide a quick fix. Holding any one power broker to certain account would require a team of investigators and public servants tracking his activities, networks, and funding sources over time: reporters connecting the dots; attorneys and regulators picking up on reporters' work and subpoenaing documents that reporters cannot; and legislators dedicating themselves to passing laws to reflect changes in the environment and hold culprits to account. Because the potential influence and "corruption" of these players are interrelated, that would involve a holistic approach, one that considers all the components collectively and how they interact.

In the broadest sense, it would be wise for us all to take an interest in legislation that involves accountability and disclosure. These are not traditionally sexy topics that you see very often on the nightly news or "trending" on Twitter, and yet they are important. That said, as we have noted, there are considerable limits to what legislation can do. Moreover, regulation often results in unintended consequences and even can be counterproductive. The influence of these players is often embedded in the power structure, no matter the political party in power, so such measures are likely to meet with significant resistance or be outgamed.

And even when tougher laws are enacted, the players are adept at skirting the rules. (One need only look at how big banks are circumventing financial-reform provisions.)

So when pressing for legislation, voters should demand that regulations encompass the new forms of influence that might not fall into existing parameters: when a former politician joins a lobbying firm and tells his younger colleagues who to call and to use his name, is that politician not a lobbyist? Perhaps he should be compelled to register as one.

We should also press for legislation to crack down on political activities by those political-influence groups that proliferated after *Citizens United*. In the fall of 2013, the Obama administration proposed a crackdown. While Republicans took the lead early on creating these groups, Democrats of course are trying their hand as well, with the president's own former campaign machine, now called Organizing for Action, being one.[28]

Aside from legislation, we should encourage codes of professional conduct among consultancies, academe, government, business, media, and think tanks. Even the American Economic Association adopted a code, but only after shaming by the 2010 documentary *Inside Job*, which exposed blatant conflicts on the part of certain star economists. Aside from requiring more disclosure when submitting research papers, "the AEA urges its members and other economists to apply the . . . principles [of greater disclosure] in other publications: scholarly journals, op-ed pieces, newspaper and magazine columns, radio and television commentaries, as well as in testimony before federal and state legislative committees and other agencies."[29]

Of course, no one can expect that "urging" will be a magic bullet. But as anthropologists have shown in research on ethics in financial conduct, people are very much motivated by what their peers and neighbors think of them.[30]

One profession that is vital in restoring accountability is the old or "legacy" media. Journalists and producers should commit to stricter standards when they quote and feature prominent players. It is helpful to directly ask a guest or source if they have any obvious conflict of interest, and many reporters still do of course try to determine conflicts. It might make sense to go one step farther and ask what affiliations they have; sometimes the players themselves, immersed in a near-hermetically sealed professional world, are only dimly aware of their own multi-layered agendas. Reporters and producers should also be made more aware of informal roles and how these can be used in ways that evade accountability.

Despite the decline of newspapers, op-eds still matter, and they are of particular concern. Editors need to make sure that the thumbnail biography attached to an op-ed contains not just the most prestigious position, like professor or former cabinet secretary, but other roles like current industry affiliations that might bear on the views being expressed in the op-ed.

—⁓—

That this material can be depressing is, of course, not lost on me. Yet by providing what I hope is clear-headed analysis, identifying what is wrong, and providing tools for scrutiny and possible solutions, I hope I have helped to equip readers to move beyond skepticism and frustration and toward understanding and action.

Having studied power and influence for several decades, and expecting to continue to do so in the years to come, I welcome comments and examples from readers highlighting players and organizations about which I might not be aware.

And if you try my strategy of singing your way through airport security, do let me know how it goes.

ENDNOTES

CHAPTER 1

1. Justin Loisseau, "The 3 Most Corrupt Countries in the World." *The Motley Fool,* January 1, 2014 (http://www.fool.com/investing/general/2014/01/01/the-3-most-corrupt-countries-in-the-world.aspx).

2. Martin Gilens and Benjamin Page, "Testing Theories of American Politics: Elites, Interest Groups, and Average Citizens." Working Paper, April 9, 2014 (http://www.princeton.edu/~mgilens/Gilens%20homepage%20materials/Gilens%20and%20Page/Gilens%20and%20Page%202014-Testing%20Theories%203-7-14.pdf).

3. Sahil Kapur, "Scholar Behind Viral 'Oligarchy' Study Tells You What It Means." *Talking Points Memo,* April 22, 2014 (http://talkingpointsmemo.com/dc/princeton-scholar-demise-of-democracy-america-tpm-interview).

4. A poll published in 2007 on declining trust globally and corruption shows that, over the last four decades, nearly all of the so-called developed, industrialized democracies have been experiencing a decrease in the public trust in government. This has not occurred at the same pace or necessarily for the same reasons everywhere, but the trend is pervasive. (Peri K. Blind, "Building Trust In Government In The Twenty-First Century: Review of Literature and Emerging Issues." 7th Global Forum on Reinventing Government: Building Trust in Government 26-29 June 2007, Vienna, Austria, November 2006 [http://unpan1.un.org/intradoc/groups/public/documents/un/unpan025062.pdf, pp. 8-23].)

    Even Swedes and Norwegians, traditionally highly trustful of their political institutions, expressed less trust in them in the 1990s (T. Christensen and P. Laegreid, "Trust in Government: The Significance of Attitudes Towards Democracy, Public Sector and Public Sector Reforms." Working Paper 7, Stein Rokkan Center for Social Studies and Bergen University Research Foundation,

April 2003, pp. 1-30). For details about these trends in the Netherlands, Austria, Canada, Germany, and Japan, see Russell J. Dalton, "The Social Transformation of Trust in Government." *International Review of Sociology*, vol. 15, no. 1, March 2005, pp. 133-154.

With regard to the United States, in a 2013 Gallup Poll respondents were asked: "Please tell me how much confidence you, yourself, have in each one—a great deal, quite a lot, some, or very little?" The following are the percentages of those who replied either "a great deal" or "quite a lot." The biggest drops in confidence were in Congress (42% in 1973 to 10% in 2013, more than a 76% fall), banks (from 60% in 1979 to 26% in 2013, nearly a 57% decline), TV news (46% in 1993 to 23% in 2013, a 50% decrease), schools (58% in 1973 to 32% in 2013, nearly a 45% decline), newspapers (39% in 1973 to 23% in 2013, a 41% decline), with diminished confidence also in unions (30% in 1973 to 20% in 2013, a 33% decline), the president (52% in 1975 to 36% in 2013, nearly a 31% decline), churches (65% in 1973 to 48% in 2013, greater than a 26% decrease), the Supreme Court (45% in 1973 to 34% in 2013, nearly a 24% decrease), and big business (26% in 1973 to 22% in 2013, more than a 15% decrease). Small increases in confidence were noted for the police, medical system, criminal justice, small business, and HMOs, and a big increase for the military. The first dates listed in each comparison are the year that Gallup first conducted the poll. See: Gallup, "Confidence in Institutions," Gallup Poll, June 13, 2013 (http://www.gallup.com/poll/163055/confidence-institutions-2013-pdf.aspx and http://www.gallup.com/poll/1597/confidence-institutions.aspx).

5. The English word *accountability* warrants close scrutiny. As political scientist Melvin J. Dubnick has written, there is a traditional meaning and a more recent usage that came into prominence in the 1980s. Dubnick argues that what distinguishes the traditional accountability notion from other governance solutions is that it depends on the existence of a "moral community"—a community "that shapes (and is shaped by) the expectations, rules, norms and values of social relationships." Thus, the traditional notion of *accountability* emerges as a primary characteristic of governance in contexts where there is a sense of agreement about the legitimacy of expectations among community members. Dubnick writes that "Conceptually, *accountabilityc* [the traditional concept] can thus be regarded as a *form of governance that depends on the dynamic social interactions and mechanisms created within of* [sic] *such a moral community*." (Melvin J. Dubnick, "Seeking Salvation for Accountability," Paper presented at the annual meeting of the American Political Science Association, August 29-September 1, 2002, pp. 6-7, emphasis in original [http://pubpages.unh.edu/dubnick/papers/salv2002.htm].)

    It's also important to note, as I discuss in the last chapter, that "accountability" does not travel easily across cultures.

6. See, for instance, Claire Cain Miller, "Tech Companies Concede to Surveillance Program." *New York Times*, June 7, 2013 (http://www.nytimes.com/2013/06/08/technology/tech-companies-bristling-concede-to-government-surveillance-efforts.html?pagewanted=1&hp&_r=0).

7. See, for example, Abbas J. Ali, *Islamic Perspectives on Management and Organization*. Cheltenham, UK: Edward Elgar, 2005; Syed Hussein Alatas,

Corruption: Its Nature, Causes and Functions. Brookfield, VT: Gower, 1990, pp. 13-14; Maxime Rodinson, *Islam and Capitalism.* London: Saqi Books, 2007 (1966); Richard Rubenstein, *Thus Saith the Lord.* New York: Harcourt, 2006; and Iqbal Zafar and Mervyn K. Lewis, "Governance and Corruption: Can IslamicSocieties and the West Learn from Each Other?" *American Journal of Islamic Social Sciences,* vol.19, issue 2, pp. 1-33.

8.   World Bank, *Helping Countries Combat Corruption: The Role of the World Bank.* Washington, D.C.: World Bank: PREM, 1997, p. 8.

9.   The timeframe here is approximately 2004 to 2007.

     The U.S. government did sue Standard & Poor's. As *International Business Times* reports (Malik Singleton, "Federal Judge Rules Justice Department Can Sue Standard & Poor's For Fraud In $5 Billion Case Stemming From Ratings," July 17, 2013 [http://www.ibtimes.com/federal-judge-rules-justice-department-can-sue-standard-poors-fraud-5-billion-case-stemming-ratings]):

> The U.S. government can pursue its $5 billion civil fraud lawsuit against Standard & Poor's following a ruling by a U.S. federal judge in Santa Ana, Calif. . . .
>
> The DOJ (Department of Justice) accuses the credit rating agency of inflating ratings so that it could win more fees from mortgage issuers and bankers that pay for its ratings. The government alleges that S&P misled investors by not being objective in its ratings from 2004 to 2007.

     In 2011, Standard & Poor's downgraded the U.S. debt rating.

10.   Louise Story, Landon Thomas, Jr., and Nelson D. Schwartz, "Wall St. Helped to Mask Debt Fueling Europe's Crisis." *New York Times,* February 13, 2010, p. A1 (http://www.nytimes.com/2010/02/14/business/global/14debt.html?pagewanted=1).

11.   Susan Beck, "The SEC's Internal Battles over Goldman Sachs Probe." *The Am Law Daily,* April 7, 2014 (http://www.americanlawyer.com/home/id=1202650075059/The+SECs+Internal+Battles+over+Goldman+Sachs+Probe%3Fmcode=1382379838036&curindex=2).

12.   Robert Schmidt, "SEC Goldman Lawyer Says Agency Too Timid on Wall Street Misdeeds." *Bloomberg,* April 8, 2014 (http://www.bloomberg.com/news/2014-04-08/sec-goldman-lawyer-says-agency-too-timid-on-wall-street-misdeeds.html).

13.   Greg Smith, "Why I Am Leaving Goldman Sachs." *New York Times,* March 14, 2012, p. A27 (http://www.nytimes.com/2012/03/14/opinion/why-i-am-leaving-goldman-sachs.html?pagewanted=all&_r=0p).

14.   Robert Mendick, "Blair Inc: How Tony Blair Makes His Fortune." *The Telegraph,* January 7, 2012 (http://www.telegraph.co.uk/news/politics/tony-blair/8999847/Blair-Inc-How-Tony-Blair-makes-his-fortune.html).

15.   On advising Gaddafi: Robert Mendick, "Tony Blair's Six Secret Visits to Col. Gaddafi." *The Telegraph,* September 24, 2011 (http://www.telegraph.co.uk/news/politics/tony-blair/8787074/Tony-Blairs-six-secret-visits-to-Col-Gaddafi.html); Peter Oborne, "On the Desert Trail of Tony Blair's Millions." *The*

Telegraph, September 23, 2011 (http://www.telegraph.co.uk/news/politics/tony-blair/8784596/On-the-desert-trail-of-Tony-Blairs-millions.html).

On serving as Middle East peace envoy: BBC, "Blair Appointed Middle East Envoy," BBC News, June 27, 2007 (http://news.bbc.co.uk/2/hi/6244358.stm).

16. James Fallows, "An Unfortunate Decision by Peter Orszag." *The Atlantic,* December 10, 2010 (http://www.theatlantic.com/politics/archive/2010/12/an-unfortunate-decision-by-peter-orszag/67822/).

17. Monika Bauhr and Naghmeh Nasiritousi, "Why Pay Bribes? Collective Action and Anticorruption Efforts." Working Paper Series 2011:18, QOG The Quality of Government Institute, December 2011, pp. 1-23.

18. The case has been made that at least some derivatives are designed to obscure reality. Warren Buffett was particularly prescient about this issue, writing this in his 2003 Berkshire Hathaway annual letter to shareholders:

> Another commonality of reinsurance and derivatives is that both generate reported earnings that are often wildly overstated. That's true because today's earnings are in a significant way based on estimates whose inaccuracy may not be exposed for many years. [T]he parties to derivatives also have enormous incentives to cheat in accounting for them. Those who trade derivatives are usually paid (in whole or part) on 'earnings' calculated by mark-to-market accounting [a model built on speculation and subjective prediction]. But often there is no real market (think about our contract involving twins) and 'mark-to-model' is utilized. This substitution can bring on large-scale mischief. . . . I can assure you that the marking errors in the derivatives business have not been symmetrical. Almost invariably, they have favored either the trader who was eyeing a multi-million dollar bonus or the CEO who wanted to report impressive 'earnings' (or both). The bonuses were paid, and the CEO profited from his options. Only much later did shareholders learn that the reported earnings were a sham."

(See: Warren E. Buffett, "Letter to Shareholders," February 21, 2003 (http://www.berkshirehathaway.com/letters/2002pdf.pdf).

In discussing the use of derivatives to conceal public debt by European governments, *New York Times* financial columnist Floyd Norris wrote in 2013:

> For some derivatives, a desire for deception is the only reason they exist. That deception can allow those who own derivatives to evade taxes or accounting rules. It can allow activity that might otherwise be illegal, were it not called a derivative, or that would face regulation if it were labeled what it truly is. Sometimes, banks use derivatives they create to help their clients deceive the public. Other times, they enable the banks to deceive those clients.

(Floyd Norris, "Wielding Derivatives as a Tool for Deceit." *New York Times,* June 27, 2013 [www.nytimes.com/2013/06/28/business/deception_by_derivative.html]).

Norris's colleague Peter Eavis describes the rare case that has actually triggered criminal prosecution: the so-called "London Whale" that saddled JPMorgan Chase with $6 billion in trading losses. As Eavis puts it, "[o]n Wall Street, bets worth hundreds of billions of dollars are valued using a considerable amount of guesswork. The problem with using this approach is that it may not be fully based on prices that occurred in actual transactions. Instead, it may rely heavily on indicative prices, which is the term Wall Street gives to the price quotes that a broker puts out to the market but isn't obligated to use in a transaction." (See: Graham Bowley, "Fast Traders, in Spotlight, Battle Rules." *New York Times*, July 17, 2011 [http://www.nytimes.com/2011/07/18/business/fast-traders-under-attack-defend-work.html?pagewanted=1&ref=highfrequencyalgorithmictrading]; and Peter Eavis, "Unreliable Guesswork in Valuing Murky Trades, Deal Book. *New York Times*, August 14, 2013 [http://dealbook.nytimes.com/2013/08/14/how-hard-is-it-to-value-derivatives-see-the-details-of-the-jpmorgan-case/].)

Philosopher-historian Joseph Vogl has elaborated on the juxtaposition of markets and politics and the relationship between markets and truth. (See Joseph Vogl, "Sovereignty Effects." Paper presented at the Institution for New Economic Thinking [INET] conference in Berlin, April 12, 2012.) See also Joseph Vogl, *The Specter of Capital*, Stanford, CA: Stanford University Press, forthcoming, 2014.

19. Vincent Antonin Lepinay, *Codes of Finance: Engineering Derivatives in a Global Bank*. Columbia University doctoral dissertation, 2011, p. xxiii.

The work finds, in the words of the author, "a self-defeating form whereby a bank's organization undermines its financial practices, and unstable securities designed by the bank destroy its infrastructure" (p. iv).

Lepinay asks: "If we have lost the hope of assigning a site to value creation (labor, land, etc.) and must now live with long cascades of derivation, how do we set the criteria for good and bad cascades?" (p. xxiv).

20. Ouroussoff's ethnography shows that rating agencies were pawns of corporate executives hoping for favorable ratings. She argues that it is the other way around: rating agencies are pushing for risk-free profit and CEOs are willing to comply, even if that means grossly understating their strategic risk.

21. Alexandra Ouroussoff, *Wall Street at War: The Secret Struggle for the Global Economy*. Cambridge, U.K. and Malden, MA: Polity Press, 2010, p. 24.

22. Some Western Europeans warned that the pipeline would saddle Europe with greater dependency on Russian gas. And with the Russian navy ordered to protect the pipeline, critics foresaw new potential for espionage. Moreover, Russia's and Germany's Central European, Baltic, and Ukrainian neighbors, bypassed by the pipeline's sea route, were outraged at being relegated to non-partner status. In Poland, the deal unleashed sentiment recalling the Hitler–Stalin pact that had carved up the nation like a side of beef. (For further detail, see Janine R. Wedel, *Shadow Elite: How the World's New Power Brokers Undermine Democracy, Government, and the Free Market*. New York: Basic Books, 2009, p. 208, notes 8-12).

23. See: http://www.washingtonpost.com/wp-dyn/content/article/2005/12/09/AR2005120901755.html. Schroeder remains chair of the Nord Stream shareholders' committee, which is 51 percent controlled by Gazprom. Gazprom

nominated him to that position (Nord Stream Pipeline Project, Management, http://www.nord-stream.com/about-us/our-management/).

24. Tony Paterson, "Merkel Fury after Gerhard Schroeder Backs Putin on Ukraine." *The Telegraph*, March 14, 2014 (http://www.telegraph.co.uk/news/worldnews/europe/ukraine/10697986/Merkel-fury-after-Gerhard-Schroeder-backs-Putin-on-Ukraine.html).

25. Nicholas Confessore and Amy Chozick, "Unease at Clinton Foundation Over Finances and Ambitions." *New York Times,* August 13, 2013 (http://www.nytimes.com/2013/08/14/us/politics/unease-at-clinton-foundation-over-finances-and-ambitions.html?pagewanted=all).

26. Of course, these patterns apply not only to former heads of state. For instance, just a week after stepping down in 2006, Alan Greenspan took in a reported $250,000 for a dinner with top hedge-fund managers hosted by Lehman Brothers (http://nypost.com/2006/02/11/stolen-thunder-critics-rip-greenspans-big-bucks-shadow-fed/). Counterparts overseas did not always follow this pattern. Masaaki Shirakawa said he would say nothing for six months after stepping down as governor of the Bank of Japan (see, for instance, Henry Sender, "Geithner Joins Top Table of Public Speakers with Lucrative Appearances," *Financial Times,* July 7, 2013 [http://www.ft.com/intl/cms/s/0/3dd59602-e42c-11e2-91a3-00144feabdc0.html#axzz34M54g3bL]).

27. Graham Bowley, "The Academic-Industrial Complex." *New York Times,* July 31, 2010 (http://www.nytimes.com/2010/08/01/business/01prez.html?pagewanted=all).

28. The critic, John Gillespie, wrote a book on corporate boards, *Money for Nothing* (see Bowley, op. cit.).

29. Within the military, some referred to Petraeus as King David, a brainy figure with boundless ambition. See, for instance, this report published after the fact: Mark Thomas, "The Rise and Fall of 'General Peaches." *Time,* November 14, 2012. This article says he also was unpopular with the CIA rank and file (Joe Nocera, "Hacking General Petraeus." *New York Times,* November 16, 2012 [http://www.nytimes.com/2012/11/17/opinion/nocera-hacking-general-petraeus.html]).

30. See *Vanity Fair:* Mark Bowden, "The Professor of War." *Vanity Fair,* May 2010 (http://www.vanityfair.com/politics/features/2010/05/petraeus-201005); and *Foreign Policy*: Blake Hounshell, "David Petraeus: Smart Like That." *Foreign Policy,* October 17, 2008 (http://blog.foreignpolicy.com/posts/2008/10/17/david_petraeus_smart_like_that).

   See also these book reviews in *Foreign Affairs*: "COIN of the Realm: Is There a Future for Counterinsurgency?" (reviews by Colin H. Kahl of these books: The U.S. Army and Marine Corps, *The U.S. Army/Marine Corps Counterinsurgency Field Manual*; and William R. Polk's *Violent Politics: A History of Insurgency, Terrorism, and Guerrilla War, from the American Revolution to Iraq. Foreign Affairs*, Council on Foreign Relations, vol. 86, no. 6, November-December 2007, pp. 169-176 [http://www.jstor.org/stable/20032516].)

   See also Fred Kaplan's article in *Foreign Affairs* ("The End of the Age of Petraeus: The Rise and Fall of Counterinsurgency." *Foreign Affairs*, vol. 92, no. 1, Jan.-Feb. 2013, pp. 75-90); and his book (*The Insurgents: David Petraeus and the Plot to Change the American Way of War.* New York: Simon & Schuster, 2013).

31. Halah Touryalai, "An Unlikely Alliance? KKR Hires Former US General, CIA Director, David Petraeus." *Forbes,* May 30,

2013 (http://www.forbes.com/sites/halahtouryalai/2013/05/30/
an-unlikely-alliance-kkr-hires-former-us-general-cia-director-david-petraeus/).

    As *Forbes* put it, "The [KKR Global] institute will deal with macro-economic issues like the role of central banks in the world since the crisis, changes in public policy and other areas where KKR has interests like environmental and social issues that would influence its investment decisions. There's no doubting Petraeus has a powerful Rolodex—one that KKR is likely to leverage."

32.   George Anders, "The Real Reason Why KKR Wants Petraeus On Call." *Forbes,* May 30, 2013 (http://www.forbes.com/sites/georgeanders/2013/05/30/the-real-reason-why-kkr-wants-petraeus-on-call/).

    KKR explicitly has Petraeus under its "thought leadership" business (http://www.kkr.com/leadership/david-h-petraeus).

33.   "The Crash: Risk and Regulation, What Went Wrong." Anthony Faiola, Ellen Nakashima, and Jill Drew, *Washington Post,* October 15, 2008, p. A01 (http://www.washingtonpost.com/wp-dyn/content/story/2008/10/14/ST2008101403344.html); and Manuel Roig-Franzia, "Brooksley Born, the Cassandra of the Derivatives Crisis." *Washington Post,* May 26, 2009 (http://www.washingtonpost.com/wp-dyn/content/article/2009/05/25/AR2009052502108.html).

34.   Cyrus Sanati, "10 Years Later, Looking at Repeal of Glass-Steagall." *New York Times,* November 12, 2009 (http://dealbook.nytimes.com/2009/11/12/10-years-later-looking-at-repeal-of-glass-steagall/?_r=0).

    Ironically, there were few policymakers more capable of understanding derivatives or their real world impact than Clinton Treasury Secretary Robert Rubin and his deputy Lawrence Summers. And both were there when derivatives could have been at least partially reined in before they became, to quote Warren Buffett, "financial weapons of mass destruction." Instead, they did exactly the opposite, blocking key regulation at pivotal moments, with both Rubin and Summers moving on to benefit from this deregulated Wild West when they left Washington.

35.   Myron S. Scholes and Robert C. Merton, principals at LTCM, received the 1997 Nobel Prize in Economics for a "new method to determine the value of derivatives."

36.   U.S. Department of the Army & U.S. Marine Corps, *The U.S. Army/Marine Corps Counterinsurgency Field Manual,* with forward by David H, Petraeus and James N. Mattis, December 15, 2006, December 2006 (http://www.fas.org/irp/doddir/army/fm3-24.pdf). See also United States Department of the Army, David Howell Petraeus, James F. Amos, John A. Nagl, and Sarah B. Sewall, *The US Army/Marine Corps counterinsurgency field manual: US Army field manual no. 3-24: Marine Corps warfighting publication no. 3-33.5,* Chicago, IL: University of Chicago Press, 2007.

37.   See, for example, Fred Kaplan, *The Insurgents. David Petraeus and the Plot to Change the American Way of War* (New York: Simon & Schuster, 2013).

38.   See, for example, Eleni Tsingou, "Transnational Policy Communities and Financial Governance: The Role of Private Actors in Derivatives Regulation." CSGR Working Paper, 111/03, 2003 (http://wrap.warwick.ac.uk/2009/1/WRAP_Tsingou_wp11103.pdf). See also Diane Stone, "Transfer Agents and Global Networks in the 'Transnationalisation' of Policy," *Journal of European Public Policy,* vol. 11, issue 3, 2004.

39. Interview with Stuart Mackintosh, executive director, Group of Thirty, June 13, 2014.

40. The first quote is from: Leonard Seabrooke and Eleni Tsingou, *Revolving Doors and Linked Ecologies in the World Economy: Policy Locations and the Practice of International Financial Reform*, University of Warwick, 2009 (http://wrap.warwick.ac.uk/1849/1/WRAP_Seabrooke_26009.pdf), p. 20. The second quote is from: Eleni Tsingou, "Club governance and the making of global financial rules," *Review of International Political Economy*, March 2014, p. 2 (http://dx.doi.org/10.1080/09692290.2014.890952).

41. Group of Thirty, Consultative Group on International Economic and Monetary, Inc. (http://www.group30.org/members.shtml).

Here's how the *Washington Post* described the G30 in early 2013: Neil Irwin, "How do we fix the global economy? Here's the answer from the secretive group of 30 bankers that runs the world." *Washington Post,* February 11, 2013 (http://www.washingtonpost.com/blogs/wonkblog/wp/2013/02/11/how-do-we-fix-the-global-economy-hes-the-answer-from-the-secretive-group-of-30-bankers-that-runs-the-world/).

See also Zero Hedge, a well-trafficked financial news aggregator and commentator site, which called it the "Goldman Sachs-sponsored G30" ("Tyler Durden," "ECB Head Forced to Defend His Goldman 'Conflicts of Interests'." Zero Hedge, December 6, 2012 (http://www.zerohedge.com/news/2012-12-06/ecb-head-forced-defend-his-goldman-conflicts-interest]).

42. Interview with Stuart Mackintosh, executive director, Group of Thirty, June 13, 2014.

43. Eleni Tsingou, *Club Model Politics and Global Financial Governance: The Case of the Group of Thirty.* Doctoral dissertation, University of Amsterdam, 2012 (http://dare.uva.nl/document/364210), p. 87. The G-30 report she references is: Group of Thirty, *Derivatives: Practices and Principles.* Global Derivatives Study Group, Washington D.C., July 1993.

44. Gillian Tett, *Fool's Gold: The Inside Story of J.P. Morgan and How Wall Street Greed Corrupted Its Bold Dream and Created a Financial Catastrophe.* New York: Free Press, 2009, p. 34.

45. See http://www.nytimes.com/1993/07/22/business/market-place-group-approves-use-of-derivatives.html.

46. Gillian Tett, *Fool's Gold: The Inside Story of J.P. Morgan and How Wall Street Greed Corrupted Its Bold Dream and Created a Financial Catastrophe.* New York: Free Press, 2009, p. 35.

47. Tett's quote reads in full. (Gillian Tett, *Fool's Gold: The Inside Story of J.P. Morgan and How Wall Street Greed Corrupted its Bold Dream and Created a Financial Catastrophe.* New York: Free Press, 2009, p. 35.)

> The tome . . . did it drop any hint that the derivatives world might benefit from a centralized clearing system, like that for commodities derivatives and the New York Stock Exchange, to settle its trades. These clearing systems not only recorded the volume of trades, providing a valuable barometer of activity that signaled signs of trouble, but also protected investors from the eventuality that the

party on the other side of the trade—the counterparty—might fall through on a deal, leaving the trade in limbo.

Of course, this very counterparty issue was to rear its ugly head—and in a big way—in the 2008 financial crisis, when big banks scrambled to assess the massive exposure they had to collapsing deals. This report shows that the struggle to measure counterparty risk continues (http://www.newyorkfed.org/newsevents/news/banking/2014/an140115.html).

48. See http://www.nytimes.com/2009/01/04/magazine/04risk-t. html?pagewanted=all&_r=0

49. Interview with Stuart Mackintosh, executive director, Group of Thirty, June 13, 2014.

50. Ibid. He also said the Group has "elements of [both] formality and informality" and that most members "have straddled both . . . public and private [roles of influence]."

51. Ibid.

52. See Eleni Tsingou, *Club Model Politics and Global Financial Governance: The Case of the Group of Thirty*. Doctoral dissertation, University of Amsterdam, 2012, p. 249 (http://dare.uva.nl/document/364210).

53. For discussion of the impact of these transformational developments, see Janine R. Wedel, *Shadow Elite: How the World's New Power Brokers Undermine Democracy, Government, and the Free Market*. New York: Basic Books, 2009, pp. 23-45.

54. The three-quarters figure is from government scholar Paul C. Light, who compiles the most reliable figures on federal contractors in the United States. In 2008, he calculated that the contract workforce consisted of upwards of 7.6 million employees, or "three contractors for every federal employee." Paul C. Light, "Open Letter to the Presidential Candidates." Huffington Post, June 25, 2008 (http://www.huffingtonpost.com/paul-c-light/open-letter-to-the-presid_b_109276.html).
     See Chapter 6 for further information on government contracting.

55. The excesses in Iraq of the now infamous Blackwater (renamed Xe and renamed again Academi) security firm are well known, but the public is practically unaware that the outsourcing of many government *functions* is now routine. These are functions deemed so integral to government that *only* federal employees should carry them out. See Janine R. Wedel, *Shadow Elite*, pp. 73-109; and Janine R. Wedel, *Selling Out Uncle Sam: How the Myth of Small Government Undermines National Security*. New America Foundation, August 2010 (http://www.newamerica.net/sites/newamerica.net/files/policydocs/SellingOutUncleSamAug10.pdf).

56. See these Congressional Research Service reports on federal advisory committees, published in 2009 and 2013, respectively: Wendy Ginsberg, "Federal Advisory Committees: An Overview." *Congressional Research Service*, April 16, 2009 (http://www.fas.org/sgp/crs/misc/R40520.pdf); and Matthew Eric Glassman, "Congressional Membership and Appointment Authority to Advisory Commissions, Boards, and Groups." Congressional Research Service, February 5, 2013 (http://www.fas.org/sgp/crs/misc/RL33313.pdf).
     President Obama put limits on registered lobbyists serving on these boards when he took office; but obviously that doesn't include those who don't register

(see Chapter 3 on "shadow lobbyists"). A *New York Times* editorial praises the Obama White House for banning registered lobbyists from the boards, but says the unregistered ones fall through the cracks (*New York Times* Editorial, "No Place for (Registered) Lobbyists." *New York Times,* December 4, 2009 [http://www.nytimes.com/2009/12/04/opinion/04fri4.html]).

57. See Chapter 9 for analysis of the role of think tanks. The Supreme Court's 2010 *Citizens United* decision unleashed a massive amount of independent election advertising, often from so-called "nonprofits," some of which are not required to release their donor information.

58. See Chapter 7 for detailed analysis of this issue. Think tanks, traditionally focused more on substantive studies, even while often influenced by ideology—leaning to the left, the right, or the "free" market—and by agenda-laden sponsors, today have turned more attention to advocacy and to branding their message for the media.

59. See, for instance, Linette Lopez, "Elizabeth Warren Wants to Take This Goldman Sachs Aluminum Story and Run Right Over Wall Street with It." *Business Insider,* July 23, 2013 (http://www.businessinsider.com/senate-banking-on-wall-st-commodities-2013-7).

60. A June 2013 letter signed by four members of Congress expressed concern to the Federal Reserve about banks' (including Goldman Sachs, Morgan Stanley, and JPMorgan Chase) expanding commercial operations. They pointed out that these extracurricular activities have nothing to do with the business of banking, and that it is not clear how the Fed or other bank regulators can actually regulate the activities. The four members of Congress are Representatives Alan Grayson (D-Fla.), Raul Grijalva (D-Ariz.), John Conyers (D-Mich.), and Keith Ellison (D-Minn.). Footnotes in the letter provide some useful information about what the banks are currently doing. See: Zach Carter, "House Dems Press Ben Bernanke on Risks of Bank Expansion." Huffington Post, July 2, 2013 (http://www.huffingtonpost.com/2013/07/02/ben-bernanke-banks_n_3533821.html).

In a major investment in nonfinancial business, enabled by special exemptions granted by the Federal Reserve Board, manipulation by "Goldman and other financial players [of the aluminum market] has cost American consumers more than $5 billion over the last three years, say former industry executives, analysts and consultants." David Kocieniewski, "A Shuffle of Aluminum, But to Banks, Pure Gold." *New York Times,* July 20, 2013.

61. Kocieniewski, op. cit.

62. For the definition of a flexian, see Wedel, *Shadow Elite,* pp. 15-19. For examples of flexians, see this book, *Shadow Elite,* and Janine R. Wedel, "Is the Government in Charge, or is it the Shadow Elite?" Huffington Post, January 7, 2010 (http://www.huffingtonpost.com/janine-r-wedel/who-can-you-trust-tom-das_b_414403.html); and Arianna Huffington, "The First HuffPost Book Club Pick of 2010: Shadow Elite by Janine Wedel." Huffington Post, January 6, 2010 (http://www.huffingtonpost.com/arianna-huffington/the-first-huffpost-book-c_b_412999.html).

63. Louise Story and Annie Lowrey, "The Fed, Lawrence Summers, and Money." *New York Times,* August 11, 2013 (http://www.nytimes.com/2013/08/11/business/economy/the-fed-lawrence-summers-and-money.html).

64.　See, for example, Story and Lowrey, op. cit.; Damian Paletta and Jon Hilsenrath, "Summers Faces Hit on Potential Fed Nod Over His Wall Street Ties." *Wall Street Journal*, July 26, 2013 (http://online.wsj.com/article/SB100 014241278873239712045786300061896947112.html); Louise Story, "A Rich Education for Summers (after Harvard)." *New York Times*, April 6, 2009 (http://www.nytimes.com/2009/04/06/business/06summers.html?pagewanted=all); and Lawrence Summers, "Austerity Would Hurt U.S. Jobs and Growth." *Washington Post*, June 2, 2013 (http://articles.washingtonpost.com/2013-06-02/opinions/39697948_1_revenue-collection-deficit-financing-deficit-reduction).

65.　Kris Benson, "Breaking: Goldman Sachs Did Not Break Any of Those Laws It Wrote." Wonkette, August 10, 2012 (http://wonkette.com/480740/breaking-goldman-sachs-did-not-break-any-of-those-laws-it-wrote).

66.　Susan Strange, *The Retreat of the State*. Cambridge, U.K.: Cambridge University Press, 1996. I argue that ethics have become disconnected from the mores of a larger public or community and detached from the authority that states and international organizations, boards of directors, and even shareholders once provided. (See Chapter 10 and Janine R. Wedel, "Rethinking Corruption in an Age of Ambiguity." *Annual Review of Law and Social Science*, vol. 8, 2012, pp. 453-498.)

67.　E-mail, May 9, 2014, from John Clarke, emeritus professor, Faculty of Social Sciences, The Open University.

CHAPTER 2

1.　Hugh Son, "Bank of America CEO Faces Shareholder Ire Amid Protests." Bloomberg News, May 9, 2012 (http://www.bloomberg.com/news/2012-05-09/bank-of-america-meets-shareholders-as-protests-swirl.html).

2.　In centrally planned systems, where political authorities made decisions about production and distribution, demand outpaced supply. The Hungarian-born economist János Kornai, calls this an "economy of shortage." (János Kornai, *Economics of Shortage*, Amsterdam, the Netherlands: North-Holland Press, 1980.) In shortage economies, too much money chased too few goods.

3.　The term was coined in Claudia Honegger, Sighard Neckel, and Chantal Magnin, *Strukturierte Verantwortungslosigkeit: Berichte aus der Bankenwelt*. Berlin: Suhrkamp Verlag GmbH und Co. KG, 2010.

4.　Of course, Weber expounds on bureaucracy as an ideal type.

　　　Weber dealt with bureaucracy in both government and private enterprise. For instance, he wrote as follows: "The management of the modern office is based upon written documents ('the files'), which are preserved in their original or draft form. There is, therefore, a staff of subaltern officials and scribes of all sorts. The body of officials actively engaged in a 'public' office, along with the respective apparatus of material implements and the files, makes up a 'bureau.' In private enterprise, 'the bureau' is often called 'the office'." (Max Weber, "Bureaucracy," Hans H. Gerth and C. Wright Mills, eds., *From Max Weber*. New York: Oxford University Press, 1946, p. 197.)

5.　If followed in letter and spirit, some scholars argue, bureaucracy would produce an organization with self-paralyzing routines. Anthropologists who expound on bureaucracy include: Don Handelman, *Models and Mirrors: Toward an Anthropology of Public Events*. New York and Oxford: Berghahn Books, 1998,

Michael Herzfeld, *Cultural Intimacy: Social Poetics in the Nation-State*. New York and London: Routledge, 2005; Philip Parnell, "The Composite State," *Ethnography in Unstable Places: Everyday Lives in Contexts of Dramatic Political Change*, Carol J. Greenhouse, Elizabeth Mertz, and Kay B. Warren, eds. Durham and London: Duke University Press, 2002.

With regard to bureaucracy in practice in the United States, see, for instance, two key works published several decades ago that address how American consumers complain when dissatisfied with a product or service (Laura Nader, ed., *No Access to Law: Alternatives to the American Judicial System*. New York: Academic Press, 1980; and Arthur Best, *When Consumers Complain*. New York: Columbia University Press, 1981). A chapter on complaint letters in anthropologist Nader's edited book explains that while there is a huge range in the content and form of the letters, they nonetheless convey a "common theme—a loss of trust" (p. 161). As one reviewer writes: "Experience with incompetent plumbers, dishonest professionals, derelict and corrupt officials, deceptive advertisers, and unresponsive merchants has sapped consumers' confidence in the market and eroded their previously held assumption that most people and most organizations can be presumed to be concerned and responsible and able" (Susan S. Silbey, "Review Essay: Who Speaks for the Consumer? Nader's *No Access to Law* and Best's *When Consumers Complain*," American Bar Foundation Research Journal, no. 2, American Bar Foundation, 1984, pp. 455-456).

6. Jamil Afaqi e-mail to Janine Wedel, January 8, 2014. My thanks to Afaqi for discussion and insights on these points.

Stripping the customer of individuality adversely affects him, according to sociologist Barry Schwartz. In *Queuing and Waiting* (Chicago: University of Chicago Press, 1975, p. 30), he writes:

> To be kept waiting—especially to be kept waiting for an unusually long while—is to be the subject of an assertion that one's own time (and, therefore, one's social worth) is less valuable than the time and worth of the one who imposes the wait.

Afaqi asserts that one's sense of personal worthlessness is heightened when queuing is virtual—such as on the computer or telephone—as there is nothing tangible to grasp on to (Afaqi e-mail, January 8, 2014).

7. In addition to Tett, sociologist of finance Donald MacKenzie, who has studied how market participants create "knowledge about financial instruments" (Donald MacKenzie, "The Credit Crisis as a Problem in the Sociology of Knowledge." *American Journal of Sociology*, vol. 116, no. 6, May 2011, p. 1778), argues that "The organizational division of labor inside credit rating agencies" played a crucial part in the financial crisis. He adds: "what I have found is more often reminiscent of the rigidities and barriers to information flow in the background of the Challenger disaster (Vaughan 1996)" (Diane Vaughan, *The Challenger Launch Decision: Risky Technology, Culture, and Deviance at NASA*. Chicago: University of Chicago Press, 1996, p. 1831).

For more general insights in the sociology of finance, see, notably, Donald MacKenzie, *Material Markets: How Economic Agents Are Constructed*. Oxford:

Oxford University Press, 2009; and his *An Engine, Not a Camera: How Financial Models Shape Markets.* Cambridge, MA, and London: MIT Press, 2006.

Silo-ization was a factor in a previous crisis, the collapse of Enron. As the *New York Times* put it in 2002, "the company's divisions had enjoyed so much autonomy that they were referred to as stand-alone silos. Each had its own system for determining salaries and bonuses and its own culture. But despite their differences, all the units were big on risk and reward. And they were arrogant, thinking themselves invincible." (John Schwartz, "As Enron Purged Its Ranks, Dissent Was Swept Away." *New York Times,* February 4, 2002 [http://www.nytimes.com/2002/02/04/business/as-enron-purged-its-ranks-dissent-was-swept-away.html?pagewanted=all&src=pm].)

While many reports noted the problem with silos at Enron, it appears that Wall Street banks did not heed the lesson in the years following its collapse. It's worth noting that the Enron debacle led to arrests and convictions, whereas the derivatives culture was mostly viewed as just the way the business worked, certainly not as criminal behavior. On derivatives culture, see, for instance, http://www.pbs.org/wgbh/pages/frontline/oral-history/financial-crisis/frank-partnoy/.

On Enron et al., see, for instance, John Cassidy, "The Greed Cycle." *The New Yorker,* September 23, 2002 (http://www.newyorker.com/archive/2002/09/23/020923fa_fact_cassidy).

8.   Lorenz Khazaleh, "Anthropologist: Investors Need to Understand the Tribal Nature of Banking." *Antropologi.info,* January 26, 2008 (http://www.antropologi.info/blog/anthropology/2008/anthropologist_investors_need_to_underst).

9.   See: Gillian Tett, *Fool's Gold: The Inside Story of J.P. Morgan and How Wall Street Greed Corrupted its Bold Dream and Created a Financial Catastrophe.* New York: Free Press, 2009; http://www.culanth.org/?q=node/580; lecture by Tett in the School of Public Policy at George Mason University, April 15, 2011, http://vimeo.com/25567890; and interviews with Tett (for instance, Brian McKenna, "How Will Gillian Tett Connect with the Natives of the US Left?" *CounterPunch* magazine, March 4-6, 2011 [http://www.counterpunch.org/2011/03/04/how-will-gillian-tett-connect-with-the-natives-of-the-us-left/]; and "Gillian Tett: The Anthropology of Finance." *Pop-Up Ideas,* BBC Radio 4, July 17, 2013 [http://www.bbc.co.uk/programmes/b036tz9w]).

10.   White adds: "For this last fact, I blame both the central bankers and the belief system of the academic community whose students gradually came to dominate the research agenda of central banks. Perhaps the most pernicious aspect of the belief system was that macro economics was a 'science' and that economic processes could be (indeed had to be) modeled using quantitative data establishing relationships between a relatively small number of variables. The problem, as [Friedrich August von] Hayek put it in his 1974 Nobel Prize lecture, is that 'for essentially complex phenomena' like a modern economy, 'the events to be explained for which we can obtain quantitative data are necessarily limited and may not include the important ones.'" (see http://williamwhite.ca/content/what-has-gone-wrong-global-economy-why-were-warnings-ignored-what-have-we-learned-experience).

11.   Some of these bankers would not entertain any responsibility for enabling the crisis, saying they knew only their own piece (read: silo) of the operation. Structured unaccountability, sociologists Honegger, Neckel, and Magnin

concluded, not only abetted the crisis, but also relieved the bankers of culpability. (Claudia Honegger, Sighard Neckel, and Chantal Magnin. *Strukturierte Verantwortungslosigkeit: Berichte aus der Bankenwelt.* Berlin: Suhrkamp Verlag GmbH und Co. KG, 2010.)

12. Honegger et al., op. cit., pp. 306-307.

13. Gillian Tett, "An Anthropologist on Wall Street." Fieldsights—Theorizing the Contemporary, Cultural Anthropology Online, May 16, 2012 (http://www. culanth.org/?q=node/580).

14. Analysts from different fields have noted how Wall Street and corporate compensation practices have encouraged short-term gains at the expense of long-term stability.

Anthropologist of finance Karen Ho conducted fieldwork among investment bankers. With layoffs common, she found that the "here-today-somewhere-else-tomorrow" mentality led to the cult of the annual bonus and the focus on making as many deals as possible, regardless of the deal's long-term merits. (Karen Zouwen Ho, *Liquidated: An Ethnography of Wall Street.* Durham, NC: Duke University Press, 2009.)

Finance professor Raghuram Rajan warned about compensation practices encouraging risk well before the 2008 crash. He also has argued that "significant portions" of banker and manager bonuses should be held in escrow until the full effect of a risk-taking decision can play out. (See Raghuram Rajan, "Monetary Policy and Incentives." Address at Central Banks in the 21st Century, *Bank of Spain Conference,* June 8, 2006 [http://www.imf.org/external/np/speeches/2006/060806.htm]; and Raghuram Rajan, "Bankers' Pay Is Deeply Flawed." *Financial Times,* January 9, 2008 [http://www.ft.com/intl/cms/s/0/18895dea-be06-11dc-8bc9-0000779fd2ac.html#axzz2dSZuUXwk].)

Economic journalist John Cassidy has noted compensation problems among corporate CEOs and top executives. Paying them with stock options encouraged a more short-term focus, in which they sought to keep the stock price high at the right times at the expense of long-term wisdom. (John Cassidy, "The Greed Cycle." *The New Yorker,* September 23, 2002 [http://www.newyorker.com/archive/2002/09/23/020923fa_fact_cassidy].)

So-called options backdating also had the effect of obscuring a company's true profit picture, as noted by various commentators (see, for instance, Bill Mann, "The Danger of Stock Option Grants." *The Motley Fool,* June 20, 2001 [http://www.fool.com/news/foth/2001/foth010620.htm]). Complaints eventually led to a crackdown on options backdating (U.S. Securities and Exchange Commission, "SEC Charges Former Apple General Counsel for Illegal Stock Option Backdating." SEC, Press Release, April 24, 2007 [http://www.sec.gov/news/press/2007/2007-70.htm]). In 2002, the Sarbanes-Oxley Act was supposed to put an end to the practice. But Berkeley Law School Professor Jesse Fried argues that it continued well after Sarbanes-Oxley (Jesse Fried, "Option Backdating and Its Implications." *Washington and Lee Law Review,* vol. 65, no. 3, Summer 2008, pp. 853-866 [http://www.law.harvard.edu/faculty/jfried/option_backdating_and_its_implications.pdf]).

15. See Caitlin Zaloom, "The Ethics of Wall Street." Fieldsights—Theorizing the Contemporary, *Cultural Anthropology Online,* May 15, 2012 (http://www.culanth.org/?q=node/570).

16.   See, for instance, the work of cultural analyst John Clarke, "Performing for the Public: Doubt, Desire and the Evaluation of Public Services," *The Values of Bureaucracy*, Paul du Gay, ed. Oxford: Oxford University Press, 2005, pp. 211-232.

17.   See, for example, Gillian Tett, "An Anthropologist on Wall Street." Fieldsights—Theorizing the Contemporary, *Cultural Anthropology Online*, May 16, 2012 (http://www.culanth.org/?q=node/580).

    See also Alexandra Ouroussoff, *Wall Street at War: The Secret Struggle for the Global Economy*. Cambridge, U.K., and Malden, MA: Polity Press, 2010.

18.   Tett's quote is at: Gillian Tett, "An Anthropologist on Wall Street." Fieldsights—Theorizing the Contemporary, *Cultural Anthropology Online*, May 16, 2012 (http://www.culanth.org/?q=node/580).

    Dominant finance's excessive influence and favoring of "short-term shareholder value and large-scale gambling . . . has actually diverted, transferred, and extracted wealth from productive enterprises, workers, houses, and communities, generating rampant socioeconomic inequality not seen since the Great Depression," argues anthropologist of finance Karen Ho (Karen Ho, "Occupy Finance and the Paradox/Possibilities of Productivity." Fieldsights— Theorizing the Contemporary, *Cultural Anthropology Online*, May 15, 2012 [http://www.culanth.org/?q=node/573]). She adds: "And yet, in explicitly non-ironic terms, Wall Street actors and advocates continually naturalize and make direct claims about their connection to social purpose through production."

19.   With regard to the U.S. Securities and Exchange Commission (SEC), see this July 1997 question-and-answer commentary that the SEC issued six months after adopting new rules for derivatives accounting, which included VaR: Office of the Chief Accountant & the Division of Corporation Finance, "Questions and Answers About the New 'Market Risk' Disclosure Rules." U.S. Securities and Exchange Commission, July 31, 1997 (http://www.sec.gov/divisions/ corpfin/guidance/derivfaq.htm#qvar).

    With regard to the Bank of International Settlements, VaR was part of the first pillar of the Basel II international banking standards adopted around the same time (Bank for International Settlements, "Part 2: The First Pillar—Minimum Capital Requirements" [http://www.bis.org/publ/ bcbs128b.pdf]). In 2009, the *New York Times* described how the banks' own propriety VaR models became part of the regulatory framework. Joe Nocera, "Risk Mismanagement." New York Times, January 2, 2009, http://www. nytimes.com/2009/01/04/magazine/04risk-t.html?pagewanted=all.

> In the late 1990s, as the use of derivatives was exploding, the [SEC] ruled that firms had to include a quantitative disclosure of market risks in their financial statements for the convenience of investors, and VaR became the main tool for doing so. Around the same time, [the] Basel Committee on Banking Supervision went even further to validate VaR by saying that firms and banks could rely on their own internal VaR calculations to set their capital requirements. So long as their VaR was reasonably low, the amount of money they had to set aside to cover risks that might go bad could also be low.

20. Joe Nocera, "Risk Mismanagement." New York Times, January 2, 2009, http://www.nytimes.com/2009/01/04/magazine/04risk-t.html?pagewanted=all.

21. With regard to VaR as a risk management tool, this article presents the basic story: Joe Nocera, "Risk Mismanagement." *New York Times,* January 2, 2009 (http://www.nytimes.com/2009/01/04/magazine/04risk-t.html?pagewanted=all). Nocera writes:

> Built around statistical ideas and probability theories that have been around for centuries, VaR was developed and popularized in the early 1990s by a handful of scientists and mathematicians—"quants," they're called in the business—who went to work for JPMorgan. . . . After pointing out that a Nobel Prize had been awarded for work that led to some of the theories behind derivative pricing and risk management, [Greenspan] said: "The whole intellectual edifice, however, collapsed in the summer of last year because the data input into the risk-management models generally covered only the past two decades, a period of euphoria. Had instead the models been fitted more appropriately to historic periods of stress, capital requirements would have been much higher and the financial world would be in far better shape today, in my judgment." Well, yes. . . . People tend not to be able to anticipate a future they have never personally experienced.
>
> With regard to risk, see the work of economic historian Harold James who points out: ". . . calculations about likely risks . . . are terribly . . . misleading. If we think there's one-in-a-1000-year chance of something happening, we're inclined to ignore it. But then we find suddenly that these one-in-a-1000-year chances . . . seem to be happening every 10 minutes. . . ." (Harold James, speaking at the 2011 Institute for New Economic Thinking conference in Bretton Woods, New Hampshire, organized by the Institute for New Economic Thinking. See: Harold James, "The Emerging Political and Economic Order: What Lies Ahead?" Presented at Bretton Woods Conference, Institute for New Economic Thinking, April 8, 2011 [http://ineteconomics.org/net/video/playlist/conference/bretton-woods/B]; Janine R. Wedel, "Capitalism's Crisis Within, and How Larry Summers Still Doesn't Get It." Huffington Post, April 21, 2011).

22. Quoted in Joe Nocera, "Risk Mismanagement." New York Times, January 2, 2009, http://www.nytimes.com/2009/01/04/magazine/04risk-t.html?pagewanted=all.

23. Jonathan Weil, "Hardy har VAR: How JPMorgan is like Enron: Value-at-risk measurement proved to be way off for both companies." InvestmentNews, May 18, 2012 (http://www.investmentnews.com/article/20120518/FREE/120519926#).

24. Gillian Tett, "An Anthropologist on Wall Street." Fieldsights—Theorizing the Contemporary, Cultural Anthropology Online, May 16, 2012 (http://www.culanth.org/?q=node/580).

25. Bill Maurer, quoted in Janine R. Wedel, "Shadow Elite: Derivatives, A Horror Story." Huffington Post, May 20, 2010 (http://www.huffingtonpost.com/janine-r-wedel/emshadow-eliteem-derivati_b_583014.html).

26. Lawrence Summers, "The Commodity Futures Trading Commission Concept Release." Testimony before the Senate Committee on Agriculture, Nutrition, and Forestry, 105th Congress, July 30, 1998 (http://ustreas.gov/press/releases/rr2616.htm).

27. I spoke with Sony Kapoor on April 11, 2014 at the Institute for New Economic Thinking Annual Conference in Toronto. More on Kapoor can be found at re/define.org.

28. E-mail message from William White, May 13, 2014.

29. Think, for instance, of Edward Snowden, who exposed many U.S. government secrets while working for a government contractor, Booz Allen Hamilton, an established company with a long history of contracting.

30. We take up the issue of government contracting in Chapter 6. See also Janine R. Wedel, *Shadow Elite: How the World's New Power Brokers Undermine Democracy, Government, and the Free Market.* New York: Basic Books, 2009, pp. 73-109 (http://janinewedel.info/books.html); and Janine R. Wedel, "Selling Out Uncle Sam: How the Myth of Small Government Undermines National Security." New America Foundation, August 2010 (http://www.newamerica.net/sites/newamerica.net/files/policydocs/SellingOutUncleSamAug10.pdf).

31. *The New York Times* has reported on the troubling use of "little-known private databases" that is effectively keeping perhaps 10 million low-income Americans from getting even a bank account, because they ended up in these databases for often very small credit offenses. A low-income financial counselor, Kristen Euretig, said this: "Most of my clients have no idea these databases exist, let alone what they did to end up in them." *New York Times*, July 30, 2013 (http://dealbook.nytimes.com/2013/07/30/over-a-million-are-denied-bank-accounts-for-past-errors/).

32. In testimony before the Privacy and Civil Liberties Oversight Board, an independent agency within the Executive Branch, the NSA's general counsel affirmed that tech companies were aware of, and helped with, data collection under the s0-called PRISM program. Alexis Kleinman, "NSA: Tech Companies Knew About PRISM The Whole Time." Huffington Post, March 20, 2014 (http://www.huffingtonpost.com/2014/03/20/nsa-prism-tech-companies_n_4999378.html).

Google has denied its involvement in turning over its users' personal data to NSA (although investigative reporting has tried to refute this). Director of National Intelligence James Clapper, several months before the NSA revelations of June 2013, also denied in congressional testimony that the NSA was gathering such information. (See, for instance, Dan Roberts, "Intelligence chief James Clapper apologizes to Congress for 'erroneous' NSA claims." *The Raw Story*, July 1, 2013 [http://www.rawstory.com/rs/2013/07/01/intelligence-chief-james-clapper-apologizes-to-congress-for-erroneous-nsa-claims/].)

After the revelations, top congressional "overseers" Senators Dianne Feinstein and Saxby Chambliss, the Democratic and Republican leaders, respectively, of the Senate Intelligence Committee, stood by Clapper and his earlier testimony. As Feinstein said, "There is no more direct or honest person than Jim Clapper." (Feinstein, appearing on ABC's *This Week*, June 9, 2013.)

33.   See, for instance, Somini Sengupta, "The Pentagon as Silicon Valley's Incubator." *New York Times*, August 22, 2013 (http://www.nytimes.com/2013/08/23/technology/the-pentagon-as-start-up-incubator.html?pagewanted=all&_r=0).

34.   James Risen and Nick Wingfield, "Web's Reach Binds N.S.A. and Silicon Valley Leaders." *New York Times*, June 19, 2013 (http://www.nytimes.com/2013/06/20/technology/silicon-valley-and-spy-agency-bound-by-strengthening-web.html?pagewanted=all).

35.   Nathan Heller, "Bay Watched: How San Francisco's New Entrepreneurial Culture is Changing the Country." *The New Yorker*, October 14, 2013.

     This model of success differs from the more traditional notion, as Karen Ho points out. Karen Ho, "Occupy Finance and the Paradox Possibilities of Productivity." Fieldsights—Theorizing the Contemporary, *Cultural Anthropology Online*, May 15, 2012 (http://www.culanth.org/?q=node/573).

36.   Conversation with Sony Kapoor on April 11, 2014.

37.   This issue is already presenting itself. See, for instance, Aarti Shahani, "Should Uber Be Responsible for Driver Recklessness?" *all tech considered*, NPR, February 2, 2014 (http://www.npr.org/blogs/alltechconsidered/2014/02/02/270359642/is-uber-responsible-for-driver-recklessness).

38.   William White, "What Has Gone Wrong with the Global Economy? Why Were the Warnings Ignored? What Have We Learned from the Experience?" Presented at the Official Monetary and Financial Institutions Forum in London, October 24, 2013, http://williamwhite.ca/content/what-has-gone-wrong-global-economy-why-were-warnings-ignored-what-have-we-learned-experience

CHAPTER 3

1.   William D. Cohan, "Mystery Men of the Financial Crisis." *New York Times*, February 4, 2010 (http://opinionator.blogs.nytimes.com/2010/02/04/mystery-men-of-the-financial-crisis/).

2.   Louise Story and Gretchen Morgenson, "In U.S. Bailout of A.I.G., Forgiveness for Big Banks." *New York Times*, June 29, 2010 (http://www.nytimes.com/2010/06/30/business/30aig.html?hp=&pagewanted=all).

3.   Jason Kelly, "Daschle's Demise Linked to Hindery's Private-Equity Lifestyle." *Bloomberg*, February 4, 2009 (http://www.bloomberg.com/apps/news?pid=news archive&sid=abRm8pGXtr4Q).

4.   Christopher Lee, "Daschle Moving to K Street." *Washington Post*, March 14, 2005, p. A17 (http://www.washingtonpost.com/wp-dyn/articles/A32604-2005Mar13.html); Michael Scherer, "The Secret Life of Tom Daschle, Moonlighting for the Insurance Industry." *Time*, August 17, 2009 (http://swampland.time.com/2009/08/17/the-secret-life-of-tom-daschle-moonlighting-for-the-inurance-indutry/).

5.   Sam Stein, "Daschle's Firm and Group Have Ties to Private Health Care Industry." Huffington Post, July 19, 2009 (http://www.huffingtonpost.com/2009/06/18/daschles-firm-and-group-h_n_217594.html).

6.   Fred Schulte and Emma Schwartz, "Daschle Had Public and Private
      Role in Push for Digital Health Records." Center for Public Integrity,
      December 15, 2009 (http://www.publicintegrity.org/2009/12/15/7020/
      daschle-had-public-and-private-role-push-digital-health-records).
7.   Kenneth P. Vogel, "Health Care Groups Paid Daschle $220K." *Politico*, January
      30, 2009 (http://www.politico.com/news/stories/0109/18237.html).
8.   Carrie Levine, "Daschle Departing Alston for DLA
      Piper." National Law Journal, November 17, 2009 (http://
      www.nationallawjournal.com/id=1202435565631/
      Daschle-departing-Alston-for-DLA-Piper?slreturn=20140318204027).
9.   On meeting with the president, see Office of the Press Secretary, "Readout of the
      President's meeting with former Senate Majority Leader Tom Daschle Today." The
      White House, August 21, 2009 (http://www.whitehouse.gov/the-press-office/
      readout-presidents-meeting-with-former-senate-majority-leader-tom-daschle-
      today); with the vice president: Alexander Bolton, "Daschle is Still Go-to Guy
      on Healthcare." *The Hill*, November 19, 2009 (http://thehill.com/homenews/
      senate/68533-tom-daschle-is-still-the-go-to-guy-on-healthcare); in general: John
      Fritze, "Daschle Still Key Player on Health Care." *USA Today*, May 21, 2009
      (http://usatoday30.usatoday.com/news/washington/2009-05-20-daschle_N.htm).
10.   See Schulte and Schwartz, op. cit. Alston & Bird, the law and lobbying firm
      where Daschle was on the payroll, recruited him to help create a health-
      information technology unit charged with assisting clients in taking advantage
      of stimulus funds, according to the firm.
11.   A description of the Daschle Loophole can be found in a February 19, 2014
      Nation investigation by Lee Fang (http://www.thenation.com/article/178460/
      shadow-lobbying-complex#).
          Arthur Delaney, "How Tom Daschle Lobbies in Secret: Influence
      Laundering." Huffington Post, March 18, 2010 (http://www.huffingtonpost.
      com/2009/11/25/how-tom-daschle-lobbies-i_n_367634.html).
12.   Elizabeth O'Bagy, "Elizabeth O'Bagy: On the Front Lines of Syria's Civil War."
      Wall Street Journal, August 30, 2013 (http://online.wsj.com/article/SB10001424
      1278873244636045790446427947111158.html).
13.   Jay Newton-Small, "The Rise and Fall of Elizabeth O'Bagy." *Time,*
      September 17, 2013 (http://swampland.time.com/2013/09/17/
      the-rise-and-fall-of-elizabeth-obagy/).
14.   *Fox News Insider,* "Syrian Expert: Rebel Forces 'Let Down' by
      President Obama's Decision." *Fox News Insider,* August 31, 2013
      (http://foxnewsinsider.com/2013/08/31/rebel-forces-syria-let-
      down-president-obamas-decision); Renee Montagne, "Assessing
      Role Extremists Play in Syrian Opposition." National Public Radio,
      September 6, 2013 (http://www.npr.org/2013/09/06/219560320/
      assessing-role-extremists-play-in-syrian-opposition).
15.   Here is McCain referencing "Doctor" O'Bagy: https://www.youtube.com/
      watch?v=_7JqP8MMLYM; Greg Myre, "From Anonymous to Media Star
      to Unemployed in a Week." *The Two-Way*, National Public Radio, September
      11, 2013 (http://www.npr.org/blogs/thetwo-way/2013/09/11/221402205/
      from-anonymous-to-media-star-to-unemployed-in-a-week).

16. The Institute for the Study of War no longer has Elizabeth O'Bagy's biography on its website (http://www.understandingwar.org/press-media/staff-bios/elizabeth-obagy).

17. O'Bagy is properly identified here in the *Atlantic*, although the article doesn't explain what the Syrian Emergency Task Force is. Media outlets that did not properly identify her could have found this affiliation without much difficulty. Michael Weiss and Elizabeth O'Bagy, "Why Arming the Rebels Isn't Enough." *The Atlantic*, June 14, 2013 (http://www.theatlantic.com/international/archive/2013/06/why-arming-the-rebels-isnt-enough/276889/).

18. Gordon Lubold and Shane Harris, "Exclusive: McCain Hires Controversial Syria Analyst Elizabeth O'Bagy." *Foreign Policy*, September 27, 2013 (http://thecable.foreignpolicy.com/posts/2013/09/27/mccain_hires_controversial_syria_analyst_elizabeth_obagy).

19. Linda Keenan and Janine R. Wedel, "10 Shadow Elitists of the Decade." Huffington Post, December 23, 2010 (http://www.huffingtonpost.com/linda-keenan/10-shadow-elitists-of-the_b_800634.html#s211985title=Neocon_Core).

20. My 2011 and 2012 interviews with top government auditors from countries such as India, Russia, Uganda, and Jamaica suggest that the phenomenon here described is widespread (Janine R. Wedel, unpublished interviews). Recent or current comptrollers or auditors general of their countries, these veteran officials all represented their countries in the UN Independent Audit Advisory Committee. It is striking that, independently of one another, they cite the privatizations and public/private partnerships introduced in the 1990s into their respective countries (often under sponsorship of international financial institutions) as creating unprecedented opportunities for corruption. These public/private arrangements and partnerships, which often involve more money and players who transcend geographical boundaries, are more complex and difficult to monitor than in the past, according to the auditors. As one auditor general expressed: "It's fair to say that the privatization era was the onset of the grand corruption era. People became bolder and went for bigger stakes. Before, it was smaller amounts."

21. Miller is quoted in Eliza Newlin Carney, "The Transparency Lobby." *National Journal*, March 21, 2011 (http://www.nationaljournal.com/columns/rules-of-the-game/the-transparency-lobby-20110321).

22. Here ALL considers a name change: Megan R. Wilson, "Group founded to defend K Street considers dropping 'lobbyist' from name." *The Hill*, September 9, 2013 (http://thehill.com/business-a-lobbying/321121-association-founded-to-defend-k-street-considers-dropping-lobbyist-from-its-name).

    Here ALL agrees to the name change: Dave Levinthal, "American League of Lobbyists changes name." Center for Public Integrity, November 18, 2013 (http://www.publicintegrity.org/2013/11/18/13789/american-league-lobbyists-changes-name).

23. Francis X. Clines, "Lobbyists Look for a Euphemism." *New York Times*, September 21, 2013 (http://www.nytimes.com/2013/09/22/opinion/sunday/lobbyists-look-for-a-euphemism.html?_r=0).

24. The letter was obtained by *Politico* (http://images.politico.com/global/2013/09/10/letter_to_all_members_-_final.html).

25. Clines, op. cit.

26. Editorial, "The Power Broker." *New York Times,* January 23, 2012 (http://www. nytimes.com/2012/01/24/opinion/the-power-broker.html).

27. Tavis Smiley, "Interview with Former Lobbyist: Jack Abramoff." PBS, April 4, 2012 (http://www.pbs.org/wnct/tavissmiley/interviews/ former-lobbyist-jack-abramoff/).

28. OpenSecrets.org, "Lobbying Database," Center for Responsive Politics (http:// www.opensecrets.org/lobby/).

29. This *New York Times* piece (Thomas Edsall, "The Shadow Lobbyist," *New York Times,* April 25, 2013 [http://opinionator.blogs.nytimes.com/2013/04/25/ the-shadow-lobbyist/]) pointed me to the Center for Responsive Politics report: OpenSecrets.org, "Lobbying Database," Center for Responsive Politics (http:// www.opensecrets.org/lobby/firmsum.php?id=D000021679&year=2008).

30. See, for example, Gerald Epstein and Jessica Carrick-Hagenbarth, "Financial Economists, Financial Interests and Dark Corners of the Meltdown: It's Time to Set Ethical Standards for the Economics Profession." Working Paper Series, Number 239, Political Economy Research Institute. University of Massachusetts-Amherst, October 2010 (http://www.peri.umass.edu/fileadmin/ pdf/working_papers/working_papers_201-250/WP239.pdf).

31. Simon Johnson, "Senior Goldman Adviser Criticizes Greece—Without Disclosing His Goldman Affiliation." *The Baseline Scenario,* February 15, 2010 (http://baselinescenario.com/2010/02/15/senior-goldman-adviser- criticizes-greece-without-disclosing-his-goldman-affiliation/); Issing's piece is at: Otmar Issing, "Europe Cannot Afford to Rescue Greece." *Financial Times,* February 15, 2010 (http://www.ft.com/intl/cms/s/0/9b8e66a6-1a3c- 11df-b4ee-00144feab49a.html?siteedition=uk#axzz2rjRk9ita). See also Frances Robinson, "Greek Bailout Would Deal 'Major Blow' to Euro, Issing Says." *Bloomberg,* February 15, 2010 (http://www.bloomberg.com/apps/ news?pid=newsarchive&sid=aOZ0Ol_v7DIM&pos=4).

32. Scott Shane, "For Obscure Iranian Exile Group, Broad Support in U.S." *New York Times,* November 26, 2011 (http://www.nytimes.com/2011/11/27/us/politics/ lobbying-support-for-iranian-exile-group-crosses-party-lines.html); Joby Warrick and Julie Tate, "High-priced advocacy raises questions for supporters of Iranian exile group," *Washington Post,* July 5, 2012 (http://www.washingtonpost.com/ world/national-security/high-priced-advocacy-raises-questions-for-supporters-of- iranian-exile-group/2012/07/05/gJQABoacQW_story.html).

With regard to other politicians written about in connection with the Iranian exile group, the *New York Times* indicated that two former CIA directors, a former FBI director, a former attorney general, President Bush's first homeland security chief, President Obama's first national security adviser, big-name Republicans like former New York mayor Giuliani and Democrats like former Vermont governor Dean had been well paid, collecting fees of $10,000 to $50,000 for speeches on behalf of the Iranian group.

The *Washington Post* is much more vague on the issue of payment, mentioning almost the same list of names plus a few more, but not delving into how much they were paid aside from a free trip to Paris for a rally.

Three of the people mentioned above acknowledge having accepted money (see Elizabeth Flock, "Iranian Terrorist Group M.E.K. Pays Big to Make

History Go Away," *US News*, July 6, 2012 [http://www.usnews.com/news/articles/2012/07/06/iranian-terrorist-group-mek-pays-big-to-make-history-go-away-iranian-group-mek-lobbies-hard-pledges-peace-as-it-pleads-case-to-be-delisted-dc-listening-terror-group-pays-to-make-history-go-awayseries?page=2]).

33. Anna Fifield, "Iranian exiles pay US figures as advocates." *Financial Times*, July 29, 2011 (http://www.ft.com/intl/cms/s/0/cc6d5774-b23d-11e0-9d80-00144feabdc0.html#axzz2XwkM5RQK).

34. See, for instance, http://truth-out.org/news/item/13031-the-privatization-of-us-foreign-policy-an-interview-with-the-author-of-the-foreign-policy-auction.

35. John Newhouse, "Diplomacy, Inc. The Influence of Lobbies on U.S. Foreign Policy." *Foreign Affairs*, May/June 2009 (http://www.foreignaffairs.com/articles/64941/john-newhouse/diplomacy-inc; http://www.viet-studies.info/kinhte/Diplomacy_Inc_FA.pdf).

36. Matthew J. Lauer is the Qorvis partner. Sara Jerome, "Lobbying firm Cassidy & Associates loses highest-paying client." *The Hill*, August 6, 2010 (http://thehill.com/business-a-lobbying/113117-lobbying-firm-cassidy-a-associates-loses-highest-paying-client).

37. *Viereck vs. United States*, 318 US 236, 1943 (https://bulk.resource.org/courts.gov/c/US/318/318.US.236.458.html).

38. Armeniapedia, "Dick Gephardt" (http://www.armeniapedia.org/index.See, for example: With regard to Feith: http://www.sourcewatch.org/index.php/International_Advisors,_Inc.
     With respect to Livingston: http://www.nytimes.com/2007/10/17/washington/17lobby.html
     With regard to Gephardt: http://www.newrepublic.com/article/politics/final-resolution

39. The fundraisers were John Merrigan and Matthew "Mac" Bernstein. See: http://abcnews.go.com/Blotter/story?id=4228113

40. Ara Khachatourian, "Clinton Calls Genocide Recognition a 'Dangerous Door.'" Asbarez.com, January 26, 2012 (http://asbarez.com/100552/clinton-calls-genocide-recognition-a-'dangerous-door'/).

41. Josh Rogin, "The Inside Story on the exploding Egypt 'envoy,' Frank Wisner." *Foreign Policy*, February 7, 2011 (http://thecable.foreignpolicy.com/posts/2011/02/07/the_inside_story_on_the_exploding_egypt_envoy_frank_wisner); Jake Tapper, David Kerley, and Kirit Radia, "Obama Administration Distances Self from Own Envoy to Mubarak," ABC News, February 5, 2011 (http://abcnews.go.com/blogs/politics/2011/02/obama-administration-distances-self-from-own-envoy-to-mubarak/).

42. The State Department spokesman was P. J. Crowley; Rogin, op. cit.

43. Eric Lichtblau, "Arab Uprisings Put Their Lobbyists in Uneasy Spot." *New York Times*, March 1, 2011 (http://www.nytimes.com/2011/03/02/world/middleeast/02lobby.html). For information about the termination of the contract, see: Chris Good, "With Aid on the Line, Egypt Has No Lobby." ABC News, July 9, 2013 (http://abcnews.go.com/blogs/politics/2013/07/with-aid-on-the-line-egypt-has-no-lobbyists/).

44. Interview with author Ben Freeman: http://truth-out.org/news/item/13031-the-privatization-of-us-foreign-policy-an-interview-with-the-author-of-the-foreign-policy-auction.

Ben Freeman's book is The Foreign Policy Auction. Create Space Independent Publishing Platform, 2012.

45. Freeman, op. cit., p. 3.

46. Adam Bernstein, "Tyrants' Lobbyist, Flamboyant to the End." *Washington Post*, May 3, 2005 (http://www.washingtonpost.com/wp-dyn/content/article/2005/05/02/AR2005050201380.html); Richard Leiby, "Fall of the House of von Kloberg," Washington Post, July 31, 2005 (http://www.washingtonpost.com/wp-dyn/content/article/2005/07/30/AR2005073001401.html). Von Kloberg apparently committed suicide in 2005.

47. Freeman, op. cit.

48. The member of the Washington Strategic Consulting Group here cited is Adwoa Dunn-Mouton; the former ambassador to Angola is Donald Steinberg. Both are referenced in: *Mother Jones*: Joshua Kurlantzick, "Putting Lipstick on a Dictator." *Mother Jones*, May 7, 2007 (http://www.motherjones.com/politics/2007/05/putting-lipstick-dictator).

49. This is based on a database by ProPublica and the Sunlight Foundation that tracks firms, their work, and campaign contributions to various politicians by firms, whose clients often include foreign countries (http://foreignlobbying.org/).

50. Rosie Gray, "Covert Malaysian Campaign Touched a Wide Range of American Media." Buzzfeed, March 1, 2013 (http://www.buzzfeed.com/rosiegray/covert-malaysian-campaign-touched-a-wide-range-of-american-m). I'm just looking at what Trevino said again—this was at the bottom of the piece—an update—I'm not exactly sure how to characterize it. From Buzzfeed:

> Trevino called back to say that he had actually checked with his legal counsel in 2011 after being questioned by Politico, but had been told at the time that he didn't need to register anywhere.
>
> "Ben Smith had actually asked me if I was a foreign agent back in 2011," Trevino said.
>
> "I asked a lawyer friend, my counsel. I said, hey, is there anything I need to comply with? He came back and said no."
>
> "After the Guardian thing, I reached out to a different counsel, and I did some googling and found out about FARA," Trevino said.
>
> Page 85—not an error at all but I guess I'd question putting Daschle in as a one off. He seems a consummate insider to me. He does seem relatively confined to health care, though.
>
> Page 91—Endnote 95. The 2007 Mishkin report sentence is better cited with this: http://blogs.wsj.com/economics/2007/08/01/the-past-lucrative-life-of-feds-mishkin/

51. Ibid. In an update towards the end of the article, Gray reports having heard more from Trevino, as follows:

> Trevino called back to say that he had actually checked with his legal counsel in 2011 after being questioned by Politico, but had been told at the time that he didn't need to register anywhere.

"Ben Smith had actually asked me if I was a foreign agent back in 2011," Trevino said.

"I asked a lawyer friend, my counsel. I said, hey, is there anything I need to comply with? He came back and said no."

"After the Guardian thing, I reached out to a different counsel, and I did some googling and found out about FARA," Trevino said.

52. See, for example, FARA's FAQ (http://www.fara.gov/fara-faq.html).

53. As John Newhouse of the World Security Institute said in 2009: "Since 1966, when FARA was amended, there have been only three indictments on alleged FARA violations and no successful criminal prosecutions" (John Newhouse, "Diplomacy, Inc: The Influence of Lobbies on U.S. Foreign Policy." *Foreign Affairs,* May/June 2009 [http://www.viet-studies.info/kinhte/Diplomacy_Inc_FA.pdf]). Since then, the case referenced in this article has been prosecuted: Jan Witold Baran and Robert L. Walker, "Former congressman Mark Siljander sentenced for FARA violation." Wiley Rein LLP, March 15, 2012 (http://www.lexology.com/library/detail.aspx?g=8120140b-2495-4b9f-86cf-54c12a53d5c6).

54. John Kurlantzick, "When Lobbyists Work for Authoritarian Nations." *Newsweek,* July 26, 2010 (http://www.thedailybeast.com/newsweek/2010/07/26/the-hired-guns.html).

55. Office of Senator Claire McCaskill, "Schumer, McCaskill, Obama Call on Justice Department Watchdog to Probe Lax and Uneven Enforcement of Foreign Law." Office of Senator Claire McCaskill, July 10, 2008 (http://www.mccaskill.senate.gov/newsroom/record.cfm?id=300414); Larry Margasak, "Foreign Agents Law Said Full of Loopholes." *AP News Archive,* June 19, 1991 (http://www.apnewsarchive.com/1991/Foreign-Agents-Law-Said-Full-of-Loopholes/id-3a396ea11e1aa55b51c8564611287530).

56. Rosie Gray, "How Foreign Governments Make Sure You Don't Know They're Lobbying You." *BuzzFeed,* March 21, 2013 (http://www.buzzfeed.com/rosiegray/how-foreign-governments-make-sure-you-dont-know-theyre-lobby).

57. Eli Lake, "Ukraine's DC Lobbyists in Disarray as Dictator Flees." *The Daily Beast,* February 25, 2014 (http://www.thedailybeast.com/articles/2014/02/25/ukraine-s-d-c-lobbyists-in-disarray-as-dictator-flees.html).

58. Kevin Bogardus, "Justice amps up enforcement of law on foreign advocacy." *The Hill,* October 28, 2011 (http://thehill.com/business-a-lobbying/190379-officials-turn-up-enforcement-of-foreign-lobby-law).

59. For more on that, Ben Freeman, author of *The Foreign Policy Auction*, is interviewed by Michael K. Busch, who teaches international relations at City College of New York. "FDL Book Salon Welcomes Ben Freeman, *The Foreign Policy Auction: Foreign Lobbying in America*," FDL Book Salon, December 2, 2012 (http://fdlbooksalon.com/2012/12/02/fdl-book-salon-welcomes-ben-freeman/).

60. John Newhouse, "Diplomacy, Inc: The Influence of Lobbies on U.S. Foreign Policy." *Foreign Affairs,* May/June 2009 (http://www.viet-studies.info/kinhte/Diplomacy_Inc_FA.pdf).

61. Ken Silverstein, "How Bahrain Works Washington." *Salon,* December 8, 2011 (http://www.salon.com/2011/12/08/how_bahrain_works_washington/).

62. John Kurlantzick, "Putting Lipstick On A Dictator." *Mother Jones*, May 7, 2007 (http://www.motherjones.com/politics/2007/05/putting-lipstick-dictator).

63. Flexibility is so much a part of the shadow elite MO that I coined these "flex" terms to describe them: "flexians" (players who work on their own), and "flex nets" (when they operate as part of a network). For definitions and characteristics, see Janine R. Wedel, *Shadow Elite: How the World's New Power Brokers Undermine Democracy, Government, and the Free Market*. New York: Basic Books, 2009, pp. 13-21; and endnote below.

   "Flex nets" are, among other things, circles of shadow elites who work together over many years and keep coming up in different incarnations vis-à-vis each other. For definition and characteristics, see endnote below and also Wedel, *Shadow Elite* (pp. 15-19). The dozen or so players I call the "Neocon Core," who helped push the United States to war in Iraq in 2003, are perhaps the quintessential case to date of a flex net (see Wedel, *Shadow Elite*, pp. 147-191). Since the 1970s, members of this Neocon core have pioneered practices at the nexus of official and private power.

   For recent or relatively recent examples of "flexians," see cases in this book and in Arianna Huffington, "The First HuffPost Book Club Pick of 2010: Shadow Elite by Janine Wedel," January 6, 2010 (http://www.huffingtonpost.com/arianna-huffington/the-first-huffpost-book-c_b_412999.html).

64. The following features make flex nets effective and distinguish them from other influencers such as lobbyists, interest groups, conspiratorial groups, Mafias, cliques, and elites. (Of course, these groupings have by no means disappeared; some are even nourished by the same transformational developments that feed flex nets, as described in Chapter 1.)

   First, flex nets form an exclusive informal network that serves as *an intricate spine*. While their roles and the organizational and political environments in which they operate may change, the group provides continuity. Unlike lobbyists (who offer politicians support and resources in exchange for access and preference in policies) and interest groups (which defend the interests of a particular group or promote a political cause [see, for instance, Vernon Bogdanor, ed., *The Blackwell Encyclopedia of Political Institutions*. Oxford: Basil Blackwell, 1987, p. 295; W. Grant, 2004. "Interest Groups," *The Concise Oxford Dictionary of Politics*, eds. Iain McLean and Alistair McMillan. Oxford, U.K.: Oxford University Press, 2003; and David Robertson, *The Routledge Dictionary of Politics*, 3rd Edition. London and New York: Routledge, 2004, p. 41]), flex nets are not formal or permanent entities and do not aspire to being so. Although members of flex nets are united by shared activities and interpersonal histories, the existence of the network is unannounced. Flex nets also are not conspiracies, whose members must keep their activities and, often, the very existence of their group, secret. While some of the group's activities in support of its goals are publicly unrevealed, others are fully in the open, invite media attention, and may even be crafted by public relations specialists.

   Group cohesion is aided by the second feature of flex nets: *shared conviction and action*. Members of a flex net act as a continuous, self-propelling team to achieve goals that are grounded in their common world view. Flex nets thus differ from the powerful "Wise Men" of the American past such as the influential advisers who refashioned American foreign policy at the end of World War II and John F. Kennedy's "Best and Brightest," who executed the Vietnam War in the 1960s. These men were mainly instruments of the presidents whose policies they pursued, whereas flex nets are self-sustaining teams with their own agendas. There was little of the long-term constancy or independent pursuit of group goals that defines flex nets.

The third characteristic that defines flex nets is that they form *a resource pool*. The influence of a flex net derives in part from its members' effort to amass and coordinate both material and interpersonal resources. As members parlay their roles and standing into influence opportunities by placing themselves in positions and venues relevant to their goals, the network as a whole can wield far more influence than an individual on his own.

While flex nets, like Mafias, work at the interstices of state and private (see, for instance, Anton Blok, "Mafia," *International Encyclopedia of the Social and Behavioral Sciences*, vol. 13. Amsterdam: Elsevier, 2001, p. 9126), pursue common goals, and share rules of behavior, flex nets should not be confused with Mafias (which, in the classic usage, are a type of patronage system, run by family enterprises, that developed in Sicily and Calabria, Italy). Unlike flex nets, which primarily seek to influence policy, Mafias pursue illegal transactions to gain power or wealth and employ violence to achieve their objectives (see, for example, Federico Varese, "Mafia," *The Concise Oxford Dictionary of Politics*, eds. Iain McLean and Alistair McMillan. Oxford, U.K.: Oxford University Press, 2003).

Finally, flex nets help create *a hybrid habitat*—their fourth feature. A flex net's strength lies in its coordinated ability to reorganize governing processes, authorities, and bureaucracies to suit the group's purposes. Members of flex nets both use and supplant standard governing structures, often setting up alternative might-be-official, might-be-unofficial organizations or authorities.

For all these reasons, flex nets also are not simply "cliques," as anthropologists and sociologists have defined them (a core group whose members contact one another for multiple purposes and advance their own interests [see, notably, Jeremy Boissevain, *Friends of Friends: Networks, Manipulators and Coalitions*. Oxford, U.K.: Basil Blackwell, 1974, p. 174; and C. Seymour-Smith, *Dictionary of Anthropology*. Boston: G. K. Hall & Co., 1986, p. 40]). Although flex nets can be seen as a type of clique (Jacek Kurczewski, ed., *Lokalne Wzory Kultury Politycznej*. Warsaw: Wydawnictwo Trio, 2007), not all cliques possess all of the characteristics of the flex net *modus operandi* that define its operations.

Flex nets also are not quite political elites. While elites in many contexts do exert power and control, as anthropologists (see, for example, Cris Shore and Stephen Nugent, eds., *Elite Cultures: Anthropological Perspectives*. New York: Routledge, 2002; and Mattei Dogan, ed., *Elite Configurations at the Apex of Power*. Leiden-Boston: Brill, 2003) have shown, flex nets—small, mobile, and with a particular *modus operandi*—are far from synonymous with political elites. With regard to elites in the United States, important historical work has been done to dissect the structure and function of influence groups, including the networks that propel them. Political scientist Phillip H. Burch's *Elites in American History* (Philip H. Burch Jr., *The Civil War to the New Deal*. New York: Holmes & Meier, 1981), a study of American political power from the Civil

War to the New Deal, depicts the web of ties among government officials and
the threat that those connections pose to the notion of democratic government.
Most famously, a half century ago, in his treatise *The Power Elite*, sociologist C.
Wright Mills (C. Wright Mills, *The Power Elite*. New York: Oxford University
Press, 1956) coined the term to describe the pyramid of power—the tiny,
singular group of elites at the pinnacle of America's business, military, and
political establishment. This interlocking constellation of government officials,
military leaders, and corporate executives, he argued, effectively "controlled"
major political and social decisionmaking. By contrast, members of flex nets
inhabit a space that lies beyond either traditional or new positions of authority.
They flex power by pooling resources within their networks and juggling roles,
operating through informal channels and undermining standard process even as
they work within formal institutions.

65. Personal communication with Simon Reich, professor in the Division of Global
Affairs and Department of Political Science, Rutgers Newark.

66. For the definition of a "flexian," see the earlier endnote in this chapter.

67. For my definition of a "flex net," see two earlier endnotes in this chapter.

68. Geithner, long at the Federal Reserve Bank of New York, is now president and
managing director of private equity firm Warburg Pincus; Orszag is now at
Citigroup with several roles including, as mentioned earlier, "Chairman of the
Public Sector Group." The circle also includes Jason Furman, Deputy Director
of the National Economic Council and later chairman of the Council of
Economic Advisers in the Obama administration.

69. Matt Taibbi, "The Big Sellout." *Rolling Stone*, December 1, 2009.

70. Quoted in Jackie Calmes, "Rubinomics Recalculated." *New York Times*,
November 23, 2008 (http://dealbook.nytimes.com/2008/11/24/
rubinomics-recalculated/).

71. Rubinomics became the rallying cry for pro-business Democrats, emphasizing
low interest rates through deficit reductions, free trade, and deregulation. See,
for example, ibid.

Proponents of Rubinomics held that the "free market" generally knew best;
that banks should be allowed to "innovate" and diversify their businesses; and
that a balanced budget would help lead to lower interest rates and hence a
thriving economy.

Gabriel Sherman in *New York* Magazine stresses the role of mindsets and
shared experience as a hugely important dynamic: "Wall Street has Washington
over a barrel—and the values of one can't help but be the values of the other.
Even in Democratic administrations like the current one, once and future Wall
Streeters are in position to pull the teeth out of regulations—for what they
see as perfectly sensible, perfectly ordinary reasons. There's no need to cue the
scary music; it's not a conspiracy. It's just that having lived in the same worlds,
read the same textbooks, imbibed the same maxims, been tutored by the same
mentors, attended the same confabs in Aspen and Davos—and, of course, been
paid with checks from the same bank accounts—they naturally think the same
thoughts. To these people, the way things are done is, more or less, the way they
have to be done. To change the system, you have to change the people; but the
people are the only ones who know how the system works" (Gabriel Sherman,

"Revolver." *New York Magazine*, April 11, 2011 [http://nymag.com/news/business/wallstreet/peter-orszag-2011-4/index1.html]).

72. Manuel Roig-Franzia, "Brooksley Born, the Cassandra of the Derivatives Crisis." *Washington Post*, May 26, 2009 (http://www.washingtonpost.com/wp-dyn/content/article/2009/05/25/AR2009052502108.html).

73. Anthony Faiola, Ellen Nakashima, and Jill Drew, "What Went Wrong." *Washington Post*, October 15, 2008 (http://www.washingtonpost.com/wp-dyn/content/story/2008/10/14/ST2008101403344.html).

74. Manuel Roig-Franzia, op. cit.

75. Ryan Lizza, "The Contrarian." *The New Yorker*, July 6, 2009 (http://www.newyorker.com/reporting/2009/07/06/090706fa_fact_lizza?currentPage=all).

76. Ibid.

77. Bonnie Kavoussi, "Sheila Bair: Timothy Geithner Did 'What Citigroup Needed'." Huffington Post, September 27, 2012 (http://www.huffingtonpost.com/2012/09/27/sheila-bair-timothy-geithner_n_1918753.html).

78. Rolfe Winkler (interviewer), "The Big Interview: Sheila Bair." *Wall Street Journal Live*, September 25, 2012 (http://live.wsj.com/video/the-big-interview-sheila-bair/A8FC152E-8F84-4A5E-BF25-70D499A62CB3.html#!A8FC152E-8F84-4A5E-BF25-70D499A62CB3).

79. Ron Suskind, *Confidence Men: Wall Street, Washington, and the Education of a President*. New York: HarperCollins, 2011, p. 379.

80. Timothy Geithner, *Stress Test*. New York: Crown, 2014.

81. Members of the Summers-Rubin circle appear to be enormously influential with the Obama administration, even while many are no longer in official roles.

82. Summers is routinely praised as "brilliant." Until the summer of 2013, it was difficult to find a single article in the *New York Times*, the *Washington Post*, or other mainline American outlets that neglected to do so. The narrative of "brilliant" is obligatory, parroted by virtually everyone, even if, nowadays, it stands alongside demonstrated policy failure.

    I first encountered Summers and his modus operandi indirectly, while studying Western aid to Russia after the Cold War (see Janine R. Wedel, *Collision and Collusion: The Strange Case of Western Aid to Eastern Europe*. New York: Palgrave, 2001, pp. 123-174). Early in his career at Treasury during the Clinton administration, Summers backed a U.S.-funded aid-and-advisory program to help reform the economy of the new post–Cold War Russia with his close friend and co-author from Harvard, economist Andrei Shleifer, leading the effort. In his official capacity, Summers helped Shleifer and Harvard win noncompetitive government awards through arrangements that flouted standard government procedure, according to other U.S. officials at the time.

    Shleifer headed the Harvard team, which managed virtually the entire nearly $400 million U.S. flagship economic-aid portfolio. And, while itself a chief recipient of aid, the Harvard Institute—the umbrella through which the Harvard-Russia players received U.S. funding—also was charged with overseeing the portfolio they ran. That is, the Harvard players were to watch over themselves and their competitors. Shleifer himself played indistinct and overlapping roles as he lobbied in favor of his projects and advised both the United States and Russia while presenting himself as an independent expert.

The Harvard "consultants" morphed into far more than dispensers of advice: they enmeshed themselves in the Russian power structure via their in-country cronies, gaining access to inside information. Backed by Summers and hundreds of millions of dollars in U.S. and Western aid and loans from international financial institutions, the Harvard-Russia partners made end runs around the democratically elected parliament, operated through top-down decree, and fused their own agendas with that of the state. Far from helping create a market economy with a legal and regulatory backbone, with which they had been tasked, they facilitated the expansion of an unaccountable state with a democratic façade. This all took place with the help of Summers and Rubin in the saddle at Treasury.

Meanwhile, Shleifer and another Harvard principal invested personally in many of the same areas in which they were being paid by U.S. taxpayers to provide "impartial" advice to help develop the Russian economy—including securities, equities, oil and aluminum companies, real estate, and mutual funds. They do not deny these investments (for the lawsuit and related documents, see http://janinewedel.info/harvardinvestigative.html#1). They also helped a wider circle meddle in the spoils of an unraveling resource-rich empire. The endowments of both Harvard and Yale gained access to valuable investments through networks inhabited by Shleifer or his wife, the currency trader and hedge fund manager Nancy Zimmerman. (She had worked at Goldman Sachs in the 1980s for Rubin, who was also a sometime board member of the Harvard Management Company that oversees Harvard University's investments and remained close to him when he was secretary of the Treasury.) When these activities began coming to light, the Harvard players, with help from Summers, enfeebled multiple U.S. investigations of Harvard's activities, including one by the Justice Department for fraud (eventually settled out of court) and for which Harvard paid $30 million to the U.S. government, the largest lawsuit in Harvard's history. For the settlement paid by Harvard being a record one, see David McClintick, "How Harvard Lost Russia," *Institutional Investor* magazine, January 24, 2006, p. 3.

Summers, after a two-year stint as Treasury Secretary from 1999 to 2001, returned to Harvard, this time as president. Two people who lobbied hard on his behalf to get him there: his old boss Rubin and his friend Shleifer, for whom he had covered and would continue to do so. See these articles by a Harvard dean at the time, Harry R. Lewis (Harry R. Lewis, "Larry Summers, Robert Rubin: Will The Harvard Shadow Elite Bankrupt the University and the Country?" Huffington Post, January 12, 2010; and Harry R. Lewis, "Larry's Conflicts," Huffington Post, July 31, 2013 [http://www.huffingtonpost.com/harry-r-lewis/larry-summers-conflict-of-interest_b_3679160.html]).

At Harvard, Summers was a walking conflict of interest. He soon brought in Rubin as a member of the Harvard Corporation, the university's board of directors. While president, it turned out, Summers also moonlighted as a private investor. (See Frank Rich, "Awake and Sing!" *New York Times*, April 11, 2009; Frank Rich, "Obama's Make-or-Break Summers." *New York Times*, June 21, 2009; Louise Story, "A Rich Education for Summers (After Harvard)." *New York Times*, April 5, 2009, Matt Taibbi, "The Big Sellout." *Rolling Stone*,

December 1, 2009; and Matt Taibbi, "Inside the Great American Bubble Machine." *Rolling Stone*, July 2, 2009.)

At the same time, Summers gambled with the university's operating budget by betting on derivatives (one bank Harvard used: Goldman Sachs), investments that would prove disastrous. In addition, while advising a hedge fund and serving as a member of the board of the Harvard Management Corporation, which oversees the investment of Harvard's endowment, Summers also "pressure[d] the university's asset manager to buy more hedge funds for the University's portfolio," according to Harry Lewis. (Harry R. Lewis, "Larry's Conflicts." Huffington Post, July 31, 2013 [http://www.huffingtonpost.com/harry-r-lewis/larry-summers-conflict-of-interest_b_3679160.html].)

Summers also virtually succeeded in pushing the Harvard-Russia affair and the wrongdoing of his friend Shleifer under the rug, despite Shleifer's being a principal subject of the U.S. government's lawsuit against the university. (The settlement required Harvard to pay $26.5 million in fines for defrauding the U.S. government, Shleifer $2 million, and Hay [the other principal player named in the lawsuit] between $1 and $2 million (Marcella Bombardieri, "Harvard, teacher, and lawyer to pay US$30m." *Boston Globe*, August 4, 2005). Only in 2006, after Harvard settled the government lawsuit, did Summers resign amid public-relations troubles within and outside the university.

83.   In 2010, Rubin rebutted his many critics, saying that he did, in fact, support such regulation in the broader sense. But as journalist Dan Froomkin points out, even if he was theoretically worried about derivatives, he hardly did enough practically to stem the threat and, in fact, was part of the group opposing Brooksley Born's 1998 push to regulate. Rubin said that the 1998 opposition stemmed from very specific legal advice he received, not from an ideological opposition to regulation in general. See Dan Froomkin, "Rubin: I Actually Supported Regulating Derivatives." Huffington Post, June 6, 2010 (updated May 25, 2011) (http://www.huffingtonpost.com/2010/04/20/rubin-i-actually-supporte_n_545113.html).

In a late 2009 *Newsweek* article titled "Getting the Economy Back on Track," Rubin counsels the public on economic recovery and on what went wrong. Though he had top jobs at Citigroup and Goldman, he describes his career in a most vague way: "many years involved in financial matters." *Newsweek*'s author bio lists him as a former Treasury secretary, co-chairman of the Council on Foreign Relations, and a fellow of the Harvard Corporation, but no corporate title is to be found therein. Robert E. Rubin, "Getting the Economy Back on Track." *Newsweek*, December 28, 2009 (http://www.thedailybeast.com/newsweek/2009/12/28/getting-the-economy-back-on-track.html).

84.   Institute for New Economic Thinking, "Panel Discussion—Rising to the Challenge: Equity, Adjustment and Balance in the World Economy." Bretton Woods Conference, hosted by the Institute for New Economic Thinking, April 10, 2011 (http://ineteconomics.org/net/video/playlist/conference/bretton-woods/R).

85.   Jeffrey Brown, "Newsmaker Interview with Lawrence Summers." PBS, April 22, 2010 (http://www.pbs.org/newshour/bb/business/jan-june10/summers_04-22.html). Summers also warned against the demonization of

mainstream economics by people who "don't do math" and flagged the dangers of overregulating in the wake of a crisis.

86. In a quick Google search of "Summers apologies," I found myself on the literary journal *McSweeney's*, which had a compilation of Summers apologizing, except that they were satirical apologies. They were takeoffs from embarrassing remarks made in 2005, while president of Harvard, about women and science, and his subsequent non-apology apologies. See: Laurence Hughes, "The Collected Apologies of Lawrence H. Summers, President of Harvard." *McSweeney's*, February 25, 2005 (http://www.mcsweeneys.net/articles/the-collected-apologies-of-lawrence-h-summers-president-of-harvard). Those hoping Summers will offer a full-throated "I was wrong" about a far bigger misstep—the deregulation he championed during his tenure—may be in for the long haul.

87. For an initial report, see, for example, "Cracks in the Crust: Iceland Banking Collapse." *Economist*, December 11, 2008. For a report on lasting devastation, see, for example, Omar Vladimarsson, "Half of Icelanders Still Struggle to Make Ends Meet, Poll Shows." *Bloomberg*, April 5, 2013 (http://www.bloomberg.com/news/2013-04-05/half-of-icelanders-still-struggle-to-make-ends-meet-poll-shows.html).

88. With regard to neoliberalism, I employ this term only sparingly because it can describe considerably different policies, not to mention differing local adaptations to them. For further detail, see Janine R. Wedel, *Shadow Elite: How the World's New Power Brokers Undermine Democracy, Government, and the Free Market*. New York: Basic Books, 2009, p. 213, note 11.

89. The scholar at the University of Iceland is Stefan Olafsson. See Stefan Olafsson, "Icelandic Capitalism—From Statism to Neoliberalism and Financial Collapse," *The Nordic Varieties of Capitalism*, ed. Lars Mjøset. Bingley, U.K.: Emerald Publishing, 2011, pp. 1-52 (http://books.google.com/books/about/The_Nordic_Varieties_of_Capitalism.html?id=a13pWg-Az4oC). The quote is on p. 24.

90. These articles give a sense of Iceland's go-go Iceland feel: Jake Halpern, "Iceland's Big Thaw." *New York Times*, May 13, 2011 (http://www.nytimes.com/2011/05/15/magazine/icelands-big-economic-thaw.html?pagewanted=all); and Michael Lewis, "Wall Street on the Tundra." *Vanity Fair*, April 2009 (http://www.vanityfair.com/politics/features/2009/04/iceland200904).

91. Roger Boyes, *Meltdown Iceland: How the Global Financial Crisis Bankrupted an Entire Country*. New York: Bloomsbury USA, 2009.

92. See Thorvaldur Gylfason, "From Crisis to Constitution." *VOX*, October 11, 2011 (http://www.voxeu.org/article/crisis-constitution-insights-iceland). and Robert Wade and Silla Sigurgeirsdóttir, "Lessons from Iceland." *New Left Review*, 65, September-October 2010 (http://newleftreview.org/II/65/robert-wade-silla-sigurgeirsdottir-lessons-from-iceland)

93. See: "The Past (Lucrative) Life of Fed's Mishkin," *The Wall Street Journal*, August 1, 2007, http://blogs.wsj.com/economics/2007/08/01/the-past-lucrative-life-of-feds-mishkin/

94. "The Rick Mishkin Steak n Shake Connection." *Time*, August 1, 2007 (http://business.time.com/2007/08/01/the_rick_mishkin_steak_n_shake/).

95. Wade and Sigurgeirsdóttir, op. cit.

96. Ibid.

97.   The FME stands for Financial Supervisory Authority. See Robert Wade and Silla Sigurgeirsdóttir, "Lessons from Iceland." *New Left Review*, 65, September-October 2010 (http://newleftreview.org/II/65/robert-wade-silla-sigurgeirsdottir-lessons-from-iceland), p. 27.

98.   Luca Lombardi, "The Case of Iceland—the Illusion of an Amicable Default." *Socialist Democracy*, November 2, 2011 (http://www.socialistdemocracy.org/RecentArticles/RecentTheCaseOfIcelandTheIllusionOfAnAmicableDefault.html); for a timeline of the crisis, see *BBC News*, "Timeline: Iceland economic crisis." *BBC News*, February 2, 2009 (http://news.bbc.co.uk/2/hi/7851853.stm).

99.   From the Wade and Sigurgeirsdóttir article: "In conditions where the currency was already tumbling, the foreign-exchange reserves were exhausted and there were no capital controls, the peg lasted for only a few trading hours; it was perhaps the shortest-lived currency peg ever. But it was long enough for cronies-in-the-know to spirit their money out of the króna at a much more favourable rate than they would get later. Inside sources indicate that billions fled the currency in these hours" (Wade and Sigurgeirsdóttir, op. cit.).

100.   Rowena Mason, "David Oddsson, Iceland's former prime minister and central banker, turns editor." *The Telegraph*, September 28, 2009 (http://www.telegraph.co.uk/finance/financialcrisis/6240803/David-Oddsson-Icelands-former-prime-minister-and-central-banker-turns-editor.html).

101.   Wade and Sigurgeirsdóttir, op. cit.: http://newleftreview.org/II/65/robert-wade-silla-sigurgeirsdottir-lessons-from-iceland#_edn34

        The name of the leading Reykjavik daily is *Morgunbladid*. Roger Boyes writes that the paper "was a mouthpiece for David Oddsson's Independence Party. *Morgunbladid* had been founded in 1913 and was the grand dame of the Icelandic press, so grand, and enjoying such monopoly, it chose not to publish on Monday so that its editors could go for long weekends. Parliamentary reporters often sat in on—and contributed to—internal sessions of the Independence Party" (Roger Boyes, *Meltdown Iceland: How the Global Financial Crisis Bankrupted an Entire Country*. New York: Bloomsbury, 2009, p. 64).

102.   Andrew Higgins, "Iceland, Fervent Prosecutor of Bankers, Sees Meager Returns." *New York Times*, February 2, 2013 (http://www.nytimes.com/2013/02/03/world/europe/iceland-prosecutor-of-bankers-sees-meager-returns.html?pagewanted=all).

103.   This is a "Special Prosecutor" in the then-newly created Office of the Special Prosecutor. See: Stephan Faris, "Iceland Prosecutor Investigates, Convicts Bankers for Financial Crimes." *Bloomberg BusinessWeek*, September 12, 2013 (http://www.businessweek.com/articles/2013-09-12/iceland-prosecutor-investigates-convicts-bankers-for-financial-crimes).

104.   See Robert Wade and Silla Sigurgeirsdóttir, "Iceland's rise, fall, stabilisation and beyond." *Cambridge Journal of Economics*, 2012, vol. 36, pp. 127-144.

CHAPTER 4

1.   The subtitle of the "Washington Conference on Corruption" was "Fighting Corruption in Developing Countries and Emerging Economies." According to the conference brochure, the conference was held on February 22-23, 1999 in

the Carlton Hotel (now the St. Regis). The suggested accommodation was the Carlton Hotel.

2. Joshua Cooper Ramo, "The Three Marketeers." *Time*, February 15, 1999 (http://content.time.com/time/world/article/0,8599,2054093,00.html).

3. Steven Sampson, "The anti-corruption industry: from movement to institution," *Global Crime*, vol. 11, issue 2, 2010, p. 262.

4. The quote is from the conference brochure.

5. Nicholas Stein, "The World's Most Admired Companies. How Do You Make the Most Admired List? Innovate, innovate, innovate. The winners on this year's list, compiled by the Hay Group consultancy, tell how they do it." *Fortune Magazine, CNN Money*, October 2, 2000 (http://money.cnn.com/magazines/fortune/fortune_archive/2000/10/02/288448/).

6. U.S. Bureau of Labor Statistics, "The Employment Situation: February, 1999." U.S. Bureau of Labor Statistics, March 5, 1999 (http://www.bls.gov/news. release/history/empsit_030599.txt); U.S. Bureau of Labor Statistics, "Lowest unemployment rates in decades at end of 1999." *TED: The Editor's Desk, U.S. Bureau of Labor Statistics*, March 29, 2000 (http://www.bls.gov/opub/ted/2000/mar/wk4/art03.htm).

7. U.S. Inflation Calculator, "New Inflation Rates with Chart, Graph and Table," August 3, 2008 (http://www.usinflationcalculator.com/site-information/new-inflation-rates-with-chart-graph-and-table/1000137/).

8. See, for instance, Transparency International, "The Fight Against Corruption: Is the Tide Now Turning?" *Transparency International (TI) Annual Report*, Berlin, April 1997, pp. 61-63 (http://archive.transparency.org/publications/publications/annual_reports/annual_report_1997); and Johann G. Lambsdorff, "Consequences and Causes of Corruption," Susan Rose-Ackerman, ed., *International Handbook on the Economics of Corruption*. Cheltenham, U.K.: Edward Elgar, 2006, p. 3.

    TI's 1997 annual report states (Transparency International, "The Fight Against Corruption: Is the Tide Now Turning?" Transparency International (TI) Annual Report, Berlin, April 1997, p. 63):

> The index is a 'poll of polls.' It has been prepared using ten sources, including three from the World Competitiveness Report, Institute for Management Development, Lausanne, three from the Political & Economic Risk Consultancy Ltd., Hong Kong, one small survey by Peter Neumann, published in the monthly German magazine, *Impulse*, No. 4/1994, two assessments by DRI/McGraw-Hill Global Risk Service and by the Political Risk Services, East Syracuse, NY and at last the first incoming replies to the internet service (http://www.uni-goettingen.de/~uwvu/icr.htm) of Göttingen University which gives contributors the possibility for anonymous contributions and also directly approaches employees of multinational firms and institutions.

9. A grade of ten indicates "clean" government, whereas zero denotes widespread corruption. The United States had a corruption score of 7.5 on a scale of 10.

See Phillip Kurata, "Transparency International Issues 1999 Corruption Rankings." *Washington File,* October 26, 1999 (https://www.fas.org/irp/news/1999/10/991026-corrupt-usia1.htm).

10. Steven Sampson, "The anti-corruption industry: from movement to institution." *Global Crime,* vol. 11, issue 2, 2010, p. 273. In this 2010 article, he wrote that these developments had occurred over the past decade.

11. Ibid., pp. 272-273.

12. See Transparency International, "The Fight Against Corruption: Is the Tide Now Turning?" *Transparency International (TI) Annual Report,* Berlin, April 1997 (http://archive.transparency.org/publications/publications/annual_reports/annual_report_1997) and Transparency International, "Annual Report 1999." *Transparency International (TI),* Berlin, 1999 (http://archive.transparency.org/publications/publications/annual_reports/annual_report_1999).

More specifically, these are AIG USA, 1997 and 1999; Arthur Andersen USA, 1997 and 1999; Bank of America USA, 1999; Bechtel USA, 1999; Boeing USA, 1999; Bristol-Myers Squibb USA, 1999; Coopers & Lybrand UK, 1997 (and, later, PriceWaterhouseCoopers UK, USA, 1999); Deloitte & Touche South Africa, 1999; Enron Corporation USA, 1997 and 1999; Exxon USA, 1999; Ford USA, 1999; General Electric Company USA 1997 and additionally Canada, 1999; General Motors USA, 1999; IBM Germany, 1997, and additionally USA, 1999; KPMG the Netherlands, 1999; Lockheed Martin USA, 1999; Merck USA, 1999; Motorola USA, 1999; Raytheon USA, 1999; Shell USA, 1999; Texaco USA, 1999; Pfizer Pharmaceuticals USA, 1997 and 1999; Weil Gotshal & Manges USA, 1999, and Westinghouse USA, 1999.

13. This is in part because "the cost of corruption is divided between a large number of actors and taxpayers," the analysts write. Monika Bauhr and Naghmeh Nasiritousi, "Why Pay Bribes? Collective Action and Anticorruption Efforts." Working Paper Series 2011:18, QOG The Quality of Government Institute, December 2011, pp. 1-23. Quotes are from p. 3.

14. Social anthropologist and *Financial Times* journalist Gillian Tett makes this analogy in "Ready for Your Banking Bulletin?" *Financial Times,* September 16, 2011. Consider, for instance, the mystique of wisdom and aura of authority enshrouding Alan Greenspan as chairman of the Federal Reserve and the reverence with which politicians and the media received his every pronouncement.

15. Corruption was not always the hot issue it became in the 1990s and beyond, when corruption scholars were exposed to a new set of global influences. The editors of a 1964 article on bureaucratic corruption in *The American Behavioral Scientist* (Nathaniel H. Leff, "Economic Development through Bureaucratic Corruption, *American Behavioral Scientist,* 1964, vol. 8, no. 8, p. 8) prefaced it with this statement: "Among scholars the subject of corruption is nearly taboo." Today, it is highly unlikely that editors of a major scholarly journal would feel the need to justify an article on corruption. For discussion of scholarly approaches to corruption during the Cold War, see Janine R. Wedel, "Rethinking Corruption in an Age of Ambiguity," *Annual Review of Law and Social Science,* vol. 8, December 2012, pp. 454-460.

16. Transparency International, "The Fight Against Corruption: Is the Tide Now Turning?" *Transparency International (TI) Annual Report,* Berlin, April 1997, p. 106.

17. Ibid., p. 13.
18. E-mail from a former TV financial news producer who asked to remain anonymous, March 19, 2012.
19. Ivan Krastev, *Shifting Obsessions: Three Essays on the Politics of Anticorruption.* Budapest: Central European University Press, 2004, p. 33. See also, for example, Kalin S. Ivanov's article on "The Limits of a Global Campaign Against Corruption" in *Corruption and Development: The Anti-Corruption Campaigns,* Sarah Bracking, ed. New York: Palgrave Macmillan, 2007, pp. 32-33.
20. Robert Klitgaard, *Controlling Corruption.* Berkeley/Los Angeles/London: University of California Press, 1988, p. 69.
21. The principal-agent theory is broadly influential in economics and public policy.
22. In terms of scholarship, as economists Andrei Shleifer and Robert W. Vishny wrote in 1993, most economic studies of corruption "focus on the principal-agent model of corruption" (Andrei Shleifer and Robert W. Vishny, "Corruption." *The Quarterly Journal of Economics,* vol. 108, no. 3, August 1993, p. 599). For gold-standard treatment of the principal-agency theory by an economist, see the work of Susan Rose-Ackerman, who has been publishing on the economics of corruption since 1975. She attributes the "wide range of productive research" in the field largely to a focus on "the piece of the broader concept most susceptible to economic analysis—monetary payments to agents." These payments are intended to "induce agents to ignore the interests of their principals and to favor . . . the bribers instead" (Susan Rose-Ackerman, ed., *International Handbook on the Economics of Corruption.* Cheltenham, UK/ Northampton, MA: Edward Elgar, 2006, p. xiv). (A summary of additional approaches to corruption in the economics literature is found in Vincent G. Fitzsimons, "Economic Models of Corruption," *Corruption and Development: The Anti-Corruption Campaigns,* Sarah Bracking, ed. New York: Palgrave Macmillan, 2007, pp. 46-51.)

    With regard to the principal-agent theory as undergirding anti-corruption efforts, see, among others, Monika Bauhr and Naghmeh Nasiritousi. They write: "Following the logic of the principal-agent framework, the anticorruption regime has adopted a large set of policies, or anti-corruption 'toolkits,' that improves the opportunities for these principals to monitor agents: increased transparency, a free press, democratization, checks and balances, decentralization and privatization. However, if corruption is unobtrusive, its effects indirect and costs divided between a large number of actors or taxpayers, the very condition upon which these measures build may not be met. If corruption is unobtrusive, a very limited number of actors may engage in activities against corruption and anticorruption measures will suffer from a lack of 'principals'" (Monika Bauhr and Naghmeh Nasiritousi, "Why Pay Bribes? Collective Action and Anticorruption Efforts." Working Paper Series 2011:18, QOG The Quality of Government Institute, December 2011, pp. 3-4).
23. Robert Klitgaard, *Controlling Corruption.* Berkeley/Los Angeles/London: University of California Press, 1988, pp. 7, 21.
24. Susan Rose-Ackerman, ed., *International Handbook on the Economics of Corruption.* Cheltenham, UK/Northampton, MA: Edward Elgar, p. xvii. Susan Rose-Ackerman's 1975 article in the *Journal of Public Economics* analyzed

penalties for corrupt transactions in U.S. laws and conditions (pp. 197-198) and policy implications also grounded in those laws and conditions (pp. 202-203) (Susan Rose-Ackerman, "The economics of corruption." *Journal of Public Economics*, vol. 4, 1975.) Her subsequent 1978 *Corruption: A Study in Political Economy* referenced numerous examples at the federal, state, and municipal levels in the United States and the laws that apply to them (pp. 187-203) (Susan Rose-Ackerman, *Corruption: A Study in Political Economy*. New York: Academic Press, 1978).

25. Medical metaphors are common, not only in the development and corruption literature, but in the economics literature more broadly (see János Kornai, "The health of nations: reflections on the analogy between economics and medical science," *Kyklos* 36, 1983, pp. 191-212).

26. *The End of History*, of course, is the title of Francis Fukuyama's influential book, *The End of History and the Last Man* (New York: Free Press, 1992).

27. See, for example, Gary S. Becker, "To Root Out Corruption, Boot Out Big Government." *Business Week*, January 31, 1994 (http://www.businessweek.com/stories/1994-01-30/to-root-out-corruption-boot-out-big-government); Gary S. Becker, "If You Want to Cut Corruption, Cut Government." *Business Week*, December 11, 1995, p. 26 (http://www.businessweek.com/stories/1995-12-10/if-you-want-to-cut-corruption-cut-government). Becker's oft-cited academic work on the subject is: Gary S. Becker and George J. Stigler, "Law Enforcement, Malfeasance, and Compensation of Enforcers." *Journal of Legal Studies*, vol. 3, no. 1, January 1974, pp. 1-18.

28. For further detail, see Janine R. Wedel, *Collision and Collusion: The Strange Case of Western Aid to Eastern Europe*. New York: Palgrave, 2001, pp. 27-28.

29. See, for example, "Corruption Charges Force Top Polish Police Officers to Quit." *New York Times*, August 14, 1994 (http://www.nytimes.com/1994/08/14/world/corruption-charges-force-top-polish-police-officers-to-quit.html); and Alan Cowell, "East Europe Is a Land of Opportunity to the Mafia." *New York Times*, September 2, 1993 (http://www.nytimes.com/1993/09/02/world/east-europe-is-a-land-of-opportunity-to-the-mafia.html).

30. The article reads: "As enemies go, the global corruption hydra has proven a frustrating one: lop off one of their heads and dozens more continue with their hideous damage." Review & Outlook, "Commercial Corruption." *The Wall Street Journal Europe*, January 3-4, 1997.

31. During the Cold War, economists, political scientists, sociologists, anthropologists, criminologists, and legal specialists contributed to the literature on corruption. See Janine R. Wedel, "Rethinking Corruption in an Age of Ambiguity." *Annual Review of Law and Social Science*, vol. 8, December 2012, pp. 454-460.

32. The term "Third World" began to gain wide currency in the 1950s to denote countries that were not aligned with either the United States or the Soviet Union during the Cold War (see, for instance, the work of social critic Pascal Bruckner, *The Tears of the White Man: Compassion as Contempt*. New York: Free Press, 1986). Economists Peter T. Bauer and Basil S. Yamey (Peter T. Bauer and Basil S. Yamey, "East-West/North-South: peace and prosperity?" *Commentary* 70, 1980, pp. 57-63) and Bruckner (op. cit.) demonstrated that what Third World or underdeveloped countries had in common (with few

exceptions) was that they were actual or potential recipients of international economic development schemes and foreign aid, not hunger, poverty, stagnation, exploitation, or race. Bauer and Yamey explained: "Official foreign aid has been the unifying characteristic of this huge, variegated, and utterly diverse collectivity ever since its components began to be lumped together from the late 1940s onward as, successively, the 'underdeveloped world,' the 'Third World,' and now, the 'South.' These expressions never made any sense except as references to a collectivity of past, present, or prospective aid recipients" (Bauer and Yamey, op. cit., p. 58).

33. Economists who encountered developing countries often stumbled on the issue of corruption. Political scientists, too, were often introduced to corruption while studying the Third World, albeit while concentrating on colonial and postcolonial states, not economic development, as was the case with the economists.

34. Nye emphasized, however, that corruption is not "a uniquely Afro-Asian-Latin American problem" (Joseph S. Nye, "Corruption and political development: a cost-benefit analysis." *American Political Science Review*, vol. 16, 1967, p. 418).

Grappling with the intellectual debates of the day, political scientists pondered corruption in the context of real-world events and emerging systems. Their definitions and approaches to corruption emphasized the violation of norms and formal rules. Nye defined corruption as "behavior which deviates from the *formal* duties of a public role because of private-regarding (personal, close family, private clique) pecuniary or status gains; or violates *rules* against the exercise of certain types of private-regarding influence." Joseph S. Nye, "Corruption and political development: a cost-benefit analysis," *American Political Science Review*, vol. 16, 1967, p. 419 [emphasis added].

35. Robert Klitgaard, *Controlling Corruption*. Berkeley/Los Angeles/London: University of California Press, 1988, p. x. Klitgaard also assessed that "corrupt activities are more widespread—and more systematically embedded—in many governments of the developing world than in the West" (p. 10).

36. See, for instance, Nathaniel H. Leff, "Economic Development through Bureaucratic Corruption." *American Behavioral Scientist*, vol. 8, 1964, pp. 8-14.

37. Nye considered not only economic development but added a political twist to also examine national integration and governmental capacity (Joseph S. Nye, "Corruption and political development: a cost-benefit analysis," *American Political Science Review*, vol. 16, 1967, p. 419).

38. Ibid., p. 427. See also Janine R. Wedel, "Rethinking Corruption in an Age of Ambiguity." *Annual Review of Law and Social Science*, vol. 8, December 2012.

39. See, for example, Jonathan S. Landay, "Foreign Aid on the Chopping Block." *The Christian Science Monitor*, December 20, 1994 (http://www.csmonitor.com/layout/set/r14/1994/1220/20021.html/%28page%29/2).

40. Julie Bajolle, "The origins and motivations of the current emphasis on corruption: the case of Transparency International." Presented at Workshop: The International Anti-Corruption Movement, *European Consortium for Political Research Joint Sessions of Workshops*, April 25-30, 2006, Nicosia, Cyprus, p. 6.

41. James D. Wolfensohn, "People and Development." Annual Meetings Address, The World Bank, October 1, 1996 (http://web.worldbank.org/WBSITE/EXTERNAL/EXTABOUTUS/ORGANIZATION/EXTPRESIDENT/

EXTPASTPRESIDENTS/PRESIDENTEXTERNAL/0,,contentM
DK:20025269~menuPK:232083~pagePK:159837~piPK:159808~theSite
PK:227585,00.html).

42. It would be difficult to argue convincingly that corruption scholarship after the Cold War was unaffected by prevailing approaches of the World Bank and TI. See Janine R. Wedel, "Rethinking Corruption in an Age of Ambiguity," *Annual Review of Law and Social Science*, vol. 8, December 2012, pp. 453-498.

   After the Cold War, political-science, sociological, anthropological, criminological, and legal perspectives on corruption played second fiddle to economic ones. Economists were the most inclined and best positioned to connect scholarship with policy consulting and advocacy. Economists like Klitgaard had a head start. He had already proffered (thoughtful) recommendations in his 1988 *Controlling Corruption* (with chapter titles such as "Policy Measures" and "Graft Busters: When and How to Set up an Anticorruption Agency"), informed by working with policymakers in developing countries. Robert Klitgaard, *Controlling Corruption*. Berkeley/Los Angeles/London: University of California Press, 1988.

43. Daniel Kaufmann, an economist at the Bank (from 1999 to 2008 a senior manager or director at the World Bank Institute), was prominently associated with the Bank's anti-corruption work during the height of its anti-corruption cachet (although, according to sources inside the Bank, he was not a prime mover in its main policy and operational work). Bank-employed economists who were most influential and visible outside the Bank were not necessarily those who were the most influential inside it.

   Susan Rose-Ackerman, among the most frequently cited economists of corruption, wrote her 1999 book while a visiting research fellow at the institution and remarks that her year was a "transformative experience" (Susan Rose-Ackerman, *Corruption and Government: Causes, Consequences, and Reform*. New York: Cambridge University Press, 1999, p. xi).

44. These include co-founder Frank Vogl and at least one TI director, Michael Wiehen. Eigen, Vogl, and Wiehen previously served in senior positions at the Bank. (See also Elizabeth Harrison, "The 'Cancer of Corruption.'" *Between Morality and Law: Corruption, Anthropology and Comparative Society*, Italo Pardo, ed. Aldershot, U.K.: Ashgate, 2004, p. 140.)

45. Transparency International website: http://archive.transparency.org/news_room/latest_news/press_releases/1997/1997_07_31_cpi.

46. At present its corporate donors include Shell Oil, Ernst and Young, and KKR.

47. Transparency International, "Annual Report 1999." *Transparency International (TI)*, Berlin, 1999, p. 2 (http://archive.transparency.org/publications/publications/annual_reports/annual_report_1999).

48. The Sampson quotes are from: Steven Sampson, "The anti-corruption industry: from movement to institution." *Global Crime*, vol. 11, issue 2, 2010, p. 272.

49. Janine R. Wedel, *Collision and Collusion: The Strange Case of Western Aid to Eastern Europe*. New York: Palgrave, 2001, pp. 1-43.

50. The issue of political corruption could, however, be raised with savvy and creative leadership on the part of the World Bank. Helen Sutch, a prime mover behind the effort to put corruption on the Bank's agenda and to make

anti-corruption a priority, did just that. As principal economist leading the governance and anti-corruption work in Poland and Latvia from 1997 to 2000 (later Bank-wide sector manager for governance and anti-corruption from 2000 to 2003), Sutch, at the request of the Minister of Finance, conducted a study in Poland that included political corruption. The study drew on opinion polls, parliamentary committee reports, and other relevant available information, as well as some 50 confidential interviews that Sutch carried out with leaders in a variety of sectors. The results of the study were then discussed with public officials, parliamentary representatives, and the media, drawing rare and useful public attention to the issue of corruption (Jacek Wojciechowicz, former World Bank Polish official, e-mail correspondence, July 5, 2012; my personal experience with World Bank office and media in Poland).

51.   In *The Tyranny of Experts: Economists, Dictators, and the Forgotten Rights of the Poor* (New York: Basic Books, 2013), William Easterly takes on the development enterprise, critiquing the role—and built-in unaccountability—of the foreign expert.

52.   Exceptions include works by Kwame Sundaram Jomo (for example, Kwame Sundaram Jomo, "Governance, rent-seeking, and private investment in Malaysia." *Corruption: The Boom and Bust of East Asia*, Jose Edgardo Campos, ed. Quezon City, Philippines: Ateneo de Manila University Press, 2001, pp. 131-162); and Mushtaq Husain Khan (for example, Mushtaq Husain Khan & Kwame Sundaram Jomo, eds., *Rents, Rent-Seeking and Economic Development: Theory and Evidence in Asia.* Cambridge, U.K.: Cambridge University Press, 2000).

53.   Johann G. Lambsdorff, "Consequences and Causes of Corruption." International Handbook on the Economics of Corruption, Susan Rose-Ackerman, ed. Cheltenham, U.K.: Edward Elgar, 2006, p. 4.

54.   For a statement about this by TI co-founder Eigen, see: Michael Montgomery, "Interview excerpts with Peter Eigen." The Cost of Corruption, *American Radio Works* (http://americanradioworks.publicradio.org/features/corruption/eigen.html).

55.   Transparency International, "The Fight Against Corruption: Is the Tide Now Turning?" *Transparency International (TI) Annual Report*, Berlin, April 1997, pp. 23-54.

56.   As I have said, attention was paid to foreign bribe-givers in the countries of the Other. During the same general time frame, the OECD was working on and promoting acceptance of its Convention on Combating Bribery of Foreign Public Officials in International Business Transactions, which targeted the OECD countries.

57.   Some indices have as their unit of analysis firms (national or international), sectors, or political institutions, yet still *within* a country. See this chapter's section on "Seducing with Numbers" for some of these indices.

58.   Foreign influences were largely overlooked despite documentation at the time that development assistance and foreign aid can facilitate corruption. Some studies, monographs, and media reports documented cases in which aid spurred corruption (see, for instance, Robert Klitgaard, *Tropical Gangsters: One Man's Experience with Development and Decadence in Deepest Africa.* New York: Basic Books, 1990).

       With regard to the World Bank, although anti-corruption Bank programs did include audits of contracts and add oversight staff, the notion that corruption could be spurred in any substantial way from the outside did not, for the most part, figure into the Bank's approach to studying corruption.

59.   See, for example, World Bank, *Helping Countries Combat Corruption: The Role of the World Bank*. Washington, D.C.: World Bank, Poverty Reduction and Economic Management, 1997, p. 11.

60.   Gary S. Becker, "To Root Out Corruption, Boot Out Big Government." *Business Week*, January 31, 1994, p. 18.

  Kalin S. Ivanov explains this view: "For Becker (1995) and many other economists, 'the source of official corruption is the same everywhere: large government with the power to dispense many goodies to different groups.' Therefore, smaller and more 'businesslike' government is 'the only surefire way to reduce corruption' (Becker, 1995) [Gary S. Becker, "If You Want to Cut Corruption, Cut Government," *Business Week*, December 11, 1995, p. 26.]." (Kalin S. Ivanov, "The Limits of a Global Campaign Against Corruption," *Corruption and Development: The Anti-Corruption Campaigns*, Sarah Bracking, ed. New York: Palgrave Macmillan, 2007, p. 34.)

61.   Michael Johnston, *Syndromes of Corruption: Wealth, Power, and Democracy*. New York: Cambridge University Press, 2005, p. 6.

62.   With respect to the first aid approach, for instance, a 1999 Bank program for the Europe and Central Asia region specifies: *(a)* "Economic policy reform (deregulation, tax simplification)," *(b)* "Civil service reform (moving to a professional, merit-based, well-paid civil service)," *(c)* "Public finance management (strengthening audit and procurement)," *(d)* "Legal and judicial reform (an independent and strong judiciary, development of the legal profession)," and *(e)* "Awareness building and public oversight (Ombudsman, client surveys, NGOs)" (World Bank, *Anti-Corruption Program in the ECA Region*. Washington, D.C.: World Bank Poverty Reduction and Economic Management, 1999, p. 2).

  Regarding the second aid approach (shrinking opportunities for corruption), that idea is reflected in the World Bank's institutional initiatives to reform the "performance" of the public sector, such as the recruitment, training, and promotion of public employees. This was one of two major areas of its anti-corruption work. (The other major area of anti-corruption work was public education.) (World Bank, *Helping Countries Combat Corruption: The Role of the World Bank*. Washington, D.C.: World Bank, Poverty Reduction and Economic Management, 1997, p. 8).

63.   Privatization almost at any cost—at the expense of attention to creating regulatory and governance institutions as the backbone of a market economy and issues such as the potential for privatization-induced corruption—prevailed as a near religion among economists and many decisionmakers in the 1990s (Janine Wedel, *Collision and Collusion: The Strange Case of Western Aid to Eastern Europe*. New York: Palgrave, 2001, pp. 49-50).

  The anti-corruption industry and the privatizers of the 1990s pursued a mutual goal—privatization—with limited debate in the standard economics literature. Key architects of Russian privatization schemes, including Maxim Boycko, a central player, and Harvard professor Andrei Shleifer, argued that privatization would diminish corruption as well as increase efficiency (Maxim

Boycko, Andrei Shleifer, and Robert W. Vishny, "A Theory of Privatization." *The Economic Journal*, vol. 106, no. 435, March 1996, pp. 309-319; see also Maxim Boycko, Andrei Shleifer, and Robert W. Vishny, *Privatizing Russia*. Cambridge, MA: MIT Press, 1995). A shrunken state sector would simply not have as many opportunities to extract bribes or concessions (Shleifer and Vishny 1998). (This idea has roots in Bhagwati's analysis of the "welfare consequences" of DUP [directly unproductive, profit-seeking] activities [Jagdish N. Bhagwati, "Directly unproductive profit-seeking (DUP) activities." *Journal of Political Economy*, vol. 90. No. 5, October 1982, pp. 988-1002]; see also Jagdish N. Bhagwati and T. N. Srinivasan, "The welfare consequences of directly unproductive profit-seeking (DUP) lobbying activities: price versus quantity distortions." *Journal of International Economics*, vol. 13, issues1-2, 1982, pp. 33-44.) For further detail, see Janine R. Wedel, "Rethinking Corruption in an Age of Ambiguity." *Annual Review of Law and Social Science*, vol. 8, December 2012, pp. 463-470.

64. This is the case not only with regard to former Soviet and Eastern Bloc countries (see, for example, Elizabeth Harrison, "The 'Cancer of Corruption.'" *Between Morality and Law. Corruption, Anthropology and Comparative Society*, Italo Pardo, ed. Aldershot, U.K.:Ashgate, 2004, p. 143).

65. See, for example, Svetlana P. Glinkina, "Privatizatsiya and kriminalizatsiya: how organized crime is hijacking privatization." *Demokratizatsiya*, vol. 2, 1994, pp. 385-391; Gernot Grabher and David Stark, eds., *Restructuring Networks in Post-Socialism: Legacies, Linkages, and Localities*, Oxford: Oxford University Press, 1997; Anthony Levitas and Piotr Strzałkowski, "What does 'Uwłaszczenie Nomenklatury' (Propertisation of the Nomenklatura) really mean?" *Communist Economies*, vol. 2, 1990, pp. 413-416; Domenico Mario Nuti, "Mass privatisation: costs and benefits of instant capitalism." Discussion Paper, Series No. 9, CIS-Middle Europe Centre, London Business School, 1994; Louise Shelley, "Privatization and crime: the post-Soviet experience." *Journal of Contemporary Criminal Justice*, vol. 11, 1995, pp. 244-245; David Stark, "Privatization in Hungary: from plan to market or from plan to clan?" *East European Politics & Societies*, vol. 4, 1990, pp. 351-392; David Stark and Lazlo Bruszt, *Postsocialist Pathways: Transforming Politics and Property in East Central Europe*. Cambridge: Cambridge University Press, 1998.

66. Although the ideology of privatization reigned supreme, the view from the ground revealed the rearranging of state assets into might-be-state, might-be-private entities, often with powerful players—themselves mergers of official and private power—at the helm (for instance, Antoni Kamiński, "The new Polish regime and the spector of economic corruption." Presentation at Woodrow Wilson International Center for Scholars, April 3, 1996; Antoni Kamiński, "Corruption under the post-communist transformation." *Polish Sociological Review*, vol. 2, 1997, pp. 91-117, 1997; Antoni Kamiński and Joanna Kurczewska, "Main actors of transformation: the nomadic elites," Eric Allardt and Wlodzimierz Wesolowski, eds., *The General Outlines of Transformation*. Warsaw: IFIS PAN 1994, pp. 132-153; Janine R. Wedel, "Corruption and organized crime in post-communist states: new ways of manifesting old patterns." *Trends in Organized Crime*, vol. 7, 2001, pp. 3-61; Janine R. Wedel, "Blurring the state-private divide: Flex organisations and the decline of

accountability," in Max Spoor, ed., *Globalisation, Poverty and Conflict: A Critical Development Reader*. Dordrecht, Netherlands/Boston: Kluwer Academic, 2004, pp. 217-235).

In Russia, voucher privatization fostered the concentration of vouchers and property in a few hands (through unregulated voucher investment funds, for instance); managers retained control over most industries, and investors wound up owning very little (Hilary Appel, "Voucher privatisation in Russia: structural consequences and mass response in the second period of reform." *Europe-Asia Studies*, vol. 49, no. 8, pp. 1433-1449; Lynn D. Nelson and Irina Y. Kuzes, *Property to the People: The Struggle for Radical Economic Reform in Russia*. Armonk, NY: M. E. Sharpe, 1994, pp. 25-26; Janine R. Wedel, *Shadow Elite: How the World's New Power Brokers Undermine Government, Democracy, and the Free Market*. New York: Basic Books, 2009, pp. 124-125).

Privatization was rendered "a de facto fraud," as economist James R. Millar put it (James R. Millar, "From utopian socialism to utopian capitalism: the failure of revolution and reform in post-Soviet Russia." George Washington University 175th Anniversary Papers, No. 2. George Washington University, Washington, D.C., 1996, p. 8), and the parliamentary committee that had judged the privatization scheme to "offer fertile ground for criminal activity" was proved right (Lynn D. Nelson and Irina Y. Kuzes, *Radical Reform in Yeltsin's Russia: Political Economic and Social Dimensions*. Armonk, NY: M. E. Sharpe, 1995, p. 51). Then Russia suffered the mother of all privatizations: the loans-for-shares scheme, which crystallized the ascendancy of a breed of oligarchs who would fundamentally configure the nation's politics, economics, and society for years to come (for example, Max Bivens and Jonas Bernstein, "The Russia you never met." *Demokratizatsiya*, vol. 6, 1998, pp. 613-647; Stefan Hedlund, *Russia's "Market" Economy: A Bad Case of Predatory Capitalism*. London: UCL Press, 1999; Leonid Kosals, "Interim outcome of the Russian transition: clan capitalism." Kyoto Institute of Economic Research, Discussion Paper no. 610, 2006, pp. 1-36; Leonid Kosals, "Essay on clan capitalism in Russia." *Acta Oeconomica*, no. 57, 2007, pp. 67-85; Stephen Kotkin, "Stealing the State." *The New Republic*, April 13, 1998; Ol'ga Kryshtanovskaya, "Illegal Structures in Russia." *Trends in Organized Crime*, no. 31997, pp. 14-17; Ol'ga Kryshtanovskaya, "The real masters of Russia," *RIA Novosti Argumenty I Fakty*, No. 21, May 1997).

Involvement in the loans-for-shares scheme, which depended entirely on access to inside information, transferred control of many of Russia's prime assets for token sums to seven preselected bank chiefs. Boris Fyodorov, a former finance minister, characterized the scheme as "a disgusting exercise of a crony capitalism, where normal investors were not invited. . . . [O]nly those who were friends of certain people in the government were invited. . . . These loans-for-shares unleashed a wave of corruption like never before" (Boris Fyodorov, "Return of the Czar." Interview with Boris Fyodorov, *Frontline*, PBS, May 9, 2000 [http://www.pbs.org/wgbh/pages/frontline/shows/yeltsin/interviews/fyodorov.html]). E. Wayne Merry, who had a bird's-eye view of the process as chief political analyst at the U.S. embassy in Moscow, later observed: "We created a virtual open shop for thievery at a national level and for capital flight in terms of hundreds of billions of dollars, and the raping of natural resources"

(E. Wayne Merry, "Return of the Czar." Interview with E. Wayne Merry, *Frontline,* PBS, 2000 [http://www.pbs.org/wgbh/pages/frontline/shows/yeltsin/interviews/merry.html]).

67. See, for instance, this 2000 World Bank report: World Bank, *Anti-Corruption in Transition: A Contribution to the Policy Debate.* Washington, D.C.: World Bank, 2000, p. xiii. The term "oligarchs" appears on pages xviii, 1, 4, and 46; "clans" on pages xxvi, 31, and 64; and "organized crime" on pages 23 and 97.

John Nellis, who worked extensively on privatization at the Bank did a mea culpa with regard to enthusiasm for privatization without effective regulatory control (see, for instance, John Nellis, *Time to Rethink Privatization in Transition Economies?* The World Bank, June 1999; Nancy Birdsall and John Nellis, "Privatization's bad name isn't totally deserved," *The Christian Science Monitor,* September 26, 2002, p.11; and Sunita Kikeri and John Nellis, "An Assessment of Privatization," *The World Bank Research Observer,* vol. 19, no. 1, Spring 2004, pp. 87-118.

68. For early (Cold War-era) economists on corruption, see, for example, Gary S. Becker and George J. Stigler, "Law Enforcement, Malfeasance, and Compensation of Enforcers." *Journal of Legal Studies,* vol. 3, no. 1, January 1974, pp. 1-18; and Susan Rose-Ackerman, "The economics of corruption." *Journal of Public Economics,* vol. 4, issue 2, 1975, pp. 187-203. For 1990s scholarship, see, for instance, Andrei Shleifer and Robert Vishny, "Corruption." *The Quarterly Journal of Economics,* vol. 108, no. 3, 1993, pp. 599-617; and Susan Rose-Ackerman, *Corruption and Government: Causes, Consequences, and Reform.* New York: Cambridge University Press, 1999.

With regard to the "new consensus" about corruption that developed during the 1990s, political scientist Michael Johnston has written that it "treats corruption mostly as bribery" (Michael Johnston, *Syndromes of Corruption: Wealth, Power, and Democracy.* New York: Cambridge University Press, 2005, p. 6). Bribery continues to be the essential definition of corruption, according to TI co-founder Frank Vogl, currently adviser to its managing director (Janine Wedel, interview with Frank Vogl, November 26, 2013).

69. Susan Rose-Ackerman, ed., *International Handbook on the Economics of Corruption.* Cheltenham, U.K./Northampton, MA: Edward Elgar, 2006, p. xv.

70. Decades earlier, political scientist James C. Scott had made a similar argument. He argued that developing countries were more likely than developed ones to be labeled corrupt, because the forms of corruption in the former are more visible and less likely to be legal (James C. Scott, "The Analysis of Corruption in Developing Nations." *Comparative Studies in Society and History,* vol. 11, no. 3, June 1969, pp. 315-341).

71. The fact that the early (Cold War-era) economists of corruption (such as Gary S. Becker and George J. Stigler and Susan Rose-Ackerman) employed the principal-agent theory with regard to corruption in the United States (not in the "Third World") makes the post-Cold War wholesale (mis)application to the entire world more understandable, although no less flawed. (See Gary S. Becker and George J. Stigler, "Law Enforcement, Malfeasance, and Compensation of Enforcers." *Journal of Legal Studies,* vol. 3, no. 1, January 1974, pp. 1-18; and Susan Rose-Ackerman, "The economics of corruption." *Journal of Public Economics,* vol. 4, issue 2, 1975, pp. 187-203.)

72.   Monika Bauhr and Naghmeh Nasiritousi, "Why Pay Bribes? Collective Action and Anticorruption Efforts." Working Paper Series 2011:18, QOG The Quality of Government Institute, December 2011, pp. 1-23.

73.   According to the CPI, the United States has been relatively uncorrupt, gracing the top quartile in 1998 (18th of 85) (table in Seymour Martin Lipset and Gabriel Salman Lenz, "Corruption, Culture, and Markets," Lawrence E. Harrison and Samuel P. Huntington, *Culture Matters: How Values Shape Human Progress.* New York: Basic Books, 2000, p. 113), the top ninth in 2005 (17th of 158), and the top seventh in 2011 (24th of 182) (Transparency International, "Corruption Perceptions Index." Transparency International [http://www.transparency.org/research/cpi/overview]).

74.   See: Transparency International, "2008 Corruption Perceptions Index." Transparency International (http://archive.transparency.org/news_room/in_focus/2008/cpi2008/cpi_2008_table).

        See also: Simon Rogers, "Corruption, country by country. The 2009 Transparency International index in full." *The Guardian,* November 17, 2009 (http://www.theguardian.com/news/datablog/2009/nov/17/corruption-index-transparency-international); and Phillip Kurata, "Transparency International Issues 1999 Corruption Rankings." *Washington File,* October 26, 1999 (https://www.fas.org/irp/news/1999/10/991026-corrupt-usia1.htm).

75.   The Goldman Abacus deal, discussed in Chapter 1, took place in 2007.

76.   Transparency International, "2008 Corruption Perceptions Index," Transparency International (http://archive.transparency.org/news_room/in_focus/2008/cpi2008/cpi_2008_table). Transparency International, "2009 Corruption Perceptions Index," Transparency International (http://www.transparency.org/research/cpi/cpi_2009#results).

77.   Roger Boyes, *Meltdown Iceland: Lessons on the World Financial Crisis from a Small Bankrupt Island.* New York: Bloomsbury USA, 2009, p. 41.

78.   See, for instance: European Commission, "Profile on Ireland" (http://ec.europa.eu/ireland/economy/irelands_economic_crisis/index_en.htm).

79.   Johann G. Lambsdorff, "Consequences and Causes of Corruption," Susan Rose-Ackerman, ed., *International Handbook on the Economics of Corruption.* Cheltenham, U.K.: Edward Elgar, 2006, p. 3.

80.   Transparency International, "The Fight Against Corruption: Is the Tide Now Turning?" *Transparency International (TI) Annual Report.* Berlin, April 1997, pp. 61-63.

81.   Simon Rogers, "Corruption, country by country. The 2009 Transparency International index in full." *The Guardian,* November 17, 2009 (http://www.theguardian.com/news/datablog/2009/nov/17/corruption-index-transparency-international).

82.   Such indices often lack epistemological rigor and are frequently misused. See, for instance, Raymond June, Afroza Chowdhury, Nathaniel Heller, and Jonathan Werve, *A Users' Guide to Measuring Corruption,* Marie Laberge and Joachim Nahem, eds. Oslo: UNDP/Global Integrity, June 2008, p. 6; Christiane Arndt and Charles Oman, *Uses and Abuses of Governance Indicators.* Paris: OECD Development Centre, 2006 (http://www.oecd.org/document/2 5/0,2340,en_2649_33731_37081881_1_1_1_1,00.html); Michael Johnston, "Measuring Corruption: numbers versus knowledge versus understanding,"

Arvind K. Jain, ed., *The Political Economy of Corruption*. New York: Routledge, 2001, pp. 157-179; and Melissa Thomas, "What Do The Worldwide Governance Indicators Measure?" *European Journal of Development Research*, vol. 22, no. 1, 2010, pp. 31-54, among others.

This *Guardian* article discusses some of the perceived drawbacks of the CPI: http://www.theguardian.com/global-development/poverty-matters/2013/dec/03/transparency-international-measure-corruption-valid.

Lambsdorff recognizes "the limitations of perception-based indices . . .", adding that ". . . researchers have nevertheless been able to use them to significantly advance the study of corruption." Johann G. Lambsdorff, "Consequences and Causes of Corruption." *International Handbook on the Economics of Corruption*, Susan Rose-Ackerman, ed. Cheltenham, U.K.: Edward Elgar, 2006, p. 3.

For an analysis of the most common methods of measuring corruption, see Eric M. Uslaner, *Corruption, Inequality, and the Rule of Law: The Bulging Pocket Makes the Easy Life*. Cambridge: Cambridge University Press, 2008, pp. 11-17.

83. Ivan Krastev, *Shifting Obsessions: Three Essays on the Politics of Anticorruption*. Budapest: Central European University Press, 2004, pp. 18-19. For further analysis and critique, see Kalin S. Ivanov's article on "The Limits of a Global Campaign Against Corruption." *Corruption and Development: The Anti-Corruption Campaigns*, Sarah Bracking, ed. New York: Palgrave Macmillan, 2007, pp. 32-33.

84. Ivanov, op. cit., p. 33.

85. For the quote from TI, see: Transparency International, "1998 Corruption Perceptions Index." Press release, September 21, 1998 (http://archive. transparency.org/news_room/latest_news/press_releases/1998/1998_09_22_cpi).

With regard to aid agencies telling countries that they need to improve their TI (or similar) scores to qualify for assistance, see the following information and sources.

The U.S. Millennium Challenge Corporation currently uses the World Bank's Worldwide Governance Indicators as one of the indicators to determine a country's eligibility for funds (see: http://www.mcc.gov/pages/selection/indicator/control-of-corruption-indicator).

Hans Krause Hansen writes: "Over the years corruption perception indices of various sorts have been widely publicized in global media and shaped decisionmaking processes concerning significant financial and political matters, including the investment decisions of corporations and the allocation of development aid by government agencies" (Arndt and Oman, 2006) [Christiane Arndt and Charles Oman, *Uses and Abuses of Governance Indicators*. Paris: OECD Development Centre, 2006 {http://www.oecd.org/document/25/0,2340, en_2649_33731_37081881_1_1_1_1,00.html}]. They have also spurred many controversies amongst experts and triggered protests from lower ranking countries finding themselves trapped in processes of 'naming and shaming' (e.g., Löwenheim, 2008:261). Similar to other rankings and forms of benchmarking, such indices seem [to] have taken a life on their own. Even contestation of their adequacy or appropriateness somehow bolsters their materiality (Larner and Le Heron, 2004)" (Hans Krause Hansen, "Corruption and Risks: Managing Corruption Risks," *Review of International Political Economy*, vol. 18, no. 2, May 2011, p. 260).

86. See this article by Lambsdorff for prominent indices used by corruption researchers. Johann G. Lambsdorff, "Consequences and Causes of Corruption,"

Susan Rose-Ackerman, ed., *International Handbook on the Economics of Corruption.* Cheltenham, U.K.: Edward Elgar, 2006, p. 3.

Playing a part in corruption indices are prespecified variables, such as the nine corruption variables named by Susan Rose-Ackerman (Susan Rose-Ackerman, *Corruption and Government: Causes, Consequences, and Reform.* New York: Cambridge University Press, 1999, p. xi; Susan Rose-Ackerman, ed., *International Handbook on the Economics of Corruption.* Cheltenham, U.K./ Northampton, MA: Edward Elgar, 2006); and Johann G. Lambsdorff (Johann G. Lambsdorff, "Consequences and Causes of Corruption," *International Handbook on the Economics of Corruption,* Susan Rose-Ackerman, ed. Cheltenham, U.K.: Edward Elgar, 2006, p. 4). Most of the variables specified by these authors are identical, including the size of the public sector, the quality of regulation, the degree of economic competition, the structure of government, the amount of decentralization, and the impact of cultures.

The use of metrics as analysis in cross-country studies bred a body of corruption literature, some of it with rather sweeping conclusions. Although economists did not abandon their earlier (Cold War–era) focus on modeling hypothetical transactions, the economics of corruption largely turned to employing indices and large data sets—data purportedly comparable across countries—to make their arguments. Political scientist Michael Johnston writes that "[m]uch recent work has been cross-sectional, often applying statistical measures and models to large numbers of countries to account for their scores on various single-dimension corruption indices" (Michael Johnston, *Syndromes of Corruption: Wealth, Power, and Democracy.* New York: Cambridge University Press, 2005, p. 4). Especially popular have been correlative studies, containing varying degrees of persuasive evidence regarding causality. We have learned, for instance, that corruption is:

- positively associated with the extent to which "government regulations are vague and lax" in a sample of 26 African countries (Lambsdorff and Cornelius 2000, cited in Johann G. Lambsdorff, "Consequences and Causes of Corruption," Susan Rose-Ackerman, ed., *International Handbook on the Economics of Corruption.* Cheltenham, U.K.: Edward Elgar, 2006, p. 7);
- significantly associated with income inequality (Sanjeev Gupta, Hamid Davoodi, and Rose Alonso-Terme, "Does corruption affect income inequality and poverty?" *Economics of Governance,* vol. 3, issue 1, March 2002, pp. 23-45);
- significantly correlated with "higher military spending and higher arms procurement (as a share of either GDP or total government spending)" (Johann G. Lambsdorff, "Consequences and Causes of Corruption." *International Handbook on the Economics of Corruption,* Susan Rose-Ackerman, ed. Cheltenham, U.K.: Edward Elgar, 2006, p. 33);
- possibly associated with negative GDP growth, though the many studies on this topic are often flawed methodologically and yield contradictory conclusions (according to Johann G. Lambsdorff, "Consequences and Causes of Corruption." *International Handbook on the Economics of Corruption,* Susan Rose-Ackerman, ed. Cheltenham, U.K.: Edward Elgar, 2006, pp. 25-27); and

• possibly negatively correlated with democracy. (A long-standing argument is that democracy limits corruption by heightening competition for political positions and that, through elections, voters can hold officeholders accountable [Johann G. Lambsdorff, "Consequences and Causes of Corruption," *International Handbook on the Economics of Corruption*, Susan Rose-Ackerman, ed. Cheltenham, U.K.: Edward Elgar, 2006, pp. 10-11]. Lambsdorff's literature review yields the conclusion that only robust democracy limits corruption, and only over the long-term.) (For contextual analysis of the dynamics of democracy and corruption, see, for example, Donatella Della Porta & Yves Mény, eds., *Democracy and Corruption in Europe*. London: Pinter, 1997.)

87. Kalin S. Ivanov, "The Limits of a Global Campaign Against Corruption." *Corruption and Development: The Anti-Corruption Campaigns*, Sarah Bracking, ed. New York: Palgrave Macmillan, 2007, p. 34.

88. This trend has been criticized by scholars who have examined how ranking and measurement using impact and outreach variables are being employed to judge the activities of organizations (John Clarke, "Performing for the public: doubt, desire, and the evaluation of public services," Paul du Gay, ed., *The Values of Bureaucracy*. Oxford: Oxford University Press, 2005, pp. 211-232; Raymond June, "The discreet charm of flexians," reviewing Janine R. Wedel's *Shadow Elite*. *Global Integrity*, January 18, 2010 [http://www.globalintegrity.org/node/491]; Marilyn Strathern, *Audit Cultures: Anthropological Studies in Accountability, Ethics, and the Academy*. Oxford/New York: Routledge, 2000).

89. Although not attracting as much splash, an emphasis, both in scholarship and practice, emerged on "good governance" nearly in parallel and overlapping with the anti-corruption push. The World Bank publishes governance data on its website going back to 1996 (http://data.worldbank.org/data-catalog/worldwide-governance-indicators).

Also playing a role in corruption indices are governance indicators. Kaufmann and two other Bank economists developed six governance indicators (Daniel Kaufmann, Aart Kraay, and Massimo Mastruzzi, "Measuring governance using cross-country perceptions data." *International Handbook on the Economics of Corruption*, Susan Rose-Ackerman, ed. Cheltenham, U.K.: Edward Elgar, 2006, pp. 56-57). These governance indicators consist of political stability and absence of violence, government effectiveness, voice and accountability, regulatory quality, rule of law, and control of corruption. See also Daniel Kaufmann, Aart Kraay, and Pablo Zoido-Lobaton, "Aggregating governance indicators." World Bank Policy Research Working Paper 2195. Washington, D.C.: World Bank, 1999; and Daniel Kaufmann, Aart Kraay, and Massimo Mastruzzi, "Governance matters IV: governance indicators for 1996-2004." World Bank Policy Research Working Paper 3630. Washington, D.C.: World Bank, 2005.

The *Wall Street Journal* and the Heritage Foundation, a Washington, D.C.-based conservative think tank, came out with their Index of Economic Freedom in 1995, according to the foundation's website (http://www.heritage.org/index/about). The Cato Institution, a Washington, D.C.-based libertarian think tank, published its first Economic Freedom of the World report the same year (http://www.cato.org/economic freedom world). *The Economist* Intelligence Unit publishes a Democracy Index (https://www.eiu.com/public/topical_report.aspx? campaignid=DemocracyIndex12).

90. Hans Krause Hansen and Tony Porter, "What Do Numbers Do in Transnational Governance?" *International Political Sociology*, vol. 6, 2012, pp. 409-426.

91. Ibid., p. 415.

92. See Lakoff and Johnson for an analysis and typology of metaphors (George Lakoff and Mark Johnson, *Metaphors We Live By*. Chicago: University of Chicago Press, 1980, pp. 10-13).

93. Anthropologist Mark Hobart has pointed out that "when the metaphorical images so frequently used in development discourse to justify policies are removed, the degree to which many theories require modification or rethinking is remarkable" (Mark Hobart, *An Anthropological Critique of Development: The Growth of Ignorance*. London: Routledge, 1993, p. 6).

94. See Chapter 1 and Janine R. Wedel, *Shadow Elite: How the World's New Power Brokers Undermine Government, Democracy, and the Free Market*. New York: Basic Books, 2009, pp. 1-15, 23-45.

95. For the definition of "representational juggling," see: *Shadow Elite*, pp. 17-18, 129-135.

    For budding flexians performing multiple roles across multiple spaces with multiple sponsors, see: Janine R. Wedel, *Collision and Collusion: The Strange Case of Western Aid to Eastern Europe*. New York: Palgrave, 2001, pp. 45-49.

96. With regard to Shleifer cited by corruption scholars, see, for example, World Bank, "Helping Countries Combat Corruption. The Role of the World Bank," *Poverty Reduction and Economic Management, The World Bank*, September 1997, p. 20.

    With respect to Shleifer's definition of and approach to corruption, see, for instance, Andrei Shleifer and Robert W. Vishny, "Corruption." *Quarterly Journal of Economics*, vol. 108, no. 3, August 1993. Regarding Shleifer's activities: he played overlapping roles as he secured aid funding to reform Russia's economy in the form of (highly unusual) noncompeted U.S. awards (with help from Larry Summers, his friend, coauthor, Harvard colleague, and, in the Clinton administration, a high U.S. Treasury official). See also endnote below.

97. With regard to Shleifer's role in privatization, he helped design voucher privatization in Russia and was supported by U.S. aid awards for Russian reform to do so.

    With regard to Shleifer's personal investments, see: United States District Court, District of Massachusetts, United States of America, Plaintiff, v. The President and Fellows of Harvard College, Andrei Shleifer, Jonathan Hay, Nancy Zimmerman, and Elizabeth Hebert, Defendants, Civil Action No. OOCV11977DPW, September, 26, 2000. See also: Janine R. Wedel, *Shadow Elite*, op. cit., pp. 117-121.

    In Russia, Shleifer and the other Harvard principal, Jonathan Hay, invested in the lucrative securities market; equities, aluminum, oil, and other companies (including the energy giant Gazprom); real estate; and mutual funds. They do not deny making these investments (United States District Court, op. cit., p. 30; see also, for example, Thanassis Cambanis, "US seeking $102m from Harvard pair." *Boston Globe*, June 27, 2002). The U.S. Department of Justice concluded that "Harvard's actions, instead of fulfilling their intended purpose of fostering trust and openness in the nascent mutual fund market, in fact involved exactly the type of favoritism and perceived and actual barriers to entry and success that the United States was spending hundreds of millions of dollars to dispel."

Following a multiyear investigation, in 2000, the Justice Department had brought a $120 million fraud lawsuit against Harvard University and the Harvard principals in the USAID-funded project, Shleifer and Jonathan Hay (and their wives, later dismissed from the case). Justice alleged that Shleifer and Hay had been "using . . . inside information . . . influence . . . [and] USAID-funded resources, to advance . . . personal business interests and investments" (United States Attorney, District of Massachusetts, *United States sues Harvard and others for false claims relating to USAID programs in Russia.* Press release, United States Department of Justice, September, 26, 2000). The case culminated in 2005 with a negotiated settlement and the fee paid by Harvard a record one (David McClintick, "How Harvard Lost Russia." *Institutional Investor Magazine,* Americas and International Editions, January 24, 2006, p. 3). Harvard was fined $26.5 million, Shleifer $2 million, and Hay between $1 and $2 million (Marcella Bombardieri, "Harvard, teacher, and lawyer to pay US$30m." *Boston Globe,* August 4, 2005).

98.   Andrei Shleifer and Daniel Treisman, "A normal country." *Foreign Affairs,* March/April 2004 (www.foreignaffairs.org/20040301faessay83204/andreishleifer-daniel-treisman/a-normal-country.html).

99.   *Foreign Affairs* declined to publish a letter to the editor making this point. The letter was coauthored by myself, the lead investigator from the Office of Inspector General of the U.S. Agency for International Development (Phil Rodokanakis), two former political officers from the U.S. embassy in Moscow (Donald Jensen and E. Wayne Merry), an eminent economist specializing in the Soviet and Russian economies (Steven Rosefielde), and a prominent political scientist (Peter Reddaway), also a specialist on Russian affairs. In response, *Foreign Affairs* told us that none of the Russia experts and economists they consulted with objected to Shleifer publishing the Shleifer article. Thus, in the midst of the U.S. government's lawsuit against Harvard, Shleifer, and another Harvard principal, *Foreign Affairs* gave Shleifer a respected platform to legitimate his activities and thus his defense. At the very least, the magazine should have identified Shleifer's involvements.

100.   Economist Lambsdorff concluded as early as 2000 that, as a result of privatizing, "[c]orruption might just be shifted from the public to the private sector" (Johann G. Lambsdorff and Peter Cornelius, "Corruption, Foreign Investment, and Growth," Klaus Schwab, Lisa D. Cook, Peter K. Cornelius, Jeffrey D. Sachs, Sara E. Sievers, and Andrew Warner, eds., *The Africa Competitives Report 2000/2001 (A Joint Publication of the World Economic Forum and the Institute for International Development, Harvard University),* pp. 70-78. Oxford: Oxford University Press, pp. 76-77).

101.   Daniel Kaufmann, Aart Kraay, and Massimo Mastruzzi, "Measuring governance using cross-country perceptions data," Susan Rose-Ackerman, ed., *International Handbook on the Economics of Corruption.* Cheltenham, U.K./Northampton, MA: Edward Elgar, 2006, p. 52.

102.   World Bank, *Anti-Corruption in Transition: A Contribution to the Policy Debate.* Washington, D.C.: World Bank, 2000, p. xv.

Much work on state capture was devoted to business, such as "the efforts of firms to shape the laws, policies, and regulations of the state to their own advantage by providing illicit private gains to public officials," as two World Bank authors put it (Joel Hellman and Daniel Kaufmann, "Confronting the challenge of state capture in transition economies." *Finance & Development*, vol. 38, no. 3, September 2001, p. 1 [http://www.imf.org/external/pubs/ft/fandd/2001/09/hellman.htm]).

103.　See, for example, Paul Krugman, "Crony Capitalism, U.S.A." *New York Times*, January 15, 2002 (http://www.nytimes.com/2002/01/15/opinion/crony-capitalism-usa.html).

104.　Steven Sampson, "The anti-corruption industry: from movement to institution." *Global Crime*, vol. 11, issue 2, 2010, pp. 272-273.

105.　See, for instance, economist Pranab Bardhan's indictment of the CPI (Pranab Bardhan, "The Economist's Approach to the Problem of Corruption." *World Development*, vol. 34, no. 2, 2006, pp. 342-343).

Scholars such as Rose-Ackerman and Lambsdorff have acknowledged some limitations of cross-country statistical research (Susan Rose-Ackerman, ed., *International Handbook on the Economics of Corruption*. Cheltenham, U.K./Northampton, MA: Edward Elgar, 2006, p. xxiv; Johann G. Lambsdorff, "Causes and consequences of corruption: What do we know from a cross-section of countries?" *International Handbook on the Economics of Corruption*, op. cit., p. 42). These limitations include the fact that corruption that is clustered in different sectors can still produce similar rankings (when like sectors are not compared with like sectors). (Obviating this, Randi Ryterman and some other World Bank economists developed and deployed separate anti-corruption surveys for enterprises, households, and public officials. See, for instance, James Anderson, *Corruption in Latvia: Survey Evidence*. Washington, D.C.: World Bank, 1998.)

Among other limitations acknowledged: the perceptions of businesspeople (the basis for some indices) may be different from those of regular citizens. Some adverse practical implications that flow from the focus on metrics have also been acknowledged.

106.　With regard to the state-of-the-art metrics, see the work of the European Research Centre for Anti-Corruption and State-Building (http://www.againstcorruption.eu/) (for instance, "14Mar Corruption Indicators, the Next Generation," http://anticorrp.eu/news/corruption-indicators-the-next-generation/) and, specifically, the work of Alina Mungiu-Pippidi, director of the center. See also, for instance, Alina Mungiu-Pippidi, ed., *Controlling Corruption in Europe. The Anticorruption Report. Volume 1*. Berlin: Barbara Budrich Publisher, 2013 (http://anticorrp.eu/publications/a-comparative-assessment-of-regional-trends-and-aspects-related-to-control-of-corruption-in-the-middle-east-and-north-africa-asia-and-the-pacific-sub-saharan-africa-latin-america-and-the-caribbean/). See, too, the work of Alena V. Ledeneva (for instance, "Russia's Practical Norms and Informal Governance: The Origins of Endemic Corruption," *Social Research*, vol. 80, no. 4, Winter 2013, pp. 1135-1162.

107.　Hans Krause Hansen, "The Power of Performance Indices in the Global Politics of Anti-Corruption," *Journal of International Relations and Development*, vol. 15, no. 4, 2012, p. 510.

108.　Ibid., pp. 455-465.

109.　Ibid., pp. 506-531. Hansen adds: ". . . performance indices are not simply techniques of *reporting* about things, but are themseves a *performative* part of social action in general and of governmental and managerial action in particular" (p. 509).

CHAPTER 5

1.　Research of anthropologist Hülya Demirdirek (as yet unpublished). A brief description appears here: Janine R. Wedel and Linda Keenan, "*Shadow Elite*: Truthiness, Porn and the Real Problem With Reality TV." Huffington Post, November 18, 2010 (http://www.huffingtonpost.com/janine-r-wedel/emshadow-eliteem-truthine_b_785258.html).

2.　See, for example, David Rosen, "Is the internet killing the porn industry?" *Salon*, May 30, 2013 (http://www.salon.com/2013/05/30/is_success_killing_the_porn_industry_partner/).

3.　See: National Security Agency, "Commitment" (http://www.nsa.gov/commitment/index.shtml).

4.　Consider, for instance, that "In 1984 the number of companies owning a controlling interests [sic] in America's media was 50　today that number is six" (http://www.pbs.org/moyers/moyersonamerica/net/timeline.html).

5.　Dominic Boyer and Alexei Yurchak, "American Stiob: Or, What Late-Socialist Aesthetics of Parody Reveal about Contemporary Political Culture in the West." *Cultural Anthropology*, vol. 25, issue 2, May 2010, pp. 179-221.

6.　Ibid., p. 192.

7.　Ibid.

8.　Boyer and Yurchak add this example in an endnote: "In a famous episode of the political program 'Crossfire' on CNN (October 15, 2004) Stewart accused the hosts Tucker Carlson and Paul Begala of performing political discussion in form only, at the expense of any real debate of issues: 'You're doing theater, when you should be doing debate, which would be great'; see Media Matters for America, "Jon Stewart on *Crossfire:* 'Stop, stop, stop, stop hurting America.'" *Media Matters for America*, October 15, 2004 (http://mediamatters.org/research/200410160003), accessed December 10, 2009.

　　Boyer and Yurchak, op. cit., p. 216.

9.　The quote from Boyer and Yurchak is from op. cit., p. 184.

　　Regarding viewership: *The Daily Show*'s ratings average viewership hovers around the 1.5 million mark for new episodes; *The Colbert Report*, around 1.1 million. *South Park*'s 2013 premiere pulled in 2.9 million, which was up 10 percent from the last season premiere. This 2014 tally is relatively consistent with other ratings: Sara Bibel, "Thursday Cable Ratings: NBA Playoffs Wins Night, 'Vikings', 'Pawn Stars', 'The Challenge', 'Sirens', & More." *TV By The Numbers*, May 2, 2014 (http://tvbythenumbers.zap2it.com/2014/05/02/thursday-cable-ratings-nba-playoffs-win-night-vikings-pawn-stars-the-challenge-sirens-more/259696/). See also: Rick Kissell, "'South Park' Returns to Three-Year Ratings High." *Variety*, September 26, 2013 (http://variety.com/2013/tv/news/south-park-returns-to-three-year-ratings-high-1200671493/).

　　An indication of Colbert's popularity is that he is slated to assume one of the most-watched nighttime perches with the retirement of David Letterman from the *Late Show*.

10. Ibid., p. 208.

11. Both late communism and Western political culture of today produce formalized "repeatable genres of political performance," Boyer and Yurchak write. And, in both contexts, "successful political messaging" equals "the circulation of formulaic political rhetoric" (Boyer and Yurchak, op. cit., p. 209).

12. The four trends Boyer and Yurchak cite as causing this state of affairs effectively all have to do with the decimation or mutation of the media caused by the rise of the Internet (Boyer and Yurchak, op. cit., pp. 206-209).

    New information technologies are specified as a crucial transformational development and elaborated in Janine R. Wedel, *Shadow Elite: How the World's New Power Brokers Undermind Democracy, Government, and the Free Market*. New York: Basic Books, 2009, Chapter 2.

13. Amy Mitchell, Tom Rosenstiel, and Leah Christian, "Mobile Devices and News Consumption: Some Good Signs for Journalism." *The State of the News Media 2012*, Pew Research Center (http://stateofthemedia.org/2012/mobile-devices-and-news-consumption-some-good-signs-for-journalism/?src=prc-section).

14. Jesse Holcomb, Jeffrey Gotfriend, and Amy Mitchell, "News Use Across Social Media Platforms." Pew Research Journalism Project, Pew Research Center, November 14, 2013 (http://www.journalism.org/2013/11/14/news-use-across-social-media-platforms/).

15. Political scientist Jeremy Mayer calls this "cocooning." He writes (Jeremy D. Mayer, *American Media Politics in Transition*. New York: McGraw Hill, 2008, pp. 315-317):

    > The growth of technology's role in American life may contribute to a sense of hyperindividualism as we cocoon ourselves away not only from politics but also from real-world human connections. . . . True believers can cocoon themselves away from troubling facts by surrounding themselves with websites that deny the truth. The mainstream media print corrections; many political blogs simply repeat their errors until they and their readers believe them.

16. Bill Keller of the *New York Times* is a prime example of someone made fun of mercilessly for being a dinosaur. See, for instance, Bill Keller, "Is Glenn Greenwald the Future of News?" *New York Times*, October 27, 2013 (http://www.nytimes.com/2013/10/28/opinion/a-conversation-in-lieu-of-a-column.html); or Hamilton Nolan, "Farewell, Bill Keller's Awful Magazine Column." *Gawker*, July 25, 2011 (http://gawker.com/5824375/farewell-bill-kellers-awful-magazine-column). In February 2014, Keller announced that he was leaving the *Times* for a nonprofit news startup.

    This article reflects the same view: Jack Shafer, "From Tom Paine to Glenn Greenwald, we need partisan journalism." *Reuters*, July 16, 2013 (http://blogs.reuters.com/jackshafer/2013/07/16/from-tom-paine-to-glenn-greenwald-we-need-partisan-journalism/).

17. According to the *New York Times*, Greenwald portrays himself "as an activist and an advocate" (Noam Cohen and Leslie Kaufman, "Blogger, With Focus on Surveillance, Is at Center of a Debate." *New York Times*, June 6, 2013 [http://www.nytimes.com/2013/06/07/business/media/anti-surveillance-activist-is-at-center-of-new-leak.

html?pagewanted=all]). Greenwald later told the *Times*: "It is not a matter of being an activist or a journalist; it's a false dichotomy. . . . It is a matter of being honest or dishonest. All activists are not journalists, but all real journalists are activists. Journalism has a value, a purpose—to serve as a check on power" (David Carr, "Journalism, Even When It's Tilted." *New York Times*, June 30, 2013 [http://www. nytimes.com/2013/07/01/business/media/journalism-is-still-at-work-even-when-its-practitioner-has-a-slant.html?pagewanted=all&_r=1&]).

18. Nick Confessore (https://twitter.com/nickconfessore); David Carr (https:// twitter.com/carr2n); Jeff Elder (https://twitter.com/JeffElder); (https://twitter. com/thefix); Chris Cillizza (https://twitter.com/TheHyperFix).

19. John Clarke, "Performing for the public: doubt, desire and the evaluation of public services." *The Values of Bureaucracy*, Paul du Gay, ed. Oxford: Oxford University Press, 2005, pp. 211-232.

20. Boyer and Yurchak, op. cit., p. 208.

21. This was sometimes at the expense of long-term wisdom. While "dynamic" CEOs were being (personally) rewarded with a pop in the stock price, the layoffs they were ordering weren't necessarily wise long term decisions for their companies.

   Presumably to impress the board and warrant bigger raises, CEOs also seemed intent on appearing "bold," as Linda Keenan writes. This became a central animating force in a CEO's identity—and core identity is not easily changed. "That attitude brought a shift in how managers both treated and viewed their employees," Keenan observes. "CEOs who slash payrolls might get called 'dynamic'; ones who do not might be viewed as 'lumbering.'" (Linda Keenan and Janine R. Wedel, "Shadow Elite: Wall Street Culture—They Still Don't Get It [Except Their Bonuses]." Huffington Post, May 27, 2010 [http://www.huffingtonpost.com/linda-keenan/emshadow-eliteem-wall-str_b_591537.html]).

   Anthropologist of finance Karen Ho makes a similar point (Karen Ho, *Liquidated: An Ethnography of Wall Street*. Durham, NC: Duke University Press, 2009).

22. The idea sounded good on paper: stock options tied an executive's own personal fortune to his shareholders' fortunes through the stock price, ostensibly making him more likely to act, as he should, in their interest. The result was different, Cassidy shows. In practice, top managers were tempted to mislead investors, and boards could play with option dates and prices to give senior management maximum personal gain (John Cassidy, "The Greed Cycle." *The New Yorker*, September 23, 2002, p. 64 [http://www.newyorker.com/archive/2002/09/23/020923fa_fact_cassidy]).

23. Linda Keenan and Janine R. Wedel, "Shadow Elite: Wall Street Profiteers—Capitalists or Communists?" Huffington Post, April 29, 2010 (http://www. huffingtonpost.com/linda-keenan/emshadow-eliteem-wall-str_b_556472.html).

24. See Frank Dobbin and Dirk Zorn, "Corporate malfeasance and the myth of shareholder value," Julian Go (ed.), *Political Power and Social Theory* 17. Bingley, U.K: Emerald, 2005, pp. 179-198. They write that the financial analysts who issue firms' quarterly profit projections became the new sources of power in the contemporary business world.

25. This was compiled by PBS's *Frontline* (http://www.pbs.org/now/politics/wallstreet.html).

26. Blodget got caught and was sued for fraud and banned from the industry for life. However, in a classic case of "failing up"—being promoted despite recognized failure in previous positions—he is now the founder/CEO of a popular business news outlet called *Business Insider*, as well as a frequent contributor to well-regarded journalistic outlets including Slate and *Newsweek*.

Ten top investment firms reached a settlement in 2003 to erect more barriers between analysts and bankers within the same firm, a measure to avert such conflict of interest.

27. According to a study conducted by the *Financial Times*, from 1999 to the end of 2001, out of the 25 biggest business collapses, executives and directors still took in $3.3 billion in salary, bonuses, and stock/stock-option sales. Even when the stock did fall, companies could reprice the options lower, giving executives yet another chance to strike gold ("US Corporate Excess—Barons of Bankruptcy." *Finfacts Ireland*, August 1, 2002 [http://www.finfacts.ie/irelandeconomy/bankruptcy.htm]).

Executive-pay expert Graef Chrystal observed that repricing options in a volatile environment allows top players to "[create] . . . an anti-gravity device, which guarantees that . . . executives will get super rich." Quoted in John Cassidy, "The Greed Cycle." *The New Yorker*, September 23, 2002 (http://www. newyorker.com/archive/2002/09/23/020923fa_fact_cassidy).

28. U.S Securities and Exchange Commission, "Ten of Nation's Top Investment Firms Settle Enforcement Actions Involving Conflicts of Interest Between Research and Investment Banking." Press release, U.S. Securities and Exchange Commission, April 28, 2003 (http://www.sec.gov/news/press/2003-54.htm).

29. In the ensuing chapters, we will look at various examples of how power brokers in different arenas have used TV (and other media, new and old) to press their agendas. This Huffington Post article by Nick Wing is one of many articles covering the logo petition: Nick Wing, "White House Petition: Make Lawmakers Wear Logos of Financial Backers on Clothing, Like In NASCAR." Huffington Post, March 20, 2013 (http://www.huffingtonpost. com/2013/03/20/white-house-petition-logos_n_2912087.html).

30. Chertoff's firm maintained that the firm represented Rapiscan only very briefly, and well before his Christmas-Day-bombing media blitz. See: http://www. huffingtonpost.com/2010/11/23/fear_pays_chertoff_n_787711.html

31. Chertoff penned an op-ed on the same topic in the *Washington Post*, in which his firm and its relationship to "a security and risk-management firm whose clients include a manufacturer of body-imaging screening machines" was disclosed in his bio, although the name of the firm was not mentioned. See: http://www. washingtonpost.com/wp-dyn/content/article/2009/12/31/AR2009123101746.html

32. Clark Hoyt, "The Sources' Stake in the News." *New York Times*, January 16, 2010 (http://www.nytimes.com/2010/01/17/opinion/17pubed.html?_r=2&).

33. Sebastian Jones, "The Media Lobbying Complex." *The Nation*, March 1, 2010 (http://www.thenation.com/article/media-lobbying-complex).

34. Pew 2013 State of the Media report: Mark Jurkowitz, Paul Hitlin, Amy Mitchell, Laura Santhanam, Steve Adams, Monica Anderson, and Nancy Vogt, "The Changing TV News Landscape." *2013 State of the Media*, Pew Research Center (http://stateofthemedia.org/2013/special-reports-landing-page/ the-changing-tv-news-landscape/).

35.   http://variety.com/2014/tv/news/cnn-reassigns-up-to-50-employees-as-breaking-news-gets-more-emphasis-1201169734/. See also: http://www.thewrap.com/cnn-layoffs-news-digital.

36.   These are so-called Super PACs (Political Action Committees)—supposedly independent of candidates and "nonprofits" (technically "social welfare" nonprofits) with generic names and often undisclosed sponsors. Super PACs are typically 527s, which can spend unlimited funds but have to disclose their sources of funding. The entities can also be 501(c)(4)s, which are limited in spending but need not disclose. The 527s and 501(c)(4)s are often paired together, like the Karl Rove-associated American Crossroads and Crossroads GPS.

37.   Hamilton Nolan, "Qorvis embroiled in speaker compensation dispute." *PR Week US*, October 29, 2004 (http://www.prweekus.com/qorvis-embroiled-in-speaker-compensation-dispute/article/50906/); Alex Berenson, "Big Insurer Denies Any Ties to Plans to Attack Spitzer." *New York Times*, October 29, 2004 (http://www.nytimes.com/2004/10/29/business/29spitzer.html?pagewanted=print&position=).

38.   Andrew Beaujon, "New York Times passes USA Today in daily circulation." *Poynter*, April 30, 2013 (http://www.poynter.org/latest-news/mediawire/211994/new-york-times-passes-usa-today-in-daily-circulation/).

39.   Pew Research Center, "State of the News Media 2012: New Devices, Platforms Spur More News Consumption." *Pew Research Center*, March 19, 2012 (http://www.pewresearch.org/2012/03/19/state-of-the-news-media-2012/).

40.   *The Newsroom* has been attacked by some critics for its overly idealist vision of what news should be.

41.   Mark Jurkowitz, Paul Hitlin, Amy Mitchell, Laura Santhanam, Steve Adams, Monica Anderson, and Nancy Vogt, "The Changing TV News Landscape." 2013 State of the Media Report, Pew Research Center (http://stateofthemedia.org/2013/special-reports-landing-page/the-changing-tv-news-landscape/).

42.   Quoted in Sandra Oshiro, "How laid-off journalists can stay afloat while the industry moves 'to new moorings.'" *Poynter*, February 13, 2014 (http://www.poynter.org/latest-news/top-stories/238425/how-laid-off-journalists-can-stay-afloat-while-the-industry-moves-to-new-moorings/).

43.   Pew Research Center, "New Devices, Platforms Spur More News Consumption." 2012 State of the Media Report, *Pew Research Center* (http://www.pewresearch.org/2012/03/19/state-of-the-news-media-2012/). See also Slate: Evgeny Morozov, "A Robot Stole My Pulitzer!" Slate, March 19, 2012 (http://www.slate.com/articles/technology/future_tense/2012/03/narrative_science_robot_journalists_customized_news_and_the_danger_to_civil_discourse_.html).

44.   Editorial, "Mary Jo White at the SEC." *New York Times*, February 7, 2013 (http://www.nytimes.com/2013/02/08/opinion/mary-jo-white-at-the-sec.html).

45.   Arthur Levitt, "Mary Jo White Is Rockstar in SAC Deal." *Bloomberg*, November 5, 2013 (http://www.bloomberg.com/video/on-sac-stage-mary-jo-white-is-the-rockstar-levitt-qtjssLQMTQaZIszipG82cQ.html).

46.   Annie-Rose Strasser, "What You Should Know About Mary Jo White, Obama's Appointment to the SEC." *Think Progress*, January 24, 2013 (http://thinkprogress.org/economy/2013/01/24/1489131/what-to-know-about-mary-jo-white-obamas-appointment-to-the-sec/); David Lat, "Just How Rich Is Mary Jo White, Debevoise Partner and Likely Future SEC Chair?" *Above the*

Law, February 12, 2013 (http://abovethelaw.com/2013/02/just-how-rich-is-mary-jo-white-debevoise-partner-and-likely-future-sec-chair/); http://www.thelawyer.com/debevoises-mary-jo-white-picked-by-obama-to-head-the-sec/1016631.article

47. See: http://www.newyorker.com/online/blogs/johncassidy/2013/01/send-mary-jo-white-to-justice-not-the-sec.html.

   For a description of some of Mary Jo White's white-collar crime work, see: "Mary Jo White: White Knight." *Columbia Law School Magazine,* Winter 2010 (http://www.law.columbia.edu/magazine/5361/mary-jo-white).

48. Nicholas Lemann, "Street Cop." *The New Yorker,* November 11, 2013 (http://www.newyorker.com/reporting/2013/11/11/131111fa_fact_lemann).

49. Ibid.

50. Gary Rivlin, "How Wall Street Defanged Dodd-Frank." *The Nation,* April 30, 2013 (http://www.thenation.com/article/174113/how-wall-street-defanged-dodd-frank).

51. Mary Walton, "Investigative Shortfall." *American Journalism Review,* September 2010 (http://www.ajr.org/Article.asp?id=4904). It is worth noting that Walton's extensive report was aided by a grant from a philanthropic nonprofit: the Open Society Institute, founded and chaired by billionaire investor George Soros.

52. With that caveat in mind, figures from Investigative Reporters and Editors, the professional association that most such American journalists belong to, show that its membership plunged from 5,000 in 2005 to 3,400 in 2009 (Ken Doctor, "The newsonomics of going deeper." *Nieman Journalism Lab,* November 29, 2012 [http://www.niemanlab.org/2012/11/the-newsonomics-of-going-deeper/]). By 2012, it had bumped back up to 4,300 after an aggressive outreach effort (Mary Walton, op. cit.).

53. The 2010 Pew "State of the Media" report (http://stateofthemedia.org/2010/).

54. Pew Research Center, "Overview: The State of News Media 2013," *An Annual Report on American Journalism,* Pew Research Center's Project for Excellence in Journalism, 2013, p. 3, http://stateofthemedia.org/files/2013/08/SOTNM-low-rez-pdf.pdf

55. Ibid., pp. 3-4.

56. The number of people surveyed was 595. Robert Hodierne, "Is There Life After Newspapers?" *American Journalism Review,* February/March 2009 (http://www.ajr.org/article.asp?id=4679).

57. Rosanna Fiske, "Why journalists don't always make the best PR pros." *Poynter,* August 15, 2011 (http://www.poynter.org/latest-news/top-stories/142682/why-journalists-dont-always-make-the-best-pr-pros/). In addition to serving as chair and CEO of the Public Relations Society of America until 2011, the article the chairwoman wrote has this additional tag line: "She is also program director of the Global Strategic Communications master's program in the School of Journalism and Mass Communication at Florida International University in Miami."

58. John Sullivan, "PR Industry Fills Vacuum Left by Shrinking Newsrooms." ProPublica, co-published with *Columbia Journalism Review,* May 1, 2011 (http://www.propublica.org/article/pr-industry-fills-vacuum-left-by-shrinking-newsrooms).

59. Robert Waterman McChesney and John Nichols, *The Death and Life of American Journalism: The Media Revolution that Will Begin the World Again.* New York: Nation Books, 2010.

60. John Sullivan, op. cit.

61. See, for example, Richard W. Pollay, "Propaganda, Puffing and the Public Interest: The Scientific Smoke Screen for Cigarettes." *Public Relations Review*, vol. 16, no. 3, 1990, pp. 39-54 (http://works.bepress.com/richard_pollay/22).

62. Hawley talked to marketing strategist David Meerman Scott on his blog *Web Ink Now*. David Meerman Scott, "How Raytheon Implemented a Brand Journalism Approach to Content Marketing." *WebIncNow*, April 10, 2013 (http://www.webinknow.com/2013/04/how-raytheon-implemented-a-brand-journalism-approach-to-content-marketing.html). Raytheon's news-like company website is at: http://www.raytheon.com/.

63. David Meerman Scott, op. cit.

64. Jeff Sonderman, "What the Forbes model of contributed content means for journalism." *Poynter*, May 29, 2012 (http://www.poynter.org/latest-news/top-stories/173743/what-the-forbes-model-of-contributed-content-means-for-journalism/).

65. He started at Public Strategies in April 2009. See: "Richard Wolffe, MSNBC Political Analyst," October 1, 2009 (http://www.nbcnews.com/id/33123380/ns/msnbc_tv-meet_the_faces_of_msnbc/t/richard-wolffe/#.Uu_oOvlkSSo).

   Glenn Greenwald exposed this. See: Glenn Greenwald, "GE's Silencing of Olbermann and MSNBC's Sleazy Use of Richard Wolffe: Two new major MSNBC scandals reveal much about how corporate journalism functions." *Salon*, August 1, 2009 (http://www.salon.com/2009/08/01/ge/). See also: Zachary Roth, "Richard Wolffe's Two Hats: MSNBC Host and Corporate Spin-Meister." *Talking Points Memo*, August 3, 2009 (http://tpmmuckraker.talkingpointsmemo.com/2009/08/richard_wolffes_two_hats_msnbc_guest_host_and_corp.php).

66. Noah Shachtman, "Think-Tanks and the Reporters Who Heart Them." Danger Room, *Wired.com*, December 18, 2009 (http://www.wired.com/dangerroom/2009/12/think-tanks-and-the-reporters-who-heart-them/).

67. Nathan Hodge, "Danger, Brookings Institution!," Danger Room, *Wired.com*, May 28, 2010 (http://www.wired.com/dangerroom/2010/05/danger-brookings-institution/).

68. The former FCC commissioner is Michael Copps. The relative size of Comcast is discussed here: Yinka Adegoke and Dan Levine (reporting) and Eric Beech (editing), "Comcast completes NBC Universal merger." *Reuters*, January 29, 2011 (http://www.reuters.com/article/2011/01/29/us-comcast-nbc-idUSTRE70S2WZ20110129).

69. Bill Moyers, "Former FCC Commissioner: Big Media Dumbs Down Democracy." *Moyers & Company*, December 4, 2012 (http://billmoyers.com/2012/12/04/former-fcc-commissioner-michael-copps-on-the-past-and-future-of-news/).

70. Interview can be found here on Gawker: Michelle Dean, "Is The Internet Making Us More Unequal? A Q&A with Astra Taylor." *Gawker*, April 15, 2014 (http://gawker.com/is-the-internet-making-us-more-unequal-a-q-a-with-astr-1563177911). Her book is: Astra Taylor, *The People's Platform: Taking Back Power and Culture in the Digital Age*. New York: Metropolitan Books, Henry Holt and Company, 2014.

71. Jon Russell, "The Intercept, the first online publication from eBay founder Pierre Omidyar, is now live." *The Next Web*, February 10, 2014 (http://thenextweb.com/

media/2014/02/10/the-intercept-the-first-online-publication-from-ebay-founder-pierre-omidyar-is-now-live/).

72. "Philanthro-Journalism: Reporters Without Orders: Can journalism funded by private generosity compensate for the decline of the commercial kind?" *The Economist*, June 9, 2012 (http://www.economist.com/node/21556568).

73. Mary Walton, "The Non-Profit Explosion." *American Journalism Review*, September 2010 (http://www.ajr.org/article.asp?id=4906).

74. See: Michael Moss and Geraldine Fabrikant, "Once Trusted Mortgage Pioneers, Now Scrutinized," *New York Times*, December 24, 2008, http://www.nytimes.com/2008/12/25/business/25sandler.html?adxnnl=1&adxnnlx=1268665238-1SuHK+1ZW7SAGIrmY7lNPA; and Jeff Horwitz, "The Education of Herb and Marion Sandler," *Columbia Journalism Review*, March 18, 2010, http://www.cjr.org/feature/the_education_of_herb_and_marion.php?page=all

75. Jack Shafer, "Non-Profit Journalism Comes at a Cost." Slate, September 30, 2009 (http://www.slate.com/articles/news_and_politics/press_box/2009/09/nonprofit_journalism_comes_at_a_cost.html).

76. Jesse Holcomb, Tom Rosenstiel, Amy Mitchell, Kevin Caldwell, Tricia Sartor, and Nancy Vogt, "Assessing a New Landscape in Journalism." Non-Profit News, Pew Research Journalism Project, July 18, 2011, p. 1 (http://www.journalism.org/2011/07/18/non-profit-news/).

77. The original *Washington Post* article is here: Elaine S. Povich and Eric Pianin, "Support grows for tackling nation's debt," *Washington Post*, December 31, 2009, http://www.washingtonpost.com/wp-dyn/content/article/2009/12/30/AR2009123002576.html. This article discusses the *Post*'s defense: Richard Pérez-Peña, "Sourcing of Article Awkward for Paper," *New York Times*, January 5, 2010, http://www.nytimes.com/2010/01/06/business/media/06post.html

78. S.C. Lewis, "From Journalism to Information: The Transformation of the Knight Foundation and News Innovation." *Mass Communication & Society*, 2012 (http://conservancy.umn.edu/bitstream/123291/1/MC%26S%20-%20From%20Journalism%20to%20Information%20-%20the%20Transformation%20of%20the%20Knight%20Foundation%20and%20News%20Innovation.pdf).

79. Shortly before the United States invaded Iraq, the Center posted the draft "Patriot II" legislation that had hitherto been secret. Later in 2003, it published all the contracts the United States had issued in Iraq and Afghanistan. Its report *Windfalls of War*, which won a George Polk Award, was the first to identify that the bulk of the contracts were to Halliburton, Vice President Dick Cheney's former employer. Five years later, Lewis co-authored a lengthy analysis and chronology of the George W. Bush administration's pre-war rhetoric on the Iraq invasion, identifying 935 "false statements" about Saddam Hussein's threat to U.S. national security.

80. Like the Center for Public Integrity, ICIJ also relies on grants from foundations and individual donations: "We rely heavily on charitable foundations and on financial support from the public." See: http://www.icij.org/about and http://www.razoo.com/story/Icij.

81. See ICIJ's website (http://www.icij.org/blog). In addition to these initiatives, in 2009 Lewis co-created the Investigative News Network, "a nonprofit consortium of over 90 nonprofit, non-partisan newsrooms around the country dedicated to investigative and public-service journalism."

82. "Philanthro-Journalism: Reporters Without Orders: Can journalism funded by private generosity compensate for the decline of the commercial kind?" *The Economist*, June 9, 2012 (http://www.economist.com/node/21556568).

83. Harry Browne, "Foundation-Funded Journalism: Reasons to be Wary of Charitable Support." *Journalism Studies*, vol. 11, no. 6, 2010, pp. 889-903. See also: http://www.slate.com/articles/news_and_politics/press_box/2009/09/nonprofit_journalism_comes_at_a_cost.html.

84. Tellingly, Barnes gets played by one nefarious power broker who eventually kills her.

85. Alexander C. Kaufman, "Matt Yglesias Named Executive Editor of Ezra Klein's New Vox Media Venture." *FishbowlNY*, January 27, 2014 (http://www.mediabistro.com/fishbowlny/matt-yglesias-named-executive-editor-of-ezra-kleins-new-vox-media-venture_b200941).

86. http://krugman.blogs.nytimes.com/2014/03/23/tarnished-silver/?_php=true&_type=blogs&_r=0.
    See also: http://www.nytimes.com/2014/03/22/opinion/egan-creativity-vs-quants.html?src=me&ref=general.

87. Mayhill Fowler's account of "Bittergate" is in a November 5, 2009 post in the Huffington Post (http://www.huffingtonpost.com/mayhill-fowler/bittergate-the-untold-sto_b_346342.html).

88. Patrick Radden Keefe, "Rocket Man. How an unemployed blogger confirmed that Syria had used chemical weapons." *The New Yorker*, November 25, 2013 (http://www.newyorker.com/reporting/2013/11/25/131125fa_fact_keefe).

89. The 2010 Pew report discussing citizen journalism is at: http://stateofthemedia.org/2010/overview-3/.

90. *Alternet*'s "Bubble Barons" project can be seen here: Kevin Connor, "Exposing the Great American Bubble Barons: Join Us in the Investigation." *AlterNet*, February 23, 2010 (http://www.alternet.org/story/145735/exposing_the_great_american_bubble_barons%3A_join_us_in_the_investigation).

91. Katharine Q. Seelye, "Times Reporter Agrees to Leave the Paper." *New York Times*, November 10, 2005 (http://www.nytimes.com/2005/11/10/business/media/10paper.html).

92. Raffi Khatchadourian, "No Secrets." *The New Yorker*, June 7, 2010 (http://www.newyorker.com/reporting/2010/06/07/100607fa_fact_khatchadourian).

93. John Burns and Ravi Somaiya, "Wikileaks Founder On the Run, Trailed by Notoriety." *New York Times*, October 23, 2010 (http://www.nytimes.com/2010/10/24/world/24assange.html?pagewanted=all).

94. A description of the *Times*' reasoning for not linking to the WikiLeaks site can be found in this January 2011 piece: Bill Keller, "Dealing With Assange and the Wikileaks Secrets." *New York Times*, January 26, 2011 (http://www.nytimes.com/2011/01/30/magazine/30Wikileaks-t.html?pagewanted=all).
    Later Assange leaked a massive number of U.S. State Department cables. While the *New York Times* got access to them from another paper, that was not his wish. He apparently wanted to retaliate against the *Times* and was willing to be far less than open, even though the *Times* would certainly be the ideal place to spread his information far and wide. (Paul Farhi, "WikiLeaks Spurned New York Times, But *Guardian* Leaked State Department Cables." *Washington Post*, November 29, 2010 [http://www.washingtonpost.com/wp-dyn/content/article/2010/11/29/AR2010112905421.html].)

In the midst of all this, Assange was mired in allegations of sexual abuse and financial difficulties.

95.   Leonard Downie, Jr. is the former *Washington Post* executive editor. Reported in: John Sullivan, "PR Industry Fills Vacuum Left by Shrinking Newsrooms." ProPublica, co-published with *Columbia Journalism Review*, May 1, 2011 (http://www.propublica.org/article/pr-industry-fills-vacuum-left-by-shrinking-newsrooms).

96.   Ken Silverstein, "Undercover, under fire." *Los Angeles Times,* June 30, 2007 (http://www.latimes.com/la-oe-silverstein30jun30,0,3345659.story).

97.   The name of the former State Department official plugged by *Washington Life*, Matt Lauer, can be found, alongside such figures as Anna Lefer Kuhn, head of a human-rights social-justice foundation; photographer Trevor Frost; and women's-rights activist Shaunna Thomas. See: "Features: 2013: The Young and the Guest List. The 8th annual guide to Washington's most influential 40-and-under young leaders." *Washington Life Magazine,* April 3, 2013 (http://www.washingtonlife.com/2013/04/03/features-2013-the-young-and-the-guest-list./), p. 46.

       For Qorvis staff, see: http://www.qorvis.com/people. The Capitol Hill legislative assistant worked for Congressman James Maloney; the former top Senatorial policy and communications adviser worked for Senator Mary L. Landrieu.

98.   Joshua Green, "J-School for Jerks. How you, too, can learn to behave like Bill O'Reilly." *The Atlantic,* March 1, 2005 (http://www.theatlantic.com/magazine/archive/2005/03/j-school-for-jerks/303732/).

99.   See: http://www.qorvis.com/clients.

100.   See: http://www.qorvis.com/clients/kingdom-bahrain.

101.   See: http://www.qorvis.com/clients/republic-fiji.

102.   Kevin McCauley, quoted in *Mother Jones*, which covered the trend in 2007 when it was still relatively new: Joshua Kurlantzick, "Putting Lipstick on a Dictator." *Mother Jones,* May 7, 2007 (http://www.motherjones.com/politics/2007/05/putting-lipstick-dictator).

103.   Qorvis was believed to be orchestrating a mysterious radio ad campaign that popped up in dozens of cities in 2002 from the "Alliance for Peace and Justice in the Middle East," praising a plan for resolving the Israel/Palestinian fight that was being floated by Saudi Crown Prince Abdullah, who was about to visit President Bush at his Texas ranch. When news of the radio ads surfaced, it reportedly caused an uproar among some partners and clients at K-Street legal and lobbying mainstay Patton Boggs, which owned a stake in Qorvis and had its own contract with Saudi Arabia (Josh Gerstein, "Saudi Account Caused a Row At Patton, Boggs." *New York Sun,* December 21, 2004 [http://www.nysun.com/national/saudi-account-caused-a-row-at-patton-boggs/6578/]; Philip Shenon, "Saudis Face New Problem With Publicity." *New York Times,* December 5, 2002 [http://www.nytimes.com/2002/12/05/business/saudis-face-new-problem-with-publicity.html?n=Top%2fReference%2fTimes%20Topics%2fSubjects%2fT%2fTerrorism]).

104.   Obiang had a lucrative contract with Qorvis, along with other more traditional legal-lobby firms. The firms McDermott Will & Emery LLP and Cassidy and Associates also have had substantial contracts with Equatorial Guinea (Lanny J. Davis & Associates LLC vs. Republic of Equatorial Guinea, http://unitedrepublic.org/why-are-dc-lobbyists-helping-dictator/).

(See also: Sara Jerome, "Lobbying firm Cassidy & Associates loses highest-paying client." *The Hill*, August 6, 2010 [http://thehill.com/business-a-lobbying/113117-lobbying-firm-cassidy-a-associates-loses-highest-paying-client].) Apparently, the money was well spent. Obiang got the diplomatic money shot in 2006, so to speak, a handshake photo-op with Secretary of State Condoleezza Rice, who noted that Obiang, well-known for his repressive ways, was a "good friend." (See: Al Kamen, "Photo-Op Frames a Shot at Iran." *Washington Post*, April 17, 2006 [http://www.washingtonpost.com/wp-dyn/content/article/2006/04/16/AR2006041600737.html].) Later he would get another one with President Obama (see: http://commons.wikimedia.org/wiki/File:Teodoro_Obiang_Nguema_Mbasogo_with_Obamas.jpg). According to William Sands of the Pulitzer Center on Crisis Reporting, U.S. corporate interests got something as well, even if that meant supporting a despotic kleptocrat like Obiang.

International oil companies also spent large sums on lobbying in support of the Equatorial-Guinean regime: approximately $6.6 million by ExxonMobil Corp. in 2008; $1.3 million by Amareda Hess Corp. in 2009; and an estimated $5 million by Marathon Corp. in 2010, according to information provided under the Lobbying Disclosure Act. This lobbying and political pressure created a quid pro quo situation where the United States wouldn't openly criticize the regime, and the regime guaranteed the US oil industry near-exclusive access to the country's national oil reserves. Due to the lack of transparency, no one knows how much oil revenue the Obiang regime has siphoned out of the economy or how much revenue oil companies have earned in their operations in Equatorial Guinea. (See: William Sands, "Equatorial Guinea: Legitimizing Obiang." Pulitzer Center on Crisis Reporting, April 24, 2012 [http://pulitzercenter.org/reporting/equatorial-guinea-president-teodoro-obiang-legitimization-corruption-oil-unesco-eiti-dodd-frank].)

In the years following the Rice photo-op, Obiang took on another lobbyist, former Clinton administration official Lanny Davis, who insisted that he was helping Obiang reform, telling the *New York Times* "I've kidded him he'd do better to win [re-election] by 51 percent than 98 percent" (Celia Dugger, "African Leader Hires Adviser and Seeks an Image Change." *New York Times*, June 28, 2010 [http://www.nytimes.com/2010/06/29/world/africa/29obiang.html]). The joke, though, was on Davis, who sued Obiang for stiffing him on a six-figure bill about a year later: Ryan J. Reilly, "Lanny Davis Sues Brutal African Regime For Stiffing Him on Legal Bill." *Talking Points Memo*, October 13, 2011 (http://tpmmuckraker.talkingpointsmemo.com/2011/10/lanny_davis_sues_brutal_african_regime_for_stiffing_him.php).

105. See: Thor Halvorssen, "PR Mercenaries, Their Dictator Masters, and the Human Rights Stain." Huffington Post, May 19, 2011 (http://www.huffingtonpost.com/thor-halvorssen/pr-mercenaries-their-dict_b_863716.html).

106. See: Tom Squitieri, Huffington Post (http://www.huffingtonpost.com/tom-squitieri).

107. Squitieri continues to occasionally tweet about Qorvis, but one wouldn't know he works there from just reading his columns. And one would have to read his entire Twitter feed to glean that he works there. His tweets to the Bahrain

pieces he did for the Foreign Policy Association blog were still up as of May 2014; below that are tweets that serve the interests of the client (Bahrain).

Here are some of his tweets:

> Tom Squitieri@TomSquitieri 21 Nov 11
> A look at life and death on Bahrain's streets: http://foreignpolicyblogs.com/2011/11/21/intersections-of-fate-in-bahrain/ . . .
> Tom Squitieri@TomSquitieri 19 nov 11
> Independent commission details attacks on Bahrain Asian citizens http://foreignpolicyblogs.com/2011/11/19/attacks-on-bahrain …'s-asian-citizens-documented-by-independent-commission/http://foreignpolicyblogs.com/2011/11/21/intersections-of-fate-in-bahrain/ . . .
> Tom Squitieri@TomSquitieri 10 Aug 2012
> Qorvis Communications celebrates 12 years of creative success. Read all about it! http://qorvis-blogs.com/?p=80 @qorvis @qorvisdigital @qorvisgps.
> Retweeted by Tom Squitieri
> عاليات #البحرين@bhactivities 16 Nov 2011
> Do you know that #NabeelRajab is talking freely in #Bahrain without being arrested!? Isn't that #Democracy? #JustSaying #bbc #cnn #uk #usa
> Tom Squitieri ¶@TomSquitieri 16 Nov 2011
> More than 30 journalists plan to come to Bahrain to cover release of independent commission report.
> Tom Squitieri ¶@TomSquitieri 1 Nov 2011
> Bahrain moves to reduce, drop charges against some medical personnel who unlawfully disrupted hospitals during protests earlier this year.

108. Kevin Morris, "PR firm accused of editing Wikipedia for government clients." *The Daily Dot,* March 8, 2013 (http://www.dailydot.com/news/qorvis-lauer-wikipedia-paid-editing-scandal/).

109. Ibid. The name of the Qorvis partner is Matt J. Lauer.

110. Melanie Newman, "Lobbying's Hidden Influence. PR Uncovered: Top Lobbyists boast of how they influence the PM." *Bureau of Investigative Journalism,* December 5, 2011 (http://www.thebureauinvestigates.com/2011/12/05/pr-uncovered-top-lobbyists-boast-of-how-they-influence-the-pm/).

111. Ken Silverstein, "How Bahrain Works Washington." *Salon,* December 8, 2011 (http://www.salon.com/2011/12/08/how_bahrain_works_washington/).

112. The journalist is Anna Lenzer. Anna Lenzer, "'Team Fiji' Co-opts the 99%." Huffington Post, December 23, 2011 (http://www.huffingtonpost.com/anna-lenzer/fiji-_b_1165175.html).

113. Marcus Baram, "Lobbyists Jump Ship in Wake of Mideast Unrest." Huffington Post, March 25, 2011 (http://www.huffingtonpost.com/2011/03/24/lobbyist-mideast-unrest-departures_n_840231.html). The reporter is Marcus Baram; the lobbyist Amos Hochstein.

114. Joshua Kurlantzick, "When Lobbyists Work for Authoritarian
     Nations." *Newsweek*, July 26, 2010 (http://www.thedailybeast.com/
     newsweek/2010/07/26/the-hired-guns.html).
115. Evgeny Morozov identifies two -isms he deems dangerous, recounted in a
     Columbia Journalism Review profile: "The first is 'solutionism,' the idea that we
     should recast our problems, from political gridlock to weight loss, as things to
     be solved primarily through technological efficiency. The second is 'internet-
     centrism,' which he describes as the 'firm conviction that we are living through
     unique, revolutionary times, in which the previous truths no longer hold'"
     (Michael Meyer, "Evgeny vs. the Internet." *Columbia Journalism Review*,
     January/February 2014, p. 29). See also Evgeny Morozov, *To Save Everything,
     Click Here, The Folly of Technological Solutionism*. New York: Public Affairs
     Books, 2013; and Evgeny Morozov, *The Net Delusion: The Dark Side of Internet
     Freedom*. New York: Public Affairs Books, 2011.
         A number of observers have argued that the Internet is definitely not the
     democratizing force that tech utopians think it is. Besides Morozov, see, for
     instance, Sherry Turkle, *Alone Together, Why We Expect More from Technology and
     Less from Each Other*. New York: Basic Books, 2011.
116. Matthew Yglesias, "The Glory Days of Journalism." Slate, March 19, 2013
     (http://www.slate.com/articles/business/moneybox/2013/03/pew_s_state_of_
     the_media_ignore_the_doomsaying_american_journalism_has_never.html).

CHAPTER 6
1. Jack Mirkinson, "Daniel Ellsberg Calls Edward Snowden a 'Hero,' Says NSA
   Leak Was Most Important in American History." Huffington Post, June 10,
   2013 (http://www.huffingtonpost.com/2013/06/10/edward-snowden-daniel-
   ellsberg-whistleblower-history_n_3413545.html).
2. See, for instance, "Edward Snowden Impersonated NSA Officials:
   Report." Huffington Post, August 29, 2013 (http://www.huffingtonpost.
   com/2013/08/29/edward-snowden-impersonated-nsa_n_3837459.html).
       Snowden had worked for another contractor, Dell, before Booz Allen.
3. The three-quarters figure is from government scholar Paul C. Light. In
   2008, he calculated that the contract workforce consisted of upwards of 7.6
   million employees, or "three contractors for every federal employee." Paul C.
   Light, "Open Letter to the Presidential Candidates." Huffington Post, June
   25, 2008 (http://www.huffingtonpost.com/paul-c-light/open-letter-to-the-
   presid_b_109276.html). See also: Paul C. Light, *A Government Ill Executed: The
   Decline of the Federal Service and How to Reverse It*. Cambridge, MA: Harvard
   University Press, 2008.
       The cost of services alone (not counting goods) provided by contractors
   soared from some $125 billion in 2001 to an estimated $320 billion-plus in
   2008. Where once the government procured mainly manufactured goods from
   the private sector, a huge (and steady) portion of government purchases is now
   for services that would once have been performed by the civil service.
       With respect to the rise in federal dollars spent on contractors' services:
   These figures are calculated from data available on the Federal Procurement
   Data System (FPDS) (https://www.fpds.gov/). While the FPDS database

shows the 2001 service figures by category, the 2008 database does not. The total combined figure of goods and services for 2008 is $534 billion. Because procurement spending on services currently accounts for more than 60 percent of total procurement dollars, the $320 billion figure given is 60 percent of $534 (see http://www.fpdsng.com/downloads/agency_data_submit_list.htm). For the assessment that "procurement spending on services accounts for more than 60 percent of total procurement dollars," see *Report of the Acquisition Advisory Panel to the Office of Federal Procurement Policy and the United States Congress,* January 2007, p. 3 (http://acquisition.gov/comp/aap/24102_GSA.pdf).

The latest FPDS data in which services are compiled by category are for 2006, and the figure for that year is $244.7 billion. See Federal Procurement Data System, *Federal Procurement Report 2006: Section 1 Total Federal Views,* pp. 31-32 (http://www.fpdsng.com/downloads/FPR_Reports/2006_fpr_section_I_total_federal_views.pdf). The number was calculated by adding total spending on R&D (p. 31), plus total spending on other services (p. 32). No more recent compilation of these numbers become available after as of July 2009.

[With regard to the portion of government purchases now spent on work previously performed by the civil service: The proportion of services, as compared with total procurement (goods and services) went from 39 percent at the end of the Reagan administration (FY 1988) to 46.5 percent at the beginning of the Clinton presidency (FY 1993) to approximately 60 percent in 2006 (see https://www.fpds.gov/). See also Project on Government Oversight, "Pick Pocketing the Taxpayer: The Insidious Effects of Acquisition Reform, Revised Edition." March 11, 2002 (http://www.pogo.org/pogofiles/reports/contract-oversight/pickpocketing-the-taxpayer/co-rcv-20020311.html). The 2007 report of the Acquisition Advisory Panel assessed that "procurement spending on services accounts for more than 60 percent of total procurement dollars" (*Report of the Acquisition Advisory Panel to the Office of Federal Procurement Policy and the United States Congress,* January 2007, p. 3 {http://acquisition.gov/comp/aap/24102_GSA.pdf}).

While the total dollar value of federal procurement spending has declined since 2011, the proportion of services (including construction) to products has remained constant at about 60 percent. Federal procurement spending for 2013 was $461.3 billion (calculated from figures available at www.usaspending.gov [accessed May 20, 2014]), while spending for services (including construction) was $276.2 billion.

For detailed analysis of and information regarding U.S. government contracting-out, see Chapter 4—"U.S. Government, Inc."—of Janine R. Wedel's *Shadow Elite: How the World's New Power Brokers Undermine Democracy, Government, and the Free Market.* New York: Basic Books, 2009. For analysis of outsourcing in the national security arena, see Janine R. Wedel's *Selling Out Uncle Sam: How the Myth of Small Government Undermines National Security.* New America Foundation, Washington, D.C., August 2010 (http://newamerica.net/publications/policy/selling_out_uncle_sam).

Legal scholar Paul Verkuil additionally discusses the implications of outsourcing government functions in *Outsourcing Sovereignty: Why Privatization of Government Functions Threatens Democracy and What We Can Do About It* (New York: Cambridge University Press, 2007).

4. Core or "inherently governmental" functions, which the government itself deems so integral to its work that only federal employees should carry them out, are specified in an OMB circular of 2003 (Office of Management and Budget, 2003. "Circular No. A-76 (Revised) to the Heads of Executive Departments and Establishments" on the "Performance of Commercial Activities, May 29, 2003, "B - Categorizing Activities Performed by Government Personnel as Inherently Governmental or Commercial," A-2, http://www.whitehouse.gov/sites/default/files/omb/assets/circulars/a076/a76_incl_tech_correction.pdf).

5. For a perspective on how the nation's Founding Fathers (James Madison and others) might have reacted to this state of affairs, based on their writings, see: Janine R. Wedel, *"Federalist* No. 70: Where Does the Public Service Begin and End?" *Public Administration Review,* December 2011, pp. S118-S127.

6. The *Wall Street Journal* titled a front-page article "Is U.S. Government 'Outsourcing Its Brain'?" (Bernard Wysocki Jr., "Is U.S. Government 'Outsourcing Its Brain'?" *Wall Street Journal,* March 30, 2007, p. A1.)

7. Ingrid Lunden, "Endgame Raises Another $23M to Take its Gov't Security Solutions to a Wider Commercial Market." *TechCrunch,* March 13, 2013 (http://techcrunch.com/2013/03/13/endgame-raises-another-23m-to-take-its-govt-security-solutions-to-a-wider-commercial-market/).

8. James Bamford, "NSA Snooping Was Only the Beginning. Meet the Spy Chief Leading Us Into Cyberwar." *Wired,* June 12, 2013 (http://www.wired.com/threatlevel/2013/06/general-keith-alexander-cyberwar/all/).

9. I studied these reports and documents as part of the research for my book *Shadow Elite: How the World's New Power Brokers Undermine Democracy, Government, and the Free Market* (New York: Basic Books, 2009) and in a follow-on study (supported by the Ford Foundation), *Selling Out Uncle Sam: How the Myth of Small Government Undermines National Security* (New America Foundation, Washington, D.C., August 2010). In addition to gathering data from myriad published and unpublished sources, I conducted interviews with government and contractor officials.

10. According to *Wired,* U.S. annual expenditures on cybersecurity goods and services are approximately $30 billion. Other contractors working in this area, in addition to Booz Allen Hamilton, include General Dynamics, SAIC, Boeing, and Raytheon. James Bamford, "NSA Snooping Was Only the Beginning. Meet the Spy Chief Leading Us Into Cyberwar." *Wired,* June 12, 2013 (http://www.wired.com/threatlevel/2013/06/general-keith-alexander-cyberwar/all/).

11. Booz Allen as the "shadow intelligence community" is reported in Tim Shorrock, *Spies for Hire: The Secret World of Intelligence Outsourcing.* New York: Simon & Schuster, 2008, p. 47. See his Chapter 2, "Booz Allen Hamilton and the 'Shadow IC'" (pp. 38-71).
    See also: Drake Bennett and Michael Riley, "Booz Allen, the World's Most Profitable Spy Organization." *Bloomberg BusinessWeek,* June 20, 2013 (http://www.businessweek.com/articles/2013-06-20/booz-allen-the-worlds-most-profitable-spy-organization#p1).

12. Bennett and Riley, op. cit. See also Booz Allen Hamilton, "Excellence At Work: Fiscal Year 2013 Annual Report." Booz Allen Hamilton, June 21, 2013 (http://

www.boozallen.com/content/dam/boozallen/media/file/Booz-Allen-FY13-annual-report.pdf).

13. *Washington Post* Investigation, "Top Secret America." *Washington Post,* http://projects.washingtonpost.com/top-secret-america/companies/booz-allen-hamilton/print/

> *Vault* ranked Booz Allen number one in public-sector consulting in 2013 and 2014 and number three in defense consulting (Vault Career Intelligence, "Company Reviews & Rankings: Best Consulting Firms." *Vault,* http://www.vault.com/company-rankings/consulting/best-firms-in-each-practice-area/?sRankID=279).

14. According to *Bloomberg BusinessWeek,* "About 70 percent of the 2013 U.S. intelligence budget is contracted out, according to a Bloomberg Industries analysis; the Office of the Director of National Intelligence (ODNI) says almost a fifth of intelligence personnel work in the private sector" (Drake Bennett and Michael Riley, "Booz Allen, the World's Most Profitable Spy Organization." *Bloomberg BusinessWeek,* June 20, 2013 [http://www.businessweek.com/articles/2013-06-20/booz-allen-the-worlds-most-profitable-spy-organization#p1]).

15. With regard to the percentage of Booz's business from government contracts, for the fiscal year that closed in March 2013, the percentage is 99 (U.S. Securities and Exchange Commission, "Booz Allen Hamilton: Prospectus Supplement," February 12, 2014 [http://www.sec.gov/Archives/edgar/data/1443646/000119312514054835/d674987d424b4.htm]).

> The company's 2013 annual report states: "For fiscal year 2013, 2012, and 2011, approximately 99%, 98%, and 97% respectively, of the Company's revenue was generated from contracts with U.S. government agencies or other U.S. government contractors" (Booz Allen Fiscal Year 2013 Annual Report, p. 64 [http://www.boozallen.com/media/file/Booz-Allen-FY13-annual-report.pdf]).

> With regard to the portion of Booz's annual revenue that comes from U.S. intelligence and military agencies, see David Sanger and Nicole Perlroth, "After Profits, Defense Contractor Faces the Pitfalls of Cybersecurity." *New York Times,* June 15, 2013 (http://www.nytimes.com/2013/06/16/us/after-profits-defense-contractor-faces-the-pitfalls-of-cybersecurity.html?pagewanted=all&_r=0); and Binyamin Appelbaum and Eric Lipton, "Leaker's Employer is Paid to Maintain Government Secrets." *New York Times,* June 9, 2013 (http://www.nytimes.com/2013/06/10/us/booz-allen-grew-rich-on-government-contracts.html?_r=0).

> About one quarter of Booz's business came from intelligence contracts in the fiscal year ended in March 2013 (Drake Bennett and Michael Riley, "Booz Allen, the World's Most Profitable Spy Organization." *Bloomberg BusinessWeek,* June 20, 2013 [http://www.businessweek.com/articles/2013-06-20/booz-allen-the-worlds-most-profitable-spy-organization#p1]).

16. As the *Washington Post* explains, for "the fiscal year ended March 31, 2010, the company reported operating income of less than $200 million on revenue of $5.1 billion, as almost every dollar it brought in went out the door to employees. In the three years since, revenue has risen only modestly to $5.8 billion, but operating income has more than doubled to $446 million. In other words, sales are rising slowly, but profit margins

rose dramatically. That explains how bottom line earnings went from $25 million in fiscal 2010 to almost nine times that in 2013." Neil Irwin, "Seven Facts About Booz Allen Hamilton." *Washington Post,* June 10, 2013 (http://www.washingtonpost.com/blogs/wonkblog/wp/2013/06/10/seven-facts-about-booz-allen-hamilton/).

17.   Booz leases 3.2 million square feet of office space across many facilities, which is more space than the Empire State Building (Neil Irwin, op. cit.). In 2010, Booz had more than 16,000 employees in the Washington area alone. Marjorie Censer, "Booz Allen Hamilton by the numbers." *Washington Post,* November 22, 2010 (http://www.washingtonpost.com/wp-dyn/content/article/2010/11/19/AR2010111906280.html).

18.   With regard to Snowden's salary: Booz Allen, "Booz Allen Statement on Reports of Leaked Information." Press release, June 11, 2013 (http://www.boozallen.com/media-center/press-releases/48399320/statement-reports-leaked-information-060913).

       This figure appears to be considerably higher than that of your average systems analyst (see: Bureau of Labor Statistics, "Occupational Employment and Wages: Computer Systems Analysts." U.S. Department of Labor, May 2013 [http://www.bls.gov/oes/current/oes151121.htm#ind]; http://work.chron.com/average-salary-computer-system-analysts-8853.html; and Bureau of Labor Statistics, "Occupation Outlook Handbook: Computer Systems Analysts." U.S. Department of Labor, January 8, 2014 [http://www.bls.gov/ooh/computer-and-information-technology/computer-systems-analysts.htm]).

19.   See Tim Shorrock, *Spies for Hire: The Secret World of Intelligence Outsourcing.* New York: Simon & Schuster, 2008. Chapter 2, "Booz Allen Hamilton and the 'Shadow IC,'" p. 39.

20.   Mark Mazzetti and David E. Sanger, "Bush Announces Pick for Intelligence Post." *New York Times,* January 5, 2007 (http://www.nytimes.com/2007/01/05/washington/05cnd-intel.html?hp&ex=1168059600&en=ccb62c6b48201e10&ei=5094&partner=homepage&_r=0).

21.   Glenn Greenwald, "Mike McConnell, the WashPost & the dangers of sleazy corporatism." *Salon,* March 29, 2010 (http://www.salon.com/2010/03/29/mcconnell_3/).

22.   Siobhan Gorman, "McConnell to Return to Booz Allen." *Wall Street Journal,* January 27, 2009 (http://online.wsj.com/news/articles/SB123301068820817223).

23.   INSA's 2011 tax documents.

24.   See: "INSA: An Alliance of Expertise and Experience," http://www.insaonline.org/i/a/i/a/index2.aspx?hkey=10d3ba7c-b95b-4298-9cdb-8cb4a343e161; and INSA, "Robust Public-Private Partnership Essential to our National Security," Statement Regarding the Nation's Security Infrastructure, Press Release, June 13, 2013, http://www.insaonline.org/i/f/pr/07.12.13_PublicPrivatePartnership.aspx.
       See also Glenn Greenwald, op. cit.

25.   Besides Clapper and McConnell, the company has employed top executives who previously served in key positions in intelligence agencies (James Woolsey, who headed the CIA; as well as Joan Dempsey, Melissa Hathaway, Richard Wilhelm, and Dov Zakheim).

The company also has had a number of former defense and intelligence officials on its board (http://www.boozallen.com/about/leadership). See also: Julian Borger, "Booz Allen Hamilton: Edward Snowden's US Contracting Firm." *The Guardian*, June 9, 2013 (http://www.theguardian.com/world/2013/jun/09/booz-allen-hamilton-edward-snowden).

26. Shane Harris, *The Watchers: The Rise of America's Surveillance State*. Penguin Press: New York, 2010, pp. 194-195.

27. Ibid., pp. 193-195.

28. Harris portrays McConnell, talking to Clapper, considering a return to DNI as a matter of timing and community: "Was this the right time to come back? Could they make a difference, get real work done and put the community back on track?" (Ibid., p. 324.)

29. Ibid., pp. 324-325.

30. Glenn Greenwald, op. cit.

31. For more on McConnell becoming "the leading spokesman for demanding full immunity for lawbreaking telecoms," see also Glenn Greenwald, "Mike McConnell's clear explanation of FISA." *Salon*, August 23, 2007 (http://www.salon.com/2007/08/23/mcconnell_2/).

32. McConnell's bio on Booz Allen's website (http://www.boozallen.com/about/leadership/executive-leadership/McConnell).

33. Ken Dilanian, Tribune Washington Bureau, "Intelligence nominee's contractor ties draw scrutiny." *Los Angeles Times*, July 25, 2010 (http://articles.latimes.com/2010/jul/25/nation/la-na-clapper-contractors-20100725). (Dilanian's byline says "Tribune Washington Bureau." Dilanian is national security correspondent in the Times Washington Bureau, "which also serves the *Chicago Tribune, Baltimore Sun*, other newspapers" (http://www.linkedin.com/pub/ken-dilanian/6/632/82b).

34. Ibid.

35. Ibid.

36. Tim Shorrock, "Put the Spies Back Under One Roof." *New York Times*, June 17, 2013 (http://www.nytimes.com/2013/06/18/opinion/put-the-spies-back-under-one-roof.html?_r=0).

   See also "Mike McConnell, Booz Allen and the Privatization of Intelligence." *Democracy Now* (http://www.democracynow.org/2007/1/12/mike_mcconnell_booz_allen).

37. Ken Dilanian, "Clapper says he would aim to expand clout of intelligence chief." *Los Angeles Times*, July 21, 2010 (http://articles.latimes.com/2010/jul/21/nation/la-na-clapper-confirmation-20100721).

38. Ken Dilanian, "Intelligence nominee's contractor ties draw scrutiny." *Los Angeles Times*, July 25, 2010 (http://articles.latimes.com/2010/jul/25/nation/la-na-clapper-contractors-20100725).

39. See also this *Washington Post* investigation into the influence of contractors and the unmanageable growth of the intelligence community since 9/11: *Washington Post Investigation*, "Top Secret America" (http://projects.washingtonpost.com/top-secret-america/).

40. Robert O'Harrow, Jr., "Costs Skyrocket as DHS Runs Up No-Bid Contracts." *Washington Post*, June 28, 2008 (http://www.washingtonpost.com/wp-dyn/content/article/2007/06/27/AR2007062702988.html).

41. James Bamford, "NSA Snooping Was Only the Beginning. Meet the Spy Chief Leading Us into Cyberwar." *Wired,* June 12, 2013 (http://www.wired.com/threatlevel/2013/06/general-keith-alexander-cyberwar/all/).

42. For more on Clapper and the Snowden leaks, see, for example: Eli Lake, "Spy Chief James Clapper: We Can't Stop Another Snowden." *The Daily Beast,* February 23, 2014 (http://www.thedailybeast.com/articles/2014/02/23/spy-chief-we-can-t-stop-another-snowden.html).

43. Glenn Kessler, "James Clapper's 'least untruthful' statement to the Senate." *Washington Post,* June 12, 2013 (http://www.washingtonpost.com/blogs/fact-checker/post/james-clappers-least-untruthful-statement-to-the-senate/2013/06/11/e50677a8-d2d8-11e2-a73e-826d299ff459_blog.html).

44. Congressmen Darrell Issa, Ted Poe, Paul Broun, Doug Collins, Walter Jones, and Alan Grayson, "Letter to the President of the United States," January 27, 2014 (http://issa.house.gov/wp-content/uploads/2014/01/FINAL-NSA-Reforms-Letter-01-23-2014-2.pdf).

45. By the quotation marks, I don't mean to imply that they're not officially retired: in fact, McConnell spent 29 years on active service in the military, Clapper 32, and 20 years of active service is all that's required for official retirement. Rather, I mean to indicate that they're both still working full-time and therefore not "retired" in the conventional, civilian meaning of the word.

46. Bryan Bender, "From the Pentagon to the Private Sector." *Boston Globe,* December 26, 2010 (http://www.boston.com/news/nation/washington/articles/2010/12/26/defense_firms_lure_retired_generals/)

47. E-mail from Julia Pfaff to author, June 13, 2014.

48. Ibid.

49. Bryan Bender, "From the Pentagon to the Private Sector." *Boston Globe,* December 26, 2010 (http://www.boston.com/news/nation/washington/articles/2010/12/26/defense_firms_lure_retired_generals/).

     The *Globe* generously provided my Mapping Shadow Influence project with its database on the retired generals and admirals; the project has doubled the size of the database. The Mapping Shadow Influence Project website is at: http://shadowelite.net/.

     See also Janine R. Wedel and Linda Keenan, "Shadow Elite: Eisenhower's Dark Vision Realized—The Military-Industrial Complex At 50." Huffington Post, January 13, 2011 (http://www.huffingtonpost.com/janine-r-wedel/emshadow-eliteem-eisenhow_b_808410.html).

50. Luke Johnson, "Report: 70 Percent of Retired Generals Took Jobs With Defense Contractors or Consultants," Huffington Post, November 19, 2012 (http://www.huffingtonpost.com/2012/11/19/defense-contractors-generals_n_2160771.html); David Barstow, "One Man's Military-Industrial-Media Complex." *New York Times,* November 30, 2008 (http://www.nytimes.com/2008/11/30/washington/30general.html?pagewanted=print).

51. Bryan Bender, op. cit.; David Barstow, "One Man's Military-Industrial-Media Complex." *New York Times,* November 30, 2008 (http://www.nytimes.com/2008/11/30/washington/30general.html?pagewanted=all).

52. David Barstow, "Behind TV Analysts, Pentagon's Hidden Hand." *New York Times,* April 20, 2008 (http://www.nytimes.com/2008/04/20/us/20generals.html?pagewanted=all&_r=1&).

53.   David Barstow, "One Man's Military-Industrial-Media Complex." *New York Times,* November 30, 2008 (http://www.nytimes.com/2008/11/30/washington/30general.html).

54.   Bryan Bender, "From the Pentagon to the Private Sector," op. cit.

55.   Ibid.

56.   The theoretical maximum length of service is thirty years, which, assuming a start in the person's early twenties, would mean retirement for officers (who have almost universally been to college) in their early fifties at the oldest. Although many senior officers are able to get permission to serve longer, retirement ages for military personnel are typically much younger than for civilians.

57.   Bryan Bender, "From the Pentagon to the Private Sector," op. cit.

58.   Joan Vennochi, "The Press had a Crush on David Petraeus,Too," *Boston Globe,* November 18, 2012,http://www.bostonglobe.com/opinion/2012/11/18/david-petraeus-seduction-media-pays-off/uMaGeGBIgV7LxjhsOS5H7M/story.html.

59.   Bryan Bender, "From the Pentagon to the Private Sector," op. cit.

60.   Ibid.

61.   Citizens for Responsibility and Ethics in Washington (CREW), "Strategic Maneuvers: The Revolving Door from the Pentagon to the Private Sector." CREW, November 16, 2012 (http://www.citizensforethics.org/page/-/PDFs/Reports/CREW_Strategic_Maneuvers_Pentagon_Generals_Revolving_Door_11_15_12.pdf?nocdn=1); see also: R. Jeffrey Smith, "Generals no longer retire to Vermont—they lobby for contractors in Washington." Center for Public Integrity, November 21, 2012 (http://www.publicintegrity.org/2012/11/21/11839/generals-no-longer-retire-vermont-they-lobby-contractors-washington).

62.   Tom Vanden Brook, Ken Dilanian, and Ray Locker, "Retired military officers cash in as well-paid consultants." *USA Today,* November 18, 2009 (http://usatoday30.usatoday.com/news/military/2009-11-17-military-mentors_N.htm).

63.   Ibid.; Tom Vanden Brook, "Pentagon reworks disclosure rule for 'senior mentors.'" *USA Today,* July 19, 2010 (http://usatoday30.usatoday.com/news/military/2010-07-19-1Amentors19_ST_N.htm).

64.   Tom Vanden Brook, "Pentagon reworks disclosure rule for 'senior mentors,'" op. cit.; and Tom Vanden Brook and Ken Dilanian, "Gates orders overhaul of Pentagon mentor program." *USA Today,* April 2, 2010 (http://usatoday30.usatoday.com/news/military/2010-04-01-mentors_N.htm)

65.   Tom Vanden Brook and Ken Dilanian, "Gates orders overhaul of Pentagon mentor program." *USA Today,* April 2, 2010 (http://usatoday30.usatoday.com/news/military/2010-04-01-mentors_N.htm)

66.   Office of the Inspector General, United States Department of Defense, "DoD Complied with Policies on Converting Senior Mentors to Highly Qualified Experts, but Few Senior Mentors Converted." Report No: DODIG-2012-009, October 31, 2011 (http://www.dodig.mil/audit/reports/fy12/audit/dodig-2012-009.pdf).

67.   Tom Vanden Brook, "Pentagon use of retired officers as 'mentors' plummets." *USA Today,* November 7, 2011 (http://usatoday30.usatoday.com/news/washington/story/2011-11-07/pentagon-uses-fewer-retired-generals-advisers-as-mentors/51116058/1).

68.   E-mail from *USA Today*'s Tom Vanden Brook, May 19, 2014, and telephone conversation of May 20, 2014.

69.   Retired Lieutenant General Joseph L. Yakovac said this Bryan Bender, "From the Pentagon to the Private Sector." (http://www.boston.com/news/nation/washington/articles/2010/12/26/defense_firms_lure_retired_generals).

70.   Conversation with Col. Gressang of April 3, 2014, and e-mail of May 19, 2014.

71.   Bryan Bender, "From the Pentagon to the Private Sector." *Boston Globe*, December 26, 2010 (http://www.boston.com/news/nation/washington/articles/2010/12/26/defense_firms_lure_retired_generals).

72.   Jeff Horwitz and Maria Aspan, "How Promontory Financial Became Banking's Shadow Regulator." *American Banker*, March 15, 2013 (http://www.americanbanker.com/magazine/123_4/how-promontory-financial-became-banking-s-shadow-regulator-1057480-1.html).

73.   For Promontory's offices and locations, see its website (http://www.promontory.com/default.aspx). Danielle Douglas, "The rise of Promontory." *Washington Post*, August 2, 2013 (http://www.washingtonpost.com/business/economy/the-rise-of-promontory/2013/08/02/c187a112-f32b-11e2-bdae-0d1f78989e8a_story.html); Jesse Hamilton, "Promontory Financial Hires Top Official from U.S. Banking Agency." *Bloomberg*, September 11, 2013 (http://www.bloomberg.com/news/2013-09-11/promontory-financial-hires-top-official-from-u-s-banking-agency.html).

74.   Ben Protess and Jessica Silver-Greenberg, "Former Regulators Find a Home with a Powerful Firm." *DealB%K, New York Times*, April 9, 2013 (http://dealbook.nytimes.com/2013/04/09/for-former-regulators-a-home-on-wall-street/); and Jesse Hamilton, "Promontory Financial Hires Top Official from U.S. Banking Agency." Bloomberg, September 11, 2013 (http://www.bloomberg.com/news/2013-09-11/promontory-financial-hires-top-official-from-u-s-bankingagency.html)

75.   Promontory Financial Group's website (http://www.promontory.com/Firm/Firm_Leadership/).

76.   Massimo Calabresi, "Promontory's Role in the Dodd-Frank Game." *Time*, September 16, 2013 (http://swampland.time.com/2013/09/16/one-firms-role-in-the-dodd-frank-game/).

77.   Robyn Meredith, "Beware of derivatives, Ludwig warns thrift executives." *American Banker*, October 1994, vol. 159, issue 202, p. 2 (http://connection.ebscohost.com/c/articles/9411072367/beware-derivatives-ludwig-warns-thrift-executives).

78.   Promontory Financial Group's website (http://www.promontory.com/).

79.   Danielle Douglas, "The rise of Promontory." *Washington Post*, August 2, 2013 (http://www.washingtonpost.com/business/economy/the-rise-of-promontory/2013/08/02/c187a112-f32b-11e2-bdae-0d1f78989e8a_story.html).

80.   The Volcker Rule holds that banks should be barred from investing depositors' dollars for institutional profit.

81.   Massimo Calabresi, "Promontory's Role in the Dodd-Frank Game." *Time*, September 16, 2013 (http://swampland.time.com/2013/09/16/one-firms-role-in-the-dodd-frank-game/).

82.   Jesse Eisinger, "A Revolving Door in Washington with Spin, but Less Visibility." *DealB%k, New York Times*, February 20, 2013 (http://dealbook.nytimes.com/2013/02/20/a-revolving-door-in-washington-that-gets-less-notice/?_php=true&_type=blogs&_r=0).

83.   The nonprofit referenced is the Sunlight Foundation.
        Source: Ben Protess and Jessica Silver-Greenberg, "Former Regulators Find a
        Home with a Powerful Firm." *DealbB%K, New York Times,* April 9, 2013 (http://
        dealbook.nytimes.com/2013/04/09/for-former-regulators-a-home-on-wall-street/).

84.   Jeff Horwitz and Maria Aspan, "How Promontory Financial Became
        Banking's Shadow Regulator." *American Banker,* March 15, 2013 (http://www.
        americanbanker.com/magazine/123_4/how-promontory-financial-became-
        banking-s-shadow-regulator-1057480-1.html).

85.   Ibid.

86.   Ibid., p. 168.

87.   Ibid., p. 169.

88.   MF Global, Inc., "2011 CFTC Order Review." Presentation to the Audit and
        Risk Committee of the Board of Directors, Promontory Financial Group, May
        12, 2011 (http://av.r.ftdata.co.uk/files/2012/03/12-00047.pdf).

89.   Ben Hallman and Eleazar David Melendez, "Foreclosure Review Insiders
        Portray Massive Failure, Doomed from the Start." Huffington Post, January 14,
        2013 (http://www.huffingtonpost.com/2013/01/14/foreclosure-review-failure-
        start_n_2468988.html).

90.   Paul Kiel, "Is BofA's Foreclosure Review Really Independent? You Be the
        Judge." ProPublica, October 11, 2012 (http://www.propublica.org/article/
        is-bofas-foreclosure-review-really-independent-you-be-the-judge).

91.   ProPublica gave some of the documents supporting its conclusions to Senator
        Robert Menendez, who was heading an oversight hearing. Menendez responded
        to ProPublica thusly:

        > Congress was led to believe that the consultants would be
        > analyzing homeowner foreclosures completely independently of the
        > Wall Street banks, but these memos raise serious questions as to
        > whether that's true. If banks are trying to skew the results in their
        > favor, regulators should stop that immediately.

92.   Ben Hallman and Eleazar David Melendez, "Foreclosure Review Insiders
        Portray Massive Failure, Doomed from the Start." Huffington Post, January 14,
        2013 (http://www.huffingtonpost.com/2013/01/14/foreclosure-review-failure-
        start_n_2468988.html).

93.   Board of Governors of the Federal Reserve System and Office of the
        Comptroller of the Currency, "Amendments to Consent Orders Memorialize
        $9.3 Billion Foreclosure Agreement." Press release, Board of Governors of the
        Federal Reserve System, February 28, 2013 (http://www.federalreserve.gov/
        newsevents/press/enforcement/20130228a.htm).

94.   "Full transcript of the 4/11/13 Senate Independent Foreclosure Review
        hearing." *Corrente Wire,* April 15, 2013 (http://www.correntewire.com/
        full_transcript_of_41113_senate_independent_foreclosure_review_hearing).

95.   Ibid.

96.   Danielle Douglas, "The rise of Promontory." *Washington Post,* August 2, 2013 (http://
        www.washingtonpost.com/business/economy/the-rise-of-promontory/2013/08/02/
        c187a112-f32b-11e2-bdae-0d1f78989e8a_story.html).

97. Lisa Myers and Rich Gardella, "Foreclosure compensation checks arrive, but anger some homeowners." NBC News, May 2, 2013 (http://investigations. nbcnews.com/_news/2013/05/02/18022071-foreclosure-compensation-checks-arrive-but-anger-some-homeowners?lite).

98. Ben Hallman and Eleazar David Melendez, "Foreclosure Review Insiders Portray Massive Failure, Doomed from the Start." Huffington Post, January 14, 2013 (http://www.huffingtonpost.com/2013/01/14/foreclosure-review-failure-start_n_2468988.html?).

99. See documents posted on the *New York Times* website in 2010 (http:// documents.nytimes.com/documents-on-marketing-cheese#annotation/a0).

100. Michael Moss, "While Warning About Fat, U.S. Pushes Cheese Sales." *New York Times*, November 6, 2010 (http://www.nytimes.com/2010/11/07/us/07fat. html?scp=1&sq=dominos&st=cse&_r=1&).

101. Ibid.

102. Ibid.

103. Ibid.

104. Russell Gold and Stephen Power, "Oil Regulator Ceded Oversight to Drillers." *Wall Street Journal*, May 7, 2010 (http://online.wsj.com/ news/articles/SB10001424052748704370704575228512237747070?m g=rcno64-wsj&url=http%3A%2F%2Fonline.wsj.com%2Farticle%2F SB10001424052748704370704575228512237747070.html).

105. Juliet Eilperin, "U.S. exempted BP's Gulf of Mexico drilling from environmental impact study." *Washington Post*, May 5, 2010 (http://www.washingtonpost.com/ wp-dyn/content/article/2010/05/04/AR2010050404118.html).

106. Ibid.

107. Russell Gold and Stephen Power, "Oil Regulator Ceded Oversight to Drillers." *Wall Street Journal*, May 7, 2010 (http://online.wsj.com/news/ articles/SB10001424052748704370704575228512237747070?mg=rcno64-wsj&url=http%3A%2F%2Fonline.wsj.com%2Farticle%2Fb SB1000142405274 8704370704575228512237747070.html).

108. Ibid.

109. Michael Isikoff, "How BP Works Washington." Newsweek, May 6, 2010 (http://www.newsweek.com/how-bp-works-washington-72727).

110. Sources: Dan Eggen, "BP is getting more political, and that may help weather oil-spill storm." *Washington Post*, May 6, 2010 (http://www.washingtonpost. com/wp-dyn/content/article/2010/05/05/AR2010050504804.html); Michael Isikoff, "How BP Works Washington." *Newsweek*, May 6, 2010 (http:// www.newsweek.com/how-bp-works-washington-72727); and "Former Senate Majority Leader, U.S. Special Envoy George Mitchell to Discuss World Hot Spots, State of Congress at National Press Club Newsmaker Tues. March 4 10 AM." *PR Newswire*, February 25, 2014 (http://www. prnewswire.com/news-releases/former-senate-majority-leader-us-special-envoy-george-mitchell-to-discuss-world-hot-spots-state-of-congress-at-national-press-club-newsmaker-tues-march-4-10am-247133101. html and http://news.psu.edu/story/296327/2013/11/22/administration/ mitchell-commends-university-leaders-athletics-integrity).

111. Isikoff, op. cit.

112. According to the http://www.boemre.gov/ website, "On October 1, 2011, the Bureau of Ocean Energy Management, Regulation and Enforcement (BOEMRE), formerly the Minerals Management Service (MMS), was replaced by the Bureau of Ocean Energy Management (BOEM) and the Bureau of Safety and Environmental Enforcement (BSEE) as part of a major reorganization" (http://www.boemre.gov/).

CHAPTER 7

1. James McGann of the University of Pennsylvania conducts an annual survey of think tanks. See: James McGann, "2013 Global Go-To Think Tank Index Report." Think Tank and Civil Societies Program, International Relations Program, University of Pennsylvania (http://gotothinktank.com/dev1/wp-content/uploads/2014/01/GoToReport2013.pdf).

2. McGann's survey shows that think-tank creation exploded especially in the decade following the end of the Cold War (1991-2000); the rate of increase has slowed down since. James McGann, "2007 Global Go-To Think Tank Index Report." Think Tank and Civil Societies Program, International Relations Program, University of Pennsylvania, p. 5 (http://www.thinktankdirectory.org/blog/wp-content/uploads/2008/02/mcgann_2007_the-global-go-to-think-tanks.pdf).

3. According to the 2013 Global Go-To Think Tank Index, there are 6,826 think tanks in the world, of which 1,828 are in the United States. The largest concentration of think tanks is in the nation's capital (395), followed by Massachusetts (176). The 2012 Global Go-To Think Tank Index notes that 31 percent of think tanks in the United States were created between 1981 and 1990 (James G. McGann, "2013 Global Go-To Think Tank Index." Think Tank and Civil Societies Program, University of Pennsylvania, January 22, 2014; James G. McGann, "2012 Global Go-To Think Tank Index." Think Tank and Civil Societies Program, University of Pennsylvania, January 28, 2013.)

4. Bryan Bender, "Many D.C. think tanks now players in partisan wars." *Boston Globe,* August 11, 2013 (http://www.bostonglobe.com/news/nation/2013/08/10/brain-trust-for-sale-the-growing-footprint-washington-think-tank-industrial-complex/7ZifHfrLPlbz0bSeVOZHdI/story.html).

5. "The Corruption of Think Tanks." *JPRI Critique*, vol. 10, no. 2, 2003 (http://www.jpri.org/publications/critiques/critique_X_2.html).

6. Brookings, "Brookings Institution History." Brookings Institution (http://www.brookings.edu/about/history).

7. One effect of this blurring, Medvetz writes, is that think tanks become a place where elites can "shop for policy expertise to support their pre-held views." Thomas Medvetz, *Think Tanks in America*. Chicago: University of Chicago Press, 2012, p. 179.

8. Ibid., book jacket.

9. Ibid., p. 179.

10. Donald E. Abelson, "Old world, new world: the evolution and influence of foreign affairs think-tanks." *International Affairs,* vol. 90, issue 1, January 2014, pp. 125-142 (http://www.chathamhouse.org/sites/default/files/public/International%20Affairs/2014/90_1/INTA90_1_08_Abelson.pdf).

11. The *New York Times* notes: "The job switch should have substantial financial benefits for Mr. DeMint, whose 2010 net worth, $65,000, was among the lowest in the Senate. Edwin J. Feulner, the current head of the foundation, in 2010 earned $1,098,612 in total compensation." Jennifer Steinhauer, "Tea Party Hero is Leaving the Senate for a New Pulpit." New York Times, December 6, 2012 (http://www.nytimes.com/2012/12/07/us/politics/jim-demint-to-leave-senate-to-run-heritage-foundation.html?_r=0)

12. Ibid.; Bryan Bender, "Many D.C. think tanks now players in partisan wars." *Boston Globe*, August 11, 2013 (http://www.bostonglobe.com/news/nation/2013/08/10/brain-trust-for-sale-the-growing-footprint-washington-think-tank-industrial-complex/7ZifHfrLPlbz0bSeVOZHdI/story.html).

13. See http://www.alternet.org/story/75950/'third_way'_think_tank_pushes_telecom_agenda_on_fisa_bill.

14. Jon Cowan and Jim Kessler, "Cowan and Kessler: Economic Populism Is a Dead End for Democrats." *Wall Street Journal*, December 2, 2013 (http://online.wsj.com/news/articles/SB10001424052702304337404579213923151169790).

15. Office of Senator Elizabeth Warren, "Letter to Jamie Dimon, Brian T. Moynihan, Michael L. Corbat, John G. Stumpf, Lloyd C. Blankfein, and James P. Gorman," December 4, 2013 (http://www.warren.senate.gov/files/documents/Letter%20from%20Elizabeth%20Warren%2012-4-2013.pdf).

16. Lee Fang, "Third Way: 'Majority of Our Financial Support' from Wall Street, Business Executives." *The Nation*, December 11, 2013 (http://www.thenation.com/blog/177569/third-way-majority-our-financial-support-wall-street-business-executives#).

17. Lee Fang, "GOP Donors and K Street Fuel Third Way's Advice for the Democratic Party." *The Nation*, December 3, 2013 (http://www.thenation.com/blog/177437/gop-donors-and-k-street-fuel-third-ways-advice-democratic-party).
    For background on the lobbying activities of Peck Madigan, Jones & Stewart, see OpenSecrets.org, "Lobbying Spending Database: Peck Madigan Jones." Center for Responsive Politics (http://www.opensecrets.org/lobby/firmsum.php?id=D000034920&year=2013).

18. Lee Fang, "Third Way," op. cit.

19. Ryan Grim, "Third Way Memo on Public Health Care Stirs Progressive Outrage." Huffington Post, July 9, 2009 (http://www.huffingtonpost.com/2009/06/08/third-ways-anti-public-he_n_212816.html).

20. "Matt Renner | Telecom Group Key Player in Immunity Battle." Truthout, January 31, 2008 (http://www.truth-out.org/archive/item/76005:matt-renner--telecom-group-key-player-in-immunity-battle).

21. Eric Lichtblau and Scott Shane, "Companies Seeking Immunity Donate to Senator." *New York Times*, October 23, 2007 (http://www.nytimes.com/2007/10/23/washington/23nsa.html?_r=0).

22. William K. Black, "Wall Street Uses Third Way to Lead Its Assault on Social Security." Huffington Post, November 13, 2012 (http://www.huffingtonpost.com/william-k-black/third-way-wall-street_b_2121372.html). See also Jim Kessler, David Kendall, Ryan McConaghy, and Jonathan Cowan, "The Case for Taking Up Entitlement Reform." *Third Way*, March 2011 (http://www.thirdway.org/publications/380).

23.   Carlos Lozada, "Setting Priorities for the Afghan War: When CNAS talks, people listen." *New York Times*, June 7, 2009.

24.   Center for a New American Security (http://www.cnas.org/about).

25.   Michael Hastings, "The Runaway General." *Rolling Stone*, June 22, 2010 (http://www.rollingstone.com/politics/news/the-runaway-general-20100622?page=2).

26.   COINdinistas and disciples: Michael Keane, "The Pentagon's Insurgents: David Petraeus and the Rise and Fall of the 'Coindinistas.'" *The Blaze*, March 24, 2013 (http://www.theblaze.com/contributions/the-pentagons-insurgents-david-petraeus-and-the-rise-and-fall-of-the-coindinistas/).

      Adherents: Andrew C. McCarthy, "Moving forward in Afghanistan." *National Review Online*, December 9, 2009 (http://m.nationalreview.com/articles/228763/moving-forward-afghanistan/andrew-c-mccarthy).

      Prophets: Laleh Khalili, "The New (and Old) Classics of Counterinsurgency." *Middle East Research and Information Project*, vol. 40, Summer 2010 (http://www.merip.org/mer/mer255/new-old-classics-counterinsurgency).

      Guru: Toby Dodge, "General Petraeus Goes to Kabul." *IDEAS*, London School of Economics, Issue 5, September 2010 (http://www.lse.ac.uk/IDEAS/publications/ideasToday/05/dodge.pdf).

      Zeal: Herschel Smith, "Counterinsurgency Zeal." *captainsjournal.com*, April 25, 2010 (http://www.captainsjournal.com/2010/04/25/counterinsurgency-zeal/).

27.   William A. Galston, "A Question of Life and Death: U.S. Policy in Afghanistan." The Brookings Institution, June 15, 2010 (http://www.brookings.edu/research/opinions/2010/06/15-afghanistan-galston).

28.   Kelley Beaucar Vlahos, "One-Sided COIN." *The American Conservative*, August 1, 2009 (http://www.theamericanconservative.com/articles/one-sided-coin/).

29.   Center for a New American Security's Supporters (http://www.cnas.org/content/cnas-supporters).

30.   Nathan Hodge, "Coalition of the Shilling." *The Nation*, March 11, 2010 (http://www.thenation.com/article/coalition-shilling).

31.   Richard Fontaine and John Nagl, "The New Reality about U.S. Contractors." CBS News, December 21, 2009 (http://www.cbsnews.com/news/the-new-reality-about-us-contractors/).

32.   Jason Horowitz, "Hot Policy Wonks for the Democrats: The New Realists." *New York Observer*, August 15, 2007 (http://observer.com/2007/08/hot-policy-wonks-for-the-democrats-the-new-realists/).

33.   U.S. Department of Defense, Michèle Flournoy, Under Secretary of Defense for Policy (http://www.defense.gov/bios/biographydetail.aspx?biographyid=172).

34.   Yochi J. Dreazen, "Obama Dips Into Think Tank Talent." *Wall Street Journal*, November 17, 2008 (http://online.wsj.com/news/articles/SB122688537606232319).

35.   Donald E. Abelson, "Old world, new world: the evolution and influence of foreign affairs think-tanks." *International Affairs*, vol. 90, issue 1, January 2014, pp. 125-142 (http://www.chathamhouse.org/sites/default/files/public/International%20Affairs/2014/90_1/INTA90_1_08_Abelson.pdf).

36.   Center for a New American Security, "John Nagl and Robert Kaplan Named Members of Defense Policy Board." CNAS press release, July 2, 2009

(http://www.cnas.org/files/documents/press/CNAS%20Appointments%20
to%20Defense%20Policy%20Board.pdf).

37. Project Vote Smart, "Hearing of the Senate Foreign Relations Committee—
The Nomination of Kurt Campbell to be Assistant Secretary of State for
East Asian and Pacific Affairs, by Dick Lugar, Jim Webb, Jr., and Ted
Kaufman," June 10, 2009 (http://votesmart.org/public-statement/430684/
hearing-of-the-senate-foreign-relations-committee-the-nomination-of-kurt-
campbell-to-be-assistant-secretary-of-state-for-east-asian-and-pacific-a-
ffairs#.UypIcvldUtM).

38. Michael Crowley, "COIN Toss." *New Republic*, January 4, 2010 (http://www.
newrepublic.com/article/world/coin-toss).

39. For analysis of the COIN strategy, see Andrew Bacevich. In *Breach of Trust*, he
writes (Andrew Bacevich, *Breach of Trust: How Americans Failed Their Soldiers
and Their Country*. New York: Metropolitan Books, 2013, p. 109):

> . . . even granting the extravagant claims made by those likening
> Petraeus to Patton or ascribing to him the qualities of a "maverick
> savior," the surge posed a problem. If its "success" in Iraq defined
> the army's principal contribution to national security, the service
> was in trouble.
>
> Indeed, when General Stanley McChrystal's attempt to export
> COIN to Afghanistan in 2009-10 fizzled, the counterinsurgency
> balloon quickly deflated.

See also: http://www.theatlantic.com/magazine/archive/2008/10/
the-petraeus-doctrine/306964/; http://www.theamericanconservative.
com/prof-bacevich-deflates-coin-happy-crowd-of-1400/; http://www.
theamericanconservative.com/larison/bacevich-reviews-accidental-guerrilla/.

40. Spencer Ackerman, "CNAS Whale Swallows National-Security Journalists
Whole." *Attackerman*, October 15, 2009 (http://attackerman.firedoglake.
com/2009/10/15/cnas-whale-swallows-national-security-journalists-whole/).

41. CBS, "Veterans Talk Troop Deployment." CBS News, December 2, 2009
(https://www.youtube.com/watch?v=X0C1gC0LJhM).

42. Center for a New American Security's Writers-In-Residence Program (http://
www.cnas.org/programs/writers-residence).

43. Shanker, Schmitt, and Sanger just before Shanker and Schmitt took their book
leave at CNAS: David E. Sanger, Thom Shanker, and Eric Schmitt, "Obama
Gives Way to Rate Efforts in Afghan Region." *New York Times*, September 17,
2009 (http://query.nytimes.com/gst/fullpage.html?res=9D04E5DE113AF9
34A2575AC0A96F9C8B63&ref=thomshanker); "People: Thom Shanker."
New York Times (http://topics.nytimes.com/top/reference/timestopics/people/s/
thom_shanker/?offset=660&s=newest); Thomas E. Ricks, "A Military
Tactician's Political Strategy." *Washington Post*, February 9, 2009 (http://www.
washingtonpost.com/wp-dyn/content/article/2009/02/08/AR2009020802321.
html?sid=ST2009020702304).

44. The ambassador at the time was Karl Eikenberry. *Politico*, "Cloud Returns to
journalism; joins *Tribune*." *Politico*, March 4, 2010 (http://www.politico.com/

blogs/michaelcalderone/0310/Cloud_returns_to_journalism_joins_Tribune.
html?showall).

45. See Peter Osnos, "Meet Captain Matt Pottinger, United States Marine Corps." The Atlantic, April 11, 2014 (http://www.theatlantic.com/national/archive/2011/04/ meet-captain-matt-pottinger-united-states-marine-corps/236825/).

Here is the report: Major General Michael T. Flynn, Captain Matt Pottinger, and Paul D. Batchelor, "Fixing Intel: A Blueprint for Making Intelligence Relevant in Afghanistan." Voices from the Field, Center for a New American Security, January 2010 (http://www.cnas.org/files/documents/press/ AfghanIntel_Flynn_Jan2010_code507_voices.pdf).

46. McChrystal is quoted in: Julian E. Barnes, "U.S. Intelligence chief in Afghanistan wages battle for resources." *Los Angeles Times,* November 25, 2009 (http://articles.latimes.com/2009/nov/25/world/la-fg-afghanistan25-2009nov25). See also: Julian E. Barnes, "The 'chief operating officer' in Afghanistan." *Los Angeles Times-Washington Post News Service,* December 4, 2009 (http://gulfnews.com/about-gulf-news/al-nisr-portfolio/weekend-review/ articles/the-chief-operating-officer-in-afghanistan-1.542963).

47. Nathan Hodge, "How a Plugged-In DC Think Tank Published a General's Brutal Intel Critique." *Wired,* January 8, 2010 http://www.wired.com/2010/01/ how-a-plugged-in-dc-think-tank-published-a-generals-brutal-intel-critique/

48. *Politico*'s Laura Rozen, "Mil intel report sig of more defiance by the generals?" *Politico,* January 6, 2010 (http://www.politico.com/blogs/laurarozen/0110/ Mil_intel_report_sign_of_more_defiance_by_the_generals_.html?showall).

49. Thomas E. Ricks, "Travels with Paul (I): A time to build." *Foreign Policy,* January 13, 2011 (http://ricks.foreignpolicy.com/posts/2011/01/13/ travels_with_paula_i_a_time_to_build).

50. Paula Broadwell with Vernon Loeb, *All In: The Education of General Petraeus.* New York: Penguin Books, 2012 (http://www.amazon.com/ All-In-Education-General-Petraeus/dp/B00F6IM5CW).

51. Tara McKelvey, "Too Close for Comfort? Tom Ricks and the military's new philosophical embeds." *Columbia Journalism Review,* September 9, 2009 (http:// www.cjr.org/cover_story/too_close_for_comfort.php?page=all&print=true).

52. Center for a New American Security, "CNAS Releases Afghanistan Policy Brief by Andrew Exum." *Center for a New American Security,* October 20, 2009 (http://www.cnas.org/media-and-events/press-release/cnas-releases-afghanistan-policy-brief-by-andrew-exum#.UyH0GfldUtM).

53. SWJ Editors, "CNAS Releases Afghanistan Policy Brief." *Small Wars Journal,* October 20, 2009 (http://smallwarsjournal.com/blog/cnas-releases-afghanistan-policy-brief); *Frontline,* "Obama's War: Interview with Andrew Exum." PBS, August 5, 2009 (http:// www.pbs.org/wgbh/pages/frontline/obamaswar/interviews/exum.html).

54. *Frontline,* "Obama's War," op. cit.

55. Nathan Hodge, "How the Afghan Surge Was Sold." *Wired,* December 3, 2009 (http://www.wired.com/dangerroom/2009/12/ how-the-afghan-surge-was-sold/).

56. Andrew Alexander, "Undisclosed conflict in a review of Jon Krakauer's book on Pat Tillman." *Washington Post,* November 15, 2009 (http://www.washingtonpost. com/wp-dyn/content/article/2009/11/13/AR2009111303346.html).

57. Exum blogged at Abu Muqawama, his nom de guerre. See: Abu Muqawama, "On Defense Policy Analysts and Conflicts of Interest." January 12, 2012 (http://www.cnas.org/blog/on-defense-policy-analysts-and-conflicts-of-interest-5862#.U6slwvldXyG).

58. Nathan Hodge, "Coalition of the Shilling." *The Nation*, March 11, 2010 (http://www.thenation.com/article/coalition-shilling).

59. Joan Vennochi, "The press had a crush on David Petraeus, too." *Boston Globe*, November 18, 2012 (http://www.bostonglobe.com/opinion/2012/11/18/david-petraeus-seduction-media-pays-off/uMaGeGBIgV7LxjhsOS5H7M/story.html).

60. Jon Lee Anderson, "The Petraeus Illusion." *The New Yorker*, November 13, 2012 (http://www.newyorker.com/online/blogs/comment/2012/11/the-petraeus-illusion.html).

61. SWJ Editors, "CNAS Releases Afghanistan Policy Brief." *Small Wars Journal*, October 20, 2009 (http://smallwarsjournal.com/blog/cnas-announces-new-research-agenda-and-website).

62. Center for a New American Security, "CNAS Announces 2014 Next Generation National Security Leaders." Press release, Center for a New American Security, February 11, 2014 (http://www.cnas.org/next-generation-2014-release#.UyD8SfldXiE).

CNAS leaders are still finding high-level positions at the White House: in 2014, CNAS CEO Robert Work was nominated by President Obama to be Deputy Secretary of Defense after just a year as CNAS CEO; before that, he was Under Secretary of the Navy (Center for a New American Security, "CNAS CEO Robert Work Nominated as Deputy Secretary of Defense." Press release, Center for a New American Security, February 7, 2014 [http://www.cnas.org/CNAS-CEO-Robert-Work-Nominated-Deputy-Secretary-Defense#.UypQ1vldUtM]).

Former Secretary of State Madeleine Albright is on the board of directors, as are former BAE Systems CEO Linda Hudson and former senator Joseph Lieberman (Center for a New American Security, "CNAS Announces Changes to Board of Directors." Press release, Center for a New American Security, November 4, 2013 [http://www.cnas.org/files/documents/press/Board%20Changes%20PR%20(10.04.13).pdf]).

Michèle Flournoy is scheduled to serve as interim CEO of CNAS until its board selects a successor for Work; she has also decamped as a "senior adviser" for Boston Consulting Group's (BCG) "growing Public Sector" portfolio (Center for a New American Security, "CNAS CEO Robert Work Nominated as Deputy Secretary of Defense." Press release, Center for a New American Security, February 7, 2014 [http://www.cnas.org/CNAS-CEO-Robert-Work-Nominated-Deputy-Secretary-Defense#.U0WG1_ldVqV]).

Andrew Exum became a consultant for BCG (Carnegie Council for Ethics in International Affairs, "Ethics Matter: The Future of War, with Andrew Exum." Carnegie Council for Ethics in International Affairs, December 12, 2013 [https://www.carnegiecouncil.org/calendar/data/0467.html]; Boston Consulting Group, "Former DoD Under Secretary Michèle Flournoy Joins BCG as Senior Adviser." Press release, Boston Consulting Group, July 16, 2012 [http://www.bcg.com/media/PressReleaseDetails.aspx?id=tcm:12-109698]).

Tom Ricks, over on the "The Best Defense," is trying to make sense of the new "anti-COIN" movement, with longtime COIN backer David Kilcullen

(Thomas E. Ricks, "Kilcullen speaks: On COIN going out of style, his recent book, Syria, and more." *Foreign Policy,* February 12, 2014 [http://ricks. foreignpolicy.com/posts/2014/02/12/kilcullen_speaks_on_coin_going_out_of_ style_his_recent_book_syria_and_more]).

And Hillary Clinton, of course, is still in the picture.

63.   See Janine R. Wedel, *Shadow Elite: How the World's New Power Brokers Undermine Democracy, Government, and the Free Market.* New York: Basic Books, 2009, pp. 165-176.

64.   See the "Neocon Core" graphic (http://janinewedel.info/shadowelite.html).

65.   Wedel, *Shadow Elite,* op. cit., pp. 177-191.

66.   This quote from Stubbs is in: Paul Stubbs and Janine Wedel, "Policy Flexians in Global Order: Contexts, Cases and Consequences," *Actors and Agency in Global Social Governance,* Alexandra Kaasch and Kerstin Martens, eds., forthcoming. See also Charles Morris, *The Sages: Warren Buffett, George Soros, Paul Volcker, and the Maelstrom of Markets.* New York: Public Affairs, 2009.

67.   See: http://www.opensocietyfoundations.org/about/programs/think-tank-fund

68.   See Paul Stubbs, "'Managing' Consultancy: charisma, competence and translation in transnational spaces," Paper for American Anthropological Association Annual Conference, Montreal, November 2011 (http://www.scribd.com/doc/71677033/ Stubbs-Managing-Consultancy-Charisma-competence-and-translation-in-transnational-spaces) (accessed 2 January 2013); Paul Stubbs, "Blitz Statement on the Role of NGOs" (http://www.moneynations.ch/topics/euroland/text/paulblitz. htm) (accessed 2 January 2013); Paul Stubbs, "Flex Actors and Philanthropy in (Post-)Conflict Arenas: Soros' Open Society Foundations in the Post-Yugoslav Space," *Politička misao/Croatian J. of Political Science,* vol. 50, no. 5, 2013, pp. 114-138); and Paul Stubbs and Janine Wedel, "Policy Flexians in Global Order: Contexts, Cases and Consequences," in *Actors and Agency in Global Social Governance,* Alexandra Kaasch and Kerstin Martens, eds., forthcoming.

69.   Paul Stubbs and Janine Wedel, "Policy Flexians in Global Order: Contexts, Cases and Consequences," *Actors and Agency in Global Social Governance,* Alexandra Kaasch and Kerstin Martens, eds., forthcoming.

70.   Diane Stone, "Transnational Philanthropy, Policy Transfer Networks and the Open Society Institute." CSGR Working Paper 238/08 (http://www2.warwick. ac.uk/fac/soc/csgr/research/workingpapers/2008/23808.pdf) (accessed 2 January 2013), p. 2.

71.   In an interview with a journalist of the *New Republic,* George Soros states "Just write that the former Soviet Empire is now called the Soros Empire." Michael Lewis, "The Speculator." *New Republic,* January 10, 1994 (http://www. newrepublic.com/article/politics/the-speculator).

Kim Scheppele, "The Soros Empire," presented at the Harry and Helen Gray Humanities Program Workshop, "American and German Cultural Policies in Eastern Europe: Assessing Developments in the 1990s," September 25, 1998, *American Institute for Contemporary German Studies,* October 1999, p.24 (http:// www.aicgs.org/publication/american-and-german-cultural-policies-in-eastern-europe-assessing-developments-in-the-1990s/).

72.   Diane Stone, "Transfer and Translation of Policy." *Policy Studies,* vol. 33, issue 6, 2012, pp. 483-499.

73. Călin Dan, "Soros—the dictatorship of goodwill." *nettime.org*, May 10, 1997 (http://www.nettime.org/Lists-Archives/nettime-l-9705/msg00050.html) (accessed 23 January 2013).

74. Paul Stubbs, "Flex Actors and Philanthropy in (Post-)Conflict Arenas: Soros' Open Society Foundations in the Post-Yugoslav Space," *Politička misao/Croatian J. of Political Science*, vol. 50, no. 5, 2013, p. 118.

75. Călin Dan, "Soros—the dictatorship of goodwill," op. cit.

As a result, as Stone has written, many of the foundations operated in ways that lacked transparency and the financial propriety that OSI, through its funding of transparency initiatives, demanded of others (Diane Stone, "Transnational Philanthropy," op. cit.)

76. Kim Scheppele, "The Soros Empire," presented at the Harry and Helen Gray Humanities Program Workshop, "American and German Cultural Policies in Eastern Europe: Assessing Developments in the 1990s," September 25, 1998, *American Institute for Contemporary German Studies*, October 1999, p. 24 (http://www.aicgs.org/publication/american-and-german-cultural-policies-in-eastern-europe-assessing-developments-in-the-1990s/).

77. Paul Stubbs, "Flex Actors and Philanthropy in (Post-)Conflict Arenas: Soros' Open Society Foundations in the Post-Yugoslav Space," *Politička misao/Croatian J. of Political Science*, vol. 50, no. 5, 2013, pp. 114-138.

In the late 1990s, Soros's endeavors took more of a "global turn," as Diane Stone put it (Diane Stone, "Transnational Philanthropy," op. cit.), engaging in long-term partnerships with the World Bank, UNDP, and the European Union.

78. Stubbs and Wedel, op. cit.

See also: Nicolas Guilhot, "Reforming the World: George Soros, Global Capitalism and the Philanthropic Management of the Social Sciences." *Critical Sociology*, vol. 33, 2007, pp. 447-477.

Anthropologist Nicholas Guilhot argues, persuasively, that Soros is creating a new technocratic consensus and agreed division of labor between NGOs, state agencies, and international financial institutions, with the global players he spawned proving highly "versatile" in gaining the support of diverse interests.

79. Kim Scheppele, "The Soros Empire," op. cit.

80. Paul Stubbs and Janine Wedel, "Policy Flexians in Global Order: Contexts, Cases and Consequences," *Actors and Agency in Global Social Governance*, Alexandra Kaasch and Kerstin Martens, eds., forthcoming.

81. Conversation with Paul Stubbs, June 26, 2014. See also Paul Stubbs, "Flex Actors and Philanthropy in (Post-) Conflict Arenas: Soros' Open Society Foundations in the Post-Yugoslav Space," *Politička misao/Croatian J. of Political Science*, vol. 50, no. 5, 2013.

82. Conversation with Paul Stubbs, June 26, 2014.

83. Greenpeace USA, "Dealing in Doubt: The climate denial machine vs climate science." *Greenpeace USA*, September 2013 (http://www.greenpeace.org/usa/Global/usa/report/Dealing%20in%20Doubt%202013%20-%20Greenpeace%20report%20on%20Climate%20Change%20Denial%20Machine.pdf).

84. Naomi Oreskes and Erik Conway, "*Shadow Elite: Merchants of Doubt*—Do Scientific Denialists Have No Shame?" Huffington Post, June 17, 2010 (http://www.huffingtonpost.com/naomi-oreskes/emshadow-eliteem-merchant_b_615504.html).

85. Jill Fitzsimmons, "Meet the Climate Denial Machine." *Media Matters for America*, November 28, 2012 (http://mediamatters.org/blog/2012/11/28/meet-the-climate-denial-machine/191545).

86. Jill Fitzsimmons, Jocelyn Fong, and Shauna Teel, "Who is Robert Bryce?" *Media Matters for America*, October 7, 2011 (http://mediamatters.org/research/2011/10/07/who-is-robert-bryce/181888).

87. Jill Fitzsimmons, "Meet the Climate Denial Machine." Media Matters for America, November, 28, 2012 (http://mediamatters.org/blog/2012/11/28/meet-the-climate-denial-machine/191545#heritage).
     See also: "Jonathan H. Adler," Policy Experts: The Insider Guide to Public Policy Experts and Organizations (http://www.policyexperts.org/us_experts/us_experts_results.cfm?Topic=OneTopic&Issues=153&state=ALL&Search=Verify%3E).

88. Jill Fitzsimmons, "Meet the Climate Denial Machine." *Media Matters for America*, November 28, 2012 (http://mediamatters.org/blog/2012/11/28/meet-the-climate-denial-machine/191545#cato); and Cato Institute, "Commentary: Patrick J. Michaels" (http://www.cato.org/people/25/commentary).

89. Jill Fitzsimmons, "Meet the Climate Denial Machine." *Media Matters for America*, November 28, 2012 (http://mediamatters.org/blog/2012/11/28/meet-the-climate-denial-machine/191545#heartland).

90. Jill Fitzsimmons, "Meet the Climate Denial Machine." Media Matters for America, November, 28, 2012 (http://mediamatters.org/blog/2012/11/28/meet-the-climate-denial-machine/191545#aei).
     See also: Ian Sample, "Scientists offered cash to dispute climate study." *The Guardian*, February 1, 2007 (http://www.theguardian.com/environment/2007/feb/02/frontpagenews.climatechange).

91. Riley E. Dunlap and Peter J. Jacques, "Climate Change Denial Books and Conservative Think Tanks." *American Behavioral Scientist*, vol. 57, no. 6, 2013, pp. 699-731 (http://www.ncbi.nlm.nih.gov/pmc/articles/PMC3787818/).

92. Ibid.

93. http://www.gallup.com/poll/167960/americans-likely-say-global-warming-exaggerated.aspx.

94. Dunlap and Jacques, op. cit.

95. Robert J. Brulle, Jason Carmichael, and J. Craig Jenkins. "Shifting public opinion on climate change: an empirical assessment of factors influencing concern over climate change in the US, 2002–2010." *Climatic Change*, vol. 114, no. 2, 2012, pp. 169-188.
     See also: OpEdNews, "Not Just the Koch Brothers: New Study Reveals Funders Behind the Climate Change Denial Effort." Press release, *OpEdNews*, January 5, 2014 (http://www.opednews.com/articles/Not-Just-the-Koch-Brothers-by-Press-Release-Black-Money-Secret-Donors_Climate-Change_Climate-Change-Deniers_Denial-140105-86.html).

96. Source Watch (http://www.sourcewatch.org/index.php/Atlas_Economic_Research_Foundation).

97. Karin Fischer and Dieter Plehwe, "The 'Pink Tide' and Neoliberal Civil Society Formation: Think Tank Networks in Latin America." *State of Nature*, Winter 2013 (http://www.stateofnature.org/?p=6601).

98.   http://www.forbes.com/sites/alejandrochafuen/2014/02/19/
        think-tanks-and-the-power-of-networks/.

CHAPTER 8

1.   For a description of Rodman's latest (January 2014) visit, see Rosie Gray, "How
        Dennis Rodman Got to North Korea." *BuzzFeed,* January 17, 2014 (http://
        www.buzzfeed.com/rosiegray/how-dennis-rodman-got-to-north-korea).

2.   Ed Pilkington, "US firm Monitor Group admits mistakes over $3m Gaddafi
        deal." *The Guardian,* March 3, 2011 (http://www.theguardian.com/world/2011/
        mar/04/monitor-group-us-libya-gaddafi).

3.   Laura Rozen, "Among Libya's Lobbyists." *Politico,* February 21, 2011 (http://
        www.politico.com/blogs/laurarozen/0211/Among_Libyas_lobbyists.html).
        After the affair came to light, Monitor Group, which professed ignorance of
        federal requirements, admitted to breaking the law by failing to register with
        the Justice Department as a lobbyist on behalf of a foreign government. After
        a set of reviews, the firm released a statement that some of the work it did in
        Libya between 2006 and 2008 should have been registered, and that it would
        do so retroactively (Siddartha Mahanta, "Libya Lobbyists Come Clean."
        Mother Jones, May 6, 2011 [http://www.motherjones.com/mojo/2011/05/libya-
        lobbyists-come-clean]). As the *Boston Globe* wrote: "The media attention on
        Monitor prompted the Justice Department to send a letter inquiring about the
        company's work in Libya. Failure to register can lead to fines and even jail time,
        but specialists say that as long as companies try to comply with the law, such
        penalties are rare" (Farah Stockman, "Firm says it erred on Libya consulting;
        Cambridge company will register as lobbyist." *Boston Globe,* May 6, 2011
        [https://global-factiva-com.mutex.gmu.edu/redir/default.aspx?P=sa&NS=16&
        AID=9VIV000400&an=BSTNGB0020110506e7560001d&cat=a&ep=ASI]).
           Monitor's Libya work, together with another project that "promised to help the
        Kingdom of Jordan get more influence over John Kerry—forced Monitor consultants
        to file retroactively as lobbyists. . . . Monitor admitted that some aspects of the Libya
        project were 'a mistake,' but insists that it had nothing to do with the company's
        demise" (Farah Stockman, "Why did the smartest guys in the room go bankrupt?"
        Boston Globe, January 20, 2013 [http://www.bostonglobe.com/opinion/2013/01/20/
        when-smartest-guys-room-bankrupt/lUYj7Nl8vAHhlL1iWVpSoK/story.html]).

4.   Letter from Mark B. Fuller, CEO of Monitor Group, and Rajeev Singh-
        Molares, director, to Mr. 'Abd Allah al-Sanusi, July 2, 2006, p. 12 (Mark B.
        Fuller and Rajeev Singh-Molares, "Letter to Mr. 'Abd Allah al-Sanusi," July 3,
        2006 [http://www.motherjones.com/files/monitor_letter.pdf]).

5.   For a list of Monitor Group's founders, see: Mary Mcinerney, "Tuning into
        Monitor." *Boston Business Journal,* July 23, 2001 (http://www.bizjournals.com/
        boston/stories/2001/07/23/focus1.html?s=print) or Farah Stockman, "Firm says
        it erred on Libya consulting ; Cambridge company will register as lobbyist." *Boston
        Globe,* May 6, 2011 (http://www.bostonglobe.com/opinion/2013/01/20/when-
        smartest-guys-room-bankrupt/lUYj7Nl8vAHhlL1iWVpSoK/story.html).

6.   Stockman, op. cit.

7.   Mary Mcinerney, "Tuning into Monitor." *Boston Business Journal,* July 23, 2001
        (http://www.bizjournals.com/boston/stories/2001/07/23/focus1.html?page=5).

8. Ibid.
9. The Libyan opposition group that acquired and released the documents is the National Conference of the Libyan Opposition (Laura Rozen, "Among Libya's Lobbyists." *Politico*, February 21, 2011 [http://www.politico.com/blogs/laurarozen/0211/Among_Libyas_lobbyists.html]).
10. Mark B. Fuller, CEO of Monitor Group and Rajeev Singh-Molares, director, "Letter to Mr. 'Abd Allah al-Sanusi," July 3, 2006, published by *Mother Jones*, http://www.motherjones.com/files/monitor_letter.pdf.
11. Ibid.
12. Ibid.
13. Farah Stockman, "Local consultants aided Khadafy; Cambridge firm tried to polish his image." *Boston Globe*, March 4, 2011 (http://www.boston.com/news/local/massachusetts/articles/2011/03/04/local_consultants_aided_khadafy/); https://global-factiva-com.mutex.gmu.edu/redir/default.aspx?P=sa&NS=16&AID=9VIV000400&an=BSTNGB0020110304e73400025&cat=a&ep=ASI; "Project to Enhance the Profile of Libya and Muammar Qadhafi: Executive Summary of Phase 1," 2007, pp. 5-9 (http://www.motherjones.com/files/monitor_letter.pdf).
14. Monitor Group, "Project to Enhance the Profile of Libya and Muammar Qadhafi: Executive Summary of Phase 1" (http://www.motherjones.com/files/project_to_enhance_the_profile_of_libya_and_muammar_qadhafi.pdf).
15. Joseph S. Nye, Jr., "Tripoli Diarist." *New Republic*, December 10, 2007 (http://www.newrepublic.com/article/tripoli-diarist). See also David Corn and Siddartha Mahanta, "From Libya With Love." *Mother Jones*, March 3, 2011 (http://www.motherjones.com/politics/2011/03/libya-qaddafi-monitor-group).
16. Andrew Moravcsik, "A Rogue Reforms." *Newsweek*, July 16, 2007 (http://www.thedailybeast.com/newsweek/2007/07/15/a-rogue-reforms.html).
17. Benjamin Barber, "Gaddafi's Libya: An Ally for America?" *Washington Post*, August 15, 2007 (http://www.washingtonpost.com/wp-dyn/content/article/2007/08/14/AR2007081401328.html).
18. Monitor Group, "Project to Enhance the Profile of Libya and Muammar Qadhafi: Executive Summary of Phase 1" (http://www.motherjones.com/files/project_to_enhance_the_profile_of_libya_and_muammar_qadhafi.pdf).
19. See ibid., pp. 5-6; Anthony Giddens, "The colonel and his third way." *New Statesman*, August 28, 2006; Anthony Giddens, "My chat with the colonel," *The Guardian*, March 8, 2007 (http://www.theguardian.com/commentisfree/2007/mar/09/comment.libya); and Corn and Mahanta, op. cit.
20. Farah Stockman, "Local consultants aided Khadafy; Cambridge firm tried to polish his image." *Boston Globe*, March 4, 2011 (http://www.boston.com/news/local/massachusetts/articles/2011/03/04/local_consultants_aided_khadafy/) and https://global-factiva-com.mutex.gmu.edu/redir/default.aspx?P=sa&NS=16&AID=9VIV000400&an=BSTNGB0020110304e73400025&cat=a&ep=ASI.
21. Joseph S. Nye, Jr., "Tripoli Diarist." *New Republic*, December 10, 2007 (http://www.newrepublic.com/article/tripoli-diarist?keepThis=true&TB_iframe=true).
22. Quoted in David Corn, "Monitor Group and Qaddafi: Still Spinning?" *Mother Jones*, March 3, 2011 (http://www.motherjones.com/mojo/2011/03/monitor-group-and-qaddafi-still-spinning).

23. Benjamin Pauker, "Understanding Libya's Michael Corleone." *Foreign Policy*, March 7, 2011 (http://www.foreignpolicy.com/articles/2011/03/07/understanding_libyas_michael_corleone).

24. Benjamin Barber, "A response to Jon Wiener's 'Professors Paid by Qaddafi: Providing "Positive Public Relations."'" *The Nation*, March 6, 2011 (http://www.thenation.com/article/159054/benjamin-barber-responds?comment_sort=ASC#axzz2bUxtiqcR).

25. Pletka's title and bio: Danielle Pletka, Vice President, Foreign and Defense Policy Studies, American Enterprise Institute (http://www.aei.org/scholar/danielle-pletka/).
    Source of quote: Ed Pilkington, "US firm Monitor Group admits mistakes over $3m Gaddafi deal." *The Guardian*, March 3, 2011 (http://www.theguardian.com/world/2011/mar/04/monitor-group-us-libya-gaddafi).

26. Robert D. Putnam, "With Libya's Megalomaniac 'Philosopher-King.'" *Wall Street Journal*, February 26, 2011 (http://online.wsj.com/news/articles/SB10001424052748703408604576164363053350664). See also David Corn and Siddartha Mahanta, "From Libya With Love," *Mother Jones*, March 3, 2011 (http://www.motherjones.com/politics/2011/03/libya-qaddafi-monitor-group).

27. Emily Flitter, Kristina Cooke, and Pedro da Costa, "Special Report: For some professors, disclosure is academic." *Reuters*, December 20, 2010 (http://www.reuters.com/article/2010/12/20/us-academics-conflicts-idUSTRE6BJ3LF20101220).

28. See Janine R. Wedel and Linda Keenan, "Shadow Elite: Do Economists Need a Code of Ethics?" Huffington Post, January 6, 2011, http://www.huffingtonpost.com/janine-r-wedel/emshadow-eliteem-do-econo_b_805106.html.

29. Gerald Epstein and Jessica Carrick-Hagenbarth, "Financial Economists, Financial Interests and Dark Corners of the Meltdown: It's Time to set Ethical Standards for the Economics Profession." Political Economy Research Institute, University of Massachusetts Amherst, Working Paper no. 239, October 2010 (http://www.peri.umass.edu/fileadmin/pdf/working_papers/working_papers_201-250/WP239.pdf).

30. Ibid., p.1.

31. Ibid.

32. Ibid., p. 4.

33. Ibid., pp. 5 and 19.

34. Gerald Epstein and Jessica Carrick-Hagenbarth, "Letter to Mr. Robert E. Hall, President, American Economic Association," January 3, 2011, pp. 1-2 (http://www.peri.umass.edu/fileadmin/pdf/other_publication_types/AEA_letter_Jan3b.pdf).

35. American-based codes of ethics for these professions are as follows: For journalists: Society of Professional Journalists, "Code of Ethics" (http://www.spj.org/ethicscode.asp). For engineers: National Society of Professional Engineers, "Code of Ethics" (http://www.nspe.org/resources/ethics/code-ethics). Note that different engineering fields also have their own versions of a code of ethics. For accountants: American Institute of Certified Public Accountants, "Code of Ethics" (http://www.aicpa.org/interestareas/professionalethics/Pages/ProfessionalEthics.aspx); International Federation of Accountants, "Code of Ethics" (http://www.ifac.org/publications-resources/2013-handbook-code-ethics-professional-accountants). For anthropologists: American Anthropological

Association, "Principles of Professional Responsibility" (http://ethics.aaanet. org/ethics-statement-0-preamble/). For sociologists: American Sociological Association, "Code of Ethics" (http://www.asanet.org/about/ethics.cfm).

Epstein and Carrick-Hagenbarth point out the lack of an ethics code in economics. Gerald Epstein and Jessica Carrick-Hagenbarth, "Letter to Mr. Robert E. Hall, President, American Economic Association," January 3, 2011 (http://www.peri.umass. edu/fileadmin/pdf/other_publication_types/AEA_letter_Jan3b.pdf). See also G. Martino, "A Professional Code for Economists." *Challenge*, 2005, pp. 88-104.

Lloyd J. Dumas, Janine R. Wedel, and Greg Callman examine the issue and put forth a proposed code of ethics in: *Confronting Corruption, Building Accountability: Lessons from the World of International Development Advising*. New York: Palgrave Macmillan, 2010.

36. "Submissions to the AEA journals should conform to the AEA disclosure principles which state": American Economic Association, "AEA's Disclosure Policy," July 1, 2012 (http://www.aeaweb.org/aea_journals/AEA_Disclosure_Policy.pdf).

37. Ibid.; and Pedro da Costa, "New ethics standards for economists." *Macroscope blog, Reuters,* January 6, 2012 (http://blogs.reuters.com/ macroscope/2012/01/06/new-ethics-standards-for-economists/).

38. David Kocieniewski, "Academics Who Defend Wall St. Reap Reward." *New York Times,* December 27, 2013 (http://www.nytimes.com/2013/12/28/ business/academics-who-defend-wall-st-reap-reward.html?hp&_r=0&gwh=B9 32D50B26508EF7EBB9E3BE54D79F0C&gwt=regi).

39. Ibid.

40. Gerald Epstein, "'Stronger than I expected'—Gerald Epstein on AEA disclosure guidelines." *Triple Crisis: Global Perspectives on Finance, Development, and Environment,* January 20, 2010 (http://triplecrisis.com/ stronger-than-i-expected/).

41. Coined by the sociologist Paul Lazarsfeld and his students in the 1950s, *KOL* refers to "structures of influence in politics, fashion, culture, medicine, and other domains" (Sergio Sismondo, "Key Opinion Leaders and the Corruption of Medical Knowledge: What the Sunshine Act Will and Won't Cast Light On." *Journal of Law, Medicine & Ethics,* vol. 41, no. 3, 2013, p. 636).

The term was based on their research of the 1944 U.S. presidential election (see: http://www.physician-connect.info/knowledge-center/physician-connect/ community-focus/). See also: P. F. Lazarsfeld, B. Berelson, and H. Gaudet, *The People's Choice: How the Voter Makes Up His Mind in a Presidential Election.* New York: Duell, Sloan and Pearce, 1944. E. Katz and P. F. Lazarsfeld, *Personal Influence: The Part Played by People in the Flow of Mass Communication.* Glencoe, IL: Free Press, 1955.

42. Carl Elliott, "The Secret Lives of Big Pharma's 'Thought Leaders,'" *The Chronicle Review, The Chronicle of Higher Education,* September 12, 2010 (http:// chronicle.com/article/The-Secret-Lives-of-Big/124335/), p. 3. This article is adapted from Elliott's book *White Coat, Black Hat: Adventures on the Dark Side of Medicine.* Boston: Beacon Press, 2010.

43. Sergio Sismondo, "Key Opinion Leaders and the Corruption of Medical Knowledge: What the Sunshine Act Will and Won't Cast Light On." *Journal of Law, Medicine & Ethics*, vol. 41, no. 3, 2013, p. 638.

44. Being a KOL, like any social role, is not just about pay and perks. It is also about identity and status. And there's a psychological payoff, argues Elliott. He writes (Elliott, op. cit.):

> . . . the real appeal of being a KOL is that of being acknowledged as important. That feeling of importance comes not so much from the pharmaceutical companies themselves, but from associating with other academic luminaries that the companies have recruited. Academic physicians talk about the experience of being a KOL the way others might talk about being admitted to a selective fraternity or an exclusive New York dance club. No longer are you standing outside the rope trying to catch the doorman's eye, waiting hungrily to be admitted. You are one of the chosen.

45. See, for instance, Sergio Sismondo, "Key Opinion Leaders and the Corruption of Medical Knowledge: What the Sunshine Act Will and Won't Cast Light On," *Journal of Law, Medicine & Ethics*, vol. 41, no. 3, 2013, p. 636. Sismondo writes: "companies hope to lead medical opinion in their preferred directions through a two-step model of influence by hiring and otherwise enrolling some physicians and researchers who will, in turn, influence many others."

    Marcia Angell, in *The Truth About Drug Companies*, highlights how pharmaceutical companies play a considerable role in the continuing medical education of physicians. She notes: "In 2001, drug companies paid over 60 percent of the costs of continuing medical education. . . . [F]ormerly, they directly supported the accredited professional organizations, but now they usually contract with private medical education and communication companies (MECCs) to plan the meetings, prepare teaching materials, and procure speakers" (See: Marcia Angell, *The Truth About Drug Companies: How They Deceive Us and What to Do About It*. New York: Random House, 2004, p. 139). This is one means of building and maintaining relationships with KOLs, "a top priority for the drug industry" (Piotr Ozierański, *Who Rules Postcommunism? The Case of Drug Reimbursement Policy in Poland*. Cambridge University dissertation, 2011, p. 20).

    Sheldon Rampton and John Stauber provide a variety of cases beyond medicine (for example, the use of biotechnology in agriculture, Microsoft and the antitrust invesgitation in 1998, and the tobacco industry), where independent experts or the seemingly neutral "Third Man" (p. 7) are used to lend credibility to a product. See: Sheldon Rampton and John Stauber, *Trust Us, We're Experts*. New York: Penguin Putnam, 2002.

46. Carl Elliott, "The Secret Lives of Big Pharma's 'Thought Leaders.'" *The Chronicle Review, The Chronicle of Higher Education*, September 12, 2010 (http://chronicle.com/article/The-Secret-Lives-of-Big/124335/), p. 2.

47. Sociologists Piotr Ozierański and co-author Lawrence King argue that this state of affairs applies not only to traditional medical specialties but also to highly sophisticated—and apparently science-based—fields like Health Technology Assessment (HTA). HTA is supposed to establish, based on complicated pharmaco-economic calculations, whether medicines subsidized by the state represent value for money, irrespective of physicians' individual clinical

experience. Ozierański and King detail the case of a key HTA expert in Poland who appears to have risen to prominence as a result of skillfully bridging the arenas of state, business, and nonprofits. While HTA was supposed to introduce more objectivity, thus curbing the influence of KOLs in traditional medicine, the authors show this has not happened (Piotr Ozierański and Lawrence King, "The Persistence of Cliques in the Postcommunist State," 2014, forthcoming paper).

48. Piotr Ozierański writes: "There are strong indications that key patterns of relationships among social actors, particularly those related to the mechanisms of pharmaceutical lobbying, take similar form in the US, the UK and in other countries of the 'Old European Union.' . . ." (Piotr Ozierański, *Who Rules Postcommunism? The Case of Drug Reimbursement Policy in Poland*. Cambridge University dissertation, 2011, p. 7.) See also Piotr Ozierański, Martin McKee, and Lawrence King, "Pharmaceutical lobbying under postcommunism: universal or country-specific methods of securing state drug reimbursement in Poland?" *Health Economics, Policy, and Law*, vol. 7, no.2, April 2012, pp. 175-195.

49. Sergio Sismondo, "Key Opinion Leaders and the Corruption of Medical Knowledge: What the Sunshine Act Will and Won't Cast Light On," *Journal of Law, Medicine & Ethics*, vol. 41, no. 3, 2013, p. 639.

50. Ibid.

51. Elliott, op. cit., p. 4.

52. Piotr Ozierański, *Who Rules Postcommunism?*, op. cit. See also Piotr Ozierański, Martin McKee, and Lawrence King, "Pharmaceutical lobbying under postcommunism," op. cit.

53. Sismondo, op. cit., p. 639. See also: Lazarsfeld, Berelson, and Gaudet, op. cit.; Katz and Lazarsfeld, op. cit.

54. Elliott, op. cit., pp. 4-5.

55. Elliott, op. cit., p. 5, adds: "Drug companies are prohibited from promoting a drug for conditions other than the ones for which the FDA has approved it, but because these off-label uses are often highly profitable, many companies have found creative ways of getting around the prohibition."

56. Sismondo, op. cit., p. 639.

57. Sismondo cites Jennifer R. Fishman, "Manufacturing Desire: The Commodification of Female Sexual Dysfunction." *Social Studies of Science*, vol. 34, no. 2, 2004, pp. 187-218.

58. Andrew Lakoff, "The Anxieties of Globalization: Antidepressant Sales and Economic Crisis in Argentina." *Social Studies of Science*, vol. 34, no. 2, April, 2004, pp. 262-263.

59. Elliott, op. cit., p. 2.

60. Sismondo, op. cit., p. 639.
   For additional support of these points, see also: Philip Mirowski and Robert Van Horn, "The Contract Research Organization and the Commercialization of Scientific Research." *Social Studies of Science*, vol. 35, no. 4, 2005, pp. 503-534; Hans Melander, Jane Ahlqvist-Rastad, Gertie Meijer, and Björn Beermann, "Evidence B(i)ased Medicine—Selective Reporting from Studies Sponsored by Pharmaceutical Industry: Review of Studies in New Drug Applications," *BMJ*, no. 326, May 29, 2003, pp. 1171-1173; Sergio Sismondo, "Ghost Management: How Much of the Medical Literature Is Shaped behind the Scenes by the

Pharmaceutical Industry?" *PLoS Medicine*, vol. 4, no. 9, 2007, p. e286; Sergio Sismondo, "Ghosts in the Machine: Publication Planning in the Medical Sciences," *Social Studies of Science*, vol. 39, no. 2, 2009, pp. 171-198; and Peter C. Gøtzsche, Asbjørn Hróbjartsson, Helle Krogh Johansen, Mette T. Haahr, Douglas G. Altman, and An-Wen Chan, "Ghost Authorship in Industry-Initiated Randomised Trials," *PLoS Medicine*, vol. 4, no. 1, 2007, pp. 47-52.

61. Elliott, op. cit., p. 2.
  Elliott adds: While "hunger for status . . . motivates many academic physicians to work for industry," to maintain their status, "those physicians must also cultivate the perception of independence" (Elliott, op. cit., p. 6).

62. Piotr Ozierański and Lawrence King. "The Persistence of Cliques in the Postcommunist State," 2014, forthcoming paper.

63. Piotr Ozierański and Lawrence King, *Who Rules Postcommunism? The Case of Drug Reimbursement Policy in Poland*, 2014, forthcoming paper.

64. The legislation was introduced in 2009, but failed to pass at that time (see: http://thomas.loc.gov/cgi-bin/bdquery/z?d111:s.00301). However, it was incorporated into the 2010 Patient Protection and Affordable Care Act, Section 6002 (Bill text: https://www.govtrack.us/congress/bills/111/hr3590/text). See also: http://www.gpo.gov/fdsys/pkg/FR-2013-02-08/pdf/2013-02572.pdf, http://www.aafp.org/news/government-medicine/20130215sunshineactrule.html. See also Elliott, op. cit., p. 7.

65. Elliott, op. cit., p. 6.

66. Eric Sagara, Charles Ornstein, Tracy Weber, Ryann Grochowski Jones, and Jeremy B. Merrill, "Dollars for Docs: How Industry Dollars Reach Your Doctors" (http://projects.propublica.org/docdollars/).

67. Beginning in 2010, ProPublica found in a project focused on the United States, in a series called "Dollars for Docs," that the tangle of ties between physicians and the pharmaceutical and medical-device industry was still vast and stretching into multiple . See: Eric Sagara, Charles Ornstein, Tracy Weber, Ryann Grochowski Jones, and Jeremy B. Merrill, "Dollars for Docs: How Industry Dollars Reach Your Doctors" (http://projects.propublica.org/docdollars/).
  There were the medical societies with nearly unimpeachable-sounding names that had turned into conduits of cash from Big Pharma companies to physicians; the physicians on company payrolls who had misconduct on their records and were presumably more desperate for the cash that drug companies were pleased to provide; the story that showed even schools with rigorous ethical codes had faculty who were ignoring rules and giving paid promotional talks for drug and device companies (Tracy Weber and Charles Ornstein, "Med Schools Flunk at Keeping Faculty Off Pharma Speaking Circuit." ProPublica, December 19, 2010 [http://www.propublica. org/article/medical-schools-policies-on-faculty-and-drug-company-speaking-circuit]; Charles Ornstein, Tracy Weber, and Dan Nguyen, "Docs on Pharma Payroll Have Blemished Records, Limited Credentials." ProPublica, October 18, 2010 [http://www.propublica.org/article/dollars-to-doctors-physician-disciplinary-records]).
  And there were the whistleblower lawsuits that exposed blatant attempts by companies to pay doctors who then would push their preferred drugs into the hands of patients (Charles Ornstein and Tracy Weber, "Lawsuits Say Pharma Illegally Paid

Doctors to Rush Their Drugs." ProPublica, October 18, 2010 [http://www.propublica. org/article/lawsuits-say-pharma-illegally-paid-doctors-to-push-their-drugs]).

68.   Eric Sagara, Charles Ornstein, and Ryann Grochowski Jones, "As Full Disclosure Nears, Doctors' Pay for Drug Talks Plummets." ProPublica, March 3, 2014 (http://www.propublica.org/article/ as-full-disclosure-nears-doctors-pay-for-drug-talks-plummets).

69.   Elliott, op. cit., p. 7.

70.   Conversation with Piotr Ozierański, June 26, 2014.

71.   Sismondo, "Key Opinion Leaders," op. cit., p. 636.

72.   D. Nguyen, C. Ornstein, and T. Weber, "Dollars for Docs: How Industry Dollars Reach your Doctors." ProPublica, available at http://projects.propublica. org/docdollars/ (last visited July 3, 2013).

73.   Bob Davis, "In Washington, Tiny Think Tank Wields Big Stick on Regulation." *Wall Street Journal*, July 16, 2004 (http://online.wsj.com/news/ articles/SB108994396555065646).

74.   Jane Mayer, "Covert Operations." *The New Yorker*, August 30, 2010 (http://www. newyorker.com/reporting/2010/08/30/100830fa_fact_mayer?currentPage=all). See also http://www.kochfamilyfoundations.org/ProjectsMercatus.asp.

75.   Mercatus Center (http://mercatus.org/all-people).

76.   Mercatus Center (http://mercatus.org/all-publications/congressional- testimony); Mercatus Center (http://mercatus.org/video).

77.   Lee Fang, "The Scholars Who Shill for Wall Street." *The Nation*, October 23, 2013 (http://www.thenation.com/article/176809/scholars-who-shill-wall-street#).

78.   Iibid.

79.   Mercatus Center, "J.W. Verret" (http://mercatus.org/j-w-verret).

80.   Elizabeth Warren, "The Market for Data: The Changing Role of Social Sciences in Shaping the Law." *Wisconsin Law Review*, vol. 2002, no. 1, 2002 (http://papers.ssrn.com/sol3/papers.cfm?abstract_id=332162).

CHAPTER 9

1.   According to the Oxford Dictionaries (http://www.oxforddictionaries.com/ us/definition/english/astroturfing), *astroturfing* dates from the 1990s. Other sources attribute the term's coinage to U.S. Senator Lloyd Bentsen in 1985 (http://dictionary.sensagent.com/Astroturfing/en-en/).

     The *Guardian* further explains (Adam Bienkov, "Astroturfing: what is it and why does it matter?" *The Guardian*, February 8, 2012 [http://www.theguardian. com/commentisfree/2012/feb/08/what-is-astroturfing]): "Astroturfing is the attempt to create an impression of widespread grassroots support for a policy, individual, or product, where little such support exists. Multiple online identities and fake pressure groups are used to mislead the public into believing that the position of the astroturfer is the commonly held view."

2.   See, for example, Richard W. Pollay, "Propaganda, Puffing and the Public Interest: The Scientific Smoke Screen for Cigarettes." *Public Relations Review*, vol. 16, no. 3, 1990, pp. 39-54 (http://works.bepress.com/richard_pollay/22). See also Yussuf Saloojee and Elif Dagli, "Tobacco industry tactics for resisting public policy on health." *Bulletin of the World Health Organization*, vol. 78, no. 7, 2000 (http://www.ncbi.nlm.nih.gov/pubmed/10994263); Sy Mukherjee,

"How Big Tobacco's Marketing Tactics Continue to Encourage Americans' Unhealthy Habits." *ThinkProgress,* April 8, 2013 (http://thinkprogress. org/health/2013/04/08/1836191/big-tobacco-tactics-playbook/); and Tim Lambert, "Just how many astroturf groups did tobacco fund?" *ScienceBlogs,* February 19, 2008 (http://scienceblogs.com/deltoid/2008/02/19/ just-how-many-astroturf-groups/).

3. R. J. Reynolds, "Building A 'Public Constituency,'" R.J. Reynolds Report, 1987 (http://legacy.library.ucsf.edu/tid/xvg33d00).

4. With regard to the history of these categories, please note the following. With regard to 501(c)(4)s, it appears that a hundred years ago, legislation opened the door for "organizations which could not qualify as charitable, educational, or religious, but whose activities somehow benefited the general public" (Case Western Reserve University law professor Laura B. Chisolm in a 1988 article for the *Indiana Law Journal,* cited in the *Wall Street Journal*; Jacob Gershman, "The Surprisingly Muddled History of the 501(c)(4) Exemption." Law Blog, *Wall Street Journal,* May 16, 2013 [http://blogs.wsj.com/law/2013/05/16/the-surprisingly-muddled-history-of-the-501c4-exemption/]). "Over the years, the IRS expanded the exemption into more political territory, allowing 501(c)(4) groups to engage in lobbying and other political activity. The 'notion that the section 501(c)(4) social welfare organization category is an appropriate classification for politically active charitable organizations seems to have originated with the IRS in the 1950's,' wrote Ms. Chisolm." This IRS document suggests that these groups were formed and given tax-exempt status because they were filling in the gaps for spotty government assistance a century ago, and also because people didn't trust government, generally, still wary of a "rebirth" of monarchy/bureaucracy (Paul Arnsberger, Melissa Ludlum, Margaret Riley, and Mark Stanton, "A History of the Tax-Exempt Sector." *Statistics of Income Bulletin,* Internal Revenue Service, Winter 2008 [http://www.irs.gov/pub/irs-soi/tehistory.pdf]).

5. Caroline E. Mayer and Amy Joyce, "The Escalating Obesity Wars." *Washington Post,* April 27, 2005 (http://www.washingtonpost.com/wp-dyn/content/ article/2005/04/26/AR2005042601259.html).

6. Ibid.

7. The Center for Consumer Freedom, "CCF Warns Congress not to Fall for Propaganda." Center for Consumer Freedom, February 6, 2014 (http://www.consumerfreedom.com/2014/02/ ccf-warns-congress-not-to-fall-for-propaganda/).

8. The Center for Consumer Freedom (http://www.consumerfreedom.com/about/).

9. The Center for Consumer Freedom, "The Nanny" (http://www. consumerfreedom.com/wp-content/uploads/2012/06/nannybloombergad.png).

10. Stephanie Strom, "Nonprofit Advocate Carves Out a For-Profit Niche." *New York Times,* June 17, 2010 (http://www.nytimes.com/2010/06/18/us/ politics/18berman.html?pagewanted=all&_r=0).

11. "Facts and Stats about the Labor Movement." *UnionFacts.com,* Center for Union Facts (http://www.unionfacts.com/).

12. Strom, op. cit.

13. The Greenpeace-member-turned-PR-consultant is Patrick Moore. The former U.S. trade ambassador and one-time mayor of Dallas is Ron Kirk.

14.　CASEnergy Coalition (http://casenergy.org/).

15.　The journalist is Judy Pasternak, formerly of the *Los Angeles Times.* Judy Pasternak, "Nuclear energy lobby working hard to win support." Investigative Reporting Workshop, American University School of Communication, January 24, 2010 (http://investigativereportingworkshop.org/investigations/nuclear-energy-lobbying-push/story/nuclear-energy-working-hard-win-support/).

16.　Ibid.

17.　Christine Todd Whitman, "Oil Spill Mustn't End Offshore Drilling: Christine Todd Whitman." *Bloomberg,* May 3, 2010 (http://www.bloomberg.com/news/2010-05-04/oil-spill-mustn-t-end-offshore-drilling-christine-todd-whitman.html.

18.　Pasternak, op. cit.

19.　See Timothy P. Carney, "Christine Todd Whitman writes op-ed advancing her client's interests—NYT runs it." *Washington Examiner,* August 5, 2013 (http://washingtonexaminer.com/christine-todd-whitman-writes-op-ed-advancing-her-clients-interest-nyt-runs-it/article/2533875); http://www.nytimes.com/2013/08/02/opinion/a-republican-case-for-climate-action.html.

20.　Diane Farsetta, "The Other Half of the Nuclear Industry's Power Couple: Christine Todd Whitman," *PR Watch,* August 27, 2007, http://www.prwatch.org/news/2007/08/6370/other-half-nuclear-industrys-power-couple-christine-todd-whitman

21.　Many of Whitman's articles can be found here: CASEnergy, "News and Events" (http://casenergy.org/category/news/).

22.　See, for instance, Piotr Ozierański, *Who Rules Postcommunism? The Case of Drug Reimbursement Policy in Poland.* Cambridge University dissertation, 2011, p. 101.

23.　Shannon Brownlee, Overtreated: Why Too Much Medicine Is Making Us Sicker and Poorer. New York: Bloomsbury, 2007, p. 193.

24.　Jessica Marshall and Peter Aldhous, "Patient groups special: Swallowing the best advice?" *NewScientist,* Issue 2575, October 27, 2006 (http://www.newscientist.com/article/mg19225755.100).

25.　Robert Pear, "Drug Company Ads Attack Medicare Coverage of Drugs." *New York Times,* July 29, 1999 (http://www.nytimes.com/1999/07/29/us/drug-company-ads-attack-medicare-coverage-of-drugs.html).

26.　Public Citizen, "Organizing Astroturf: Evidence Shows Bogus Grassroots Groups Hijack the Political Debate; Need for Grassroots Lobbying Disclosure Requirements." *Public Citizen,* January 2007 (http://www.citizen.org/documents/Organizing-Astroturf.pdf).

27.　Senator Chuck Grassley, "Grassley works for disclosure of drug company payments to medical groups." Press release, December 8, 2009 (http://www.grassley.senate.gov/news/Article.cfm?customel_dataPageID_1502=24413).

28.　Gardiner Harris, "Drug Makers Are Advocacy Group's Biggest Donors." *New York Times,* October 21, 2009 (http://www.nytimes.com/2009/10/22/health/22nami.html).

29.　Ibid.

30.　Barry Meier, "Senate Inquiry Into Painkiller Makers' Ties." *New York Times,* May 8, 2012 (http://www.nytimes.com/2012/05/09/health/senate-panel-to-examine-narcotic-drug-makers-financial-ties.html).

31.　William Ackman, "Who Wants to Be a Millionaire?" (http://www.businessweek.com/pdf/who_wants_to_be_a_millionaire.pdf).

32. Dan Ritter, "Has Bill Ackman's Billion-Dollar Bet on Herbalife Gone Bad?" *Wall St. Cheat Sheet*, March 11, 2014 (http://wallstcheatsheet.com/business/has-bill-ackmans-billion-dollar-bet-on-herbalife-gone-bad.html/?a=viewall).

33. DealB%k, "Ackman vs. Herbalife, a History." *Dealb%k, New York Times*, March 10, 2004 (http://dealbook.nytimes.com/2014/03/10/ackman-versus-herbalife-a-history/?_php=true&_type=blogs&_r=0).

34. Michael S. Schmidt, Eric Lipton, and Alexandra Stevenson, "After Big Bet, Hedge Fund Pulls the Levers of Power." *New York Times*, March 9, 2014 (http://www.nytimes.com/2014/03/10/business/staking-1-billion-that-herbalife-will-fail-then-ackman-lobbying-to-bring-it-down.html; Dewey Square Group website: http://www.deweysquare.com/who-we-are/).

35. Eric Lipton, "The Herbalife War." *New York Times*, March 9, 2014 (http://www.nytimes.com/interactive/2014/03/10/business/10ackman-herbalife-documents.html#document/p82/a148087).

36. Michael S. Schmidt, Eric Lipton, and Alexandra Stevenson, "After Big Bet, Hedge Fund Pulls the Levers of Power." *New York Times*, March 9, 2014 (http://www.nytimes.com/2014/03/10/business/staking-1 billion that herbalife will fail-then-ackman-lobbying-to-bring-it-down).

37. Pershing Square Capital Management, L.P., "Facts About Herbalife" (http://factsaboutherbalife.com/) (explicit link with Ackman). "Is Herbalife A Pyramid Scheme?" (http://www.isherbalifeapyramid.com/http://herbalife-scam.com/).

38. Anti-Herbalife Coalition, Facebook Group, Joined Facebook October 2, 2011 (https://www.facebook.com/pages/Anti-Herbalife-coalition/297644976917815).

39. Matthew Mosk and Brian Ross, "Latino Group Demands Herbalife Probe." ABC News, February 13, 2014 (http://abcnews.go.com/Blotter/latino-group-demands-herbalife-probe/story?id=22504371&singlePage=true).

40. Svea Herbst-Bayliss, "Ackman outspent by Herbalife in lobbying battle." *Reuters*, March 9, 2014 (http://www.reuters.com/article/2014/03/09/us-herbalife-idUSBREA280OH20140309).

41. Michael S. Schmidt, Eric Lipton, and Alexandra Stevenson, "After Big Bet, Hedge Fund Pulls the Levers of Power." *New York Times*, March 9, 2014 (http://www.nytimes.com/2014/03/10/business/staking-1-billion-that-herbalife-willfail-then-ackman-lobbying-to-bring-it-down).

42. Michelle Celarier, "Herbalife donated money to 5 supported Hispanic Groups." *New York Post*, February 26, 2014 (http://nypost.com/2014/02/26/herbalife-donated-money-to-5-supportive-hispanic-groups/).

43. Michael S. Schmidt, Eric Lipton, and Alexandra Stevenson, "After Big Bet, Hedge Fund Pulls the Levers of Power." *New York Times*, March 9, 2014 (http://www.nytimes.com/2014/03/10/business/staking-1-billion-that-herbalife-will-fail-then-ackman-lobbying-to-bring-it-down).

44. Michael Luo, "G.O.P. Allies Drive Ad Spending Disparity." *New York Times*, September 13, 2010 (http://www.nytimes.com/2010/09/14/us/politics/14money.html?_r=0).

45. Andrew Mayersohn, "Four Years After Citizens United: The Fallout." *Opensecrets.org*, January 21, 2014 (http://www.opensecrets.org/news/2014/01/four-years-after-citizens-united-the-fallout.html).

46. Michael Luo, "G.O.P. Allies Drive Ad Spending Disparity," *New York Times*, September 13, 2010, http://www.nytimes.com/2010/09/14/us/politics/14money.html?_r=0.

47. *Opensecrets.org*, Political Nonprofits, updated June 23, 2014, http://www.opensecrets.org/outsidespending/nonprof_summ.php.

48. Andrew Mayersohn, "Four Years After Citizens United: The Fallout." *Opensecrets.org*, January 21, 2014 (http://www.opensecrets.org/news/2014/01/four-years-after-citizens-united-the-fallout.html).

49. CrossroadsGPS (https://www.facebook.com/CrossroadsGPS).

50. Michael Beckel, "'Shadow RNC' American Crossroads Raises Millions in August from Wealthy Individuals, Corporations." *Opensecrets.org*, September 20, 2010 (https://www.opensecrets.org/news/2010/09/american-crossroads-shadow-rnc.html).

51. Americans for Prosperity (https://www.facebook.com/fightback).

52. Matea Gold, "Koch-backed political network, built to shield donors, raised $400 million in 2012 elections." *Washington Post*, January 5, 2014 (http://www.washingtonpost.com/politics/koch-backed-political-network-built-to-shield-donors-raised-400-million-in-2012-elections/2014/01/05/9e7cfd9a-719b-11e3-9389-09ef9944065e_story.html).

53. Ibid.

54. Eni Mustafaraj and Panagiotis Metaxas, "From Obscurity to Prominence in Minutes: Political Speech and Real-Time Search," presented at WebSci 2010, *Extending the Frontiers of Society On-Line*, Raleigh, NC, April 26-27, 2010 (http://journal.webscience.org/317/2/websci10_submission_89.pdf).

55. Matea Gold, op. cit.

56. Liz Bartolomeo, "The Political Spending of 501(c)(4) Nonprofits in the 2012 Election." *Sunlight Foundation*, May 21, 2013 (http://sunlightfoundation.com/blog/2013/05/21/the-political-spending-of-501c4-nonprofits-in-the-2012-election/).

57. Carl Hulse and Ashley Parker, "Koch Group, Spending Freely, Hones Attack on Government." *New York Times*, March 20, 2014 (http://www.nytimes.com/2014/03/21/us/politics/koch-group-seeks-lasting-voice-for-small-government.html).

58. The Republican strategist was Alex Vogel. Ron Moore, "Group Organizing for America and for Obama agenda." *Examiner*, March 16, 2009 (http://www.examiner.com/article/group-organizing-for-america-and-for-obama-agenda).

59. Jim Rutenberg and Adam Nagourney, "Melding Obama's Web to a YouTube Presidency." *New York Times*, January 25, 2009 (http://www.nytimes.com/2009/01/26/us/politics/26grassroots.html?pagewanted=all).

60. Quoted in ibid., p. 243.

61. Ari Melber, "Year One of Organizing for America: The Permanent Field Campaign in a Digital Age." *techPresident*, January 2010 (http://techpresident.com/ofayear1#toc Journalist Ari Melber).

62. Michael D. Shear, "Pro-Obama Group Enters Immigration Fray." *New York Times*, March 25, 2013 (http://www.nytimes.com/2013/03/25/us/politics/organizing-for-action-group-joins-immigration-fray.html).

63. Ari Melber, "Year One of Organizing for America: The Permanent Field Campaign in a Digital Age." techPresident, January 2010 (http://techpresident.com/ofayear1#toc Journalist Ari Melber).

64. Lydia DePillis, "Disorganized." *New Republic,* October 29, 2009 (http://www.newrepublic.com/article/politics/disorganized).

65. For a recent look at patronage in American politics, see Martin Tolchin and Susan J. Tolchin, *Pinstripe Patronage: Political Favoritism from the Clubhouse to the White House and Beyond.* New York: Paradigm, 2010.

66. Sheldon Rampton, "Obama's Netroots Goes to the Dogs?" *PR Watch,* Center for Media and Democracy, December 5, 2008 (http://www.prwatch.org/node/8037).

67. Chris Cillizza, "Obama Announces 'Organizing for America.'" The Fix Blog, *Washington Post,* January 17, 2009 (http://voices.washingtonpost.com/thefix/white-house/obama-announces-organizing-for.html).

68. Melber, op. cit.

69. Nicholas Confessore, "Obama's Backers Seek Big Donors to Press Agenda." *New York Times,* February 22, 2013 (http://www.nytimes.com/2013/02/23/us/politics/obamas-backers-seek-deep-pockets-to-press-agenda.html?pagewanted=all).

70. Mike McIntire, "Pro-Obama Group Details Fund-Raising and Policy Goals." Posted on The Caucus Blog, *New York Times,* March 26, 2013 (http://thecaucus.blogs.nytimes.com/2013/03/26/pro-obama-group-details-fund-raising-and-policy-goals/).

71. Ken Thomas and Nedra Pickler, "Obama to Speak to Organizing For Action Summit." AP, March 11, 2013 (http://bigstory.ap.org/article/obama-speak-organizing-action-summit).

72. Jim Messina, "Why we're raising money to support Obama agenda." CNN, March 7, 2013 (http://www.cnn.com/2013/03/07/opinion/messina-organizing-for-action/).

73. J. Gerald Hebert and Fred Wertheimer, "Letter to President Obama about OFA." Democracy 21 and Campaign Legal Center, March 13, 2013 (http://www.democracy21.org/wp-content/uploads/2013/03/OFA-LETTER-3-13-131.pdf). See also Justin Sink, "Watchdog: Obama should abandon OFA," *The Hill,* March 11, 2014 (http://thehill.com/blogs/blog-briefing-room/200446-watchdog-obama-should-abandon-ofa).

74. Alex Rogers, "Obama's Grassroots Moneybags: The Top 19 Organizing for Action Donors." *Time,* November 11, 2013 (http://swampland.time.com/2013/11/11/obamas-grassroots-moneybags-the-top-19-organizing-for-action-donors/).

75. Michael Isikoff, "Pro-Obama Group Fires Fundraiser Who Diverted Felon's $100K Gift." NBC News, February 28, 2014 (http://www.nbcnews.com/news/investigations/pro-obama-group-fires-fundraiser-who-diverted-felons-100k-gift-n39491).

76. Ibid.

77. Ibid.

78. Isikoff, op. cit.

79. Matea Gold, "Koch-backed coalition, designed to shield donors, raised $400 million in 2012." *Washington Post,* January 5, 2014 (http://www.washingtonpost.com/politics/koch-backed-political-network-built-to-shield-donors-raised-400-million-in-2012-elections/2014/01/05/9e7cfd9a-719b-11e3-9389-09ef9911065e_story.html).

80. Teneo Holdings (http://www.teneoholdings.com/).

81. Nicholas Confessore and Amy Chozick, "Unease at Clinton Foundation Over Finances and Ambitions." *New York Times*, August 13, 2013 (http://www.nytimes.com/2013/08/14/us/politics/unease-at-clinton-foundation-over-finances-and-ambitions.html?pagewanted=all).

82. Alec MacGillis, "Scandal at Clinton Inc.: How Doug Band drove a wedge through a political dynasty." *New Republic*, September 22, 2013 (http://www.newrepublic.com/article/114790/how-doug-band-drove-wedge-through-clinton-dynasty).

83. Ibid.

84. Ibid.

85. Josh Margolin, "Jon-Bubba Twist." *New York Post*, December 6, 2011 (http://nypost.com/2011/12/06/jon-bubba-twist/).

86. Alec MacGillis, "Scandal at Clinton Inc.: How Doug Band drove a wedge through a political dynasty." *New Republic*, September 22, 2013 (http://www.newrepublic.com/article/114790/how-doug-band-drove-wedge-through-clinton-dynasty).

87. Rosalind S. Helderman, "For Hillary Clinton and Boeing, a beneficial relationship." *Washington Post*, April 13, 2014 (http://www.washingtonpost.com/politics/for-hillary-clinton-and-boeing-a-beneficial-relationship/2014/04/13/21fe84ec-bc09-11e3-96ae-f2c36d2b1245_story.html).

88. Robert Mendick, "Blair Inc: How Tony Blair makes his fortune." *Telegraph*, January 7, 2012 (http://www.telegraph.co.uk/news/politics/tony-blair/8999847/Blair-Inc-How-Tony-Blair-makes-his-fortune.html).

89. The Office of Tony Blair (http://www.tonyblairoffice.org/pages/what-we-do2/).

90. "In the Stirrups of Time" (http://www.youtube.com/watch?feature=player_detailpage&v=xaWWw1lwwpE#t=118s); Ken Silverstein, "Buckraking Around the World with Tony Blair." *New Republic*, September 14, 2012 (http://www.newrepublic.com/article/politics/magazine/107248/buckraking-around-the-world-tony-blair).

91. Peter Oborne, "On the desert trail of Tony Blair's millions." *The Telegraph*, September 23, 2011 (http://www.telegraph.co.uk/news/politics/tony-blair/8784596/On-the-desert-trail-of-Tony-Blairs-millions.html).

92. Jacob Heilbrunn, "Why Did Tony Blair Become a Pal of Col. Qaddafi's?" *National Interest*, September 25, 2011 (http://nationalinterest.org/blog/jacob-heilbrunn/tony-blairs-closest-business-partner-col-gadaffi-5931).

93. Robert Mendick, "Blair Inc: How Tony Blair makes his fortune." *The Telegraph*, January 7, 2012 (http://www.telegraph.co.uk/news/politics/tony-blair/8999847/Blair-Inc-How-Tony-Blair-makes-his-fortune.html).

94. Lionel Barber, "Tony Blair: an exclusive interview." *Financial Times*, June 29, 2012 (http://www.ft.com/intl/cms/s/2/b2ec4fd6-c0af-11e1-9372-00144feabdc0.html#axzz2xG51kTVW).

95. Mendick, op. cit.

CHAPTER 10

1. Don Kash, a scholar in the field of technological innovation, puts it thusly: "Culture shock is what happens when you go into another culture and you don't

know what the rules are. What's future shock? . . . Future shock is when you get up and open the door to a technology that changes the rules of the game and you close the door, but it is distinct from culture shock because you can never go home. You can never go back to the place where you know the rules." The author of *Future Shock* is Alvin Toffler (New York: Random House, 1970). The passage is from Don Kash, "The Role of Culture in Organizational-Technological Change," Lecture at George Mason University, November 17, 2004.

2. This was the slogan of their 2009 documentary *The Yes Men Fix the World*.
3. For the background on the chemical spill, see, for example: BaoBao Zhang, "The Bhopal Disaster." PBS, June 8, 2010 (http://www.pbs.org/wnet/need-to-know/five-things/the-bhopal-disaster/1316/); Editors, "Indian government seeks double compensation payout for Bhopal disaster." *Telegraph,* December 3, 201 (http://www.telegraph.co.uk/news/worldnews/asia/india/8179365/Indian-government-seeks-double-compensation-payout-for-Bhopal-disaster.html); Prasenjit Bhattacharya, "Court Rules Union Carbide Not Liable in Bhopal Case." *Wall Street Journal,* June 28, 2012 (http://online.wsj.com/news/articles/SB10001424052702303561504577493642502980690); and Bhopal Information Center, "U.S. Court of Appeals Upholds 2012 Judgement of District Court in Bhopal Case; Union Carbide Not Responsible for Pollution-Related, Personal Injury Claims." Bhopal Information Center (http://www.bhopal.com/court-of-appeals-upholds-2012-judgment).
4. Here's the story from the Yes Men website: The Yes Men, "Dow Does the Right Thing" (http://theyesmen.org/hijinks/bbcbhopal). Yes Men hoax interview (http://www.youtube.com/watch?v=I1vhS26GoEY). Apparently Dow Chemical paid a company to monitor the Yes Men (http://wikileaks.org/gifiles/docs/38/388134_yes-men-monitoring-03-25-11-.html).
5. The Museum of Hoaxes, "The Yes Men's Bhopal Hoax, 2004" (http://www.museumofhoaxes.com/hoax/archive/permalink/the_yes_mens_bhopal_hoax).
6. David Montgomery, "Occupy Wall Street takes lessons from The Yes Men." *Washington Post,* October 20, 2011 (http://www.washingtonpost.com/lifestyle/style/the-yes-men-use-humor-to-attack-corporate-greed/2011/09/28/gIQACyJg0L_story.html).
7. Dominic Boyer and Alexei Yurchak, "American Stiob: Or, What Late-Socialist Aesthetics of Parody Reveal about Contemporary Political Culture in the West." *Cultural Anthropology*, vol. 25, issue 2, 2010, p. 212.
8. In the 1980s, the goal of refashioning the state in the image of the private sector motivated the migration of audits from their original association with financial management to other areas of working life.
9. As I explained in an endnote in Chapter 1, Dubnick establishes that the English "accountability" has a traditional meaning, plus a more recent usage that came into prominence in the 1980s. He argues that what distinguishes the traditional "accountability" notion from other governance solutions is that it depends on the existence of a "moral community." The traditional notion of *accountability* is a primary characteristic of governance in contexts where there is agreement about the legitimacy of expectations among community members. Dubnick writes that "Conceptually, *accountabilityc* [the traditional concept] can thus be regarded as a *form of governance that depends on the dynamic social interactions and mechanisms*

created within of [sic] *such a moral community*" (Melvin J. Dubnick, "Seeking Salvation for Accountability." Paper presented at the annual meeting of the American Political Science Association, August 29-September 1, 2002, pp. 6-7 [emphasis in original] [http://pubpages.unh.edu/dubnick/papers/salv2002.htm].)

For scholarship on performance, evaluation, and audit culture, see John Clarke, "Performance paradoxes: The politics of evaluation in public services," Howard Davis and Steve Martin (eds.), *Public Services Inspection in the UK*. London, Philadelphia: Jessica Kingsley Publishers, 2008; Michael Power, *The Audit Society: Rituals of Verification*. Oxford: Oxford University Press, 1999; Michael Power, *The Audit Society: Rituals of Verification*. Oxford: Oxford University Press, 1994; and Mark Bovens, "Analysing and Assessing Public Accountability. A Conceptual Framework." European Governance Papers (EUROGOV) No. C-06-01, January 2006.

10.   E-mail correspondence with Helen Sutch, June 2014.

11.   As anthropologist Raymond June points out, "[O]ne can be transparent and demonstrate accountability without being accountable. We must be careful not to conflate terms and concepts" (Raymond June, "The discreet charm of flexians: reviewing Janine Wedel's *Shadow Elite*." *Global Integrity*, January 18, 2010 [http://www.globalintegrity.org/node/491].)

12.   The Workshop on "Building Accountability into International Development and Advising in an Age of Diffused Governance" was funded by the Ford Foundation. For the results of the workshop and larger project, and for analysis of accountability issues in international development advising, see Lloyd J. Dumas, Janine R. Wedel, and Greg Callman, *Confronting Corruption: Building Accountability: Lessons from the World of International Development Advising*. New York: Palgrave Macmillan, 2010.

13.   Kazimierz Wyka, "The Excluded Economy," Janine R. Wedel (edited, annoted, and with introductions by), *The Unplanned Society: Poland During and After Communism*. New York: Columbia University Press, 1992, p. 58.

14.   Eric Sagara, Charles Ornstein, and Ryann Grochowski Jones, "As Full Disclosure Nears, Doctors' Pay for Drug Talks Plummets." ProPublica, March 3, 2014 (http://www.propublica.org/article/as-full-disclosure-nears-doctors-pay-for-drug-talks-plummets).

15.   Tim LaPira, "Erring on the side of shady: How calling out 'lobbyists' drove them underground." *Sunlight Foundation*, April 1, 2014 (http://sunlightfoundation.com/blog/2014/04/01/erring-on-the-side-of-shady-how-calling-out-lobbyists-drove-them-underground/); The Executive Order: The White House, Executive Order 13490: Ethics Commitments by Executive Branch Personnel," January 21, 2009 (http://www.whitehouse.gov/the_press_office/Ethics-Commitments-By-Executive-Branch-Personnel).

16.   Journalist Christian Caryl explores a fascinating case in this regard: that of Burmese oppositionists and jailed pro-democracy activists who have forged alliances even with those responsible for putting them in jail (Christian Caryl, "Burmese Days." *The New York Review of Books*, July 12, 2012 [http://www.nybooks.com/articles/archives/2012/jul/12/burmese-days/]).

17.   See the work of sociologist Alena Ledeneva, *How Russia Really Works: The Informal Practices that Shaped Post-Soviet Politics and Business*. Ithaca and London: Cornell University Press, 2006.

18. "Double strategy" is from Yves Dezalay and Bryant Garth, *The Internationalization of Palace Wars: Lawyers, Economists, and the Contest to Transform Latin American States* (Chicago: University of Chicago Press, 2002), p. 11.

19. See, for example, Ali J. Abbas, *Islamic Perspectives on Management and Organization*. Cheltenham, U.K.: Edward Elgar, 2005; Syed Hussein Alatas, *Corruption: Its Nature, Causes and Functions*. Brookfield, VT: Gower, 1990, pp. 13-14; Maxime Rodinson, *Islam and Capitalism*. London: Saqi Books, 2007 (1966); Richard Rubenstein, *Thus Saith the Lord*. New York: Harcourt, 2006.

20. Lloyd J. Dumas, Janine R. Wedel, and Greg Callman, *Confronting Corruption, Building Accountability: Lessons from the World of International Development Advising*. New York: Palgrave, 2010, pp. 24-25.

21. Ibid., p. 24.

22. However corruption is conceptualized, we must keep in mind that establishing a normative definition of the phenomenon across time and place is not a fruitful starting point for understanding the dynamics and social organizational underpinnings of corruption in a given society or what that society might regard as corruption. A robust body of anthropological, sociological, and other social-science literature demonstrates that point. Corruption can be accurately studied only by examining the patterns and systems of influence that underlie it. For analysis of and further sources on this issue, see: Janine R. Wedel, "Rethinking Corruption in an Age of Ambiguity." *Annual Review of Law and Social Science*, vol. 8, December 2012.

   From Occupy Wall Street and Tea Party activists to authors of books on the financial crisis—for instance, Gretchen Morgenson's *Reckless Endangerment: How Outsized Ambition, Greed, and Corruption Led to Economic Armageddon*, with Joshua Rosner (Morgenson and Rosner, New York: Times/Henry Holt and Co., 2011)—corruption is being reconsidered.

23. I co-organized an initiative and an international Working Group, with Ford Foundation sponsorship, to create a code of ethics for international development consultants. The code we developed, if appropriately adapted and implemented, could help reduce bad projects and wasted aid dollars. See: Lloyd J. Dumas, Janine R. Wedel, and Greg Callman, *Confronting Corruption, Building Accountability: Lessons from the World of International Development Advising*. New York: Palgrave, 2010, pp. 33-63.

24. http://www.nbcnews.com/video/nightly-news/55397168#55397168

25. See Michael Gerson's biography on the *Washington Post*: http://www.washingtonpost.com/wp-srv/opinions/biographies/michael-gerson.html.

26. Sociologist Alena Ledeneva's focus on the "informal practices" of players is illuminating in this regard (Alena Ledeneva, *How Russia Really Works: The Informal Practices that Shaped Post-Soviet Politics and Business*. Ithaca and London: Cornell University Press, 2006).

27. With this framework, I have launched a Mapping Shadow Elite project to document and chart the operations of players, using cases from the finance and military sectors. The idea is to illustrate the MO of players and networks in visual terms and to offer practical tools to the public and the media to help unmask such players (see http://shadowelite.net/).

28. American Economic Association, "AEA's Disclosure Policy," July 1, 2012 (http://www.aeaweb.org/aea_journals/AEA_Disclosure_Policy.pdf).

29.   It is registered as a 501(c)(4).
30.   See, for example, the work of Annelise Riles (Annelise Riles, *Collateral Knowledge: Legal Reasoning in the Global Financial Markets*. Chicago: University of Chicago Press, 2011; Annelise Riles, "*Shadow Elite:* Move Your Money and Beyond—Reforming Market Culture from the Bottom Up." Huffington Post, January 27, 2011 [http://www.huffingtonpost.com/annelise-riles/shadow-elite-move-your-mo_b_814681.html]). See also: Karen Ho, "Disciplining Investment Bankers, Disciplining the Economy: Wall Street's Institutional Culture of Crisis and the Downsizing of American Corporations." *American Anthropologist*, vol. 111, no. 2, 2009.

Acknowledgments

T his project has benefited immensely from the wisdom, experience, and research of numerous colleagues and associates.

I am enormously indebted to Linda Keenan, who stimulated my conceptualization of the book and worked with me to shape it. The book benefits considerably from her experience, especially in the realms of media and finance. Beyond that, she conducted research, suggested examples, and assembled materials for my review. I thank her for her keen insights, camaraderie, and countless hours in conversation.

Independent editor Sarah Flynn also has been invaluable. Her ability to find the best way to express my ideas, her effectiveness as both sounding board and wordsmith, and her unflagging commitment to the project have seen me through every draft of the manuscript, from its beginnings as a proposal.

I am also grateful to Jessica Case, my editor at Pegasus. Not only did she "get" the book right away. Her enthusiasm for the project, feedback on the manuscript, flexibility, and patience have been considerable—and are very much appreciated.

Michael Carlisle, my agent, has been as usual a gem. I thank him for his confidence in me, his insights into the nature of the topic, and his steadfast help and good judgment.

A number of colleagues generously read and commented on drafts of the manuscript. For extensive and invaluable feedback on multiple chapters, I am eternally indebted to Lisa Margonelli and Adam Pomorski. I also thank Adam Pomorski for, as usual, offering guidance throughout the project. Hülya Demirdirek, John Clarke, Jack High, Jeremy Mayer, Alexandra Ouroussoff, Piotr Ozierański, Helen Sutch, and Joseph Vogl also reviewed the manuscript and made valuable suggestions. Todd R. LaPorte, Julia Pfaff, Tony Pfaff, and Bill White read parts of the manuscript (in Bill's case, multiple times) and provided supportive and detailed critiques. For feedback on specific points or sections, I thank also Jamil Afaqi, and Gary Lyndaker. I am grateful to Terry Redding and Caroline Taylor for editorial suggestions.

I am indebted to several scholars who organized workshops that provided opportunities for discussion: Karel Williams of Manchester University and Aeron Davis of the University of London (Goldsmiths College), "Fractured Power: Elites in Our Time"; Christina Garsten and the Copenhagen Business School, "Bridging Markets and Politics"; Paul Stubbs, Alexandra Kaasch, and the University of Bremen, "Actors and Agency in Global Social Governance"; Alan Smart, Filippo Zerilli, the Royal Museum for Central Africa, and the Free University Brussels, "Norms in the Margins and Margins of the Norms"; and Christina Garsten and the Stockholm Anthropology Roundtable, "Brokers and the Shaping of Transnational Markets." Featured talks kindly arranged by Harold James at Princeton University; Victor Niederhoffer at NYC Junto; the European Journalism Observatory, Lugano, Switzerland; the Freie Universität Berlin; David Miller and the University of Strathclyde; TEDxBerlin; and the Bruno Kreisky Forum for International Dialogue, Vienna, also helped me hone my arguments.

I am extremely grateful to Karelle Samuda for highly skilled research, help in crystallizing certain points, and careful fact-checking. I also thank Lydia Greenberg for pulling together research on specific aspects of corruption.

I thank the Institute for New Economic Thinking (INET), the Park Foundation, the Center for Global Studies at George Mason University, and private donors Victor Niederhoffer and Fern Goering, who funded specific research related to the project. I also thank the New America Foundation, where I began work on this book as a senior research fellow.

I thank Bryan Bender, Christopher Rowland, and the *Boston Globe* for generously sharing their database of 750 retired generals and admirals with my Mapping Shadow Influence Project. The book draws on some of these data.

The School of Public Policy at George Mason University has supplied me with a supportive academic home, for which I am most grateful. I am especially indebted to my students and former students, from whose real-world experience in their chosen professions I benefit significantly.

I am grateful to friends who both put me up (when on the road) and put up with me, in particular Michał and Irena Federowicz and the Occasional University of Lewes and Hyères. As always, I am especially and profoundly indebted to Adam and Basia Pomorscy for their generous and abiding help and friendship.

And while this project might not have come to fruition without the generous assistance of so many, I alone am responsible for the final product.

JANINE R. WEDEL
Washington, D.C.
June 2014

Index

A

Abdel-Rahman, Omar, 118
Abelson, Don, 181, 188
Abramoff, Jack, 9–10, 55
accountability. *See also* transparency; unaccountability
  deniability and, 40–42, 72
  ethics and, x, 28–29, 37–38, 259–263
  informality and, 10–11, 43–47
  lapses in, 12
  performance of, 30
  practical measures for, 272–274
  shadow lobbyists and, x, 53–57, 111, 168,
    261, 266
  strategies for, 263–274
  systems for, 33–34
  trust and, ix, 6–12, 24–33, 40–48, 67–77,
    93–94, 100–108, 159–160, 223–225,
    262–267
accountability journalism, 73, 114–121,
  126–127, 143. *See also* journalism
accountability systems, 33–34
Ackman, William, 236–238
Affordable Care Act, 50
Aidid, Mohammed Farah, 61
al-Khawaja, Maryam, 138–139
Anders, George, 17
Anderson, Jon Lee, 194
anthropology, xi, 26, 104–105, 145, 216

anti-corruption. *See also* corruption
  approaches to, xii
  High Priests and, xii, 74–100
  impact of, 12
Assange, Julian, 133–134
"astroturfing," 227, 232–233
authenticity, 102–104, 108

B

Bair, Sheila, 66, 71, 172
Band, Douglas, 15, 248–249
Barber, Benjamin, 208–211
Barstow, David, 160
Baucus, Max, 235
Baudrillard, Jean, 105, 122
Becker, Gary, 80, 89
Bender, Bryan, 120, 159–161, 164, 182
Berman, Richard, 229–230
Bezos, Jeff, 13
Bible, 8, 266
"big government," 89, 234, 242
bin Laden, Osama, 25
Blagojevich, Rod, 9–10
Blair, Tony, 10, 15–16, 92, 247, 250–252, 270
Blinder, Alan, 166
Blodget, Henry, 110–111
Bloomberg, Michael, 229
Born, Brooksley, 18–19, 23, 66, 67, 71
Boyer, Dominic, 104–105, 109, 258

Boyes, Roger, 69, 93
"brain drain," 120–121
bribery, 6–9, 28, 60, 75–77, 84–85, 90–92
Broadwell, Paula, 192, 194
Brown, Sherrod, 171–172
Brownlee, Shannon, 232–233
Brulle, Robert, 202
Bryce, Robert, 201
bureaucracy, 29–35
Bush, George H. W., 80
Bush, George W., 58, 64, 133, 154, 176, 209, 247

C
Campbell, Kurt M., 186, 189–190
Carr, David, 107
Carrick-Hagenbarth, Jessica, 214
Cassidy, John, 110
Ceauşescu, Nicolae, 60
Chafuen, Alejandro, 203
Cheney, Dick, 209
Chertoff, Michael, 112–113, 269
"churnalism," 127, 143
Cillizza, Chris, 107
civil society, 86, 98, 196–199, 264
Clapper, James R., Jr., 153–158
Clarke, John, 29
Clemons, Steve, 179
Clinton, Bill, 15–16, 25, 64, 92, 151, 166, 176, 247–252, 270
Clinton, Hillary, 58, 186, 188, 249–250
cliques, 18–19
Cloud, David, 190, 191
Coakley, Martha, 241
code of ethics, 213–217, 222, 263, 268. See also ethics
Cohen, Stevie, 118
Colbert, Stephen, 8, 14, 104–106, 108, 258
collaborators, 45–47
company-state, 147–151, 158, 173–177, 182
Confessore, Nicholas, 107
confidence in leaders, 14–17, 27–28
"contracting out," 33–34, 150, 165, 173–174
Conway, Erik, 200
Copps, Michael, 126
corruption. See also new corruption
    anti-corruption, xii, 12, 74–100
    bribery and, 6–9, 28, 60, 75–77, 84–85, 90–92
    combating, 76–77, 80–83, 268
    country rankings, 3–4
    economic approaches to, 82, 88–99, 105
    examining, 48–73
    in new world, 3–29

in old world, 5–10
public trust and, xiii, 6–12, 28–29, 47–52, 263–268
redefining, 28–29
scholars of, 96–98
of shadow lobbyists, 266–271
unaccountability and, ix–xiii, 3–29
Corruption Perceptions Index (CPI), 76–79, 83, 89, 92–95, 98–99
Corzine, Jon, 170, 249
cover-ups, 64–68
"crony capitalism," 75–76, 89, 98
"cyber-industrial complex," 149

D
Dan, Călin, 197
Danzig, Richard, 189
Daschle, Tom, 49–52, 92, 176
Daschle Loophole, 50
Dean, Howard, 56
de Blasio, Bill, 183
DeMint, Jim, 182
deniability
    accountability and, 40–42, 72
    ambiguity and, 173–174, 180
    flexibility and, 26–27, 174, 196, 215
    informality and, 221–222
    obscurity and, 227, 241
    outsourcing and, 41
    unaccountability and, 40–42, 72
digital age. See also information technologies
    astroturfing and, 227, 232–233
    impact on media, 102–103, 135–136
    simulacra and, 122–126
    Wild West approach to, 126–127
digital cowboys, 130–134
Dilanian, Ken, 154–155
Dimon, Jamie, 13
disclosure
    ethics and, 44
    performance of, 140
    rules for, 44, 51–53, 114, 140
Dodd-Frank legislation, 22, 119, 166–167, 224
Doe, Samuel K., 60
Draghi, Mario, 8
Dubnick, Melvin J., 260
Dumas, Lloyd J., 266–267
Dunlap, Riley, 201, 202

E
Eigen, Peter, 83–84
Einhorn, David, 38

INDEX

Eisenhower, Dwight D., 158, 165, 190
Elder, Jeff, 107
Elliott, Carl, 218–221, 223
Environmental Policy Act, 175
Epstein, Gerald, 214, 217
ethics
    accountability and, x, 28–29, 37–38,
        259–263
    code of, 213–217, 222, 263, 268
    disclosure and, 44
    individual choice and, 28
    professional ethics, 37–38, 87
    rules for, 44, 52
    shadow generals and, 163–165
    shame and, 28, 212, 223
Exum, Andrew, 192–193

F

"failing up," 7–8, 17, 28, 64–68, 255
fake authenticity, 108
fake news, 104–105, 116, 258
Fallows, James, 11
Feith, Douglas, 58
Fick, Nathaniel, 190
financial crisis, global, 7–8, 18, 21–22, 37, 96,
    142
financial crisis of 2008, 13–14, 35–36, 45, 49,
    108–109, 166, 213
Fink, Richard, 224
Fischer, Karin, 203
flexian, 25–26, 64, 67, 96, 198–199
flexibility, 25–27, 174, 196, 215
Flint, Alex, 231
Flournoy, Michèle A., 186, 192
Flynn, Michael, 191, 192
Fontaine, Richard, 188
Foreign Agents Registration Act, 57–63
Foreign Corrupt Practices Act, 83
"Fourth Estate," 109
free press, 109, 130
Fukuyama, Francis, 208
fund-raising groups, 25, 240–241, 246, 250

G

Gaddafi, Muammar, 10, 206–211, 251
Gates, Robert, 153–154, 163, 189
Geithner, Timothy, 65–67
Gephardt, Richard, 58
Gerson, Michael, 271
Giddens, Anthony, 209
Gissurarson, Hannes Hólmsteinn, 69
Giuliani, Rudy, 56

Giustra, Frank, 248–249
Glass-Steagall Act, 19
Gore, Al, 201
Gorelick, Jamie, 176
Gotti, John, 117
governing changes, 20–27, 52, 101–102,
    148–149, 195–199
Grassley, Charles, 234–235
"grassroots" billionaires, 236–238
"grassroots" organizations
    fund-raising groups, 25, 240–241, 246, 250
    nonprofit organizations and, 226–252
    simulacra of, 227–229
    swaying public opinion, xiii, 145
    unaccountability of, xi, 6, 128, 177, 226–252
Greenspan, Alan, 18, 66, 74
Greenwald, Glenn, 107–108, 127, 133, 151–154
Gressang, Randall, 164

H

Haarde, Geir, 69, 71
Harris, Shane, 153–154
Hawley, Chris, 123
Hayden, Michael, 154
High Priests
    anti-corruption and, xii, 74–100
    code of ethics and, 215–217
    description of, 78–82
    economics of, 186, 206, 212–213
    shadow lobbying, 206, 212–215
Hodge, Nathan, 124–125, 193
Honest Leadership and Open Government
    Act, 264
human reactions, 255–258
Hussein, Saddam, 60

I

Iksil, Bruno (the "London Whale"), 13, 39,
    190
informality
    accountability and, 10–11, 45–47
    deniability and, 221–222
    unaccountability and, 10–11, 43–47
information technologies, 33–34, 38–43, 50,
    96. See also Internet age
intelligence community, 102–103, 133–134,
    147–158
Internet, colonizing, 135–136
Internet age, 14, 24, 105, 115, 126–127,
    134–139, 227. See also digital age
investigative journalism, 73, 114, 120,
    126–130, 227. See also journalism

investigative reporting, 52, 115–116, 120–123, 126–129, 246
Isikoff, Michael, 246–247
Issing, Otmar, 56

J
Jacques, Peter, 201, 202
Jaffe, Greg, 190
Jastrow, Robert, 200
Jester, Dan, 49, 52, 59
Johnson, Simon, 56
Johnston, David Cay, 121
Johnston, Michael, 89
Jolie, Angelina, 63
journalism. *See also* media
    accountability journalism, 73, 114–121, 126–127, 143
    churnalism and, 127, 143
    downsized journalists, 121–126
    fake news, 104–105, 116, 258
    free press, 109, 130
    investigative journalism, 73, 114, 120, 126–130, 227
    mainstream media, 17, 61, 90, 104, 116, 258
    migration of, 121–126
    nonprofit journalism, 122, 127–128
    philanthro-journalism, 127–130
    public relations people, 121–126
    simulacra and, 122–126
    think tanks and, 124–130
    weakening, 115–121

K
Kaplan, Robert, 189, 190
Kapoor, Sony, 40, 44–45
Keane, Jack, 161
Keenan, Linda, 53
Kelly, Max, 43
Keough, Donald, 249
Kerry, John, 50
Key Opinion Leaders (KOLs), 206, 217–223, 232, 263–264
Kidney, James, 9
Kilcullen, David, 190
Kim, Jong Un, 206
King, Lawrence, 221
Klein, Ezra, 131
Klitgaard, Robert, 79–80
Koch brothers, 240–242, 247
Kovach, Bill, 242–243
Krastev, Ivan, 79, 93–94
Kristof, Nicholas, 120

Krugman, Paul, 98, 131
Kuttner, Robert, 65

L
Lakoff, Andrew, 220
Lambsdorff, Johann Graf, 79, 88, 93, 99
LaPira, Tim, 264
Larsen, Kaj, 116, 122
law, limits of, 264–265
leaders, confidence in, 14–17, 27–28
leadership, 14–17, 27–28
Lemann, Nicholas, 118–119
Leno, Jay, 247
Lepinay, Vincent Antonin, 13
Levitt, Arthur, Jr., 19, 66, 118, 166
Levy, Reynold, 184
Lewis, Bernard, 208–209
Lewis, Charles, 129–130
Lewis, Kenneth, 118
Livingston, Bob, 58, 59
Lobbying Disclosure Act, 62, 264
lobbying issues, 53–61. *See also* shadow lobbyists
Locomotives, 68–72, 93, 270–271
Ludwig, Eugene, 166–168

M
Mack, John, 118
Mackintosh, Stuart, 20, 22
Madoff, Bernie, 9–10
mainstream media, 17, 61, 90, 104, 116, 258. *See also* media
mandates, 150, 170, 173–177
Marcos, Ferdinand, 82, 91
Markey, Edward, 236
Mayer, Jane, 224
McCaffrey, Barry, 53, 160, 269
McCain, John, 50–51
McCarthy, Justin D., 165
McChrystal, Stanley, 191–193
McConnell, John Michael "Mike," 151–158, 165, 262
McNamara, Robert, 185
media. *See also* journalism
    abuse of, x–xii
    digital age and, 102–103, 135–136
    digital cowboys and, 130–134
    exploiting, 109–115, 134–137
    fake news, 104–105, 116, 258
    free press, 109, 130
    mainstream media, 17, 61, 90, 104, 116, 258

performance of, 4–9, 109–115
personalization of, xii, 102–108
privatizing, 101–144
Medvetz, Thomas, 180–181
Melber, Ari, 243–244
Merkel, Angela, 15
Messina, Jim, 245
metaphors, 78–80, 95, 100, 271
Michaels, Patrick, 201
military generals, 158–165
military mentors, 162–165
Miller, Judith, 132–133
Miller, Paul A., 53
Mishkin, Frederic, 70
Mitchell, George, 176
Mobutu, Sese Seko, 60, 82, 91
Moffett, Toby, 59
Moravcsik, Andrew, 209
Moynihan, Brian, 31–32
Mubarak, Hosni, 59
Murdoch, Rupert, 128

N
Nagl, John, 188, 189
National Security Agency (NSA)
    intelligence and, 43, 147–148, 151–154
    leaks about, 133–134
    privacy and, 7
    "transparency" of, 102–103
Nazarbayev, Nursultan A., 248
Negroponte, John, 209
Negroponte, Nicholas, 208–210
"Neocon Core," 53, 195
new corruption. *See also* corruption
    bureaucracy and, 29–35
    calling out, 27–39
    examining, 48–73
    explanation of, 5–10
    new world corruption, 3–29
    old world corruption, 5–10
    unaccountability and, xi–xiii, 3–29, 33,
        47–78, 84–91, 96–97, 145, 255–259,
        268
Newhouse, John, 56–57, 63
Nierenberg, William, 200
nonprofit journalism, 122, 127–128
nonprofit organizations, 25, 62, 122–124,
    226–230, 237–247. *See also* "grassroots"
    organizations
nonprofit politicians, 238–239
numbers, seducing with, 92–94
Nye, Joseph S., 82, 208–210

O
O'Bagy, Elizabeth, 50–52, 54–55, 64
Obama, Barack, 11, 25–26, 49–50, 58–59,
    64–67, 107, 132, 158, 188–189, 242–245, 264
Obama, Michelle, 108, 173
Obiang, Teodoro, 138
Occupy Wall Street protests, 4, 132
Oddsson, David, 69, 71
Oliver, John, 116
Omidyar, Pierre, 127
Open Government Act, 264
Oreskes, Naomi, 200
Orszag, Peter, 11, 65
Other, the, 87–90, 98, 265
Ouroussoff, Alexandra, 13–14
outsourcing
    accountability systems and, 33–34
    deniability and, 41
    of government duties, 165–166, 170–172, 199
    of intelligence, 150, 154–156
    think tanks and, 188
Ozieranski, Piotr, 219, 221, 223

P
Panetta, Leon, 176
Paulson, Henry, 49, 59
performance
    of accountability, 30
    of disclosure, 140
    of media, 4–9, 109–115
    professional performance culture, 105, 109,
        259
    for public, 117–119
    of television, 109–115
    of truth, xi, xii, 101–144
Perle, Richard, 53, 58, 209
Perry, William, 189
personalization of media, xii, 102–108. *See also*
    media
Peterson, Pete, 129, 185
Petraeus, David, 16–17, 19, 186–187, 190–194
Pfaff, Julia, 159
"philanthro-journalism," 127–130
Phillips, Macon, 242
Physician Payment Sunshine Act, 222, 263
physicians, 205–206, 217–223
Plehwe, Dieter, 203
Pletka, Danielle, 211
Podesta, John, 189
Podesta, Tony, 59
Poindexter, John, 153
Poitras, Laura, 108

policymaking agencies, 17–20
Popper, Karl, 196
pornography, 101–102, 106–108
Porter, Michael, 206
Portes, Richard, 70
Pottinger, Matt, 191
"power centers," 55, 120, 178. *See also* think tanks
"power cliques," 18–19
press releases, 121–126
prestige, 205–225
principal-agent theory, 79, 91–92, 97
privatization of media, 101–144. *See also* media
"professional performance culture," 105, 109, 259
professors, 205–214, 217–218, 224–225
public performance, 117–119
public relations, 121–126
public trust. *See also* trust
    corruption and, xiii, 6–12, 28–29, 47–52, 263–268
    decline of, 24, 33–35
    restoring, xiii, 253, 259, 263–268
    violation of, ix, 6–12, 26–29, 47–52, 72, 77, 100, 223, 252
Putin, Vladimir, 15
Putnam, Robert, 208, 211

Q
Qur'an, 8, 266

R
Reagan, Ronald, 68–69, 209
Reed, Jack, 159
regulation limits, 61–64
Reid, Harry, 50
research organizations, 178. *See also* think tanks
Rice, Susan, 189
Ricks, Tom, 190, 191, 192
Rivlin, Alice, 179
Rockefeller, Jay, 184–185
Rodman, Dennis, 206
Rose-Ackerman, Susan, 80
Rove, Karl, 240, 241
Rubin, Robert, 18, 23, 52, 64–68, 71, 73–75
Rudman, Warren, 176

S
Saleh, Ali Abdullah, 138
Sampson, Steven, 76, 84, 98
Sánchez, Linda, 236
Sandler, Herb, 128
Sandler, Marion, 128

Sanger, David, 190
Sarbanes-Oxley Act, 166
Scalia, Eugene, 119
Schapiro, Mary, 166
Scheppele, Kim Lane, 197–198
Schmitt, Eric, 190
Schroeder, Gerhard, 15, 53
Seitz, Frederick, 200
Selassie, Haile, 82, 91
"Senior Military Mentor" program, 163
senior military mentors, 162–164
Sewall, Sarah, 189
Shachtman, Noah, 125–126
shadow elites
    corruption of, 266–271
    damage by, 72–73
    evading accountability, 53–57, 111, 261, 266
    exploiting media, 134–137
    High Priests, 206, 212–215
    hoaxers, 258
    networks of, 64–73, 196
    think tanks, 180–185
shadow generals, 158–165
shadow government, 148–149, 156–157, 173–174
shadow intelligence community, 150–158
shadow lobbyists
    corruption of, 266–271
    damage by, 72–73
    evading accountability, x, 53–57, 111, 168, 261, 266
    exploiting media, 135–137
    High Priests, 206, 212–215
    professors as, 205–206
    shame and, 56–61
    think tanks, 55–56, 65–66, 137–145
shadow oversight, 169–170
shadow regulators, 165–173
shame
    bureaucracy and, 32
    ethics and, 28, 212, 223
    resurrecting, 72–73
    shadow lobbyists and, 56–61
"Shame is for sissies," 56, 61
Shanker, Thom, 190
Shaw, David, 246
Sherman, Wendy, 188, 189
Shleifer, Andrei, 96–97
Shorrock, Tim, 155
Sigurgeirsdóttir, Silla, 70–71
"silos," 33–34

Silver, Nate, 131
Silverstein, Ken, 63, 136–137, 140–141
Simmons, Ruth, 16
Simpson, Alan, 176
simulacra
    explanation of, 105–109
    of grassroots entities, 227–229
    strength of, 122–126
    of think tanks, 179
Sismondo, Sergio, 218–220, 223
Snowden, Edward, 24, 42, 107, 127, 133–134,
    147–148, 151–152, 157, 176
Soros, George, 75, 130, 195–199
spies, 7, 46, 107–108, 147–148
Spitzer, Eliot, 115
Squitieri, Tom, 139
Steinberg, James, 189
Stewart, Jon, 8, 104–105, 116, 258
Stiglitz, Joseph, 98
stock markets, 13–14
Stone, Diane, 196–197
"structured unaccountability," xii, 7, 30–47,
    255–258. See also unaccountability
Stubbs, Paul, 195–199
Sullivan, Andrew, 131
Sullivan, John, 122
Summers, Lawrence, 18, 23, 25–26, 40, 52,
    64–68, 71–74, 97
Sunshine Act, 222, 263
Suskind, Ron, 66–67
Sutch, Helen, 262
"SWIMNUT," 3–4, 12

T
Taibbi, Matt, 65
Taylor, Astra, 127
Taylor, James, 201
Tea Party movement, 4, 182
"technocratic competence idea," 40
technology, impact of, 38–40
television, exploiting, 109–115
"terms of use" agreements, 45–46
Tett, Gillian, 21, 36–39
Thatcher, Margaret, 68–69
think tanks
    hiring journalists, 124–130
    holding tanks, 188
    influence of, 24–26, 178–204
    outsourcing and, 188
    power centers and, 55, 120, 178
    shadow elites, 180–185
    shadow lobbyists, 55–56, 65–66, 137–145

shaping war policy, 19–24
simulacra of, 179
swaying public opinion, ix–xiii, 19–24, 195,
    202, 269–273
thought leaders and, 178–204
Tourre, Fabrice, 42
transparency. See also accountability
    age of, 41, 48, 103, 108, 126–136
    demand for, 20, 26, 72–73, 133–136,
        183–185, 264–266
    illusion of, 95
    of intelligence, 102–103
    lack of, 73–75, 88–92, 128, 149, 185, 258
    limits of, 222–223
Trevino, Joshua, 62
trust. See also public trust
    accountability and, ix, 6–12, 24–33,
        40–48, 67–77, 93–94, 100–108, 159–160,
        223–225, 262–267
    corruption and, xiii, 6–12, 28–29, 47–52,
        263–268
    decline of, 24, 33–35
    restoring, xiii, 253, 259, 263–268
    violation of, ix, 6–12, 26–29, 47–52, 72, 77,
        100, 223, 252
truth, loss of, 12–14
truth, performing, xi, xii, 101–144
"truthiness," 14, 106–108
"truthi-news," 14
Tsingou, Eleni, 20, 22

U
U. S. Foreign Corrupt Practices Act, 83
Ul-Haq, Mohammed Zia, 82, 91
unaccountability. See also accountability
    advancement of, 27
    corruption and, ix–xiii, 3–29
    deniability and, 40–42, 72
    flexibility and, 25–27
    of grassroots organizations, xi, 6, 128, 177,
        226–252
    impact of, 12
    informality and, 10–11, 43–47
    information technology and, 33–34, 38–43,
        50, 96
    new corruption and, xi–xiii, 3–29, 33,
        47–78, 84–91, 96–97, 145, 255–259, 268
    structured unaccountability, xii, 7, 30–47,
        255–258
    trust and, ix, 6–12, 24–33, 40–48, 67–77,
        93–94, 100–108, 159–160, 223–225,
        262–267

V
Value at Risk (VaR) models, 38–39, 92
Vanden Brook, Tom, 163
Vennochi, Joan, 194
Volcker Rule, 168
von Kloberg, Edward, III, 60–61

W
Wade, Robert, 70–71
Wałęsa, Lech, 33
Wall Street protests, 4, 132
Ward, Monte, 54
Warren, Elizabeth, 183, 224–225
Washington-Wall Street clique, 18–26
Weatherstone, Dennis, 21, 25
Webb, Jim, 189–190
Weber, Max, 34–35
Wertheimer, Fred, 245

White, Mary Jo, 117–120
White, William, 36, 40, 47
Whitman, Christine Todd, 176, 230–231, 269
Williams, Julie, 168
Wisner, Frank, 59
Wolfensohn, James, 83
Wolffe, Richard, 124
workaround systems, 28–29, 197, 259
Wyden, Ron, 157

Y
Yanukovych, Viktor, 62
Yglesias, Matthew, 131, 142–143
Yurchak, Alexei, 104–105, 109, 258

Z
Zaloom, Caitlin, 38